Oregon and the Collapse of *Illahee*

FIRST PEOPLES
New Directions in Indigenous Studies

GRAY H. WHALEY

Oregon and the Collapse of *Illahee*

U.S. Empire and the Transformation of

an Indigenous World, 1792–1859

The University of North Carolina Press   Chapel Hill

Publication of this book was made possible, in part, by a grant from the Andrew W. Mellon Foundation.

Designed by Courtney Leigh Baker and set in Minion Pro and Myriad Pro by Achorn International Inc. Manufactured in the United States of America. The paper in this book meets the guidelines for permanence and durability of the Committee on Production Guidelines for Book Longevity of the Council on Library Resources. The University of North Carolina Press has been a member of the Green Press Initiative since 2003.

Library of Congress Cataloging-in-Publication Data
Whaley, Gray H.
Oregon and the collapse of Illahee : U.S. empire and the transformation
of an indigenous world, 1792–1859 / Gray H. Whaley. — 1st ed.
p. cm.   Includes bibliographical references and index.
ISBN 978-0-8078-3367-4 (cloth : alk. paper) — ISBN 978-0-8078-7109-6 (pbk. : alk. paper)
1. Indians of North America—Oregon—History. 2. Indians of North America—
Government relations—1789–1869. 3. Indians, Treatment of—Oregon—History.
4. Whites—Oregon—Relations with Indians. 5. Oregon—Race relations. I. Title.
E78.O6W53 2010   979.5004'97—dc22   2009050001

Portions of this work appeared earlier, in somewhat different form, as "Oregon, *Illahee*, and the Empire Republic: A Case Study of American Colonialism, 1843–1858," *Western Historical Quarterly* 36, no. 2 (2005): 157–78, copyright by the Western Historical Association, reprinted by permission; "'Trophies' for God: Native Mortality, Racial Ideology, and the Methodist Mission of Lower Oregon, 1834–1844," *Oregon Historical Quarterly* 107, no. 1 (2006): 6–35; and "'Complete Liberty'? Gender, Sexuality, Race, and Social Change on the Lower Columbia River, 1805–1838," *Ethnohistory* 54, no. 4 (2007): 669–95.

cloth   14 13 12 11 10   5 4 3 2 1   paper   14 13 12 11 10   5 4 3 2 1

Contents

Tables, Maps, and Figures

Preface   Reconstructing an American Colonial History

The colonial history of the United States did not end with the American Revolution. Independence from the British Empire signaled the advent of U.S. colonialism. In the West, the colonial era continued through the nineteenth century and for Native peoples continues today through the ongoing imposition of federal and, increasingly, state sovereignty over Native nations. Thus, reconceiving American colonial history is not merely an intellectual exercise; it allows one to better comprehend past and present. The early American histories of Oregon and the American West are largely understood in terms of the "westward expansion" of the United States during the nineteenth century. Although historians have increasingly accepted that such expansion bears much in common with the histories of imperialism and colonialism around the world, American westward expansion still remains "exceptional."[1]

Broadly defined, *imperialism* is an abstract ordering of power, an accumulation of high-level decisions, policies, and treaties that systematize expansion. Colonialism is the ground-level reality of imperialism: actions, local decisions, and their consequences, which can defy or support empire, a process that Richard White has described as shaping the metropolis from the periphery.[2] As this book demonstrates, negotiating colonization from the periphery was both a common aspect of early Oregon history and a frustrating and only partly successful effort during a period of intense division within the American "empire republic."

This book reevaluates the colonization of modern western Oregon, one of the most important sites of imperial competition in North America during the early decades of U.S. history. It takes a critical new look at the cross-cultural practices of the fur trade, the relationship between Christian mission and colonization, imperial policies of Indian treaties and land disposal, Native sovereignty and identity, and the ideological and practical components of American settler colonialism: race, republicanism, liberal economics, and violence.

The evidence derives partly from standard sources such as the journals of fur traders, colonials, and missionaries, as well as sundry government records. However, because my perspective and thus my questions differ from much of the established historiography, these sources are transformed. For example, how were political, racial, and gender ideologies evident in land claim ledgers? Why do the records of the Oregon Mission become increasingly racialized between 1834 and 1844? Importantly, the book does not only give fresh life to old sources; it draws on previously underutilized data, particularly regarding Native perspectives. During the heyday of Boasian anthropology between the 1890s and the 1940s, scholars and graduate students poured into the Pacific Northwest, gathering languages, stories, and material culture before they "vanished" or became hopelessly "corrupted" by assimilation. The efforts of these scholars and students produced numerous interviews with elder Native consultants.

I have integrated these so-called salvage ethnographies with more traditional sources such as Indian agency reports and newspapers to produce a new composite of the Oregon Indian world: *Illahee*. No simple "Indian perspective" is presented; rather, *Illahee* encompasses the numerous, often contradictory ways in which Native peoples changed in relation to colonialism. It became possible to ask how colonization affected gender, kinship, sexuality, ethnic distinctions, prophecy narratives, and politics within Native communities. Such insights, together with lifting the veil of republican ideologies and analyzing colonial practices, have produced a much more complicated, conflicted, and representative history of the quintessential, antebellum promised land: western Oregon.

My two principal metaphors of place, Oregon and *Illahee*, describe essentially the same physical space. The terms illustrate the attempts by Native and non-Native actors to construct culturally meaningful places amid wrenching historical changes. Integrating such an approach has been variously described as spatial history (how people "turned space into place") and ethnogeography.[3] In recent decades, historians have attempted to dissolve biased, intellectual boundaries created by frontier histories and to reestablish boundaries that distinguish different historical conceptions and attempt to represent non-Western perspectives responsibly. My construction of Oregon and *Illahee* is intended to explore physical and imagined boundaries during Western colonization and conquest and, to quote Philip Deloria, "the historical consciousnesses that are the products of that world and of those changes."[4]

Acknowledgments

I am indebted to the generous advice of many individuals. At the University of Oregon, Professors Jeffrey Ostler, Peggy Pascoe, Matthew Dennis, and Madonna Moss offered insightful commentary at critical points early in the manuscript. The Coquille Indian Tribe provided a welcoming forum to air my research ideas, as did the Western History Association, the American Society for Ethnohistory, the Oregon Historical Society, the Pacific Coast Branch of the American History Association, the Oregon Humanities Center, the history faculty at Western Michigan University and Southern Illinois University, and the Oregon Historical Society, which also helped me with its Donald J. Sterling Jr. Senior Research Fellowship. I appreciate the commentary from the several blind reviewers of this manuscript and the earlier articles in *Western Historical Quarterly*, *Ethnohistory*, and *Oregon Historical Quarterly* through which I fleshed out some of my arguments. This work is stronger thanks to all the patient and critical readings. Thanks also to the many individuals from the Confederated Tribes of Coos, Siuslaw, and Lower Umpqua, the Confederated Tribes of Siletz, the Confederated Tribes of Grand Ronde, Yurok, Klamath, Chinook, and Warm Springs who contributed knowledge and criticism, particularly Robert Kentta, Jason Younker, Denni Hockema, and Patty Whereat. Special thanks to Coquille tribal elder and anthropologist George B. Wasson Jr., who shape-shifted variously into a teacher, friend, colleague, storyteller, singer, and tour guide.

Thank you, Rachel, for having enough confidence and resolve for both of us during the years of writing and revising this manuscript. Thanks to my boys, Benjamin and Devin, for providing much needed love and distractions. The Whaley and Bridges clans provided years of support and encouragement.

Oregon and the Collapse of *Illahee*

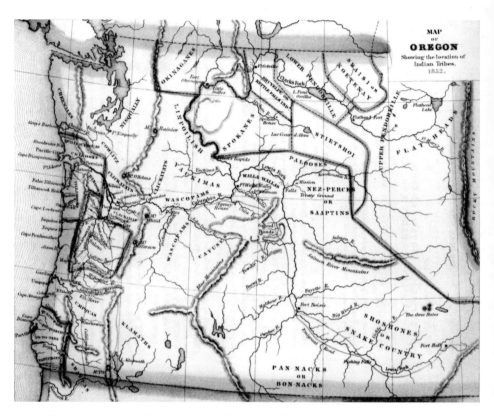

Contemporary map of Oregon showing the location of Indian tribes, 1852 (Seth Eastman, illustrator, in Schoolcraft, *Information Respecting the History, Condition and Prospects of the Indian Tribes of the United States*)

CHAPTER ONE

Introduction

Historical Constructions of Oregon and *Illahee*

When the first Western ship entered the Columbia River in 1792, Americans and Chinooks greeted each other, exchanged goods, and unknowingly launched a colonial history that would forever alter the political, cultural, economic, and ecological landscapes. The hundreds of square miles surrounding the lower Columbia River was, to Westerners, "the lower Oregon Country." To indigenous people, the region had many names, depending on context and language. Taken together however, the region might be effectively termed *Illahee*, an encompassing Chinook word for the land, soil, and home. Although Chinookan dialects dominated the numerous villages along the lower and middle Columbia River and its lower tributaries, Native speakers of several other languages lived near or regularly visited the lower country for trading, hunting and gathering, and raiding. These Native peoples adopted the term *Illahee* for various uses through the Indians' regional trade jargon, *Chinook wawa* or Chinook Jargon.

Prior to the arrival of Western traders, *Illahee* was already a dynamic and diverse place, featuring trade and kin networks that reached east of the Rocky Mountains and hundreds of miles to the north, south, and interior of the vast "Oregon Country." The subsequent colonial fur trade joined and altered the existing networks of *Illahee*; it did not create them. Indeed, according to a story maintained by lower Chinookans and first published by pioneering anthropologist Franz Boas in 1894, the Clatsops assimilated the newcomers into their world rather than the reverse.

In "The First Ship Comes to Clatsop Country," Charles Cultee offers modern readers an introduction to some crucial interpretive issues that I have attempted to weave throughout my own narrative. The story begins with an elder, grieving mother, who has "wailed . . . for a whole year" and traveled to the coast for the day. Returning to Clatsop, she was "walking along the beach . . . now she saw something. She thought it was a whale. When she came near it she saw two spruce trees standing upright on it. She thought, 'Behold! It is no whale. It is a monster!'" The old woman reached the "thing" and noted the wood, copper, and iron construction. "Then a bear came out of it . . . but his face was that of a human being." She continued home, crying, "'Oh my son is dead and the thing about which we have heard in tales is on shore!'" Her village scrambled to meet the fearful "thing" and its occupants, who now requested water for their kettles.

Note the shifting descriptions of the whale-monster-thing-ship and its inhabitants as the tale continues: One Clatsop "climbed up and entered the thing. He went down into the ship. He looked about in the interior; it was full of boxes. He found brass buttons in strings half a fathom long. He went out again to call his relatives, but they had already set fire to the ship." The Clatsop and the "bears" jumped down. "It burned just like fat." The Clatsop "gathered the iron, the copper, and the brass" and spread word of the event. The "two persons" on the ship "were taken to the chief of the Clatsop." The situation almost produced a fight between two village headmen, although they reached a compromise of sending one sailor to each village. "Now the Quinalt, the Chehalis, and the Willapa came. The people of all the towns came there. The Cascades, the Cowlitz, and the Klickitat came down the river. All those of the upper part of the river came down to Clatsop."

The Clatsops began exchanging "strips of copper" for slaves from other Native peoples. As well, "A nail was sold for a good curried deerskin. Several nails were given for long dentalia. They bought all this and the Clatsop became rich." Cultee notes the significance of the materials—"iron and brass were seen for the first time"—but he concludes with the detail, "Now they kept those two persons. One was kept by each [Clatsop] chief, one was at the Clatsop town at the cape."[1]

The non-Native historical record bears little resemblance to this tale of an initial encounter on the lower Columbia. One might be tempted to analyze the story in terms of a composite of shipwrecks and other possible correlates, but the story illustrates something much more important for one's attempt to understand *Illahee* and how it became Oregon. For lower Chinookans, the constituent parts of the story (movement, time, space and place, transformation, and identity) conveyed the essential meanings.[2]

The narrative was recorded about the time of Frederick Jackson Turner's famed frontier thesis, a time when Indian lands and resources faced a renewed onslaught. Yet, to frame it simply as "resistance" (turning the march-of-progress narrative on its head) ignores its indigenous conceptualization.[3] Cultee's tale does suggest an inverse of Turner, as newcomers with valuable possessions to which they have no inherent right enter Native space, are transformed, indigenized, and stripped of their identity. However, the analysis must be developed beyond an opposition to dominant society.

Geography and the old woman's movement through it reflect specific meanings of place and peoples' relation to it. At the heart of lower Chinookan spiritual lives was the so-called Guardian Spirit Complex, in which individuals, kin, and spirit guides moved across the landscape. They ventured to sites and enacted rituals and ceremonies that temporarily charged the spaces with sacred power. The basic strictures of the Guardian Spirit Complex infused all Chinookan beliefs and practices, including narratives.[4] Cultee's tale features nonhuman actors, according to the convention of Chinook tales, and the identity of the ship and the sailors changes as they move across space from the barely perceptible position on the water (the whale) to nearing the beach (the threatening monster) to the approach of the village in the form of its people.

Ending a year of mourning and wailing for her son, the old woman returns from the coast and spies the "whale" from the beach. In the water world of the lower Columbia, the beach was an indefinite space, a meeting place between villagers and outsiders and a place to receive gifts from the ocean, whether a beached whale or lost cargo, whether on the coast or in the vast intertidal zone of the river system. On arrival, the headmen and the townspeople claim the beach, the ship, and the crew. The outsiders enter the village under the power of Clatsops (rather than a technologically sophisticated people venturing from a great distance and penetrating the Columbia). Subsequently, *Illahee* arrives in the guise of villagers identified as Quinalt, Chehalis, Willapa, the Cascades, Cowlitz, and the Klikitat, thus accounting for many of the linguistically and ethnically diverse peoples of the Greater Lower Columbia. In this narrative, the Clatsop are at the relative center of the configuration. The metals on board are precious, but they are exchanged for indigenous goods. The identity of the sailors is effectively moot; they are enslaved. They have no village or kin identity.

Time is indigenized as well. The year was not 1792 but the end of a year of mourning, a culturally derived moral imperative on the people. Time is expressed in relation to the individual who experienced the encounter vis-à-vis her age, her motherhood, and her proper observance of Clatsop mourning ritual. As a result of their proper conduct, "the Clatsop became rich." The tale evidences a particular conception of place, *Illahee*, and the relation of the indigenous inhabitants to it.

Compare Charles Cultee's tale with a contemporary account from the famed popular historian Hubert Howe Bancroft, published in 1884: "Gray then dropped down the stream, noting the Chinook village, and landing in the boat at one point, was visited by many natives in their canoes, and obtained a good quantity of furs." Gray then waited for a good tide and left. Bancroft concludes that "[t]his achievement of Gray, which Americans chose to regard as the 'discovery of the Columbia,' figured very prominently . . . in the international discussions of later years."[5] Bancroft was not simply being terse; Capt. Robert Gray and his mate did not comment much on the Chinooks. These veterans of the growing China trade knew that their successful entry into the Columbia (named for their ship, *Columbia Rediva*) was important, but the Chinooks were simply expected features of a landscape from which they sought commodities. They and Bancroft effectively evidence "Oregon."

The region that Westerners referred to as the *Oregon Country* in the eighteenth century encompassed modern Oregon, Washington, and Idaho, as well as western Montana and western Wyoming, in the United States and the sprawling Canadian province of British Columbia. The several ecological zones included every basic type found in North America, from rugged coastlines to steep canyons to wide valleys to high peaks to deserts, and stretched from 42° N to 54° 40' N latitude. Indeed, it takes some imagination to refer to the massive area as a coherent region, let alone to call it a place, a designation that suggests some deeper connection among the distinctive spaces. To Europeans and Euro-Americans, *Oregon* referred to the lands between the Spanish claims to Alta California and New Mexico to the south, the British claims to Rupert's Land to the east, and the Russian claims to Alaska to the north. In short, competing imperial claims defined the Oregon Country.

The Native peoples imagined no such place. Although the term *Oregon* likely derived from a Native word such as *eulachon* (an oily fish and popular indigenous trade item from the Pacific to the Canadian Prairie), Oregon did not have the same meaning that Westerners subsequently gave it.[6] Much of this book focuses on the southwestern portion of the Oregon Country, modern-day western Oregon and Washington. Both the indigenous and the newcomer populations saw the lower Columbia River as a central feature, but the Indians did not conceive of a "lower Oregon" the way Westerners did. Instead, one has to imagine a cohesive Native world as a composite of

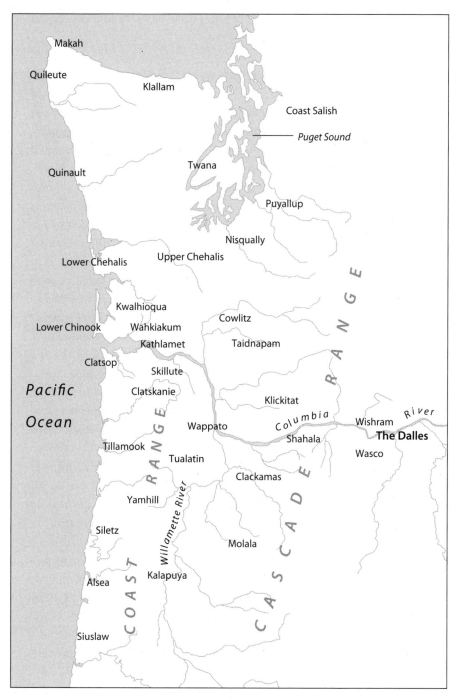

The Greater Lower Columbia (based on maps in Boyd and Hajda, "Seasonal Population Movement along the Lower Columbia River")

trade and kinship networks, a sum of interrelated parts that did not respect imperial borders.

FOR THE PURPOSES of analysis, one can cast the historical *Illahee* of the mid-nineteenth century in comparable terms as *Oregon*. Common criteria of defining place include conceptions of property ownership and resource use privileges, and connections to spirituality, identity (individual and group), and the "national" sovereignty of villages. Indian people at the time would not have used these explicitly Western terms or referred to a unified *Illahee*. This approach is meant to allow for a historical comparison across cultures and does not assume complete universalism among "rational" humans, as some scholars have recently termed such thinking.[7] The criteria allow one to compare organizing ideas, "apple to apple," kinship to citizenship, usufruct property rights to absolute title.

Economically important places of *Illahee* did not just offer excellent eulachon, salmon, or huckleberry harvesting. Such resource sites were linked to individual, familial, and communal privileges that were crucial to constructions of identity. Unlike in Euro-American society, individual ownership of productive resource sites was uncommon. In a few cases, such as Tualatin tar-weed areas in the lower Willamette Valley, Kalapuyans recognized usufruct property rights (that is, primary *use* privileges of a resource without *ownership* of the physical site). These privileges existed as allotments to specific bands or individuals. More commonly in the region, however, whole communities comprised of multiple families had usufruct rights to limited resource sites, particularly for fishing. Privileges to use larger gathering sites such as camas fields, seasonal wapato-root ponds, and shellfish beds extended to neighboring communities and to those with marriage or other kinship ties. Indeed, access to resource sites compelled many marriage arrangements, crossing languages and ethnicities.

Thus, in *Illahee*, the concept of territory was comparatively inclusive, permeable, and dynamic. It derived from personal relationships among communities that were composed of multiple kins and constantly being reshaped by marriages, births, and deaths. Importantly, place did not necessarily determine territoriality: communities restricted access to specific resources, not necessarily to fixed geographic boundaries. For example, Clackamas Chinookans prevented unrelated Kalapuyans from fishing at Willamette Falls, but those same Kalapuyans freely hunted seals in the "Chinookan territory" of the lower Columbia River.[8] Although beliefs and practices varied from the

Oregon-California borderlands to the lower Columbia River environs to the interior valleys of western Oregon, *Illahee* featured related concepts of place that helped shape identities and the political economy.

Spiritual beliefs functioned similarly to economics in Native conceptions of place. Throughout *Illahee*, specific places named in origin stories situated people in their heritage and contributed to their senses of self and community. Comparing ceremonialism in two regions of *Illahee*, the Oregon-California borderlands and the Greater Lower Columbia environs, illuminates the importance of place and its different connections to spirituality.

In the Oregon-California borderlands, sacred places housed spiritual beings who sustained communities and individuals. The so-called world renewal cult of this "southern" region (or "northern" from the California perspective) featured place-specific rituals for earth renewal, first fruits, or acquisition of doctoring powers, making it wholly dependent on the local environment. Visitor participation in this regional belief network ideally ensured intervillage harmony; and extended kin, often crossing ethnic lines, made available sufficient wealth items for successful ceremonies. On the California side of the Siskiyou Mountains, such ceremonies are better documented than on the Oregon side, because more Indian communities avoided removal, survived war, and thus could maintain their place-specific ceremonies after the 1850s. Yet, one knows from the historical record that peoples of modern southwest Oregon danced in the northern California ceremonies. As well, ceremonies of the Tolowa, Athapaskans who straddled the colonial border, included visitors from both southwest Oregon such as Tututnis of Rogue River and from northwest California such as Yuroks, Karoks, and Wiyots. Testimonies from early-twentieth-century "salvage ethnographies" and modern descendants point to similar dance sites as far north as Pistol River and Tutun on the Rogue River.[9] Thus, this place-centered ceremonialism extended well into modern southwest Oregon.

Other relationships among spirituality, people, and place also existed in *Illahee*. Religious ceremonies north of the Alsea River on the central Oregon coast to the Greater Lower Columbia region were not necessarily held at the dwellings of specific spirits. Lower Chinookans, for example, in the aforementioned Guardian Spirit Complex, commonly used five isolated sites for vision quests. The ritualized journey to these sites, involving swimming and a prescribed sequence of dives, was the key to success rather than the destination per se. The potential guardian spirits did not reside at the quest site but were called to it by the correct behavior of the youth.

Similarly, during the subsequent, annual guardian spirit dances, individual Chinookans hosted five-day ceremonies at their homes to honor their spirit powers. The spirit could then direct the dancers to move the ceremony to a specified place. Large canoes traveled abreast to maintain the drumming and singing, as participants paddled, often several miles, to the prescribed locations. Finally, the spirit dictated the principal food for the concluding feast, advising the medicine person of the place where the food would be found.[10]

Chinookan guardian spirits were, in a sense, more mobile than those invoked in the southern world renewal ceremonies, and some ceremonial places could effectively shift and fluctuate according to the demands of spirits and the behavior of humans. Still, in both regional examples, place and spirituality were clearly, if differently, connected, and they offer evidence that *Illahee* was, at once, regional and local. Proper individual and communal behavior demanded cooperation to access both spirits and places, linking villages and kin groups within regions.[11] Shared ceremonies reflected the identities of Native communities and their space within these regional networks.

The Native peoples of *Illahee* could and did move about considerably and yet retained a relatively fixed sense of their place. Communities often separated and coalesced seasonally. Some bands of Klikitats and Klamaths spent significant time away from their respective homelands and were infamous among Willamette Valley colonists as a result. Also, by 1850, intermarriages were occurring among Native groups over huge distances. An example of this intermarriage would be an Ikiraku'tsu (Bear Creek Shasta) headman of the Rogue Valley, who married his daughter to a man of the Wascopam, hundreds of miles to the north.[12] Indeed, entire bands sometimes emigrated.

The names that colonialists attributed to "tribes," or "nations," often derived from the location of peoples when the Westerners first encountered them. The so-called upper Coquille Tribe, Athapaskans of the upper Coquille River, had occupied that river drainage since only about 1800. According to Coquel Thompson, his father was a boy when his people moved from the Umpqua River to the upper forks of the Coquille.[13] Coquel Thompson's family history was hardly unique—a common method of defusing intravillage conflict was to found another town.[14]

Regardless of their movements, individuals and groups retained their core sense of identity: kinship connections to their home communities. Famed Klamath headman Lileks spent much of the early to mid-1840s among the Wascopam and at The Dalles mission. He could and did, however, return to his kin at Klamath Lake. Indeed, with Chiloquin, he used his experiences to consolidate several bands from Klamath Lake and Klamath Marsh into a "tribe" and to lead them through the tumultuous 1850s and 1860s without significant conflict with Euro-Americans, a relatively peaceful experience not shared by neighboring Modocs and Shastas.[15] The Klikitats of the Willamette Valley could similarly return to their homeland and relatives on the Columbia Plateau. Indeed, those relatives on the Plateau negotiated for the safe return of their Willamette Valley kinfolk in 1855, during the last of colonial Oregon's intermittent "Indian wars."[16] Furthermore, as discussed, social and ceremonial "visiting" was evident throughout western Oregon, binding communities across ethnic and linguistic lines. As suggested by historian Alexandra Harmon's work on Indian identity around Puget Sound, Native peoples of the Pacific Northwest were intertwined with one another, and identity was a fluid phenomenon.[17] Saying such is not to argue that "an Indian is an Indian," but rather that the simplistic tribal designations of the treaty era, which have since been reified by anthropological scholarship and government bureaucracy, poorly reflects flexible Native constructions of the mid-nineteenth century.[18] *Illahee* was a linkage of local communities, bound and sometimes divided by kinship ties.

Such weblike connections distinguished *Illahee* from the single cord of national citizenship that bound Euro-Americans, excluded "others," sanctioned Judeo-Christianity, and systematized property and government. No "middle ground" was ever going to emerge between an Oregon defined by Anglo-American society and *Illahee*.[19] Particularly by the 1850s, the conceptions of a single nation-state, citizenship, and absolute land title were too well supported by demographics and the environment of western Oregon to compel accommodation by colonials. Euro-Americans could literally set the terms, including the identities of Indian peoples; indeed, they had to. As had been true since the landing of Columbus, imperialists had to impose manipulable definitions of identity, place, and property on the indigenous people.

Thus, the legal creation of Native "nations" was essential to American colonization. The United States relied on identifying a body politic to cede specific tracts of land through treaty. The treaty then legitimized the removal of aboriginal "citizens" who had supposedly agreed to vacate the ceded territory. American empire created Indian nation-states from what were actually multikin villages that lacked centralized governmental authority. Furthermore, according to the Doctrine of Discovery, Native national status included the burden of limited sovereignty. From their inception, Native nations were thus subject to the superior sovereignty of the "discovering" and "conquering" nation, the United States. Of course, the Americans' ultimate path from discovery to conquest and colonization was hardly preordained or unchallenged.

Chapter Narrative Introduction

When Capt. Robert Gray successfully navigated the treacherous mouth of the Columbia River in 1792, he sought sea otter pelts necessary for the China trade, the jewel of trans-Pacific commerce. As well, in exploring the coastal waters of the lower Oregon Country, maritime traders sought a safe, reliable supply point in the milder climes of the southern Northwest Coast. Importantly, Gray also sailed into the world of imperial politics. As the first mariner to enter the lower Columbia River, he established a claim to the unknown lands of the lower Oregon Country for the United States by right of discovery. Gray's primary concern was peltry, not politics, but the latter proved more crucial in the long term.

Later in 1792, British ships also successfully navigated the Columbia's mouth, sailed farther upriver, and established more contacts with Chinookan peoples than Gray had. In the ensuing decades, American and British ships plying the maritime trade slowly drew the lower country into the trans-Pacific economy and into the competitive realm of imperial claims. The trade was always primary, but the politics were ever present. The early history of western Oregon, from its "discovery" in 1792 to its American statehood in 1859, featured a similar pattern: different peoples came for the promise of fulfilling specific dreams, from the monetary to the spiritual. Intentionally or not, however, they contributed to the larger imperial competitions between Great Britain and the United States, between colonial and indigenous peoples, and between colony and empire. Like people in colonial histories elsewhere, local actors and local conditions both shaped and were shaped by the forces of nineteenth-century imperialism, a global history in which the United States was intimately involved.

As early as 1804, the vast, distant, and unknown Oregon Country came to symbolize a promised land to ensure the future of the American republic. With the ink on the Louisiana Purchase barely dry, Thomas Jefferson ordered the addition of the disputed Oregon Country to the explorations of Meriwether Lewis and William Clark. To the Jeffersonian Republicans, the lands of the West would provide a "safety valve" for the growing American population and subsequent generations. Available property would allow the imagined republic of honest yeoman farmers to continue to grow and would forestall the feared decline into a corrupt, elite-dominated, wage-earning political economy like that then taking shape in Europe and the northeastern United States. Westward expansion of the United States would promote an "empire of liberty."

Jefferson's dream had its detractors. The political opposition countered that such imperial expansion would foster dangerous democratic impulses, threatening order and stability, and would ultimately fracture the nation.[20] British merchants, Canadian traders, and promoters of the British Empire feared the growth and competition of the precocious United States, rarely letting an imperial challenge to the Oregon Country go unmet. So much was invested in a place that so few Westerners actually had visited or knew much about. Indeed, it is through the experiences of those who actually did venture to the Oregon Country, rather than another study of distant elites, that one can better understand how Oregon was created from *Illahee*, a history of changes among the colonial population, Native peoples, the local environment, and the American and British empires.

With the establishment in 1811 of a small, American enterprise grandly known as Fort Astoria, both the colonial trade and the imperial competition advanced significantly. British Canadians quickly challenged the American claim of financier John Jacob Astor, and eventually an ironic sideshow to the War of 1812 resulted. Still, the ground-level realities had more to do with everyday relations between Native Oregonians and the diverse colonial population of Britons, Americans, Canadians, Eastern American Indians, Native Hawaiians, and the slowly increasing population of people whose heritage stemmed from two or more of these national and ethnic categories. Indeed, nationality often mattered less than personal conduct in an evolving colonial world where neither the people nor the relations among them remained fixed for long. Trade, sexual relations, diplomacy, conflict, and, particularly after 1830, disease made change and accommodation the only constants in the Oregon Country. Colonial life would continue to have imperial implications, but it was still the small, the local, the personal that mattered most in Oregon and *Illahee*. According to the feminist slogan of the 1970s, "the personal is political"; one should remember that the colonial was deeply personal, and themes of gender, sexuality, and individual conduct recur throughout this analysis.[21]

In 1834, another group of outsiders entered the lower country, this time bearing the Bible and the burden of Christian mission. Jason Lee and his band of Methodists believed that they must save the Indians from the perceived darkness of their culture and the corruptive influences of godless and uncivilized Western colonists. Malaria had ravaged the Native population over the past four years, and respiratory illnesses and other diseases unwittingly introduced by Westerners continued to wreak havoc on Indian people. The dismal prospects for Indian survival undermined the missionaries' faith in the mission itself. Native linguistic diversity befuddled the missionaries, and Chinook Jargon did not have the subtlety to convey a complex theology. The missionaries grew frustrated with Native reluctance to embrace evangelical Christianity and Western civilization.

Worse, between 1842 and 1844, the trickle of arriving emigrants seeking the Jeffersonian promised land grew into a flood. The Methodists' Oregon Mission became embroiled in controversies regarding the future of the Indians, colonial land claims, and imperial competition between American settlers and the British Hudson's Bay Company. Previously muted, racial constructions of Indian, mixed-blood, and white identities came to the forefront. Critical missionaries employed racial ideology to negotiate the contradictory impulses of mission and colony, to extricate themselves from their obligations of Christian mission to the Indians, and to redirect their mission efforts to the growing colonial population.[22]

Unlike traders, missionaries, and early colonists, some of whom had intermarried with local Indians, the increasing number of colonists in the 1840s and 1850s saw no place for *Illahee* in Oregon. American colonists quickly established a provisional government with which to record both their private land claims and the concomitant business transactions of selling, trading, and dividing those claims and the natural resources located on them. Without the legitimacy of either Britain or the United States, the colonists conducted private arrangements with the local Native population, believing that the United States would soon take sole imperial possession and that Congress would retroactively sanction their private claims and Indian negotiations.

The Oregon Treaty with Great Britain, the Land Donation Acts, and the Indian treaties of the 1850s exemplify both their successes and their failures at driving imperial expansion from the periphery. Native people initially negotiated treaty concessions that hindered colonial efforts. As well, federal officials, the national politics of slavery and Indian lands, and factional infighting among the Oregon colonials frustrated dreams of a colonial American world of liberal economics, republicanism, and white supremacy.[23]

Indian people sought to shape the contours of Oregon colonialism and clearly saw the treaty system as a means to this end. They and their few allies such as Rev. Josiah Parrish knew they could not prevent colonization, but they also knew that *Illahee* had to have a place in Oregon if the people were to survive. The overriding problem that Indian people faced was the near-absolute colonial conviction of racial exclusivity: the Western lands were for "whites," and Indians were to be removed and confined. The Indians were a colonized people struggling within an increasingly narrow space to define themselves and their futures. Not until recent decades have Indians been able to take advantage of the "national" status of which the United States contrived to deprive their ancestors, and to use this status to fight for basic human rights, land claims, and environmental protections, among other issues. Such was hardly the case in the 1850s, of course. Then, these people faced the horror of forced removal and confinement on the new reservations.

Indian resistance to forced removal in the 1850s from their part of *Illahee* grew from the core of who the communities were as people—to themselves, among other Indians, and to the spirit people, who were their ancestors. Euro-American colonists who noted Native "superstition" about leaving the "homes and graves of their fathers" glimpsed only the surface of the difference between *Illahee* and Oregon.[24] Western civilization conceived of Christendom as universal, existing on a plane beyond geographical boundaries; it existed wherever Christians carried and maintained it. In the mid-nineteenth century, the Indian peoples of *Illahee* would not have conceived of spirituality as being independent of place.

By the early 1850s, Native people overtly stated that they had come to rely on wage work and were becoming part of the colonial economy. They refused, however, to lose a significant part of what made them Clatsop, Nasomah, or Santiam: their sacred places. When Anson Dart, superintendent of Indian affairs, and his successor, Joel Palmer, suggested removing the western Oregon peoples to the Columbia Plateau and the Klamath Basin, Indians on both sides of the mountains condemned the proposal. Indians of the "Eastside" cited disease as one damning factor (western Oregon Indians had indeed suffered more because of their close proximity to the settlements), but they also noted reasons Palmer described as cultural.[25] To remove the Clatsops would be to steal from them a crucial piece of what it meant at that time to be Clatsop.[26] Practically, to displace the Clatsops or any western peoples among the Wascopam or Klamaths would obliterate their social status and identity.

By the mid-1850s, *Illahee* existed only in small pockets in the western valleys of the lower country (in 1853, Americans split the region into Oregon and Washington territories). In the south, however, in the borderlands between the colonial centers of Oregon and northern California, *Illahee* was much more in evidence. In 1851, an extension of the California Gold Rush attracted thousands of gold seekers, merchants, and farmers into an area that had never been fully incorporated into the fur trade or the colonial economy.

This was the "Rogue" country of southwest Oregon. So-called Rogue Indians represented several ethnicities and languages, and their reactions to the sudden arrival of colonists were similarly varied. As many Indians in the Willamette Valley and Puget Sound region had done previously and continued to do, Native peoples of southwest Oregon created economic niches in the new economy. They operated ferries, labored in mining camps and on farms and ranches, guided packers and miners, and traded food—all while trying to maintain traditional economic practices in the face of a rapidly changing ecological landscape.

Others stole, engaged in prostitution, or met hostilities from colonists with violent retribution. Many colonials resented all of these activities as infringements and threats. The Indians of southwest Oregon faced two related problems. First, a reputation as "rogues," a relic of locally undeveloped fur trade relations, became entrenched by exaggerated accounts of thievery and violence and fed an imagined threat of a pan-Indian conspiracy. Second, a frustrated, local colonial population blamed the "Rogue" Indians for a variety of political and economic problems, and some colonists viewed removing or exterminating them as a necessary first step toward progress. When federal officials and the regular army balked, colonists used a murder, which was blamed on local Shasta Indians from the Table Rock Reservation, to launch a volunteer militia effort to exterminate the "Rogues."

The ensuing "Rogue River War" of 1855–56 and its aftermath evidenced many of the most salient features of American settler colonialism. The racialization of people and place had advanced to an extremist, militant sense of Euro-American "birthright," a belief that U.S. citizenship legitimated the extermination of fully dehumanized Indians perceived to be a threat to the "public welfare."[27] The limited interracial relations had not developed a stable means of communication and conflict resolution, if such was even possible when the colonial demand for land and resources was so absolute. Imperial authority was weak, with only a token force of federal officers and regular troops to maintain order.

Additionally, the colonial fear of an intertribal confederacy from northernmost California to British Columbia fed popular hysteria about the "Indian threat" and contributed to the virulence and pervasiveness of the calls for extermination. Indeed, some evidence points to interethnic unity among Native bands of southwestern Oregon, the Columbia Plateau, and Puget Sound. Outside the local regions, however, the supposed confederacy never extended beyond the sharing of a dystopian prophecy about miserable conditions on reservations and the establishment of some unprecedentedly long-distance kin relations. Many contemporary officials noted the limitations of Indian political unity, and the pan-Indian threat was simply an excuse for attempted genocide.

In 1856, the regular army intervened and stopped the conflict, but not without engendering long-standing problems. Army officers worked against territorial claims for war remunerations, refuting many of the charges against the Indians and blaming colonial greed and racism for the war. This fight over the legacy and costs of the war stressed relations among the federal government, colonials, and Indians, with the Indians continuing to bear the brunt of local frustrations, caprice, and avarice.[28]

In 1859, Oregon achieved statehood and thus ended its colonial relationship with the United States, which had begun in 1792 with Captain Gray's "discovery." Oregon citizens, like many in the West, would long claim that their home was a "plundered province," a victim of distant capital and a distant capitol, blaming outsiders for the failure of their dreams of the promised land. Their claims, however, were and continue to be rhetorical or, at best, analogous to colonialism. Residing on reservations and in precarious homes in Oregon society, the Native population was only just entering a colonial relationship with the federal government in the 1850s. They, unlike the dominant society around them, continued to be a colonial population living under an imposed sovereignty.

Finally, as Jefferson's political opponents had feared two generations earlier, the colonization of the West did fracture the nation. The unresolved questions of race and slavery in the western territories that shaped local, regional, and national politics resulted in the Civil War only two years after the incorporation of Oregon.

Oregon, like any place, is a cultural construction of the physical landscape. After nearly seventy years, Oregon was a peripheral American state overshadowed by its southern neighbor, California, but with a citizenry that would continue attempts to make it a place where the American dream could be realized. Similarly, Native peoples re-created *Illahee* as a dynamic world that, while scattered through the margins of dominant society, continued to exist within Oregon.

This book attempts to explain this complicated and central part of American history by interweaving several "story lines" of empire, colony, and indigeneity: the personal, political, economic, cultural, environmental, and social.

CHAPTER TWO

So Many Little Sovereignties, 1792–1822

Global Trade and *Illahee*

By the late 1700s, a new era of global exchange and imperial competition had emerged: the trans-Pacific trade. The Spanish had long since consolidated their rule on the Pacific coast of the Americas and the Philippines, and the Russians colonized the far northern Pacific Rim. Relative latecomers, the British and Americans increased their commercial presence on the Pacific Ocean, attracted by the China trade and whaling. Oregon came to embody a colonial vision of the place, arriving on the ships of Western commerce. Native and Western peoples created colonial worlds together through their daily interactions, struggles for power and influence, and accommodations, as temporary and contingent as they often were. The dynamic colonial world of Oregon had to be negotiated into existence within the Native world of *Illahee*.

Although the mouth of the Columbia was dangerous and Native traders kept the costs high, the trade attracted many ships to the river. After 1792, the lower Columbia gradually emerged as a necessary stop rivaling in importance the islands above Puget Sound, particularly because the Chinooks initially forced other Native traders such as the Chehalis to trade their furs to them for subsequent exchange with the British and Americans.[1] As well, the trade ships or "coasters" sought indigenous products of the lower Columbia to trade with Indians farther north along the Northwest Coast, where sea otters—the prize of the Pacific fur trade—were more plentiful and their thicker coats more valuable.

The lower Chinookans and the neighboring Tillamooks on the coast supplied colonial traders with *clamon,* or dressed elk-skin hides that northern Native people desired as body armor, similar to the leather jerkins of medieval Europe. The *clamon* were effective for slave raids, feuds, and ceremonial wealth displays. The dressed hides were reportedly sufficient to turn an arrow as readily as a pistol ball, although the later proliferation of more powerful arms rendered them useless and quashed the market.[2] Other important Native manufactures included watertight hats and basketry. Lower Chinookans also provided some slaves, which coasters traded north of Puget Sound.[3] Coasters provided quick, direct routes for Native peoples separated by hundreds of miles of mountainous coastline. The mariners also obtained fresh water and food from the lower Columbia at the beginning and end of their Northwest Coast visits.

The same mild climate that limited the sea otter population also made the Greater Lower Columbia region a good choice for a colonial trade settlement. A lower Columbia station could gather inland peltries, supply coasting vessels and the Russian posts in southeast Alaska and northern California, and establish the trader's nation with a secure imperial claim. Still, for years, no empire attempted to establish a colony in this remote region. The situation would not begin to change until 1805, with the arrival of the Corps of Discovery from the United States traveling overland from the Missouri River east of the Rocky Mountains. That the Americans would be the first was far from a foregone conclusion.

The Russians began exploiting Aleut and Kodiak hunters to acquire sea otter pelts for trade at the northern Chinese market at Kyakhtah in the 1740s. The British did not "discover" the profitable trade for Northwest Coast sea otters until 1788, exchanging them at Canton (Guangzhou) in southern China. Justifiably distrustful of Europeans, the Chinese maintained different ports and markets for the western and eastern Europeans. This was despite repeated Russian complaints that prices were lower at Kyakhtah than at Canton and that the northern market required an excruciatingly expensive overland trek from coastal Siberia through Mongolia.[4] The western Europeans and the Americans who soon joined them made the best of their superior trading position at Canton.

By the early 1790s, English and American mariners regularly "coasted" the Northwest Coast seeking sea otter and other pelts for Canton. By the early 1800s, Hawai'i became the crucial resupply point for fur traders and whalers pursuing profits in the Pacific Basin. Markets and supply points secured, Western commerce had firmly established the trans-Pacific trade and Oregon's place within it by the 1810s.

The Native people of the Oregon Country had long maintained indigenous trade networks and welcomed the colonial trade.[5] Some of the earliest furs went directly from clothing Nuu-chah-nulth and Chinook Indians to adorning Chinese Mandarins across the Pacific. From the mouth of the

A Chinook lodge, ca. 1841 (Wilkes, *Narrative of the United States Exploring Expedition*; image courtesy of the Oregon Historical Society)

Columbia River to the middle stretches along the Columbia Plateau, Native peoples of the Oregon Country prized *tia Commashuck* (blue "chief beads") crafted by Canton artisans and obtained from coasters and Native intermediaries.[6] Although *tia Commashuck* never displaced *hyqua*, or dentalia, shells as the medium of indigenous exchange, beads from China formed the basis for much of the colonial-Native exchanges in the first decades.

By introducing new goods, markets, and trade routes, the colonial trans-Pacific trade radically altered the preexisting Native trade network of the Oregon Country. Indeed, the imperial outreach from Europe and the United States had already profoundly changed the Native Northwest before Gray's arrival: the smallpox epidemic of the 1780s had spread from colonials in the early maritime trade and then along indigenous trade routes. As well, Spanish colonization of the Southwest had changed life through the indirect introduction of horses to the Northwest. With horses, Plateau peoples drastically increased their travel distances for hunting, trading, and raiding, and horses added to their striking power.[7] Gray's visit provided the direct introduction of non-Indians and their manufactures, but the changes caused by Western colonialism had begun years before his arrival. After Gray's voyage, change accelerated. The British followed Gray in the fall of 1792, ventured farther upriver, traded, and staked their competing imperial claim to the Greater Lower Columbia River region.[8]

Several factors conflated to limit the imperial competition over the lower Oregon trade to Great Britain and the United States. The Russians were mostly interested in sea otters, or "Мяркое Зопото," literally "soft gold," rather than the furbearers of interior Oregon.[9] From their tenuous colony among the Sitka Tlingits, the Russians reached southward to Alta California, the terminus of the sea otter lands. The pelts of the sea otters became browner and thinner south of Puget Sound and consequently were less valuable to Chinese traders at Canton and Kyakhtah, partly limiting Russian activity in the Oregon Country and Alta California. The Spanish further inhibited the development of an Alta California colony, restricting the Russians to small trading posts dependent on external food supplies. An attempt by the Russians to establish a settlement in lower Oregon also was unsuccessful. In March 1806, as the Corps of Discovery was heading back to St. Louis, Capt. Nicolai Rezanov of the *Juno* failed in his attempt to cross the bar at the Columbia's mouth. The Russians did not mount another colonization attempt before 1811, when the construction of the Americans' Fort Astoria effectively preempted them.[10]

The Spanish had their silver mines in New Spain and Peru and were interested in the Northwest Coast trade only insofar as it attracted unwanted imperial competitors to the Pacific American coastline. In 1788, the Spanish ventured to the Northwest Coast to monitor the Russians; earlier Spanish voyages had only been exploratory, although the Spanish claimed the entire coastline. On encountering British ships, the Spanish established presidios among the Wakashan peoples, the Makahs on the northern tip of the Olympic Peninsula, and the Nuu-chah-nulths across the straits on western Vancouver Island, deploying Native Peruvians as soldiers. Although the Spanish advised Maquinna, the principal Nuu-chah-nulth headman of the Nootka Confederacy, that they were the reigning authority, the presidio commander refused to intervene when Maquinna complained of abuses by European and American coasters.

The ineffective Spanish presence soon dissipated with the so-called Nootka Dispute with Great Britain in 1789–90. Maquinna had granted British Capt. John Meares "a spot of ground . . . whereupon a house might be built for the accommodation of the people we intend to leave behind."[11] Francisco Eliza as presidio commander at Santa Cruz de Nootka did not want even a small British presence on the Nootka Sound and seized the property, asserting Spanish sovereignty over the Northwest Coast through the right of discovery. The

British threatened war over the matter and argued that, because the Spanish had not occupied the region until the belated and small presidios were built, their claim was void. France, embroiled in revolution, could not come to the aid of its Catholic ally, while Britain had the likely support of Prussia and the Netherlands. Spain backed off and agreed to compensate British losses and to honor neutral trade on the Northwest Coast.[12]

The British used the same argument against the Spanish that they had advanced two centuries earlier regarding the Atlantic Coast: occupation determined the legitimacy of imperial claims. Ironically, this precedent would later haunt the British when the United States vied for dominion in the Oregon Country. Spain withdrew from the Northwest Coast in 1790 and, in 1819, it officially ceded claims north of Alta California (42nd latitude) jointly to Great Britain and the United States.

Chinookan peoples of the lower Columbia cared little about Western nationalism or imperial interests, yet the trade depended on their cooperation. Their diffuse, kin-based world of villages, or "little sovereignties," as one trader termed them, prevented colonials from effectively instituting systematic trade policies or unilaterally determining relations among their employees and local Indians. Because the region's Native population did little of the actual trapping, unlike the fur trade in Eastern North America, Western traders had to acquire permission to trap in addition to permission to acquire food, resources, and living space. To the frustration of competing empires, the lower Chinookans initially considered the maritime traders individually, not nationally, in keeping with the way in which "village" identities were configured in *Illahee*. Chinookans indicated their favorites among the thirteen ships that visited biannually, basing their preferences on the captain's disposition and prices.

The Clatsops referred generally to all European traders as *pâh-shish'-e-ooks,* "cloth men" or "blanket people," for one of the common trade items.[13] This sobriquet was in keeping with the local trading scene of the Greater Lower Columbia region, where peoples sometimes received the name of their most prominent contribution.[14] For example, Clatsop meant "pounded salmon," a dried preparation comparable to pemmican that formed such a crucial part of the diet and culture of the Northwest. The Clatsop people were so called not because they produced a large surplus of that important product but because the calm, sheltered bay in which lower Chinookans obtained it from visiting upper Chinookans was the "Clatsop" place.[15] Other Native peoples of *Illahee* received names that suggested their ranking within the Native economic and cultural networks of the Greater Lower Columbia. The

Chinookans derisively called the only local Athapaskan speakers "Claxstars" (round heads), both because they did not participate in the regional practice of head flattening and because of poor relations with the prominent village of Chinook (*qwatsa'mts*).[16]

In the early decades of the fur trade, the lower Chinookan peoples benefited handsomely at the expense of both colonialists and other Native peoples. Under the nominal leadership of Concomly and his wife, "who by influence or example kept order as much as possible," the Chinooks and their lower Chinookan neighbors—the Willapa Chinooks, Clatsops, Cathlamet, Wahkiakum, and Clackamas—earned reputations as shrewd traders. Meriwether Lewis and William Clark famously wrote of them: "[T]hey are great higlers in trade . . . [and have] an avericious all grasping disposition. [I]n this respect they differ from all Indian I ever became acquainted with."[17] Unstated, the explorers were noting a "respect" that the Chinooks seemingly had in common with colonial traders. Indeed, the Chinookan traders frustrated Europeans and Euro-Americans through their adept bargaining and by refusing to accept fixed prices or cheap company goods, leading partly to trader David Thompson's characterization of them in 1811 as "the scoundrels that possess this River from its mouth up to the first Falls."[18]

According to the Nootka Dispute's resolution, the Lewis and Clark expedition down the Columbia could not secure the Oregon Country for the United States: theirs was only a temporary occupation. Still, they carefully left evidence of their stay in the form of a written statement, a map of their travels, and a listing of their names; these papers were nailed inside their "Fort Clatsop" and were given to local Native headmen.[19] The expedition improved the American diplomatic position vis-à-vis British claims, as had Gray's successful navigation of the Columbia's mouth in 1792. By design, the Lewis and Clark expedition had important imperial implications.

The Corps of Discovery followed the Louisiana Purchase of 1803, by which the young United States obtained 828,000 square miles of the northern Great Plains (between modern Canada and the American Southwest) east of the Rocky Mountains from Napoleon. Although the purchase did not include the vast and largely unknown Oregon Country, the Lewis and Clark expedition attempted to advance the commercial relationship between Euro-American and Native traders there.[20] Such could have future imperial implications if the United States could cement ties with the lower Chinookans to the exclusion of the British. Canada's Northwest Company had already established trading forts on the upper Columbia River and in much of modern British Columbia and was an obvious possible competitor for the traders of the United States.

The Corps of Discovery descended below the Cascade Mountain divide and arrived on the lower Columbia in late October 1805, too late for the fall visit of the coasters and too early for the spring trade. As was partly their mission, the explorers (particularly Clark) wrote extensively about the indigenous peoples, native flora and fauna, the climate, the geography, evidence of competing colonialists, and the economic promise of the region.[21] They witnessed much of the bustling trade among the Native peoples on the lower river, along some of the tributaries, and on the neighboring coastline; trade, as far as the explorers could judge, was conducted almost entirely by water.

The lower Chinookans employed three distinct canoe types to navigate the rough coastal and intertidal waters, the expansive estuaries, and the swift currents of the narrows and subsidiary streams. Lewis and Clark were taken by the functional designs but particularly impressed with the ornately carved décor of the canoes (and gabled plank houses), commenting that "the woodwork and sculpture of these people . . . evince an ingenuity by no means common among the Aborigines of America."[22] They noted relatively few horses, compared with the Columbia Plateau and Plains Indians, because the animals were of less use in the river economy, although lower Chinookans did obtain a few from Sahaptins upriver.[23]

The previous decade of maritime trade had left a permanent imprint on the region, with the effects of disease already taking an early, brutal toll and Chinese, American, and European trade goods abounding. Clark wrote, "The *Small Pox* had distroyed a great number of the nativs in this quarter. it provailed about 4 or 5 yrs Sinc among the Clatsops, and distroy'd Several hundreds of them, four of their Chiefs fell a victym to it's ravages." He also noted many burial canoes on land a few miles downstream from Fort Clatsop and empty villages among the Tillamooks on the coast.[24] Among the many survivors, China plates, red and blue blankets, old muskets (mostly in disrepair from lack of maintenance and firing gravel instead of scarce lead balls), kettles, pots, and *tia Commashuck*, or "chief beads," were ubiquitous.

During the winter, at least, the most common trade item among Indians was food. Roots, particularly wapato, "the most valuable of all roots," grew in the marshy river valleys and formed "a principal article of traffic between the inhabitants of the valley and those of this neighborhood or sea coast."[25] The expedition's Fort Clatsop stood between the wapato suppliers—mostly Wahkiakums and Cathlamets with ready access to the wetlands of adjacent valleys—and the three principal Clatsop villages; however, the Corps rarely obtained as much wapato as they desired from the Native traders.

Fort Clatsop: A Temporary Village in *Illahee*

As temporary occupants, the Corps of Discovery faced material and social problems during their winter on the lower Columbia (November 1805–April 1806). The Corps' supply of trade goods was largely depleted by their venture up the Missouri, across the Rockies, and down the Columbia—which limited their bargaining ability. Moreover, the Native traders seemed unwilling to trade all their foodstuffs for non-Native manufactured goods, preferring to spread out their trade and diversify the nature of what they obtained. More importantly, the Corps lacked any kin connections, which obligated Native traders in ongoing reciprocal relationships. Although the Americans did nothing to establish kin relations, they did realize the trade value of the Clatsop-manufactured goods, and the Corps resupplied their trade stores for the return journey with the crafts of the lower Chinookans. Subsequent land-based traders would continue this practice, as the Sahaptin peoples of the Plateau readily bartered for lower Chinookan manufactures.[26]

Whereas the Corps made no lasting interpersonal connections, they did necessarily interact with Chinookans and commented on the sexual relations between the men of Fort Clatsop and their Indian neighbors. Indeed, the Corps' writings provide early evidence for how Chinookan sexuality was affected by the maritime trade and provide a baseline for changes during the subsequent land-based trade beginning in the 1810s. Their observations could be problematic, however, particularly when they found their way (in altered form) into publication. Indeed, Lewis's published history of 1814 actually was written by the New York financier Nicholas Biddle, who was not an expedition member. Biddle sensationalized the original journals, changing details presumably to increase sales.

Such was true generally of the journals-cum-travel-literature written during and about the early trans-Pacific trade, which was already taking shape before the Corps laid an Oregon claim for the United States. The works became so prevalent that Ross Cox worried that "I might subject myself to the charge of plagiarism . . . if I touched on" a discussion of Hawaiian culture and "vices." Cox's complaint that charges "of lasciviousness . . . [are] too general," and his proto-relativist stance that "English chastity" is not judged by "the disgusting conduct of the unfortunate females who crowd our sea-ports and ships" was not typical of his time.[27] Nonetheless, thanks to Cox and others such as Biddle, Chinookan women received an inaccurate, lascivious reputation similar to that of Pacific Islanders, distorting our understanding of the social history of *Illahee*.[28]

Biddle's account—although none of the journals—claims that Chinookan men and women prostituted their daughters and nieces when conducting trade with the explorers.[29] The several journals mention only one group of young women as prostitutes, and prostitution seems to have been an infrequent and minor activity for them. The six women acted under the direction of a Chinook headman Delashelwilt from *qwatsa'mts* or, more accurately, his wife, commonly referred to as "the old baud." The Corps encountered the group three times: November 21, 1805; March 15, 1806; and shortly after departing Fort Clatsop, probably March 24, 1806.[30] Biddle added "her daughters & nieces" where Clark had written only "her 6 young squars."[31]

The women's supposed status as kin stemmed perhaps from conflating a separate story in which a family member was supposedly prostituted, as related by Clark to Biddle four years later in an interview. However, the man intended a custom-of-the-country marriage, not prostitution. Clark told Biddle that "[a] Clatsop whom I had cured of some disorder brought me out of gratitude his sister." Clark apparently ignored her and, after she stayed "two or three days in [the] next room with Chabono's wife [Sacajawea]" and "declined the solicitations of the men," she returned to her village.[32]

The lower Chinookan peoples were accustomed to the common fur trade practice of informal or custom-of-the-country marriages through contact with maritime traders. Most famously, one woman bore a tattoo "J. Bowman," referring most likely to a mariner from a seasonal trade ship and suggesting such a relationship.[33] Furthermore, the published accounts often conflicted with the original journals, in which authors enhanced juicy details. In the published version of Sgt. Patrick Gass's journal of 1811, for example, the number of "the old baud's" prostitutes grew from six to nine and their encounters from three to "frequently."[34] Although Gass included this statement under the entry date of March 21, 1806, it is part of longer, rambling commentary ruminating on all the "Flatheads" west of the Rocky Mountains and seems likely to have been written later and with publication in mind.

Indeed, the Corps' journals make it clear that the encounters were not frequent. On the second meeting on March 15, Lewis and Clark both commented that "this was the same party that had communicated the venerial to so many [Clark says 'several'] of our party in November last," and they advised their men to avoid contact. The attribution of so much venereal infection is noteworthy as well, because only one expedition member, Silas Goodrich, is explicitly mentioned as having contracted the disease, likely syphilis, in Oregon.[35] Finally, according to Sergeant Ordway's journal, which was not rewritten for publication, the third encounter with the "old baud" and the six young women occurred on the river and consisted of their offering "a Sea otter Skin dryed fish & hats for Sale," not themselves.[36] Compared with the original journals, the published accounts of the expedition overstated and misrepresented the prostitution of the six young women.

The last piece of evidence from the Corps' journals for the Chinookan peoples' supposed propensity to prostitute family members derives from an interaction between the captains and a young Clatsop man of some status named Cuscalar. The captains first met Cuscalar when visiting his village on December 9, 1805, shortly after the Corps established Fort Clatsop nearby on the south bank of the Columbia, where they awaited spring and their return across the Rocky Mountains. Two weeks later, on December 23, Clark learned that Cuscalar was ill and "[s]ent him a little pounded fish [because Cuscalar] could not come to See us." The following day Cuscalar, his brother "and 2 young Squar" came to Fort Clatsop, presenting mats for Lewis and Clark "and a parcel of roots" in exchange for two files, which the lower Chinookans prized for woodworking. Clark decided that he could not afford to part with the tools and refused the trade, "which displeased Cuscalah a little. [H]e then offered a woman to each of us which we also declined axcepting which also displeased them." The identity of the two women is unknown. Neither seems to have been the wife of Cuscalar, because she was identified on a visit five days later and Clark made no connection between them. The intent of Cuscalar and his brother is equally unclear; the captains assumed prostitution, but establishing a beneficial kin connection through custom-of-the-country marriage may have been their goal. Although Clark identified Cuscalar as "the young Clatsop chief," he had not bestowed on him a chief medal as he had the elders Coboway and Comowool. Cuscalar may have been seeking to advance his position vis-à-vis the new traders through their curious ranking system, viewing Clark's gift of pounded salmon as an opening. Anthropologist Theodore Stern notes that regular trading partners in the Native Columbia trade network did not barter as much as they presented reciprocal gifts. In this light, Clark's pounded salmon and the mats and roots of Cuscalar take on a different meaning, particularly because Cuscalar fully expected the files and became upset when Clark balked. Marriage facilitated such trading partnerships by establishing reciprocal kin obligations. Still, the journals do not reveal Cuscalar's and his brother's intentions or the women's social status. The women may even have been slaves, as was the young cook whom Cuscalar offered to trade to Clark for "some beeds and a gun" on February 28.[37]

The roles and treatment of Chinookan slaves caused some confusion in the Corps' ethnography, further contributing to misunderstandings about the historical development of prostitution and slavery in *Illahee* as well as the larger social changes they represented. Lewis and Clark commented that Cuscalar had purchased his cook from Tillamooks, who had taken him from a "great distance" down the coast. Both men also stated that Chinookan families adopted slaves and treated "them as their own children."[38] Such was obviously a relative assessment, a comparison with the lives of African American slaves such as York, a member of the expedition. Chinookan slaves lived, worked, and sometimes intermarried with Chinookan commoners, accounting for some confusion among Westerners regarding their identity and social status.

One marker that had distinguished slaves from higher-status individuals was head flattening. Chinookan parents tied their infants' heads to cradle boards to produce the desired mark of distinction and beauty. As the fur trade grew in the 1790s, however, so too did the practice of head flattening. By 1805, reflecting increased competition and raiding, the practice extended up to the middle Columbia, up the Willamette River, and along the coast from the Alsea River on Oregon's central coast to the Olympic Peninsula; hence the Corps' tendency to refer to most Indians west of the Rocky Mountains as "Flatheads." Some ethnic groups of lower Oregon adopted head flattening to add to their prestige regionally, to make it more likely that an advantageous marriage could be arranged with the increasingly powerful Chinooks.

Another reason was to protect women from slave raiding, which expanded with the fur trade. In the 1790s, slave raiding and trading became integral parts of Native Northwest interactions, as competition rose with colonial trade and imported disease pressured populations. Ideally, on the lower Columbia, slaves were captured or traded from "round-headed" peoples, or Claxstars. Accordingly, on the eastern and southern frontiers of the Greater Lower Columbia region, only girls' heads were flattened, because they were more likely targeted in slave raids and their communities sought some nominal protection.[39]

Although few in number, many if not all Native women that the Chinookans prostituted were likely slaves. Young women captured or obtained through trade, although not chattel, had little social status or control over their bodies. Slavery made one effectively kinless, without a local identity that others were bound to respect. Emphasizing slaves' otherness, Chinookans commonly named them for their country of origin.[40]

Slavery certainly existed prior to the fur trade, but it grew and took on new purposes. Prostitution arose as a nexus. Throughout the Pacific trade, maritime encounters between colonial male sailors and Native women were sometimes sexual and almost always fleeting. Indigenous peoples varied in their responses to the challenges posed to their constructions of gender, sexuality, and social structure. In the havoc-wrought world of the 1790s and the early 1800s, Chinookans sought social stability by using slaves for sexual labor. Women, seized in raids and traded away, arrived on the lower Columbia without kin relations, thus with no social status or protection afforded by their lineage. The transformation of women into slaves could subsequently be reversed by marriage, establishing a kin connection to the community. With the growth of the Northwest Coast fur trade, slave women filled the newly created role of prostitutes.[41]

The Corps seemed unaware of the profound social changes they were witnessing and in which they were participating. Still, the prevalence of prostitution on the lower Columbia did not match the exaggerated claims of the published Corps accounts, and the Chinookans clearly sought more stable connections through intermarriage.

It may be as James Ronda argued that "[t]he Chinookans, whose lives focused on trading and material wealth, saw sex as an equally valid way to amass the goods that signaled power and prestige."[42] Unfortunately, however, the way in which this nascent, ancillary sex trade worked in the first decade of the nineteenth century remains unclear. During the Corps' stay, two conclusions seem evident: custom-of-the-country marriages were sought by high-status and ambitious Chinookans, and prostitution existed in a limited and casual form. Seeking to maintain or improve status through marriages with the newcomers was in keeping with Chinookan practices.

The six ostensible prostitutes acted under the direction of Delashelwilt's wife. They engaged in what might be termed *prostitution* once and possibly offered a second chance to the Corps—suggesting that such material-sexual exchanges existed by 1805. With hindsight, these women may be seen as archetypal: they were directed by others, and sex work was not a principal or frequent labor. Their probable slave status suggests that the Chinooks were beginning to incorporate a form of prostitution into their version of slavery to meet the challenges of a rapidly changing world: an indigenous world of *Illahee* that was becoming a colonial world of Oregon.

Toward a Colonial Society

With the departure of the Corps of Discovery in the spring of 1806, the Pacific trade continued as a series of biannual maritime encounters until 1811 and the construction of Fort Astoria, again in Clatsop country on the south bank of the lower Columbia. The enterprise was primarily a commercial venture to benefit John Jacob Astor and his partners, but because of the competing expansionist nations involved in the Pacific trade, Fort Astoria also was an imperial venture by default. When the international entrepreneur Astor (a German who immigrated to New York via London) determined to establish a trading post on the northern Pacific American coast to boost his profits from the maritime trade, he was necessarily creating a permanent U.S. presence on the lower Columbia. Well aware of the political climate and its possible benefits, Astor approached President Jefferson for a monopoly of the land-based trade of the lower Oregon country, citing nationalist concerns. Jefferson dismissed Astor's request, preferring free competition among American traders west of the Mississippi River. East of that boundary, the central government had been operating trading houses through its factory system since 1796, attempting an imperial monopoly of Indian trade, until abolishing the system in 1822.[43] The factory system existed to maintain order and peace between Indians and frontier settlements and, more nefariously, operated at a loss to encourage Indian debt, which could then be repaid through land cessions.

The vastly distant Oregon Country without settlements or the concomitant need to "extinguish Indian title" to the land did not merit the governmental expense of operating a trading house, and, all things being equal, Jefferson and his generation eschewed monopolies. Even the British barred monopolies within their domestic markets; the Hudson's Bay Company and the East India Company were seen as necessary evils for efficiently ordering the empire at the least expense to the Crown and Parliament.[44] Jefferson also was not convinced that the Oregon Country would ever be more than a "great state" with an affinity with the United States; constituent statehood for the far-off land seemed highly unlikely at the turn of the nineteenth century. Without his desired monopoly or significant support from the central government of the United States, Astor labored to gather the capital and expertise for his proposed Oregon venture.[45]

In 1810, Astor sent one party by sea led by Duncan McDougall aboard the ill-fated *Tonquin* and a second party overland led by Wilson Price Hunt. The *Tonquin* party arrived at the Columbia in the spring of 1811. They lost two boats and eight men in attempting to cross the treacherous mouth, and gained passage only by the luck of an in-coming tide, which carried the helpless ship into the estuary and away from the rocks. The "Astorians" arrived at their selected fort site on April 12, 1811. Like the Corps of Discovery, they opted for a south-bank location on Young's Bay; indeed, the nearby remains of Fort Clatsop quickly became a colonial tourist attraction.[46] The first group of overlanders did not reach the lower Columbia until January 1812, with stragglers continuing to arrive and be collected from Indian villages into the spring.

Hunt had opted to attempt a route south of the Corps of Discovery's trek across the Bitterroot Mountains, mistakenly believing that the Snake River was navigable. Having almost drowned in whitewater and having been trapped by the towering walls of Hells Canyon, Hunt's party were fortunate to have survived the journey. On his return trip to St. Louis in 1814, Robert Stuart took advantage of lessons learned and established a relatively safe route that would come to be known as the "Oregon Trail."

Although Astor failed to strike a partnership with Montreal's Northwest Company, he did lure away a few of its "wintering partners"—traders who lived and worked in the field at Fort William on Lake Superior and were invested in the company—and he created the Pacific Fur Company. The Scots-Canadian defectors from the Northwest Company added leadership, experience, and recruiting abilities. When Hunt had attempted to engage Euro-American trappers at Mackinac and St. Louis for the initial foray into the Oregon Country, few joined. Why should they venture to distant, unknown lands when productive trapping was known and readily available east of the Rocky Mountains?

Thus, the Scots-Canadians, recently of the Northwest Company, supplied the brunt of the "American" labor force for Fort Astoria by contracting French Canadians, Kanakas of Hawai'i, and eastern Indians such as Jean Baptiste Saganakei of the Lake of the Two Mountains Nipissings and Ignace Salioheni of an unnamed Iroquois band. Watatcum, a Cathlamet Chinook, became an essential "Astorian" early on as well. Contracted as a hunter, he supplied much of the fort's meat, particularly before the arrival of Saganakei, Salioheni, and the Metis Pierre Dorion. Despite the fact that only a minority of the labor force was Euro-American, the small trading post "Fort Astoria" flew the Stars and Stripes on occasion (such as Independence Day), received its funding from New York, and was thus American—more or less. In its multiethnic and multinational composition, Fort Astoria actually resembled most contemporary colonial enterprises around the world.[47]

Writing of the daily activities in the company log, factor Duncan McDougall referred to his diverse employees simply as "the People." It would be a mistake, however, to assume that this unifying, neutral identity implied an egalitarian fort society. The structure of the enterprise reflected a complex hierarchy based on labor, race, and nationality, with Hunt (Euro-American)

Fort Astoria, ca. 1841 (Wilkes, *Narrative of the United States Exploring Expedition*; image courtesy of the Oregon Historical Society)

and partner McDougall (Scots-Canadian) at the top. They were followed by subordinate Scots-Canadian partners; a few clerks, some of whom were Euro-American; ethnically European and Native trappers; and Native hunters.[48] (Hunt was absent at sea during almost the entire tenure of the Pacific Fur Company, arranging a contract with the Russians, coasting, and getting supplies at Hawai'i, leaving McDougall as the de facto leader.)

Although the Europeans and the Kanakas worked side by side in their daily pursuits of felling trees, building, gardening, tending livestock, and burning vast numbers of trees in the coal pit for charcoal (for the blacksmiths' forge), the men's bunks were segregated and their positions were not equal.[49] A sense of the way this order was maintained can be gleaned from a drunken argument between Euro-American John Mumford and an unnamed Kanaka, in which Mumford ultimately delivered a "cut very ill." Although he was in many cases a strict disciplinarian, McDougall dismissed the incident, noting that the Kanaka had been "rather forward," having overstepped his place with the white man.[50] The Kanakas seem to have been regarded similarly to continental indigenes, and Alfred Seton referred to them as "Owyhee Indians."[51] Whereas McDougall did allow "the People" to celebrate the Hawaiian New Year on October 27, 1812, the fete was not repeated in subsequent years and seems to have been an excuse for the men to get drunk and avoid their drudgery for a day.[52]

Iroquois Ignace Salioheni, although a valued and respected hunter, saw his family unceremoniously removed from the fort to make room for stores; they were told to share the "Nepisangue's house." This incident and another in which McDougall publicly upbraided Salioheni's wife may have contributed to the Iroquois' departure for home in 1814.[53] When the Cathlamet hunter Watatcum used his company-issued musket to hunt elk for his wife's Clatsop village after they had nursed him through a debilitating sickness, McDougall had him put in irons to remind him who owned the fruits of his labors.[54]

McDougall also tried to establish the hierarchy of "the People" in terms that he thought the local Indians would comprehend and respect. According to Seton, McDougall represented himself to Concomly as the chief and the Astorian employees as his slaves.[55] Indeed, when one Canadian, Paul Jeremie, became upset with McDougall and his reportedly harsh work schedule in the construction of Fort Astoria, he led a small group of runaways. Whether or not the Chinooks viewed the Astorians through the social distinctions of *Illahee* is unclear, but headmen such as Concomly did capture and return the "slaves" to the fort and expected compensation. As trader Alexander Ross wrote of Concomly: "We had some time ago found out that the sordid hope of gain alone attached this old and crafty chief to the whites."[56] If Ross's assessment was accurate, Concomly's and the Astorians' economic interests were mutual, and their views of social status were, at least, comparable.

The Politics of Little Sovereignties

Almost immediately after arrival, McDougall and company began to assess the political and economic lay of the land. It was readily apparent that, although the Chinookan peoples lived in identifiable winter settlements along the river and thus colonials could categorize the Indians, there was no unifying polity. The only political organization was through kinship networks that loosely bound people among the villages. Headmen and headwomen had little control over their people other than over their slaves. Gabriel Franchere reflected that "the villages form so many little sovereignties."[57] The Astorians thus had to establish and maintain relationships with leading men and women in each village instead of dealing with a central authority. The decentralization of power and the lack of a clear order led visiting Northwester David Thompson to complain in 1811 that the Chinookans were "bungling blockheads," because, according to his Western sensibilities, work could not be done effectively without hierarchy and regimentation. Still, Thompson reserved some of the blame for McDougall for not enforcing standardized trading practices and allowing each group of Native men and women that visited the fort with food and furs to haggle individual transactions autonomously.[58]

That McDougall and subsequent chief factors could not force a radical altering of the Chinookans' loose political structure has led to some understatements of the fur companies' political power and influence between 1811 and the early 1830s, at the height of the lower Columbia's land-based fur trade. One recent assessment is that the fur traders "operated in a political vacuum" because they "did not exert political control over the Indians of the area."[59] Although it is true that the initial form of colonialism evident in western Oregon did not resemble the British bureaucratic control that would later be achieved in India or that of the United States in the Philippines and Indian reservations, there are many stops along the road between "political vacuum" and imperial dominance.

After only a month at Astoria, McDougall began to play an obvious role in shaping the politics and diplomacy of *Illahee*. On May 16, 1811, Dhaichowan, a Clatsop headman, brought the chief trader to his village on Point Adams "to visit with a party of 80 or 90" Tillamooks and to confer about their potentially violent dispute with the Chinooks across the estuary. All parties agreed, according to McDougall, that hostilities should be avoided among "neighbors, but [Dhaichowan] said that the Tshinook's conduct forced them into those disagreeable broils, etc., etc." The following day McDougall dispatched one of his most experienced clerks, Thomas McKay, to the Chinooks to gain their side of the story and mediate. On the eighteenth, McKay returned, saying that matters should be settled amicably, "as both parties from knowing our sentiments seem averse to commence hostilities." The Astorians had not bent anyone to their will or fired a shot, but, by declaring their neutrality and wish for settlement, they played an important diplomatic and, therefore, political role.[60]

Likely the Native adversaries were not particularly fearful of the Astorians, who had yet to be reinforced by Hunt's overlanders. Still, the newcomers had obvious economic and military clout to be respected if they chose to take sides in hostilities. Because the preferred Native conflict resolution was settlement, not war, the Indians' esteem for McKay and McDougall probably improved in the wake of this incident.

As well, trade was not easily separated from politics on the lower Columbia. After gaining the trust of headmen already experienced with maritime traders—such as Coalpo and his powerful wife of the Clatsops, Concomly of Chinook village, and Kamaquiah of a neighboring north-bank village upriver—McDougall's people accompanied them to meet other potential Native trading partners farther afield. In early June, Coalpo took Robert Stuart about 80 miles up the coast to meet the Quinaults, who were coastal Salish speakers like the Tillamooks with whom the Clatsops had a close affinity. Not to be excluded, Concomly joined them as well and managed to connect Stuart with his relatives among the Quinaults.

On his return, Stuart apprised McDougall that they would have to challenge a preexisting trade network dominated by the Quileutes of the Olympic Peninsula. The purportedly "wicked" Quileutes were currently taking "the otters, beavers etc." above Gray's Harbor and trading them for hyqua shells at Newetee on western Vancouver Island's Clayoquot Sound. Maritime traders presumably then traded with the Nuu-chah-nulths at Newetee for the furs. Stuart recommended the Russian approach of obtaining "a few good Kodiak Indians" to hunt the sea otters and take the trade away from the Quileutes, Newetee, and the coasters.[61]

The Astorians eventually established direct trade with the Quinaults, the Chehalis, and others previously dependent on Chinook mediators, and these trade relationships had clear political implications. Concomly and the Chinooks would have less advantage over their Native neighbors when they could no longer mediate the fur trade. Although he could do nothing to prevent such losses, Concomly kept his eye open for any hint that other headmen had gained some advantage over him. When McDougall exhibited obvious distrust of his intentions during the first year, Concomly sent his son Chalowane to serve aboard the Astorians' little sloop the *Dolly*, with which they plied the lower Columbia to the Cascades Rapids, obtaining food, furs, timber, and cedar bark for the fledgling settlement. Concomly's overture and Chalowane's successful performance greatly warmed relations between Astoria and the Chinook.[62]

When McDougall gave Casino, principal headman of the Clackamas, a blue greatcoat, Concomly insisted on one as well. He probably coveted the French linen coat less than what the garment might represent. Mariners, the Corps of Discovery, and the Astorians each bestowed Western garb to honor and distinguish their preferred Native trading partners. Casino was one of the most powerful figures among the cluster of villages around the confluence of the Columbia and Willamette rivers, and the Astorians had demonstrated an increasing interest in the Willamette Valley since 1811. They dispatched trapping and hunting parties, opened trade with the Kalapuyan bands above the falls, and wintered the upper Oregon trappers throughout the lower Willamette Valley before permanent stations were established on the Columbia Plateau. Concomly did not miss much nor did McDougall. The blue greatcoat McDougall gave Concomly was apparently more ornate than Casino's, "handsomely made with large Capes, the whole bound with red binding: after the manner he had expressed a wish to have such a coat."[63]

The presentation of gifts, the jockeying for trade position, and entrusting the care of one's people to others (i.e., Chalowane and Robert Stuart) were inherently political acts. Company clerk Alexander Ross described the lower Columbians as "a commercial rather than a warlike people. Traffic in slaves and furs," he explained, "is their occupation."[64] Whereas his assessment is certainly oversimplified, it strongly suggests the extent to which lower Columbia economics and politics were linked, particularly from 1811 onward. Far from existing in a political vacuum, the fur companies occupied central roles in Indian political affairs and vice versa.

The political effects of the trade sometimes manifested themselves in unpredictable ways, partly because the fort demanded so many resources from the Indians during the long, if relatively mild, winters between late September and late June. (West of the Cascades, autumn, winter, and spring blur into each other as an often chilly "rainy season" broken periodically by brief periods of welcome sun and warmth, which the traders and subsequent colonialists rarely failed to note in their journals.) As evidenced by the daily entries in the company log, the fort was nearly dependent on Native traders for nourishment, most famously salmon but also sturgeon and eulachon, "smelts" that run in the months of February and March, as well as nutritious, starchy roots such as wapato and camas. This dependence caused various political problems.

During an early February squall in 1813, two Chinooks and a Clatsop drowned while bringing salmon across the estuary to Astoria. Distraught relatives from Point Adams and Chinook blamed Concomly, who had arranged for the food delivery. According to Concomly, his position as a headman and perhaps his life were threatened by the tragedy. He turned to McDougall, who agreed to provide the mourning families with gifts to cover the dead. This action helped Concomly maintain his status as a respected headman and retained him as one of Astoria's most important trading partners.[65]

The dependence pulled Fort Astoria into the lower Columbian cultural orbit as well; as in so many early colonial endeavors around the world, the indigenous people could often set the rules. The hungry and frustrated Astorians had to wait through the First Rites observances of the Chinookans before they could obtain sufficient salmon from the late spring and fall runs. Rightfully distrusting the colonials to treat the first salmon correctly, the Indians brought only a few fish to the fort, and, to the chagrin of the Astorians, each salmon was already prepared according to cleaning and roasting customs. Specifically, the salmon could not be cross-cut into steaks but had to be filleted, and the meat could not be boiled but had to be roasted. The Astorians commonly committed both faux pas. Finally, the Chinookans often dined with the Astorians to ensure that all the fish was consumed before sundown. The preparation and consumption customs demonstrated the peoples' respect for the salmon and both encouraged and welcomed the larger run to follow.[66]

McDougall complained his first year and even prepared for attack, because he thought that the Chinookan peoples had formed an alliance and would first weaken his people with hunger before mounting a concerted assault on the fort, such as it was after two months of fevered construction. He soon decided, however, that it was only a "superstition" and that he could do nothing to alter the Native peoples' practices. In subsequent years, when planning for the fort's food supply, he estimated the arrival of each "fish season" and calculated for the initial prohibitions at the beginning of the runs.

The Astorians did grow some food, but the garden was not terribly productive, and the pigs brought from Hawai'i seem to have consumed more calories in the garden than they delivered as pork. Bears, attracted by the fort's free-range pigs and goats, provided additional calories, thanks to Watatcum's musketry.

Moreover, fur traders and trappers competed directly with Indians for resources, and food quickly became a problem in the Willamette Valley.[67] It is difficult to determine the exact number of deer and elk killed by the Astorians, because they freely interchanged three measurements: the imprecise "bales," the gross weight, and the number of carcasses; but the inexact and anecdotal evidence suggests that the figures were quite high. Within two and a half years of the establishment of Astoria, Alexander Henry noted that the "Red Deer or elk are now scarce near the fort, having been hunted so much."[68] According to Gabriel Franchere, the Willamette station near modern Salem was originally established specifically to obtain meat, although, as he complained, most of it rotted before arriving at Astoria. The colonials apparently employed drying and storage techniques better suited for the colder climes of the Great Lakes and northern Plains, where their experiential knowledge was generated.[69]

Between the end of May and the beginning of August 1813, 74 bales of dried meat came to Astoria via the Willamette Valley. The number of animals is difficult to determine, because deer and the significantly larger elk were not distinguished, but Alfred Seton indicated that one shipment of 33 bales consisted of 117 "mostly deer."[70] One month after Seton's August haul, on September 9, 1813, McDougall reported that hunters "brought about 600 lbs. dried meat and a small bale of tallows [rendered fat rolls]." Far from being satisfied, McDougall explained that the limited take was "owing chiefly to the great number of Indians, which over run the Wolamat at this season of the year."[71]

Earlier, in March, McDougall had received a report from the Willamette fort that, although Wallace and Halsey were on good terms with the Calipuyas, the Indians were curiously disinterested in company trade goods. For their roots they wanted only meat, which the traders were collecting for Astoria. In June, when Wallace and Halsey arrived with their 19 bales of dried meat, they informed McDougall that they had explored the Willamette "almost to its source" and that "[t]he inhabitants throughout [the valley] are a set of poverty-strick beings, totally ignorant of hunting Furs & scarce capable of procuring their own subsistence."[72] The traders' assessment echoes the typical disparagement of Indians not yet initiated into the fur trade, but one should not wholly dismiss the claim of malnourishment. The following winter, trappers would complain that Kalapuyans stole beavers from their traps and, worse, ate them without preserving the pelts.

These three factors—McDougall's vague reference to Indians overrunning the Willamette Valley, the local Kalapuyans' apparent inability to obtain sufficient protein, and the pressures of Astorian hunters—can be best explored through an incident in January 1814. "Grande Nepisangue" was hunting on the Willamette when ten Sahaptian horsemen from the Columbia Plateau overtook him. The accounts of the ensuing threats and communication between the Nipissing and the Sahaptians vary somewhat among the writings of Seton and Henry, but the gist was the same. According to Henry, the horsemen stated that "they did not wish white people to come up this river; that our guns had driven away the deer or made them so wild that they could no longer be killed with bows and arrows; and finally, that if we did not abandon the river, they would drive us away."[73] The less experienced and more nervous Seton insisted that the Plateau Indians threatened to exterminate the whites but that the Nipissing convinced them of the colonials' superior numbers and that an attack was unwise.[74] In the end, the Nipissing promised not to hunt in the immediate area and returned to the Willamette station without further incident.

The encounter suggests that the pressures on the deer and elk populations were becoming unsustainable as early as January 1814, less than three years after the first colonial settlement. The Plateau people, who later visited Fort Astoria, had probably been hunting seasonally in the Willamette Valley for generations, although their exploitation may have increased in the previous half century since the introduction of horses from the Spanish settlements. The result of the increased competition and pressures on the deer and elk populations for the indigenous Kalapuyans seems evident in the descriptions of Halsey and Wallace, and their weakening condition may help explain why the malarial outbreaks of the 1830s were so cataclysmic in the valley. Far from being a benign presence, the fur traders had a tremendous early effect on the region.

From 1814, the problem would only grow, as Henry began offering winter exploitation of the Willamette Valley's resources to "freemen," or unaffiliated trappers, in exchange for their summer services.[75] These winter settlements gradually grew into permanent homesteads with the freemen's retirement from trapping in the late 1820s and presaged the massive settler colonialism of the 1840s and 1850s.

Astorians in *Illahee* Society

Of course, there was more to life than furs, food, and politics: as always in the North American fur trade, the company employees established "tender ties" with Native women.[76] Indeed, these "tender ties" formed the fundamental basis of the colonial world taking shape on the lower Columbia. Unlike the sexual relations between lower Chinookans and the Corps of Discovery, the permanent colonial presence of the fur trade offered a fuller account of wide-ranging relationships and, hence, a better look at the social history of *Illahee* and Oregon. On one end of the spectrum, Chief Trader Duncan McDougall and Chinook headman Concomly negotiated a formal diplomatic and economic union through the marriage of McDougall and Concomly's daughter, Ilche ("Moon Girl"). More typical and less formal, several traders, trappers, and fort employees maintained monogamous relationships with lower Columbian women for varying durations from weeks to years. On the other end, brief sexual encounters involved a simple trade transaction by Native women who appeared to have little choice: prostitution.

If McDougall or Ilche had any affection for each other before their marriage, his company log entry from their wedding day, July 20, 1813, does not reveal it. Instead, it shows only cold calculation to benefit the trade. McDougall dryly indicated that "[f]or some time past [I] have in treaty with Concomly for a female branch of his family to remain at this place." Presumably, such an arrangement would be a step above Concomly's son Chalowane's employment on the *Dolly*, which had effectively advanced the trading relationship. McDougall claimed that "the old man" was flattered, and, for the purposes of trade, "we conceive [the union] will be the means of securing to us his friendship more effectually than any other measure that could be adopted, and for which purpose only it was proposed." McDougall described the event dispassionately, as he recorded most daily fort occurrences: "In the afternoon received a visit from him for the purpose of finally settling the agreement spoken of. The female was brought, and the presents agreed on delivered; after which his people took leave without further ceremony." Actually, the parties had not settled the agreement yet. Native marriages involved reciprocal gifts and subsequent exchanges.[77]

Indeed, approximately two weeks later, McDougall noted that "Concomly brought over forty Salmon as a present, on account of the late arrangement with him."[78] Nearly a year later, in the summer of 1813, a second round of gifts settled the marriage agreement. With obvious sarcasm and disdain, Alexander Henry recorded on April 25, 1814, that, "McDougall this afternoon completed the payment for his wife to Concomly . . . he gave 5 new guns, and 5 blankets, 2 ½ feet wide, which makes 15 guns and 15 blankets, besides a great deal of other property, as the total cost of this precious lady. This Concomly is a mercenary brute, destitute of decency."[79] An ardent critic of McDougall's management of Fort Astoria, Henry undervalued the union that joined the two villages of Chinook and Astoria. Henry's may not have been a representative opinion, however. Alfred Seton wrote that "[e]very thing went on well [at Fort Astoria in 1814] owing to Mr. McDougall's marriage with Concomly's . . . daughter."[80]

Seton's positive assessment may have been true economically and diplomatically. Socially, however, Ilche's assumption of her role as Astoria's headwoman created disruptions in the diverse fort community. In Native villages throughout coastal Oregon, headwomen and first wives commanded high social status, overseeing the labors of lower-ranked women, lesser wives, children, and slaves, and they often conducted intervillage diplomacy and trade.[81] Their power was a common cause of comment from Western men unaccustomed to the public influence of women. According to Alexander Ross, "a Chinooke matron," accompanied by slaves "obsequious to her will," would "trade and barter . . . as actively . . . as the men, and it is as common to see the wife . . . trading at the factory, as her husband."[82] Ross Cox similarly noted the power of "chieftainesses" who "possess great authority" on the lower Columbia.[83]

Indeed, the traders depended greatly on the diplomacy of "Madame Coalpo" after a conflict near The Dalles in 1814. She was a powerful figure in the trade: she was married to Clatsop headman Coalpo and was related to leading families upriver to the Cascades Rapids, and her influence stretched the length of the lower river. A decade later in 1824, George Simpson claimed that she—not Coalpo—"rules the Roost," and her 1829 threats to abandon trade with Fort Vancouver in favor of American coasting vessels brought gifts and a capitulation to her demands from Chief Factor John McLoughlin.[84]

With her 1813 marriage to the headman, Chief Trader McDougall, Ilche could reasonably expect a degree of deference and authority at Astoria and to be ranked above other women and laborers, regardless of race. Indeed, Alexander Henry complained that "the lady" was "haughty and imperious."[85]

Indian women at Astoria, however, were not all native to the lower Oregon Country. Both the Pacific Fur and the Northwest companies hired Iroquois and other eastern Native people such as Nipissing and Cree to trap, hunt, and labor for the far western fur trade. The differences between Chinookan and Iroquoian social norms were readily apparent. Iroquois women did not recognize rank in the same fashion as Chinookans.[86] Clan mothers were respected elders and had important responsibilities in Iroquoian society, but there was no position comparable to Ilche's headwoman status among the largely egalitarian horticulturalists of the Northeast.[87]

Unfortunately, the interactions of the Native women from either end of the continent rarely entered the record, with the following exception offering only a suggestive peek. Upset with Iroquois hunter Ignace Salioheni's children for "playing with some trifling things," Ilche entered the Iroquois family's tent, "took the playthings from them and set them bawling." According to Henry, Salioheni's wife [anonymous as usual] responded by slapping Ilche: "Royalty was offended, and a dreadful row ensued." A disapproving Henry noted that McDougall intervened the following day, "revenged the insult offered to his lady" by "slapping and kicking Ignace's boy."[88] Five days later, McDougall gave Concomly the second round of marriage gifts, although if there was a connection to Ilche's humiliating slap from the wife of a hunter, Henry missed it.

Unfortunately again, McDougall kept no journal after being temporarily relieved of his command after the sale of Fort Astoria to the Northwest Company six months earlier. There is no mention of whether or how Saliohioni and his wife responded to McDougall's abuse of their son, but company personnel records indicate that the Iroquois family returned to Montreal at the end of the 1814 trapping season.[89]

The majority of monogamous relationships between company employees and Native women produced a predictably scant record, compared with that of McDougall and Ilche. Alexander Ross noted one other union similar to McDougall and Ilche's: the Astorians arranged a marriage with "Chief How-How" specifically to "pave the way for our trappers and hunters to return to the Cowlitz."[90] For the most part, however, writers rarely mentioned intermarriages between Native women and colonials. Quite simply, few men besides the traders and clerks kept journals, as most trappers were illiterate. There are passing references to "William's woman" or "two women" who accompanied their husbands on a trapping expedition.[91] Mariner Peter Corney mentioned vaguely in 1817 that "[t]he whole of the settlers do not exceed one hundred and fifty men, most of whom keep Indian women."[92] Similarly, in 1828, "Rocky Mountain man" Jedediah Smith remarked on the many mixed-blood women "treated as wives" during his winter on the lower Columbia.[93] As George Roberts, an officer of the Company put it: "The flower of the lower Columbia women were wives to the Company's laboring men."[94] Such comments suggest that, by the late 1810s and 1820s, custom-of-the-country marriages were forming a crucial part of the emerging colonial world.

Still, complaints most often seemed to have caused comment regarding intermarriages, such as Donald McTavish's refusal to sleep in his quarters after his two roommates "took each of them a Chinook woman."[95] Ross Cox claimed that "[n]umbers of the women reside during certain periods of the year in small huts about the fort from which it is difficult to keep the men." Cox unequivocally considered all such sexual encounters prostitution, although he noted that the men and women might stay together for weeks. His reference to the seasonal nature of the encounters refers to the periods in the early summer and late fall in which the voyageurs were present at the lower Columbia fort. Cox did not consider that the trappers might be returning to the same women or might hold affections deeper than prostitution implies.

That the men were protective of Chinookan women, however, seems evident in an altercation between one "Mac" and Jane Barnes, an adventurous English barmaid who resided at the fort temporarily in the summer of 1814, the only "white" woman on the lower Columbia for decades. Barnes disparaged "the native and half-bred women," "violently" attacking their "characters ... and [Mac] recriminated in no very measured language on the conduct of the white ladies," presumably of lower-class Portsmouth (England) tavern society. Cox states that "Mac" subsequently complained to him of Jane's "contempt on our women, and may I be d----d if the b----h understands B from a buffalo!" Cox concluded mildly, "[H]e judged her 'poor indeed.' "[96] Trappers and traders valued Native women as much for their "tender ties" as for their practical knowledge, labor, and experience. Without them, the fur trade would not have succeeded.[97] Similarly, for Chinookans, intermarriages fostered advantageous relations in the developing fur trade.

Prostitution was one of the most commonly charged and least evidenced complaints in the traders' discussions of Chinookan women. Clearly, ethnocentrism played a major role in this and other negative depictions of lower Columbia women, as critics used the ideal of Western femininity as a gauge. For nineteenth-century Westerners, women fit roughly into one of two idealistic categories: chaste or "loose." Chastity was an ideal that Western women of "the better sorts" (wealthy or noble) embodied in their conservative dress, demeanor, and actions. Any violation might damage their reputation and render them unchaste. The colonials' models for unchaste women, on the other hand, were the working poor of early industrial England and the growing cities of the United States. Displaced rural populations and impoverished immigrants could not afford to purchase "chastity," and the economic disruptions of modernity thrust prostitution, whether occasional or full-time, onto many women as a means of survival.[98] As an ideal, chastity purposely could not be reached by many Western women; it was one of several ways of sorting the population into better and lower orders.

Not surprisingly, this language made its way into colonial discourse to demean Native women of the lower Columbia. One observer readily compared Chinookan women with "their frail sisters at Portsmouth," an English port town infamous for its taverns, brothels, and desperate poverty.[99]

Unwittingly, the Chinookan women violated Western notions of chastity. They bathed daily on the open shoreline of the Columbia and, according to the voyeuristic voyageur Alexander Henry, who deemed them "disgusting creatures," they were "devoid of shame or decency."[100] Even when dressed, Western observers frequently complained of Chinookan women's "nakedness." Where Anglo women were stifled under layers of linens, woolens, and contorting stays, Chinookan women wore only skirts woven from cedar bark that hung in strands from a waist belt. From 1805 through the 1830s, Western observers ceaselessly commented on what the cedar-bark skirts did and did not reveal in various postures.[101] The Northwester David Thompson made the connection between dress and sexuality explicit, concluding "from what I could see and learn of them they are very sensual people."[102]

Besides idealized Anglo women, colonials had another source of comparison to disparage "naked" Chinookans: Native women of the Columbia Plateau or "upper Oregon Country." Seeking to control the trade and claim the territory of the massive Columbia Basin, competing colonials raced to establish relations with Native peoples throughout the interior of the Pacific Northwest. Brigades from Astoria moved quickly upriver, and the Northwesters moved downriver from the Columbia headwaters, establishing small trade forts beginning in 1812. By the late 1810s, forts were strewn throughout the region. Not surprisingly, the Sahaptian and Shoshone women the colonials met wore more clothing than lower Chinookans; they lived in the high desert country, where the weather is colder and more severe than the sea-level Columbia estuary, which is warmed by Pacific currents. As well, the cedar-rich forests, which supplied Chinookan clothing materials, stop at the Cascade Mountains, which trap most of the substantial moisture on the west side and leave ponderosa and lodgepole pines and other species of conifers tolerant of dry conditions to dominate the eastern plateau and canyon country. East of the Cascades, people made their clothing from animal hides.

Ross Cox swooned over the Wallawalla women of the middle Columbia: "The females . . . were distinguished by a degree of attentive kindness, totally removed from the disgusting familiarity of the kilted ladies below the rapids, and equally free from an affectation of prudery. Prostitution is unknown among them; and I believe no inducement would tempt them to commit a breach of chastity."[103] David Thompson offered similar appraisals as he returned up the Columbia in 1811: "[W]e no longer had to see naked females, many were well clothed, all of [the Nez Perce women] decently with leather, and in cleanly order, it was a pleasure to see them." This report was in stark contrast to the Chinookan women downriver who, he charged "had scarcely a trace of the decency and modesty of the upper country women."[104] Furthermore, Chinookan women did not defer to men and were central to fur-trade economics. Sahaptian women on the middle Columbia, according to the traders, were demure, further endearing them to the Westerners.

The only Anglo woman on the lower Columbia for direct comparison was Jane Barnes. She arrived in April 1814 at the relatively stable colonial settlement, which had recently passed from American to British control when Astor's former Northwesters sold out to current Northwesters during the War of 1812. The establishment was renamed Fort George, and, although the United States managed to reinstate its claim diplomatically and New England ships continued to dominate the maritime trade for another decade, the British became the fixed colonial presence. Despite these imperial changes, colonial relations lost none of their fluidity and adaptive nature. Although Barnes's stay was brief, she caused considerable competition and comment among potential suitors, and her treatment points to the extent to which, in a colonial setting, gendered and sexualized racial ideologies could mitigate a "white" woman's class status by demeaning Native women.

By the standards of her day, Barnes was unchaste; as mentioned earlier, Ross Cox's "Mac" certainly thought so. Barnes had met McTavish in her capacity as barmaid in Portsmouth, and she had agreed to accompany the aging Northwester to the Oregon Country and back without being married. Cox suggested that she regretted leaving home, having agreed to the overseas adventure "in a temporary fit of erratic enthusiasm," and, on the lower Columbia, she became an object of competition between McTavish and Chief Trader Alexander Henry.[105] According to Henry, he and McTavish negotiated her position over the course of a week and arrived at a settlement, although "[w]e differ on some personal points." The continuing points of contention probably owed much to Barnes's being lodged in Henry's quarters rather than either with McTavish or aboard the *Isaac Todd*, on which she departed some weeks later to Canton, China, and eventually back to England. Both men were concerned for her physical well-being and her reputation, "to cause no misunderstanding with the young gentlemen, etc." Indeed, the two were linked: if considered unchaste, the men feared that Barnes might be raped or, as Henry called it, suffer "ill usage."[106] McTavish apparently recovered from his loss of Barnes's affections quickly and married a Chinook woman on May 19, 1814. Three days later, however, both he and Henry drowned while paddling out to the *Isaac Todd*'s anchorage.

Contrary to the elder gentlemen's fears, Barnes's status improved after their demise. Cox claimed that the "flaxen-haired, blue-eyed daughter of Albion" became an honored figure for the remainder of her stay, as suggested by his hyperbolic description. Ignoring her lowly background in England and unchaste activities since, he deemed her worth "a score of the chastest brown vestals that ever flourished among the lower tribes of the Columbia." Latent racism reared up, demeaning Native women, and the presence of an Anglo woman challenged local, colonial gender relations. Furthermore, when the Chinook headman Concomly's eldest son Cassakas approached Fort George to cement further the ties between the two peoples in the spring of 1814, his marriage proposal for Barnes was uncategorically rejected. Barnes reportedly replied in quasi-religious racial terms, based on "certain Anglican predilections respecting mankind . . . among which she [and her country] did not include a flat head, a half naked body, or a copper-coloured skin besmeared with whale oil."[107]

Interracial marriage, and any sexual interaction, worked in only one direction: male Westerner and female Native. This distinction made little sense to Cassakas, whose sister Ilche had married Chief Trader McDougall the year before. Both were children of Concomly, who was one of the most important figures in the trade and who had successfully used marriage to advance the Chinook's trading position vis-à-vis other Native villages.

Cox claimed that, after this and subsequent refusals, Cassakas had a plan to kidnap Barnes, which resulted in her having to abandon her accustomed evening walks on the beach. Barnes's status was premised on her racial identity, which included—in a colonial setting—a pass from unchaste to chaste, but this conditional uplift apparently included checks on her freedom of movement, which was integral to the ideal of chastity.[108] Moreover, Barnes's local transformation from a barmaid into a "lady" suggests both the extent and the limits of colonial accommodation. Clearly, she could transcend her lowly position in English society. However, gendered and sexualized "whiteness" remained among the strongest structuring principles of nineteenth-century Western culture and limited the extent to which colonials would join with indigenous people to create practical forms of social relations. Keeping Barnes outside of the developing world of gender and sexual relations was as implicitly understood to colonials as it was incomprehensible to the Chinooks, who had no comparable notion to race.

Although formal and informal marriages increased in the 1810s, the prostitution of slaves with all its implications of exploitation continued. For example, some weeks after his arrival on the lower Columbia, in late January 1814, Chief Trader Henry saw the corpse of one of the slaves belonging to Coalpo's family lying outside the fort. "The poor girl had died in a horrible condition, in the last stage of venereal disease, discolored and swollen, and not the least care was ever taken to conceal the parts from bystanders."[109] After some prodding, Coalpo, a principal Clatsop headman and "medal chief" since the days of Lewis and Clark, sent people to remove the body, which they dragged away and unceremoniously stuffed into a hole with canoe paddles.

The writings of consecutive chief traders McDougall and Henry suggest that prostitution around the fort increased in the early and mid-1810s. In 1805, during the Corps' stay, there had been less impetus to foster the role of prostitutes, with only the occasional coasting vessel arriving for brief periods. With the establishment of Fort Astoria, the practice had clearly developed with the regular presence of Western male traders and trappers. Subsequent chief traders tried to stop prostitution, fearing that venereal disease would hinder their laborers' productivity.

In December 1812, McDougall demanded that Coalpo send the "girls" away and became frustrated when he later learned that the Clatsops had only "concealed" them instead. McDougall ordered Coalpo and his encampment to leave their site below the fort, but he tried to ameliorate the rejection by offering tobacco. Coalpo refused the present and claimed that he would never enter Fort Astoria again.[110] Prostitution had become a lucrative part of the relationship with the colonials and not one to be readily surrendered, and, as evident from Henry's complaints two years later, Coalpo neither stayed away from the fort nor discontinued the prostitution of women whose behavior he controlled.

The Chinookans and Henry sometimes had opposing economic interests regarding sexuality. In early 1814, with two men incapacitated by venereal disease, Henry feared that "the foul malady" would affect half his men by spring "and may seriously affect our commerce."[111] Venereal disease had been evident among the Astorians long before they even reached the Columbia. McDougall recorded cases on board the *Tonquin* after leaving New York in 1810, and one of the Kanakas, Thomas Tuana, brought it with him from Hawai'i in 1811. From April 1811 through the autumn of 1813, McDougall's sick-call registry often indicated three or four men infected, receiving mercury "treatments," or recovering from bouts of venereal disease.[112] By 1814, Henry claimed that the disease, likely syphilis, was "prevalent among our people and the women in this quarter." He could not force his men to refrain from sexual interaction, although his paranoia about the disease seems to have spread. Henry noted that Cartier "discharged his lady" after discovering two pimples. Cartier's roommate "Bethune keeps his, though he is very dubious of her." Because Henry drowned two weeks later and fort record keeping suffered as a result, it is not known whether Cartier's pimples indicated anything.

Whereas venereal disease was a real problem for the Native and colonial communities, it may still have been overstated, becoming confused with skin conditions that reflected seasonal nutritional imbalances. Henry noted in mid-March that Chinookan women began bringing "a quantity of cranberries and some roots." He claimed further that "[t]his vegetable diet has the good effect of purifying the blood and cleaning them of scabs . . . even venereal disease is checked by this diet, and sometimes cured."[113] Cranberries, wapato, camas, and licorice roots do not cure syphilis any more than the colonials' concoctions of mercury "quick-silver" ointments or Paul Jeremie's experiment in which he submerged the hapless Tuana inside a horse freshly killed and disemboweled for his "cure."[114] In other words, what was reported as venereal disease among colonials was sometimes the result of seasonal nutritional deficiencies, a perennial problem during the early fur trade.

Prostitution had political effects as well. McDougall alienated Coalpo in December 1812 when he ordered him "to be off with the whole of his people immediately" and destroyed "the remains of their houses" at the Clatsops' encampment on Point George. As well, other lower Chinookans were clearly concerned that women from their villages could be taken and enslaved as prostitutes. Two days after McDougall's confrontation with Coalpo, representatives from an unnamed Chinookan group "living a few miles behind us in Young's Bay" arrived at the fort. They were searching for a woman who had been lost in an overturned canoe a couple of days earlier. One of their slaves returned to the village and reported having left her alive on the shore. With Coalpo's recent abrupt departure, they thought that she had either been taken away by the Clatsops or that was she was being held at the fort. McDougall denied any knowledge and accused their slave of lying. Four days later, McDougall noted that the missing woman had been found, ending a situation that could have fueled an altercation.[115]

In his six months on the lower Columbia, from November 1813 to his death in May 1814, Alexander Henry tried to reform fort conduct, which included the access of Native women traders. He evidenced little experience with or tolerance for women conducting trade. His inexperience on the lower Columbia led him to accuse nearly all female traders in canoes of being prostitutes, chasing them off the beach even when they were obviously toting food and their woven manufactures, and he threatened to put women in irons. He claimed, for example, that some Clatsop women who came to trade cranberries also had come to trade "their precious favors." To support his claims, he noted one specific instance in March 1814 of "[s]everal Chinooks who had slept here, mostly women, bartering their favors with the men."[116]

Gabriel Franchere, a French Canadian clerk who resided on the lower Columbia from April 1811 until September 1814, did not term such liaisons prostitution. According to Franchere, the women's behavior was culturally accepted premarital sexuality. He concluded that "few marriages would occur [among Chinookans] if the young men wished to marry only chaste young women, for the girls have no qualms as to their conduct and their parents give them complete liberty in that respect."[117] Social status, however, affected this sexual openness, at least with the advent of colonialism. In 1824, Governor George Simpson cited the case of one of Madame Coalpo's daughters to claim that chastity was protected to appeal to the preferences of colonial traders.[118] Although Simpson cast his net broadly, his example of one of the leading lower Chinookan families was less representative than Franchere's larger characterization of the general population with whom he had regular contact from 1811 to 1814.

Social status was the key: high status, which indicated a relatively higher degree of material wealth and power, necessarily limited the agency of young women from leading families such as Coalpo's. By the first decades of the nineteenth century, power and prestige were becoming tied to the colonial traders. Western gender and sexual norms (modified by the realities of distant colonial life) shaped Chinookan norms regarding premarital sexuality from the top down. Conversely, young women from less prestigious families expressed a degree of autonomy by having sexual relations with colonials and obtained "baubles" for themselves, as Franchere put it. A material exchange in interracial sexual encounters did not necessarily mean prostitution, according to the lower Chinookan perspective. Instead, much of this sexual interaction—perhaps the majority—fit into the norms of life stages—namely premarital behavior and individual material acquisition. In the 1810s, prostitution, although economically important to such Chinookan leaders as Delashelwilt and Coalpo, was less common than casual sexual encounters engaged in by Chinookan women exercising their premarital "liberties." These different types of sexual encounters reveal significant changes in social, political, and economic worlds.

Prophecy and Colonialism

Analysis of Native perspectives through a comparative lens of fur-trade relations can obviously be fruitful. Adding prophecy narratives further develops our historical perspective. Prophecies reflect Native knowledge and illustrate ways in which Indian peoples understood, communicated, and acted on the knowledge. On the Columbia Plateau, in particular, prophecy formed a core feature of aboriginal beliefs and practices. In the nineteenth century, the Prophet Dance complex emerged there and profoundly influenced the Native North American West. Indian people took some control over historical events through the incorporation of these events into ceremonies of creation and rebirth. They harnessed and directed new knowledge, technologies, and events. Scholars have compared prophecy narratives to Western traditions of constructing historical narratives, which fundamentally are attempts to seek order and meaning through chronology and causality. As anthropologist Julie Cruikshank expressed it, prophecy narratives "may be viewed as successful engagement with changing ideas" and a changing world.[119]

One woman from the lower Kutenai River on the Columbia Plateau personified many of the changes that were both already evident in Native communities along the course of the Columbia River and that portended an entirely re-created world in the future. She visited the lower Columbia in 1811, calling herself Kauxuma-nupika ("gone to the spirits.") She played a crucial role in the nascent imperial competition by informing the Astorians of the Northwest Company's expansion west of the Rocky Mountains and by helping the Astorians to map the establishment of Fort Okanagon far upriver. Okanagon inhibited further expansion by the Northwest Company into the lands of the upper Columbia. However, the woman's life has much more to tell us about *Illahee* than her effects on the political economy of the fur trade.

Kauxuma-nupika appears under many names in the historical record and in the oral traditions of Plateau and neighboring northern Plains peoples. As a young woman her Kutenai people knew her as ququnok patke, ("one standing [lodge] pole woman"). In 1808 she met the initial Northwest Company expedition west of the Rocky Mountains and married a French Canadian trapper named Boisverd. About one year later, she returned to her people alone. She proclaimed her name Kauxuma-nupika, announced herself a man, and claimed to have gained great spiritual power from the Westerners as evident in her sexual transformation. Although her family and the Kutenai people continued to deny her physical transformation, they supported her account of transgendering—that is, a behavioral transformation from female roles to male.[120] She instigated at least one raid (an infrequent activity for the Kutenai) on neighboring Kalispels and attempted to take a warrior's name, Sitting-in-the-Water-Grizzly (qánqon kámek klaúla). The Kutenai people would not accept that name, however, until they felt that she had finally earned it by sacrificing herself to protect her adopted kinfolk, the Flatheads, from a Blackfoot raiding party in 1837.[121]

Between her rebirth as a male in 1809 and her death in 1837, Kauxuma-nupika communicated various prophetic visions to Native peoples from the mouth of the Columbia to the interior of modern British Columbia. She spoke, at least, Kutenai, Salish, some Cree (Algonkian), and probably some Chipewyan (northern Athapaskan). Just as importantly, she mastered the language of prophecy. While Kauxuma-nupika's role in the growth of the reformist movement, the Prophet Dance, is unclear, her anticolonial prophecies did cause considerable commotion in Indian country.[122]

Scholars have identified what seem to be three distinct visions of Kauxuma-nupika in the historical record and oral tradition. Initially, in 1811, Trader David Thompson encountered Kauxuma-nupika on her way down the Columbia and reported that she warned upper Chinookans that "the Small Pox . . . was coming with the white Men & that 2 Men of enourmous Size [were coming] to overturn the Ground &c." The hearers were concerned because they were "strong to live." They also wanted an explanation of the epidemic and the giant white men reportedly "overturning the Ground, and burying all the Villages and lodges underneath it: is this true," they wondered, "and are we all soon to die?" Although Thompson denied that the fur traders had any disease or any designs on the lands of the "Great Spirit," the gist of her prophecy well reflects the unmistakable patterns of North American colonization: epidemic disease followed by agrarian resettlement by Euro-Americans. Thompson countered Kauxuma-nupika's prophecy, and his party protected her from any retaliation for her perceived deceptions.[123] Subsequent reports of her prophecies may seem at first contradictory but actually maintain an indigenous understanding of North American colonization.

A second message seems evident the following spring. On the trip back up the Columbia River, Kauxuma-nupika told Native audiences that "the great white chief" had sent her and her wife to present gifts but that the fur traders, instead, sold them the goods. As evidence, she presented a paper, which trader Alexander Ross dismissed as an "old letter, which they made a handle of." The story preceded the travelers, and Indian peoples presented valuable gifts to the "bold adventurous Amazons."[124] The vision repositioned the centrality of the Indian people in the larger trade and recast the increasingly powerful, regional traders as cheats and charlatans.

Keeping abreast of the expanding fur traders in 1812, Kauxuma-nupika ventured far north to Fort Chipewyan on Lake Athabasca in the subarctic of modern Alberta. Her exploits again earned comment from Westerners and help illuminate her anticolonial prophecies. According to the ill-fated British explorer John Franklin, she profoundly influenced the Et Oeneldi-dene

("Caribou-eater" Chipewyan Athapaskans): "This fellow had prophesied that there would soon be a complete change in the face of the country; fertility and plenty would succeed to the present sterility; and that the present race of white inhabitants, unless they became subservient to the Indians, would be removed and their place be filled by other traders, who would supply their wants in every possible manner."[125] Here, Kauxuma-nupika's adherents nearly enacted the prophecy with a strike against Fort Chipewyan, an act that would have reestablished the power of the indigenous population and their beliefs.

Scholars have tended to see the prophetic narratives as distinct and contradictory, that her visions changed from an ineffective scare tactic to a self-serving promise of bounty to an incitement of violence, born of frustration. The visions seem instead, however, to have been clear, cohesive reflections of Kauxuma-nupika's historical knowledge of Western colonization, as expressed through the indigenous framework of prophecy.[126] She knew and communicated with Cree, Canadians, and Catholic Iroquois, and she would have been familiar with historical processes that had already played out in the East. She was hardly alone. Gabriel Franchere wrote that trader John McTavish had met an elderly woman among the Spokans who spoke of white men plowing, mimicked the sound and motion of swinging church bells, and imitated a Catholic genuflection years before the first missionaries arrived. Similarly, Robert Stuart witnessed a Native ceremony on the upper Columbia in 1811 featuring "a crude imitation" of Catholic rites, and so he named the site Priest Rapids.[127] He surmised knowledge of Spanish creole settlements, which also were evident in the horse herds of the Plateau. Indeed, copper kettles and horses had preceded colonialists via indigenous trade routes. Knowledge had advanced as well, although the Native peoples of the Oregon Country had not seen enough to act on the prophecies of Kauxuma-nupika beyond dancing and so attempting some control over life-altering events.

"Roguery" and Conflict Resolution

Indeed, violence between the colonial and indigenous traders was rare in the first years, but perceived threats were not. From early June 1811, when the Chinookans had scared McDougall by observing the rites at the beginning of the salmon run, which he interpreted as a pre-attack starvation plot, the colonials at Fort Astoria exhibited paranoia of a pan-Indian assault. Although McDougall determined that the salmon rites were "from a superstitious idea" rather than a militaristic one, he remained convinced that the Indians would attack as soon as the *Tonquin* departed northward. (The *Tonquin* left to coast for furs and to arrange a supply contract with the Russians at Sitka.) He was somewhat relieved after hearing that Cassakas had wounded a Chehalis headman in a game of shinny, hoping that the interethnic dispute would prevent an anti-Astoria alliance, although he subsequently fretted whether the injury was just an excuse to mobilize men for a concerted attack. McDougall's mind swirled with various possible plots and intrigue amid rumors that had begun trickling into the fort that the *Tonquin* had been lost.[128]

By the end of July, McDougall ordered military drills at the fort. With the help of a group of Clatsops, he was able to convince the Chehalis of the Astorians' friendship and that the Chinooks had been misleading them about the colonialists' supposed animosity. Instead, he tried to explain that the Chinooks lied out of a desire to monopolize the trade among the Indians. The parading and target practice, not surprisingly, attracted attention, and a few Chinookans complained "about our War like appearance." In mid-August, Concomly confessed that he had known about the *Tonquin's* fate but had withheld his knowledge because he did not want to "afflict us" with the pain of losing friends. Distrusting Concomly's reasoning, McDougall "[t]urned all hands out to drill, & examined their Arms."[129]

As they would ultimately learn from the sole survivor of the *Tonquin* tragedy, the ship had indeed sunk after an altercation between the captain, John Thorn, and Wicanninish somewhere off the coast of western Vancouver Island, probably Clayoquot Sound. Joseachal, a Quinault who fished the lower Columbia in spring, had made two previous voyages up the coast onboard colonial ships and was thus recruited by the Astorians for the *Tonquin*. After the incident, he avoided the colonials for two years before Concomly finally brought him to the fort to tell his story in June 1813. Thorn had apparently humiliated Wicanninish, and the following day, under the pretense of trade, numerous Native people boarded the ship and overwhelmed the colonials. The magazine blew, sinking the ship and killing everyone on board. Wounded members of the crew may have touched off the magazine as a dying gasp of revenge. The *Tonquin's* fate would haunt the minds of the colonial traders for decades.[130]

Despite McDougall's fears, no attack followed the loss of the *Tonquin* that first summer. Paranoia at Astoria resumed in November when McDougall learned that a headman from the Cascades was reportedly trying to assemble the lower Chinookan headmen. He recalled the Iroquois hunter Ignace Salioheni to help defend the fort. Nothing came of the alleged meeting of Chinookans, and, if it occurred, there is no reason to believe that the Astorians were the cause: Concomly, Coalpo, and Casino (and likely other lower Chinookan principals) had relatives at the Cascades Rapids. Still, the stretch of the Columbia River from the Cascades Rapids to Celilo Falls had been the scene of some disturbances. The fast, rough currents forced travelers to portage. Canoes had to be emptied of trade goods, requiring extra labor or horses to carry the bales—which made the colonials dependent on local Indians with whom they otherwise had no relationship. Otherwise, canoes could be pulled against the current. As experience taught, this practice risked losing the entire load, as the swirling whitewater swamped or ripped canoes away, dispersing trade goods all along the shoreline, islands, and eddies of the river. On July 31, 1811, David Thompson reported that "Rogues" along the portage had plotted to steal his company's arms but a combination of North-wester bravado, vigilance, and "Providence" prevented an altercation.[131] Five years earlier, the Corps of Discovery had had a few problems there as well, with Lewis's dog being stolen, John Shields being harassed when he lagged behind, and a Native man raining stones down on the expedition as they made their way along the steep-sided, slippery portage. Still, a local headman apologized, explaining that all was the work of a couple of individual trouble-makers. Any altercation was averted, as it was with Thompson in 1811.[132]

In the spring of 1812, however, colonial-indigenous encounters along the portage route turned violent. David Stuart had hired some Cathlaskos to help with the portage, because he had extensive supplies and trade goods for the season in the upper country. According to Robert Stuart's account, a couple of Cathlaskos who had been engaged to help portage purposely damaged a canoe and looted some goods. The next day 400 Indians accompanied the canoes to The Dalles and volunteered to help with the last portage above Celilo Falls. Fearing further problems, David Stuart engaged some of the Indians to transport empty canoes above the falls but not the bales of trade goods. Some men apparently threatened to destroy the canoes after carrying them until an elder convinced them otherwise.

At 1 A.M. a sleepless David Stuart decided to avert further problems by portaging goods by moonlight. By daybreak, only two loads were left, when "at least 30 determined Villains" crossed from the north bank and began "an indiscriminate pillage." John Reed and Robert McClellan, whose turn it was to stay behind, intervened, and a scuffle broke out, in which two Indians were shot and killed and Reed received a nasty head injury. The rest of the party hurried back, firing their weapons, and frightened off the remaining Indians. According to Robert Stuart, 120 men then rode out from Cathlasko village and cut off the colonials heading upriver. A Cathlasko headman approached the party and explained that he was compelled to lead a war party, but he stated that bereaved relatives would be satisfied if the colonials would surrender Reed. The leaders haggled a settlement to avert further bloodshed and arrived at "3 Blankets to cover the dead, and some Tobacco to fill the Calumet of Peace."[133]

The incident produced a couple of precedents. First, for McDougall, it proved "the bad intentions" of the "daring and resolute" upper Chinookans and river Sahaptians between the Cascades Rapids and Celilo Falls. Consequently, subsequent brigades would have to be large, "well armed and on their guard."[134] Colonials transferred much of their animosity and distrust from the "roguish" Chinooks of the lower river to the "rogues" and "saucy, impudent rascals" of the upriver "fishing places." The appellations of *rogue* and *rascal* for Indian groups had a long history in the Oregon Country and elsewhere. During the Corps of Discovery initial experiences on the lower Columbia, Sgt. Patrick Gass referred to Bakers Bay as "Rogue's harbor," for the people who "call themselves the Chin-Ook nation."[135] Nearly a decade later, in 1813, Astorian Alfred Seton noted that the trappers called the headman of the Tushepa band of Nez Perce "Les Grande Coquin," the Great Rogue, for his and his band's "rascally behavior."[136]

Such names and references are common in fur-trader writings across time and space; generally, any Native group refusing to play by the mercantilist rules set by the colonials was guilty of roguery.[137] Robert Stuart used an environmentalist explanation, claiming that the region from the Cascades Rapids to Celilo Falls was inhabited by slothful, "worthless Dogs" similar to England's urban poor; both peoples were supposedly too lazy to work. In his conception, the fishing sites, like England's early industrial cities, were "the Schools of Villainy or the Head Quarters of vitiated principles." The Dalles, where Chinookan and Sahaptian of numerous bands and ethnicities "mix promiscuously" to gamble, trade, and fish was particularly loathed by fearful colonial travelers.[138] Alexander Ross similarly considered The Dalles "the general theatre of gambling and roguery."[139] Thus, until the disease epidemics of the 1830s, the Native peoples along the portage route or "fishing places" of the middle Columbia would be among the most vilified Indians in the Oregon Country. The Shasta and Takelma peoples of southwestern Oregon would later inherit the title of "Rogue Indians" in the 1840s.

Second, the means of diplomacy would be repeated, as the colonials introduced their method of "covering the dead," developed earlier in the Eastern fur trade. Relations among Eastern Algonkians, Iroquoians, and Europeans in the lower Canada and Great Lakes trade in the seventeenth century had created an amicably agreed transfer of wealth to prevent profit-sapping blood feuds. The Native peoples of the Oregon Country typically demanded slaves (often the guilty party) in addition to material goods as restitution, but they accepted the colonials' custom of trade goods and tobacco. Victorian-era historian Francis Parkman called such invented traditions "meeting the Indian half-way," and more recently Richard White has argued that, within a specific context of international and regional pressures, such interactions produced a new syncretic culture in the Great Lakes region during the mid-seventeenth and eighteenth centuries.[140] In the Oregon Country, nothing as elaborate or coherent as a syncretic middle-ground culture developed, but the colonials and Natives did have to meet each other "halfway" with their diplomacy.

Rumors of David Stuart's clash with the Cathlaskos reached McDougall at Fort Astoria within days, but he had to wait more than a month before some of the party returned from the upper country with their version of the events. In the meantime, the *Beaver* had arrived with new "settlers" and supplies for the fort. As he had done the year before, when the *Tonquin* was about to leave, McDougall prepared for an Indian attack that he was convinced would occur as soon as the *Beaver* departed. His paranoia was fed by the tales of a Chinook elder who had been banished from his village for some unknown reason; perhaps it was related to his love of intrigue. McDougall called him "Raccoon," although he did not explain why. Raccoon had McDougall's ear and appears to have convinced the nervous colonial that the Nuu-chah-nulths from Vancouver Island, Chinooks, and upper Chinookans "from above" the rapids were joining to "Massacre the whole of us." McDougall ordered militia drills and target practice and established a "strict watch." Raccoon was not the only one to terrify the colonials: Coalpo sent "slave girls" running into the fort crying that Cassackas was crossing from Chinook with a force to attack—which was, of course, not true.[141] Coalpo's motives are as unclear as Raccoon's, although each had an interest in undermining the status of Concomly and his kin.

Much of the paranoia at Astoria resulted from a convergence of unrelated events. The first was David Stuart's altercation at The Dalles in April. Second, Raccoon apparently began rumormongering, and, for whatever reason, McDougall believed him regardless of how preposterous the tale.[142] Third, Indians of different ethnicities were indeed gathering, although their gathering had nothing to do with the Astorians. A large number of Nuu-chah-nulths from Vancouver Island arrived in Bakers Bay across the estuary to fish for sturgeon and settle some affairs with the Chinooks. The northern people brought the coveted hyqua beads to the Columbia, and the Chinooks traded slaves and clamon for the northern market. As usual, lower and upper Chinookans traded and visited relatives back and forth, and Tillamooks from the coast paddled up the river to settle accounts with the Chelwits, an upper Chinookan village near the Cascades Rapids.[143] As well, the Plateau Sahaptians, particularly the "Mount St. Helen Indians," or Klikitats, would have begun assembling to hunt and obtain roots in the Willamette Valley.[144] In short, it was life as usual in *Illahee*, the bustling Native world of the lower Columbia region.

Fourth, as in 1811, McDougall's military preparations attracted attention. When Cassackas insisted on being allowed to watch, climbing the fort walls to get a view of the militia drills, he was dragged back to his canoe in humiliation. Concomly arrived, upset at the treatment of his eldest son—which, in turn, fueled McDougall's distrust of the Chinooks. This is the situation that Coalpo exploited with his "warning." Fifth, despite the heightened tensions on the lower Columbia, which emanated from Fort Astoria, McDougall decided to celebrate American Independence Day by firing off the fort's cannons twice during the day. (In 1811, they had fired only a single round of muskets before commencing a considerable consumption of grog.) The concussions of the blasts echoed up the river, alarming Native villages and Salioheni and Pierre Dorion, whose wives and children were at the fort. They hurried back to join the nonexistent battle.

Sixth and finally, McDougall had dispatched another brigade to the upper country. Rumors arrived in mid-July that a terrible battle had occurred along the portage route and that John Clarke's party had burned a house and the winter stores of the "guilty" Indians. McDougall seemed elated, hoping that the violence "may prove an example to them in future and shew what they may expect from such behaviour as they were guilty of to our former party."[145] The rumor was unfounded, however: the whitewater swamped Clarke's canoe and swept off its contents. Rather than a battle, the Cascades Indians acted "civilly," collecting some of the trade goods from the shoreline and islands, and they joined Clarke for a smoke, as he waited for his recovered bales to dry in the sun.[146] The Cascades Indians warned that others from above would attack, but the brigade passed above Celilo Falls without incident.

Significantly, however, Stuart did not recover several rifles and "fowling pieces" (shotguns). The people of the middle Columbia rapids apparently had a growing interest in guns. In the previous July, David Thompson had claimed that the "Rogues" at the portage below the Deschutes River had plotted unsuccessfully to "seize all our arms."[147] Still, the colonials would not understand the "fishing peoples'" desire for guns until they became aware of the raids of Plateau Sahaptians and Shoshones later in 1814. For the moment, the colonials, particularly McDougall, interpreted events as if Astoria was the center of attention in Oregon and a target of some diabolical Native intrigue.

Scholars have generally explained the "rascally" behavior of the upper Chinookans and river Sahaptian neighbors of the rapids in terms of the pre-existing trade network: the colonials threatened their powerful position as the bridge between the Northwest Coast and the Columbia Plateau (and, by extension, the Rocky Mountains and Great Plains). The conjecture seems logical, because The Dalles, or "Indian mart," featured hyqua from Vancouver Island, local salmon, eel, horses, canoes, and buffalo products from the Plains as well as nutritious roots from the valleys and, finally, slaves from as far away as the Oregon-California borderlands. The Native residents enjoyed a privileged position in the indigenous network, and the fur brigades may have been expected to pay a toll of sorts for their passage.

However, Robert Stuart noted an incident that might explain why the altercations between colonials and Native peoples occurred when they did. On the first portage after the April clash, he was frightened when two Indians ran into his camp. They were not attacking, however, but warning. Through their Clatsop interpreter, the colonials learned that Shoshones (generically, "people of the interior") had assailed a canoe earlier in the afternoon and killed four men and two women.[148] At this point the wealthy river peoples did not have guns. Horsemen from the Plateau did, and the river people knew the original source of the guns: the colonial traders. Traders of Astor's Pacific Fur Company did, in fact, trade guns on the Columbia Plateau. According to Alfred Seton, they provided weapons to Nez Perce, Cayuse, and other Sahaptians, because the "Snakes" (Shoshones) had driven them out of their homelands across the Blue Mountains in the Grande Ronde and Wallowa valleys. Without guns to match their enemies, those Indians could not retake their lands and, presumably, benefit the fur trade.[149]

As well, David Thompson's disdain for the Americans' failure to profit significantly from a musket trade on the lower Columbia suggests that the Northwest Company had been actively trading guns on the upper Columbia since 1810.[150] On the portage through the "fish places," the colonials offered the river peoples tobacco and beads but never guns. Indeed, throughout 1812 and 1813, McDougall paid "extravigant" prices trying to buy back the rifles and shotguns lost by Clarke at the Cascades, fearing that they would be used against his portaging brigades.[151] Only a few were recovered. In November 1813, Ross Cox's party lost two bales of goods and recovered most of the contents only after seizing some elders, women, and children as hostages and exchanging them for the property.[152] Two months later, in January 1814, the cauldron of the river peoples' fearing "Shoshone" raids, their desire for guns to defend themselves, and the mutual vilification of the colonials and the Indians of the middle Columbia rapids boiled over into a second, bloody altercation.

In the winter of 1813–1814, warfare among Native peoples had broken out on the Plateau, and many people fled to The Dalles to escape the horse-riding, gun-wielding raiders.[153] Henry noted on January 6, 1814, that an "uncommon number of Indians" had "fled down to the Banks of the Columbia, for safety and in readiness to cross the river or escape if pursued by their enemies."[154] Stuart led a supply brigade for the interior, carrying as usual bales of goods that included guns, and they walked headlong into this unstable situation. With the brigade of forty-five men split into two groups for a portage, a party of upper Chinookans attacked from the north bank, wounding David Stuart and Saganakei. The colonials left their trade goods (including some fifty rifles and ammunition), abandoned their wounded Nipissing companion, and fled back to the fort, but not before killing two of the Native assailants during the raid.[155]

Henry claimed, "These villains . . . are bent on taking revenge upon us for having furnished firearms to their enemies above," on the Columbia Plateau. He sent word to his brother William at "Fort Calipuyaw" in the Willamette Valley, warning that the Indians of the lower Country desired "firearms to put them on a footing with their enemies; plunder seems to be their main object, not blood."[156] As suggested by McDougall's reaction to the rumor that Clarke had torched a Native house in retaliation for the first altercation, the colonials decided to mount an expedition to avenge this second attack and recover their property.

The facts of the retaliatory expedition are relatively consistent among the sources, although the evaluations of its consequences varied considerably. January was probably the worst month to conduct such an operation because of the scarcity of food. McDougall knew that the fort had a chronic shortage of food from October until the February runs of eulachon and sturgeon and the early spring vegetables. Characteristically, he blamed the Indians for refusing to trade rather than the seasonal fluctuations of the local environment. His solution, as discussed earlier, was to limit the number of mouths at the fort and dispatch people to the Willamette Valley to fend for themselves.[157] With an expedition, the colonials obviously had to make a decision; instead of waiting until late spring and summer as the Native peoples of the lower

Columbia did to settle disputes, they chose to head upriver without sufficient food and hope for the best.

By 1814, the colonials were well aware of the kinship connections among the upper and lower Chinookans, and they consulted Coalpo and his wife, the Chinookans at Oak Point, and Concomly. According to Alexander Henry, Coalpo and the Oak Point Chinookans argued for war, but Madame Coalpo disagreed. She believed that with her brother-in-law Casino of Clackamas they could parley: offer a slave and other gifts in recompense for the two dead Native people and recover the trade goods. For a price, she would join the expedition, and she correctly predicted that Casino would as well.[158] The colonials opted for her plan, but if they could they would try the hostage-taking approach that had worked for Cox's party the previous autumn.

The hasty expedition of sixty-nine members left the fort on January 10, 1814, and by the thirteenth, "on the eve of encountering enemies," they ran out of food. At the first village of the Cascades, Soto, which had apparently not participated in the attack, Casino and Madame Coalpo obtained a few dogs for the expedition to eat and recovered nine guns from their relatives. Casino learned that Canook, headman of the "Cathlathlaly" village upriver, had persuaded men from the neighboring "Thlamooyackoack" village to join. According to Henry's account, Canook had told them "that we never traded anything of consequence with them, but took our property further up, to their enemies, the Nez Percés, and that here was a favorable opportunity to better themselves." According to Casino's relatives, one man from each of the villages had died in the fighting, and they were not willing to surrender the guns. As the expedition would discover, bales of other trade goods still littered the shoreline. To the frustration of the colonials' plan, Canook had learned from the previous autumn also, and he refused to allow himself to be lured away from his men, smoking a calumet offered by the colonials but keeping his distance.

Over the next three days, Casino slowly recovered a few guns and obtained barely enough food for the expedition to keep going. Henry grumbled after having to split nine dogs and a horse among all the men, consuming the intestines, blood, fat, and bone marrow, that "I could have imagined we were just in from a buffalo hunt." Tired, hungry, and impatient, the colonials seized "a chief, a boy, and a woman" whom Casino had brought to camp. They released the boy with word that they wanted all the stolen goods returned.

Then, they put on a display to make themselves appear fearsome despite their pathetic condition and utter reliance on their erstwhile enemies for sustenance. Facing the larger cluster of eight Cathlathlaly houses on the north bank, the colonials paraded, marching back and forth, as they had practiced at the fort, occasionally firing volleys into the air. During the day, they shot some rounds from their swivel gun (a small cannon) and, in the evening, fired off two skyrockets into the night sky. Villagers from above and below turned out to watch the show, and women arrived in two canoes with a dozen guns and some other goods. Yet, because the colonials had taken hostages, no one would give them food, and no more property was offered. Word came that more goods and guns were dispersed upriver; but by this time none of the colonials seems to have been interested in going up to The Dalles. The expedition retreated downriver to Strawberry Island before trying the military display again. Franchere led the drill team back to Cathlathlaly, but to no avail. According to Henry, Canook complained "that we [colonials] must be a bad lot, to want all our property back after killing two chiefs, and they would give no more."

The now desperately hungry expedition headed downriver to Soto, still holding their prisoner to avert a feared attack. There, they released him to his family, who had been following in a canoe, giving him two blankets, a Northwest Company flag, and a few other items for his troubles. The villagers at Soto refused to trade any food, and the expedition had to continue some ways downriver before finding anyone willing or able to feed them.[159]

The expedition could hardly be called a success, given the unmet, lofty goal of retrieving all the goods. Yet, was it a failure? Alexander Henry decided that it answered "our business ends," referring to the recovery of much property and display of both might and "humanity"; and further violence "would only have made a bad affair worse." Similarly, Franchere considered the endeavor a moderate success. By not recovering the balance of the goods, they had "covered the dead" and avoided long-lasting enmity at a crucial portage.[160] To have taken more lives, he figured, would have placed the colonials outside the regional norm, perhaps engendering a confederacy against them.

On the other hand, Madame Coalpo reportedly mocked the expedition's "timidity" on her return to the Clatsops, according to Henry, and said: "we ought to have killed them all." Given that it was originally her idea to avoid such bloodshed through a parley, his report seems questionable. She may have changed her mind, however, after finding the innocence of her relatives at the lower rapids and recovering their nine guns. Indeed, Casino was the Native mediator who proved to have the most filial and trade connections above Soto. Whatever their assessments of the expedition, both Madame Coalpo and Casino profited handsomely from their involvement.[161]

The colonials appear to have benefited as well, as the feared raid from the Plateau occurred in early spring and the "Rogues" of The Dalles were apparently unable to defend themselves. In mid-March, rumors reached the fort from Oak Point "that the Nez Perces and Scietogas [Cayuse] have been to war on the tribes at the falls, killed a great many, and carried off a number of slaves; which has caused the natives to abandon their villages and to fly in panic." The Chinooks similarly reported that "the natives at the falls had sustained a severe defeat by a vast number of Indians from above, who attacked the village at the Dalles in the daytime, killed as many as they could, and burned women and children in their houses—in short, that the whole village was destroyed." By early April the Clatsops confirmed that the attackers were Nez Perce, that they had killed eighteen men, "and that many were collected at the rapids; but these had no bad intentions toward us [colonials], saying that, if we could speak well, they would do so also."[162] Indeed, the April brigade passed the portages without incident.

Although Westerners would continue to deride the "rascally" Native peoples of the middle Columbia rapids, no further hostilities occurred until the 1850s, when the explosion of settler colonialism fundamentally altered the nature of interaction and engendered violent conflict in much of the Oregon Country. For the intervening four decades, no significant violence occurred there. Although not a conquest in the Western sense, Nez Perce and Cayuse peoples would continue to be a regular presence at The Dalles and may have played a significant role in preventing further raids on the fur brigades. The trading relationship between the colonials and the Plateau Sahaptians grew throughout the 1810s and 1820s. By 1824, relations were so peaceful that George Simpson recommended the "neighborhood of the Cascade Portage" for the establishment of a Christian mission. The unequal distribution of guns, to which the colonials' 1814 expedition contributed, played a significant role in altering the Native dynamics of power at The Dalles and was thus an unintended success for the colonials.[163]

Imperial War Comes to *Illahee*

The indigenous-colonial drama at The Dalles coincided with the outbreak of a long-brewing conflict between Great Britain and the United States, and the wake of distant events eventually reached the shores of Young's Bay and the gates of Fort Astoria. The advent of the War of 1812, which created a North American theater of the Napoleonic Wars, was not a surprise to the traders. The imperial conflict had been simmering for years.[164] The transoceanic trade suddenly became much more precarious for the Astorians and other American traders.

As a colonial American trade fort competing with the British Empire, Fort Astoria was a possible target, if an unlikely one. Because the colonials were fearful, the fort did not fly colors until visiting ships were identified; its defenses were meant for Chinookans in canoes, not royal frigates with cannons.[165] Still, as James Ronda has demonstrated, Astor devised his Astoria enterprise expecting the possibility of war, even hedging his bets by attempting a trade alliance with the nominally British Northwest Company. When war began, Astor pressed for protection by the U.S. Navy. Although Commodore Oliver Perry and the *Essex* were in the Pacific preying on the British whaling fleet, Astor's various schemes collapsed, and his establishment was on its own. The Northwesters had to lie to the British Admiralty in London about the nature of Fort Astoria to get a frigate dispatched.[166] The Oregon Country was not a major concern for leaders of either nation. Although congressional war hawks definitely had the conquest and colonization of indigenous lands in mind, their eyes were fixed considerably east of the Rocky Mountains for another decade.

When news of the war reached Astoria in mid-January 1813, it presented the colonials with an interesting dilemma and set the stage for a campaign that was more ironic than tragic. As the Montreal native and second-generation fur-trader Gabriel Franchere put it, "We considered seriously the fact that nearly all of us were British subjects, yet we were trading under the American flag." He and his fellow Canadians "wished ourselves in Canada" and wanted nothing to do with the Anglo-American conflict. The Astorians considered that the British would blockade American ports. This action would prevent the return of Hunt and Astor's supply ship (which had indeed been detained in Canton by the British) and meant that they would have to take the furs arduously overland.[167] Abandonment of the settlement seemed the only option. McDougall suspended trade for furs, having more than were transportable by land already.[168]

On April 11, 1813, John McTavish arrived with a force of several Northwest Company trappers-turned-militiamen and orders to besiege Fort Astoria and await the *Isaac Todd* and her escort, a royal frigate, the *Phoebe*. (He was unaware that the ships had not left England yet.) Given that Canadians in the employ of the Northwest Company were "laying siege" to a fort full of Canadians formerly in the employ of the Northwest Company, violence was unlikely, and none occurred. Indeed, only the fort's stores of food and grog were attacked. April 12 was a local holiday, the anniversary of Astoria's founding. Instead of fighting, most everyone got drunk for a couple of days.[169] After several weeks, McDougall realized that the Astorians could not manage the abandonment in time to beat the winter, and he decided to wait until the following spring. Consequently, he and Donald McTavish devised a strategy to avert imperial problems; they divided the Oregon trade between them, and the Northwesters soon departed for their new monopolies at Spokane and among the Kutenais.

Not everyone was amused by the failure to defend the fort, however; there were a few Euro-Americans on hand. A young New Yorker and trader-in-training, Alfred Seton, mocked, "[O]ur *Chiefs* think the miseries of war are far enough extended already." He described the "siege" sarcastically in his journal: "God knows that the Great NW Co. are not to be offended with impunity. 20 men therefore under the guns of the Fort display the British colours while 60 men in a good fort surrounded with guns are fearful of offending these potent men . . . so great so very, very, very, great, that my feeble imagination cannot encompass epithets great enough to express."[170] Similarly, when Hunt arrived aboard the *Albatross* in late August, he was furious about the abandonment plans. He had negotiated a lucrative contract with the Russians to supply them from the Columbia and to purchase their sea otter furs, but he could not convince the Canadians to alter their decision.[171]

In October, McTavish returned to renew the siege as the Northwest Company ordered. Company partner Angus Shaw had received word that the *Isaac Todd* and the *Phoebe* were finally on their way to the Columbia. Surprised by the Northwest brigade, McDougall and his "foe" McTavish avoided bloodshed again; they "[c]ame to an understanding."[172] In a decision that he would have to defend for the rest of his career (as a Northwester), McDougall sold Fort Astoria lock, stock, and barrel to the Northwest Company.

In mid-November, Alexander Henry and other Northwester officers arrived, followed on the 30th by the HMS *Raccoon*. As the *Raccoon* anchored across the estuary in Bakers Bay and was not flying the Union Jack, a cautious McDougall took advantage of the bi-national nature of Astoria. According to Franchere, he sent men across "with orders to call themselves Americans if the ship were American, and British subjects in the contrary case."[173] Although he was denied a naval victory, Capt. William Black was reportedly amused by the Northwest Company's gross overstatements of the "American stronghold" on the Pacific and went through the formalities of claiming the little settlement in the name of King George. Famously breaking a bottle of Madeira wine on the flagpole, he renamed it Fort George on December 13,

1813, and soon set sail. Such was the Oregon front of the War of 1812, itself partly a product of the Napoleonic Wars.

Hunt does seem to have had a sense of humor, however. In March 1814, Hunt returned to the lower Columbia aboard the *Pedlar*, an American coaster. He traded vegetables from Hawai'i at Fort George and asked for the release of the few Euro-American trappers and the Kanakas, who all "wished to see their homes." The Northwesters gladly agreed to hand over four "useless" Euro-Americans but only reluctantly "agreed to give up four Sandwich Islanders to Mr. Hunt, who had been desirous of taking them all."[174] According to Ross Cox, some of the Euro-Americans bore an "unnatural and acrimonious hatred to the land of their forefathers" and wanted to leave.[175] Henry promised the remaining Kanakas free passage home at some unspecified future date. Obviously, Hunt was upset by news of the sale, and "arguments and altercations" marked the discussion of detailed arrangements. Still, the Northwesters invited him to dine at his former establishment. Hunt brought Concomly, whom he dressed in the famous "red coat" of the British Army, notably a Scots-Canadian detachment, the New Brunswick 104th. Henry did not appreciate Concomly's dress or manners and complained in his journal about how the Americans and the Chinooks were ruining the fur trade with their undisciplined behavior.[176]

Unlike many imperial war fronts in which vying colonial powers manipulated indigenous peoples into the fighting (e.g., contemporary Ohio Valley, interior Southeast, and Red River Valley conflicts), the Astorians and Northwesters initially tried to keep the Chinookan peoples completely ignorant of the dispute. In January 1813, McDougall and McTavish had decided to keep the war and abandonment plans from the Chinookans "until it can no longer be hid." They feared that the Native traders would take advantage and play the two parties against each other to raise the prices for food. When Concomly learned of the proposed abandonment in June, he thought that it was a reaction to the theft of some of McTavish's personal effects. Not wishing to lose the fort that had helped make him wealthy and powerful, Concomly proposed staging his own kidnapping, with McTavish's property to serve as ransom. His eldest son Cassakas would then recover the goods from the Chinooks. The colonials rejected the plan.[177]

By November 1813, the Chinookans had learned enough of the Anglo-American conflict to offer military help to the Astorians. Hunt had probably informed Concomly during his August visit of the impending arrival of a British warship, and Concomly offered McDougall aid to keep the *Raccoon* from landing any men.[178] The Chinooks were well aware of the difficulties that European boats had in negotiating the dangerous currents and eddies of the river's tidal estuary, having fished many erstwhile sailors of various nationalities out of the lower Columbia in preceding years. Comcomly was, after all, McDougall's father-in-law, having allied the peoples through McDougall's marriage to Ilche several months earlier. McDougall, however, refused the help, and Franchere did his best to explain to the lower Chinookan principals the nature of the fort's transfer.[179] Thanks mostly likely to Hunt, the Chinooks considered the Astorians legitimate and the British Northwesters as interlopers.

Following the transfer, Alexander Henry noted some initial opposition from the headmen, who acted coldly toward him and his fellow Northwesters. He explained that "they are inclined to suspect we are imposters who have supplanted their first and best friends, as they conceive the Americans to be, in order to exclude them from the country, to which the natives say we have no right." In response, Henry claimed that "[p]ains are taken to make them understand the true grounds on which we stand, not as a temporary but permanent establishment, to supply them with their necessaries as long as they deserve such attention." The *Isaac Todd* had still not arrived by early April, however, and they were running low on trade goods. Fort George dropped its prices; "this [the Indians] did not like."[180] Concomly, Coalpo, and Coniah each pressed the new establishment, trying the patience of Henry. Concomly complained about the fare served at Fort George, and the ensuing disagreement may explain why his sons temporarily retrieved Ilche. Coalpo reportedly "left in a pet" after having his increased prices for furs rebuffed. In mid-May, Coniah arrived at the fort with his "American writing" to stress his importance.

Symbolically, Henry tried to eliminate the connection between the Americans and the Clatsops established by the Corps of Discovery in the winter of 1805–6, clothing Coniah and giving "him a writing in lieu of the American one, which I threw in the fire before him."[181] The "writing" Henry destroyed was a brief record of the Lewis and Clark expedition, which the captains had penned and entrusted to Coniah as proof of their achievement both for competing imperialists and in case the explorers died on the return to St. Louis.

The colonial employees did not make the transfer any easier, and their various complaints and nationalistic disputes may have fueled the Chinookans' confusion over the new state of affairs as well as their apparent jockeying for position. McDougall and several other Canadians stayed on, changing their employer from Astor's Pacific Fur Company to British Canada's Northwest Company.[182] However, as Henry complained, the voyageurs hired by Hunt at Michilimackinac and St. Louis lacked "that sense of subordination which our business requires." Instead, "the looseness and levity they acquire in the Indian country, tends to make them insolent and intriguing fellows, who have no confidence in the measures or promises of their employers."

If the men had opted not to defend Fort Astoria, they proved themselves equally disdainful of British control. With the long-expected arrival of the *Isaac Todd*, brawls between the sailors and trappers broke out. One of the French-Canadian blacksmiths, Augustin Roussell, interrupted the officers' dinner on one occasion, drunkenly "hurrahed for the Americans . . . talked more nonsense, and richly deserved a beating," although Henry and McDougall refrained until he sobered. The first and third mates of the *Isaac Todd* were suspended from duty for damning "the British navy and, etc." One of them was a naturalized U.S. citizen pressed into service after his ship was seized. The Chinookans were, as ever, well aware of the happenings at the fort. As Henry complained, the men had frequent "communication with the Chinook ladies." Henry further mused that, if the officers of the *Raccoon* were any indication, the reign of the royal navy, England's "wooden walls," would not last much longer.[183]

Over a decade of fighting had touched and terminated lives throughout the world, but the Napoleonic Wars finally ended in late 1814. Astor made certain that the Oregon Question, really the Astoria question, would remain open, however.[184] He spent years trying to use Captain Black's dramatics to his advantage: according to the Anglo-American Treaty of Ghent, all property seized in the war was to be returned. However, the fact that McDougall had previously sold the establishment to the Northwesters complicated matters, as the sale would seem to negate the remuneration clause. Still, the British capitulated in the first joint-occupation treaty, and, in 1818, American diplomat J. B. Prevost oversaw the lowering of the Union Jack and the hoisting of the Stars and Stripes over Fort George "in token both of possession and of sovereignty." *Token* was the operative word. That Prevost had to charter a British ship, the *Blossom*, from Valparaiso, Chile, to get to the Columbia suggests how unrealistic the American claims of "possession and of sovereignty" were at the time. Moreover, James Keith, who succeeded McDougall in 1817 after the latter's promotion to Fort William, continued to operate Fort George for the Northwest Company. Yet, like the pre-war Astoria days, the remote post was again considered a settlement of the United States. In other words, nothing actually changed on the ground level. Importantly for imperial politics, however, as Prevost wrote to the secretary of state, Washington and London could be assured that "collisions . . . may be now wholly avoided."[185]

The imperial situation was complicated further by the means with which the furs were disposed. In Asia the East India Company drowned the enterprise of independent British Northwest maritime traders by forcing them to exchange their furs with company traders at low, fixed rates and then dealt with the Cantonese themselves and kept the resulting profits. The merchants of the United States faced no such monopolistic constraints; American empire favored free trade, with both greater potential profits for private investors and greater risk. The predominantly Boston-based ships exploited the bureaucratic failings of the British imperial strategy of monopoly and dominated the maritime trade during its heyday from 1792 to 1824.[186] To avoid losing profits to the East India Company, the Northwest Company traded its furs from Fort George to American ships that then traded the furs free of the imperial monopoly to Cantonese merchants. The profits were ultimately split between Boston and Montreal investors. James Keith and Boston merchants J. and T. H. Perkins made four such runs in 1817, 1819, 1820, and 1822, in which Northwest furs were exchanged in Canton for Chinese goods for the Boston market. In 1820 alone, the *Levant's* furs translated into $70,000 worth of Chinese manufactures bound for Boston consumers. Prevost suggested that such arrangements occurred frequently.[187]

Fort George was not British any more than it was American. If anything, a Northwest Company flag would be all a visitor was likely to see. The demographics reported by Prevost in 1818 suggest a complex village. He listed James Keith, three clerks, a surgeon, and an overseer—all presumably ethnically European—in addition to "17 Whites including Canadians—mechanics, 26 Natives of Owyhee [Hawai'i], 1 Native of the place, 16 Trappers & Canadian Iroquois employed in gathering & many women and children."[188]

As for the Chinookans, Gabriel Franchere had commented that "[s]ince the villages form so many little sovereignties, differences often arise among them, whether from chiefs or among the peoples."[189] He considered that this complicated political economy explained the Chinookans' tendency to parlay their conflicts into settlements to avoid significant bloodshed from wars that would otherwise occur. Franchere's assessment was an apt characterization of the lower Oregon fur trade generally.

Colonial Oregon was one of the first imperial engagements of the fledgling United States and one that pitted its national interests and citizens against those of its intermittent adversary, Great Britain. Before Jay's Treaty (1795) had even settled the borders in eastern North America, a nascent colonial Oregon became a new site of imperial and colonial competition. Yet, the diversity of the imperial, colonial, and Native participants and their various, often conflicting interests complicated the scenario well beyond a simple dichotomy of American versus British. National, ethnic, and racial diversity among colonials further complicated the situation with individual identities and loyalties based on such encompassing phenomena, even as they pursued quite personalized interests.

Between 1792 and 1822 Native and colonial peoples constructed colonial Oregon by accommodating the interests of "others" but always mediating and limiting these accommodations through their own interests and core beliefs. The various participants reconstructed Native and Western norms of gender and sexuality, contributing to the formation of a distinctively colonial culture, although Western racial beliefs ultimately limited this cultural creativity. By the early 1820s, the competing British and American traders joined the Chinookan villages as "so many little sovereignties" along the lower Columbia River. Although often frustrated by a fur trade bound more by Native kinship and village obligations than by company policies and markets, the colonials adapted themselves and fit their vision of a commercial Oregon into *Illahee*.

CHAPTER THREE

Disastrous Times We Had

Expansions and Epidemics, 1821–1834

Imperial Reordering of Lower Oregon

On an international level, the muddy imperial claims to the Oregon Country began to clear somewhat with the United States signing treaties with Spain and Russia. Despite the dubious nature of the U.S. victory over Great Britain in the "second American Revolution" of 1812–14, the young republic emerged with an expansionist vigor to colonize the Indian Country from the Mississippi to the Pacific. A new generation of political leaders such as John Quincy Adams and Thomas Hart Benton replaced Jefferson's revolutionary generation and, consequently, displaced the old fears that rapid colonization of the West would destroy the democratic-republican experiment through diffusion of the population and polity. The new generation's imperial rhetoric challenged the old European powers still recovering from the Napoleonic Wars. Spain, a crumbling empire that was losing its tenuous grip in the Americas to independent-minded Creoles, ceded its claims north of Alta California in 1818 to the United States and Great Britain in exchange for recognition of its claims to the south.

In 1824 the United States successfully pushed Russia into withdrawing to the 54th parallel in exchange for recognition of its northern claims, although the Russians did maintain Fort Ross in Mexico's California for several more years. According to Russian historian Nikolai Bolkhovitinov, St. Petersburg had interpreted the so-called Monroe Doctrine of 1823 as a challenge to the Russian America colonies, specifically the policy of noncolonization of the Americas by Europeans. Britain had initiated such a policy and invited the United States to offer a joint statement. The United States opted to issue its own, which excluded its empire republic from the ban on colonization, while benefiting from Britain's actual ability to block European competition. The

United States had been in a diplomatic dustup with the Russians since 1821 over maritime trading rights above the 51st parallel, and this situation definitely factored into President James Monroe's foreign policy, but the Pacific Northwest was not the empire republic's greatest concern.

Much of the rationale for Monroe's foreign policy derived from the United States' interests in Tejas, the Caribbean, and the newly independent Latin America. Still, envoy P.I. Poletika wrote to St. Petersburg in 1819 that Euro-American settler colonists were swarming across the Mississippi in a "general mania," and the Russians would not be able to prevent them from ultimately occupying the Oregon Country. Tsar Alexander I was much more concerned with his continental colonies in Eurasia and the threat of the Ottoman Empire on his southern borders than the vastly distant Oregon and its trans-pacific partner, Hawai'i.[1] The official withdrawals of Spain and Russia left the United States and Great Britain as the remaining competitive imperial powers of the Pacific Northwest.

While the United States was in the midst of its postwar "era of good feelings," neighboring British Canada was dividing into warring factions that featured different visions of empire. Despite U.S. sectionalism, the Missouri Compromise of 1820 promised to keep Western colonization from being divisive by "solving" the dilemmas of extending slavery. To the north, the Hudson's Bay Company (HBC; the Company), the official trading monopoly and imperial representatives in the Canadian West, had worked out a relatively peaceful coexistence with the independent entrepreneurs of the Northwest Company. The HBC maintained forts and traded for furs delivered by subarctic Native peoples. The HBC officers were employees. The Northwest Company, by contrast, sent trapping parties into the field led by traders who held stock in the Montreal-based enterprise as partners. Astor had copied this arrangement with his Pacific Fur Company, and, as mentioned, his officers had been mostly former Northwest Company men who returned to that status following the sale of Fort Astoria. In the Red River Country of modern southern Manitoba, northern Minnesota, and parts of the Dakotas, the HBC and Northwesters operated in close proximity, both claiming rights to the far west of the Athabasca Country and the Pacific Slope.

The precarious balance fostered by the rivals' different business methods was upset by the introduction of a third vision. Lord Selkirk, chief stockholder of the HBC, decided to plant a settler colony in the Red River Country with Scottish tenant farmers who had been displaced by English land speculators over the previous half century. Selkirk's colony began to take shape in late 1812. By 1815 the Northwesters, fearing the loss of their investments, resisted the colony and convinced their Native and Metis allies to join them, pointing to the threat to their lands and resources, particularly the buffalo herds. Selkirk recruited Swiss mercenaries and captured the Northwester field headquarters, Fort William. In the late 1810s, the battles were fought in the field, in the courts, and in taverns across Canada. The situation deteriorated to the point where, in 1821, London forced its combative colonials to merge. In actuality, the HBC swallowed the Northwest Company, reducing the independent "wintering partners" of the field to employees of an imperial monopoly.[2]

Far from the Canadian Plains and London boardrooms, the lower Chinookans would soon feel the effects of imperial politics. In 1821 the board of the reconstituted HBC named George Simpson to govern the newly created Pacific Department, and he employed a former Northwest wintering partner John McLoughlin as chief factor of Fort George in 1824. The new leadership made some significant changes to the operations of the trade to cut expenses and preempt attempts by Americans to reestablish a presence in the region. When Simpson toured the lower Columbia in 1824, he complained that Fort George had "an air of . . . grandeur and consequence which does not become and is not at all suitable to an Indian trading post."[3]

To the chagrin of the frugal Simpson, Northwesters Duncan McDougall and his successor James Keith still relied on food supplied by Native traders and American and European ships to a considerable and expensive extent. The Northwesters at Fort George had been largely left to their own devices while their parent company scuffled with the HBC in the Red River Country. As well, the fort had been technically a possession of the United States since Prevost's ceremonial flag raising in 1818, and the British retained occupation at the whim of the president.

With the consolidation of Canada's fur companies and the arrival of Simpson and McLoughlin, British "empire and order" returned.[4] McLoughlin moved the principal fort upriver to the north bank opposite the mouth of the Willamette River, and he established a farm and purchased some livestock to cut expenses. The new establishment was named Fort Vancouver; the English explorer's name reflected the Company's effort to reaffirm the British imperial claim.[5] Significantly, McLoughlin completely abandoned the much-disputed little settlement of Fort George in 1825. In 1826 or 1827, Indians, presumably Clatsops or Chinooks, burned the fort, leaving only a single chimney standing, "a melancholy monument of American enterprise and domestic misrule," according to one observer.[6] Anthropologist Yvonne Hajda has observed that the death of Concomly in 1830 symbolized "the end of

Concomly's Tomb, Astoria, ca. 1841 (Wilkes, *Narrative of the United States Exploring Expedition*; image courtesy of the Oregon Historical Society)

Indian social dominance on the Greater Lower Columbia."[7] One also could point to the significance of the burning of Fort George a few years earlier, symbolizing the declining influence of the Chinooks in the fur trade. Perhaps the conflagration was a statement by the aging Concomly or his eldest son Cassackas, who saw his chance for power depart upriver to the domain of rival Casino and the Clackamas village at the confluence of the Columbia and Willamette rivers.

Expansions and the Encroachment of Oregon

Under McLoughlin, the Company continued to operate the lower and upper Columbia posts but also expanded northward along the coast and south into Snake River country and the southwest Oregon—northwest California borderlands. The northern expansion as far as the Russian settlements is mostly outside the scope of this discussion, but the decision relates to the uncertain future of British tenure on the Columbia. Although an indefinite extension of the joint-occupation treaty in 1828 eased McLoughlin's fears that London would suddenly relinquish its claims and abandon Fort Vancouver, the northern expansion into modern British Columbia indicates the widespread assumption that the United States would eventually secure dominion of the lower country, perhaps including the promising Puget Sound. The Company intended to maintain a presence on the Northwest Coast and hoped to forge a link to its interior Athabasca trade and so established Fort Langley on the Fraser River; thus, the northern expansion was a long-term business investment. Navigating the upper Fraser turned out to be a death-defying experience for canoeists, but Fort Langley did serve well as a British Pacific port and exporter of packed salmon and timber for markets in Monterey, Acapulco, and Lima.

The southern expansion, by contrast, was meant to check American expansion of the Rocky Mountain fur trade into the Oregon Country. By the mid-1820s, brigades from St. Louis had established supply depots in modern New Mexico and Utah—both were Mexican possessions, but neither the American nor British brigades paid much attention to Mexico's territorial rights in its northern interior.[8] The Euro-Americans were within striking distance of the Oregon Country and had international rights under the joint-occupation agreement to enter and trap. To inhibit their entry, the Company discontinued methods that encouraged a sustainable harvest of furs and chose instead to trap out, or exterminate, the beavers, making a "fur desert" as a buffer zone between the lower Snake River and the Columbia. The Company had long maintained such an extermination policy along its frontiers with competitors such as the Northwest and xy Companies in Canada. The Snake River "fur desert," however, had the added imperial dimension of enhancing Britain's treaty-negotiating position as sole occupant if it could stall American colonization.[9]

Nevertheless, Americans arrived in 1823, independent of but coinciding with their president's imperial declarations. Formerly an Astorian and Northwester and now an HBC trader, Alexander Ross led a brigade that year into the Snake Country and came upon a Euro-American brigade under Jedediah Smith. Ross took them back to visit his post and reportedly boasted of the Snake River Country's productivity. For this blunder, Ross soon found himself transferred to the Red River mission school. Indeed, Smith would soon lead the first Euro-American trapping expedition into the Oregon Country in 1827. One of Simpson's first orders in the Oregon Country in 1824 was to replace the "empty headed" Ross with Peter Skene Ogden as leader of the Snake River brigade.[10]

Astorians and Northwesters had been trapping in the region for a decade, but their goals and procurement of furs had been limited. By the late 1820s, the Snake brigades expanded west across the Great Basin to the Klamath Basin and into the southwestern Oregon—northern California border country. A second prong of fur brigades went south from the lower Columbia through the Willamette Valley into the Umpqua and Rogue river drainages and across the Siskiyous into the Sacramento Valley of northern California. Together the southern brigades carried the trade into interior and coastal river valleys previously unknown to colonials. Their actions often brought them into conflict with Native peoples, who depended on the furbearers for food and who feared the newcomers.

Ultimately, Ogden would lead six Snake River expeditions between 1824 and 1830, expanding the range increasingly south into Mexican territories and westward into the Great Basin. In the winter of 1826–1827, his brigade traveled west to the Klamath Basin. The Klamath peoples were hospitable but not terribly interested in helping Ogden find beaver and did their best to usher his brigade from their country. Ogden wrote that "one of the Chiefs of [Lost] River informed us that some distance in advance there was a small river in which there are Beaver, but having been forbid by our Guides as well as other Indians to inform us of this."[11] The headman, probably from one of the Modoc bands, escorted the brigade to Tule Lake and down the Klamath River to the border of their lands with the Shasta peoples across the Siskiyou Mountains. The guide indicated that his people "are at present at war with" those on the other side of the mountains, and indeed they later reached a "spot formerly a [Shasta] Tribe of Indians resided but have all been distroyed by the Clammett Nation."[12] The Klamath and Modoc peoples were certainly not a coherent nation any more than the "little sovereignties" of the lower Columbia, but they spoke dialects of the same Luatamian language and maintained enough interaction across the several autonomous bands for colonials to view them as a "tribe."[13] A week later in the end of January 1827, Ogden entered "an Indian hut" and met three Shasta widows of men his "Klamath guide had killed . . . the previous summer."[14] The violence among the Native peoples of the Oregon-California borderlands demonstrated ripple effects of the expanding Columbia fur trade.

The peoples of the Klamath Basin were already suffering from the introduction of horses and firearms into *Illahee*. Just as Plateau Sahaptians raided The Dalles villages by the mid-1810s and contemporaneously fought with Shoshone "Snakes" in the valleys of the Blue Mountains, both Sahaptian and Shoshone-Paiute horsemen struck at the Klamaths and Modocs of the borderlands of south-central Oregon and adjacent California. The Klamaths embodied these initial raids into a lament chant recorded a generation later in 1880: "*Kó-i ak a nä'pka gatpam'nóka*," which Victorian-era linguist Albert Gatschet translated as "Disastrous times we had when the Northern Indians arrived."[15]

Ogden noted that the Klamath peoples were anticipating a raid from Nez Perce and Cayuse horsemen from the north when he arrived in late 1826. As they had only one horse and no firearms that he could see, the Klamath peoples were at an obvious disadvantage. They also had to repel the Shoshone-Paiute raids from the Great Basin to the east. In turn, the Klamath peoples lashed out at the neighboring Shasta, Takelma, and Pitt River (Achumawi and Atsugewi) peoples. Initially, they may have intended to replace some of their lost population taken in slave raids by doing the same to their neighbors. The raiding became a way of life between the 1820s and 1850s and, as discussed later, would earn the Klamaths a more equitable position vis-à-vis the northern Indians by the late 1830s.

Anthropologist Theodore Stern described the time as "an almost endemic condition of warfare" in the region.[16] Western colonization exacerbated this situation, and Oregon colonials unwittingly entered it. Chiloquin, a Klamath headman, credited the Shoshones with introducing the raids, stating that "[w]hen the Snakes made war on us that made us keen to fight other Indians and we made war without provocation on the Pit Rivers, Shastas and Rogue Rivers, but they never made willing war on us."[17] Similarly, David Hill (*Wawa'liks*), a "sub-chief" of the Klamath Lake band, boasted to Gatschet: "Never [did other Native peoples of the Oregon-California borderlands make] slaves of the Lake tribe conquering by war those from tribes all-around; the Lake men alone enslaved all surrounding Indians in this country."[18] Understandably, the Ikiraku'tsu Shastas, Takelmas, and Latgawas of interior southwestern Oregon were apprehensive when Ogden's brigade entered their homelands from the Klamath country. As Ogden descended the Siskiyous along Bear Creek in February 1827, he entered the region that is today called the Rogue Valley or, until the mid-1850s, the "Rogue's Valley."[19]

Colonials would echo Ogden's initial assessments of the land and its people for decades: "this is certainly a fine Country and probably no Climate in any Country equal to it." The Native peoples were, however, enigmatic, and reports of them were frightening: "here we are now amongst the tribe of Sastise or (Chastise) it was this Tribe that was represented to our party of last year and also to us as being most hostilily inclined towards us."[20] To his credit, the experienced Ogden wanted to judge for himself, writing that "so far we cannot say what their intentions may be . . . we have not seen more than 30 and their conduct has been friendly." As the brigade descended Bear Creek to the main branch of the Rogue River, he received reports from the Ikiraku'tsu that Latgawa Indians who "they are at variance with" were assembling to attack the trappers. Still, Ogden noted that such intelligence was "like all other Tribes I am acquainted with," in which Indians "represent [enemies] as hostilily inclined towards us . . . from all this I am inclined to believe it was a false report." He noted that "Our [Shasta] Guides informed us that they did not intend to proceed any further with us." The Bear Creek Valley was a bloody border area, with Klamath bands raiding from the basin to the east and Shasta bands encroaching across the Siskiyou Mountains from the south.[21] Molly Orton, a Latgawa consultant for linguist John P. Harrington, stated that the northern band of Shastas "all the time fight, take away wife." Conversely, Shasta informants probably gave the upland Takelmans their name, as they referred to a principal Latgawa village as "Lawaya," meaning "knife in belly."[22]

Anthropologists compiled many Takelma and Shasta place names well within the other's claimed territory. These place names have contributed to confusion regarding indigenous territorial boundaries, which were probably never very stable or definite. Regarding the disputed Bear Creek Valley and Table Rock area of the upper Rogue Valley, descendants of both peoples gave names suggestive of aboriginal ownership and residence.[23] One cannot know how many times indigenous peoples fought each other for the region and its riverine resources, but, clearly, the early nineteenth century was one such period, and the impact of new factors introduced by Western colonization clearly exacerbated the tense relations.

Ogden would soon agree with the Ikiraku'tsu Shastas' assessments of the Latgawa and lowland Takelma peoples. While he camped at the Rogue River in mid-February, with his brigade "scattered in different directions" to trap and scout the new country, one horse was killed and three were wounded by arrows. Ogden decided that local Indians "certainly evince a most malicious disposition towards us and if not checked and that soon our Scalps will soon share the fate of our Horses." The following day the country and its people were steadily losing their appeal, as trappers complained "of the unsteady state of the Water and Natives most numerous bold and Insolant . . . they appear determined to oblige us to leave their Country."

Slowly, however, over the next few days, Native representatives began visiting and "wished to make peace with us." Ogden "consented," and they had "a Ceremony" in which he gave two dozen buttons and the Latgawas performed a dance. The brigade finally reached its first goal of 1,000 beaver pelts, indicating the success of the "fur desert" effort, as earlier expeditions had taken over 4,000 on the Snake tributaries alone. Ogden griped that he had only eight skins toward his second 1,000. The Latgawas, like the Klamath peoples, do not seem to have been eager for the brigade to remain in their country and informed Ogden that beavers could be had downstream in Takelma country, not upstream in their own.[24]

As the brigade proceeded down the Rogue River, then north into the valleys of the Umpqua drainage—the path to the Willamette and Fort Vancouver—the effects of raiding among the Indians and the fur trade became increasingly obvious. Takelman Indians fled as the trapping expedition approached. At the village of Dilomi near modern-day Gold Hill, "upwards of 100 Indians . . . left and ascended the hills with their Children and property." Ogden entered the nearly deserted village and found a few fur-trade goods and "a Sickle and two China bowls" left behind. The sickle was being used as a knife, whereas the bowls "are preserved as ornaments." Ogden was not able to determine the source of the goods, but he soon reached another village in which at least one of the Takelmas could speak "the Umpqua Language." From him he learned that the Umpqua River was still some distance away and that it was from the Umpqua Indians that they bartered for "Knives and Axes" in exchange for beavers.

Indeed, as had often been the case since leaving the Klamath Basin, the area seemed previously trapped out. The Umpquas had already introduced the Takelmas to the fur trade, as company brigades had recently ascended the Willamette and crossed into the Umpqua country. Also, in what was becoming something of a pattern, the locals told Ogden that, if he moved on, "at no great distance," he would find a "large River well stock'd in Beaver." As they traveled, the Takelmas seemed "numerous and troublesome," and the country was unknown and not particularly productive. Ogden confessed, "I feel at a loss how to act," and "the greater part" of his brigade "would wish themselves out of this Country." The brigade safely reached Cow Creek and the south Umpqua. After learning from some Takelmas that Alexander McLeod had recently trapped the area clean, they headed north to Fort Vancouver. Ogden, however, left Jean Baptiste Gervais and four trappers to work the rivers downstream and "open a communication between this quarter and Fort Vancouver which ought to have been affected many years since."[25] McLeod, Gervais, and others successfully affected working relations with the upper Umpqua peoples, and the Company later established Fort Umpqua in 1836.

Relations with the Native peoples to the south, however, would remain strained and poorly developed through the colonial wars of the 1850s. As indicated by the place names "Rogue River" and "Rogue Valley," the several bands of Takelmas, Latgawas, Shastas, and Athapaskans had earned a lasting reputation. Because the historical record is so poor, some have argued that the geographic name may have originated from a cartographer's misspelling of the French *Rouge* or the Spanish *Rio Rocque*. As discussed earlier, colonials associated the moniker with the supposedly natural roguery of its Native inhabitants, and that meaning achieved lasting significance.[26] Trappers referred to the numerous bands of Shastas, Takelmas, and Athapaskans of southwestern Oregon as "les coquin," or the Rogues, when they began exploiting the region in the 1820s.[27] Importantly, unlike other Native groups such as the Chinooks or the peoples of The Dalles, the name stuck and contributed to the fervent hostility against these peoples, including, by the late 1850s, calls for their extermination by settler colonists.

Probably the incident that cemented the "Rogue" reputation for southwest Oregon Native peoples in the minds of colonials was the Kalawatsets' massacre of the Smith party in July 1828. As feared by British traders, Jedediah Smith led a party of Euro-American trappers across the Rocky Mountains into the Oregon Country. They eventually made their way west to northern California and up the southern Oregon coast. In his journal Smith noted a similar experience to Ogden's the year previous. From the "Buenaventura Valley," or the Sacramento Valley, to the southern Oregon coast, Indians fled their villages on his party's approach. Trade took place only when the Euro-Americans made camp, and the Indians apparently had an opportunity to look them over before approaching them with food or other items for trade.

The pattern held as the Euro-Americans passed through the Sacramento Valley and the successive river mouths of the Chetco, Rogue, and Coquille. Smith was curious about the Indians' actions, but it does not seem to have occurred to him that a group of seventeen men on horseback leading a couple of hundred horses and mules and heading directly for a village could be viewed as threatening by the local population. Only on reaching the Coos River did the villagers remain at home. Likely the Hanis Coos had been forewarned of the party's approach and description. Earlier, at the nearby Coquille River, a group of Miluk Coos, or "lower Coquilles," had fled northward, demolishing their canoe before the galloping Smith could reach them, and abandoning a young, male Kalapuya slave, whom the trappers subsequently named Marion. The retreating Miluks likely notified their coastal neighbors. The Hanis Coos, or "Cahoose," Indians received the party and ferried them across the river. Nevertheless, a few individual Coos took the opportunity to fire arrows into the backsides of eight horses and mules. The expedition did not linger.

Continuing up the coast, the Smith party reached the lower Umpqua, where a party of Kalawatsets met them about four miles upriver from the mouth. It is probable that word had again preceded them, as the Coos and Kalawatsets had intermarried extensively and maintained good relations, and runners could easily outdistance the expedition's lumbering train of pack animals. As well, the Kalawatsets were familiar with HBC trapping parties that had come downriver recently in 1826 and 1827. Smith noted that the Kalawatsets had British trade goods and were familiar with the leaders' names at Fort Vancouver. Thus, unlike their neighbors south of the Coos villages, the Kalawatsets did not flee from the eighteen strangers.

The Kalawatsets also were aware of the division between the Americans and the British, deeming Alexander McLeod, leader of the recent expedition, and the HBC as their allies and trading partners. As a Kalawatset man later explained to Michel LaFramboise, "We did not take them [Euro-Americans] to be the same people as you."[28] In the eyes of the Kalawatsets, Smith's party of seventeen trappers and the slave Marion had no local standing. Consequently, they were in a precarious position, particularly considering the Kalawatsets' interpretation of Anglo-American competition in the Oregon Country. Indeed, Smith and his party told the Kalawatsets that Oregon Country belonged to the United States; this proclamation did not go over well with the indigenous people. As indicated by Alexander Henry's address to the Native principals of the lower Columbia, the British traders represented themselves as permanent occupants in the country but not as the owners.[29]

The situation called for restraint and humility on the part of the Euro-Americans, but such was not to be. The initial problem seems to have begun when one Kalawatset man helped himself to an ax. Smith's company tied up one Kalawatset, and another Native man defused the situation by convincing his mates to return the ax. However, one of the Kalawatsets, possibly the man who had prevented the confrontation and had arranged for the ax's return, attempted to take a joyride around the trappers' camp on one of their horses. Indignant, trapper Arthur Black "compelled him to dismount." The rider apparently became upset with Black's vehement reaction, and the Smith party lost an advocate.[30]

More importantly, one of Smith's men tried to rape a Kalawatset woman that night at their camp, according to HBC officers McLoughlin and Simpson. Some scholars doubt that the attempted rape occurred, because it is noted only in the two British officers' later reports. These scholars see the accusation as an intentional slur against Americans during a period of imperial rivalry. The case against the accuracy of the rape charge is based on an assessment of the character of the alleged perpetrator, Harrison Rogers, as related in Smith's journal.[31] As discussed in some detail later, however, rape of Native women occurred too frequently to dismiss the reports so easily.

The next morning a group of Kalawatsets assailed the camp, slaughtering most of Smith's men. Black managed to sneak away and was the only survivor of the men in camp. Smith and two others had been upriver scouting and also survived. Separately they worked their ways up the coast to Tillamook villages. The Tillamooks delivered the Euro-Americans to Fort Vancouver and presented McLoughlin with a quandary over how to respond to an attack by his new Native trading partners against his imperial and commercial adversaries. Opening a trade with the southern region and establishing a land route to northern California were crucially important, and both necessitated amicable relations with the Native people of southwestern Oregon.

McLoughlin did not want to sacrifice either pursuit for the sake of avenging the Americans, but he feared the precedent that the Kalawatsets' successful raid might establish as news of it disseminated through *Illahee*. Worse, McLeod, the trader who had secured relations with the Kalawatsets and whom Indians as far away as the Rogue River Valley had taken to calling "Chief of the Umpqua," was then on an expedition in northern California and was not due to return through southwestern Oregon for several months.[32] McLoughlin wrote McLeod urging his speedy return and dispatched the former Astorian and Northwester Michel LaFramboise down to the Umpqua, as he had trapped there during McLeod's expedition and the Indians knew him. He was to speak with the Kalawatsets, ascertain their side of the story, and determine the fate of the Smith party's property. LaFramboise found that the goods were dispersed irretrievably among the bands and villages of the area and that the unapologetic Kalawatsets felt that their raid had been legitimate. They determined that the Americans were a distinct group of interlopers who offended them, and that the HBC had no right to demand the return of the gifts that they had distributed. McLoughlin conveyed the information to Smith and explained that everyone would have to wait for McLeod's return. McLoughlin felt that he alone could determine whether retribution was possible and whether it would be beneficial or harmful for the future. To his traders, McLoughlin was more thoughtful on the subject than he had been with Smith and seems to have considered the Kalawatset position. "[W]e have no right to make war, on the other hand if the business is drop[p]ed, will not our personal security be endangered wherever this report reaches[?]"[33] McLoughlin awaited his most experienced trader in the region to determine a response.

Punishing *Illahee*

By 1829, there was certainly a precedent for violent retribution from Fort Vancouver. The Clallams of Hood River, on the western shore of Puget Sound, had attacked a brigade from Fort Langley in June 1828 and had killed five trappers and one of their Native wives. Another woman, the daughter of an important Native trade ally, had been captured. McLoughlin responded harshly, ordering Alexander McLeod to lead a punitive expedition. With the aid of the *Cadboro's* cannons, the colonials killed about twenty Clallams and burned their village and all their property, including forty-six canoes, the lifeblood of the people. The surviving Clallams turned over the woman. Such a response was far more brutal than the expedition to the Cascades in 1814 and, notably, ignored Native and common fur-trade practices of attempting a settlement.

McLoughlin wrote to Simpson and the board, attempting to explain and justify the massacre. His rationales were undermined by one of his clerks, Francis Ermatinger, who had taken part in the assault and penned a highly critical report of the men's overzealous conduct. According to Ermatinger, the Clallams had not been informed of the reason for the expedition, nor was any attempt made to secure the woman's release through settlement, which could have been done "at the price of a few blankets."[34] Spurred by Ermatinger's criticisms, on one side, and the many men who supported the vengeful action, on the other, the Clallam massacre remained a contentious and much-discussed topic among the colonials.

Wintering at Fort Vancouver in 1828–1829, Jedediah Smith was well aware of the Clallam expedition and pressed for a similar action on the lower Umpqua. The chief factor wrote to McLeod via a California-bound ship that "Mr. Smith's affair has a more gloomy appearance than I expected . . . we must either make War on the Murderers of his people to make them restore his property or drop the business entirely." In the end, he deferred to McLeod to make decisions "on the spot" but indicated that he wanted McLeod to avoid violence if possible, thinking it unnecessary based on their intercourse with LaFramboise.[35] The experienced trader McLeod eventually took Smith back to the lower Umpqua in 1830 and retrieved some of his party's horses and goods from the south-coast villages without bloodshed.

Among Euro-Americans, in particular, the Native peoples of southwestern Oregon never overcame the stigma of the Smith massacre, although Kalawatset elders would later unsuccessfully implore Methodist missionaries to help them rectify that dangerously provocative image in 1840.[36] The HBC, on the other hand, maintained their relations with the Kalawatsets. They established a trading fort above them in 1836, which they maintained until 1851, when a fire razed their establishment for the second time and Euro-American settlements fueled by the California Gold Rush largely displaced the enterprise.

In a nascent colonial world, retributive expeditions were not simple matters of "whites versus Indians" or total wars of conquest. McLoughlin felt that he needed to calm relations in temporarily "unsettled" regions, and his fighting force was his labor force pulled from pursuits such as trapping, farming, felling, and milling. They were no more an army than the Native bands and villages with whom they occasionally fought. In the midst of recent and pending problems on the lower Columbia, Puget Sound, the Plateau, and the lower Umpqua in March 1830, McLoughlin complained that "it is but justice to all in charge of such Expeditions to state they are the most disagreeable Duty to which a person can be appointed." His decisions regarding when to attempt revenge in light of future profits and realistic considerations of power were agonizingly complex, partly because the actual raids were so unpredictable. As Alfred Seton had stated, fur trade employees were of "divers nations & languages,"[37] and they reflected equally diverse interests. McLoughlin complained that the expeditions were "extremely difficult to manage Composed as they are of Canadians Iroquois a few Europeans Owhyees [Kanakas], and native Indians whose language we do not speak nor they ours and even hardly understand us of hired servants who consider themselves bound to defend our persons and property when attacked but conceive it no part of their duty to go to war and merely go to oblige and of freemen [seasonal-contract trappers] who may be led but will not be commanded."[38] Historians continue to debate the justness of his punitive expeditions, but none can dispute that McLoughlin took them seriously and had limited control of their actions once they left the fort.[39]

McLoughlin's decisions in 1829 were further complicated by the loss of one of the Company supply ships (the *William and Ann*), a resulting conflict with the Clatsops, and the arrival of two American coasters, which anchored in the lower Columbia as floating trade posts offering better prices than Fort Vancouver. When the *William and Ann* sank in early March 1829 in the mouth of the Columbia River, all hands drowned and approximately one third of Fort Vancouver's annual supplies spilled into the surf. The Clatsops, ever watchful for gifts from the sea, salvaged barrels of rum and hats, among other articles. Some items they traded or gave away and others they retained. Because McLoughlin had abandoned Fort George four years earlier, no colonials witnessed the tragedy or had firsthand knowledge of the Clatsops' subsequent actions. A Native man at Fort Vancouver, who, according to McLoughlin, had a grudge against the Clatsops, spread a rumor that the crew had actually survived the wreck but had been killed for the cargo. Predictably, cries for revenge erupted around the fort community, which was still divided over the Clallam massacre less than a year before.

McLoughlin did not believe the rumors but sent five of his traders and sixty Canadians, Indians, and Kanakas downriver to confront the Clatsops and reclaim the property. Although McLoughlin argued that the Clatsops were of "well known savage disposition," he noted that the sailors' bodies had washed ashore in various locations and showed no evidence of having been massacred.[40] Still, his decision to send so large a contingent from the fort invited and produced violence.

The spring 1829 clash with the Clatsops resulted from McLoughlin's fear that an appearance of weakness would create further troubles; similar reasoning had produced the Clallam massacre. He believed that "the Indians considered the property as ours and after receiving particular information of what had been collected by the different Indians if we had not made a demand of it we would have fallen so much in Indian Estimation that whenever an opportunity offered our safety would have been endangered."[41] The Company therefore must demand "restitution" to save face. His was not an ignorant calculation; the Indians in the region acted similarly in sending a sizable force to ensure adequate settlements among each other. The colonials had witnessed several such occasions on the lower Columbia since 1811, in which different villages pressed each other for settlement, often after some brief fighting or posturing, typically dismissed by Westerners as "petty war."[42]

Indeed, the Clatsops appear to have respected McLoughlin's decision and met the show of force by offering a settlement. They requested that the HBC contingent remain onboard their ship and offered some salvaged articles, which had not yet been appropriated, as well as slaves to cover the Company's losses to their stores and esteem. Yet William Connolly, leading the HBC expedition, took offense at the "insult" and "Contemptuous reply" and ordered his men ashore. As soon as they began entering the skiffs, the Clatsops opened fire, then fled to the safety of the forested hills. Connolly and company killed four people and "Burnt their village and all their Property." McLoughlin was much satisfied, because he agreed that the Clatsops had responded haughtily and in the violence; "not one of our people got the slightest wound."[43] The assault on Clatsop was similar to the earlier one on the Clallams, a definite departure from the actions of the Northwesters when Franchere and company seemed well aware of the Native norm of avoiding unnecessary bloodshed to secure a mutually acceptable settlement; but those days were over.

Although colonials considered themselves a minority, this assessment was based on the Western conception of race. Such was meaningless to Native peoples, who did not yet consider themselves a distinct people. It is misleading to consider as McLoughlin did that colonials were outnumbered: "one white man to 200 Indians."[44] There was no comparable "Indian" identity among the Native peoples to "white" among Westerners, which bound them across nationalities.[45]

As diverse as the fur-trade personnel were and as unpredictable as their retributive expeditions were, the HBC had a coherent identity and unmatched resources, and Fort Vancouver was the most powerful "little sovereignty" west of the Cascade Mountains. The 1814 expedition from Astoria had been half-starved and so concerned with fitting into *Illahee* as a means of self-preservation that Madame Coalpo and Casino were the two most important leaders, and Henry, Franchere, and others viewed the settlement at Cascades Rapids as a success. Fifteen years later, McLoughlin was not as concerned with the safety of his forts in the lower country as McDougall had been. Rather, he was worried about the individual trapping parties alone in the field, particularly as he expanded their range into new territories in the north and south. The retributive expeditions of the next decades, particularly with the rise of the Euro-American presence, would be increasingly violent, and the avenue of arranging settlements would continue to decline steadily.

McLoughlin seems to have recognized the error of abandoning Fort George, as the Company could not see ships to help pilot them across the treacherous bar. As well, the relations with the Clatsops had clearly deteriorated. He ordered Donald Manson to open a new post near the old site in March 1829. Madame Coalpo, still a leading figure in the lower Columbia trade, began leaning toward the Americans' floating trade posts, and McLoughlin feared that he might "lose the Chinooks" and perhaps the lower Columbia trade. Instead of buying out the American coasters, McLoughlin decided to undercut their prices, operating at a loss, and "as to Madam Calpo you [Donald Manson] may give her any present you think proper." He was successful, and the American coasters departed.

Fort George consisted of Manson's tent, eventually replaced by a house and a few outbuildings. Observers noted the presence of about six Indian dwellings. These individuals likely salted and packed salmon, a commodity with which McLoughlin was experimenting in the Latin American markets of California, Peru, and Chile.[46] When George Birnie took over as clerk of Fort George, he planted a sizable potato crop, but the little settlement did not approach its former "grandeur and consequence" until Euro-Americans later revived Astoria as a port town.[47] Significantly, after the return of HBC traders in 1829, there were no more conflicts with the Clatsops. The reaffirmation of the Clatsops' ongoing, if decreased, importance to the trade seems to have quelled further problems.

In 1830, new problems arose, bringing norms of *Illahee* and Oregon into conflict again. The supply ship *Isabella* sank in almost the same spot near the Columbia's treacherous mouth as had the *William and Ann* the previous year, although the crew and cargo were saved. Obtaining sufficient horses and cattle from Plateau Sahaptians was always a problem, and McLoughlin faced potential violence on the lower Umpqua and at Fort Nez Perce near the mouth of the Walla Walla on the middle Columbia. On the Plateau, a Cayuse man of significant standing had killed a Company slave, Shasty, presenting McLoughlin with a classic fur-trade scenario pitting divergent views of society and justice. Shasty was likely a Hokan-speaking Shasta Indian or, at least, a Native of the southwest Oregon-northwest California border region, whom the Chinooks and consequently the colonials generically referred to as Shastas or Shastys. Chinook women allied with the Company obtained such slaves via trading and raiding expeditions into the lands south of the lower Columbia: the upper Willamette, Umpqua, Rogue, and Shasta valleys.[48] To the consternation of Fort Vancouver's short-lived Anglican chaplaincy, the Company gladly exploited these slaves via the control of the Native women who were married by "custom of the country" to their traders and trappers.[49]

Fur expeditions were complicated family affairs, not straightforward business pursuits. They reflected perhaps as many indigenous attributes as Western. Native American women had proven crucial to the fur trade since the seventeenth century. In the Oregon Country, elite Chinook women's control of labor marked another significant contribution. Equally important, they derived power from leading fur expeditions and increasing wealth and status for their families and home villages. As elsewhere in the trade, a minority of headmen such as Concomly and Casino emerged with new forms of power and prestige among Native communities, but some women of the lower

Columbia also used the trade to enhance their positions.[50] Madame Coalpo, who successfully played the American coasters off against the HBC, is simply the most famous.

However, fur expeditions often had a Native woman at the helm. Although the actual power they had varied considerably, all legitimated the colonialists' presence to the local Native population in any given area. Also, as mentioned, they provided the slaves. Slavery both enabled power and exhibited it. Slave raiding and trading spread with the fur trade, and, by the late 1820s, people from the southern periphery were increasingly common among the slave population of the lower Columbia as well as from points north and east where Chinooks traded them.[51]

The use of slaves in the fur trade presented problems, however. McLoughlin and the HBC wanted to project a united, perhaps "tribal" image, but the standing of their slaves in the eyes of Native peoples inhibited that desire. Shasty was sent with the 1830 expedition to the Snake River, which was headed eventually to his home in the borderlands of northwestern California and southwestern Oregon. However, the expedition left Fort Vancouver with the initial malarial "fever and ague" raging, and Shasty and a handful of others were too ill to continue by the time they reached Fort Nez Perce. While recuperating and under the order of fort trader Simon McGillivray, Shasty shot a cow that belonged to a local Cayuse man who had apparently refused to sell it to McGillivray. To the Cayuses and Wallawallas, McGillivray was responsible, and he repaid the loss of the cow with the loss of a Company slave, Shasty. The matter should have been settled, according to the Cayuse.

McLoughlin decided to transfer McGillivray, at the trader's request, telling him to warn the local Cayuse and Wallawallas "that they will get a bad character among the White Chiefs and none will be willing to remain on their lands," unless they learn to be more conciliatory.[52] The Sahaptians around Fort Nez Perce were probably unimpressed. McGillivray's successor, Pierre Pambrun, did little to advance Company authority. Like all experienced traders, he balanced accommodation and resistance as best he could. The Plateau Sahaptians had been competing with Shoshones and Blackfoot for decades and were fully capable of forming large, effective war parties that could strike quickly and decisively; of this, the colonials were quite aware.

Transferring McGillivray was a good business decision, but McLoughlin was unclear as to how to proceed regarding Shasty's death. As he understood the situation, he had two systems of justice to weigh, and both seemed inapplicable. Given the distance from colonial seats of authority and the Company's decidedly limited power on the Plateau, he could not administer English common law. Yet, noting his sense of Christianity and conveniently putting aside the Company's exploitation of slaves and its increasing violence against fellow men and women, he could not quite bring himself to abide by Native beliefs. Although "the killing of Shasty is murder yet with these Indians it is considered no greater offence than killing a horse; and perhaps not so bad as shooting the Cow." McLoughlin wrote to McGillivray in apparent resignation and wistful idealism, "if a Chief among us was to Kill a slave that Chief would be killed. But as you have not the means of putting this command in execution you will leave it to the Almighty who [may] punish the murderer." Reporting to his Company superior, Governor Simpson, he amended this view to include the ever-present concerns of commerce and the realities of Native interethnic communication lines. "But even if we did Kill [the Cayuse man], it might be the cause of deranging all our business along the Communication" of the Indians of the upper Oregon Country. Worse, punishing the man might lead to war with the Cayuse "if the tribe are willing to defend him." Given "the disposition of those [Sahaptian Indians] about Walla Walla," McLoughlin refused to take the chance. McLoughlin concluded by arguing that McGillivray did nothing to provoke the killing but was "thrown off his guard and did not act with that caution so necessary to be observed in dealings with" the Cayuse and Wallawalla Indians.[53]

McLoughlin was forced by circumstance to abandon retribution for the killing of the slave Shasty and put himself in the awkward position of having condoned a Native practice with which he disagreed. That summer, in July 1830, McLoughlin had the opportunity to clarify for his traders and trappers that he supported killing as retributive policy to be effected either by dispatching a company expedition or by hiring Indians. Apparently, William Kittson "had offered two Horses to get an Indian Killed" over some dispute. The traders were aware that such contract killings occurred among Indians of different bands and ethnicities and were an accepted, although probably rare, practice in much of *Illahee*.[54] McLoughlin wrote to his local trader, William Connolly, asking "will you have the Goodness to state to Mr Kittson that the Company will not allow such proceedings and that it must not be done." He was not against hiring a killer, but that "[i]t is only when Indians have murdered any of the Companys Servants or any person belonging to the Establishment that we can have a Right to Kill the Murderer or get him Killed."[55] Kittson's dispute did not qualify.

McLoughlin later had the unfortunate opportunity to refine his ideas about retribution, in the spring of 1832, in a case involving two Eastern Indians in the company's employ who had been killed while trapping in the Coast

Range south of the Columbia by an unknown group of Tillamooks. Apparently feeling more secure in the lower country than upriver on the Plateau, thanks in part to recent malarial outbreaks, he advised LaFramboise to embark on a punitive expedition to the "Killamook [*sic*] country for the purpose of punishing the atrocious murder of Pierre Kakarquion and Thomas Canasawrette," probably two Iroquois trappers, given their surnames. As with McLeod and the Umpqua expedition, McLoughlin deferred to LaFramboise's local knowledge and experience. McLoughlin relied on him to produce the "least effusion of blood . . . some innocent beings may in such cases unavoidably become victims as well as the guilty the severity necessary, for own safety & security may always be tempered with humanity and mercy."

LaFramboise and his party killed six people. McLoughlin congratulated him on his accomplishment: "I think it but right that you send word to these sauvages . . . that we do not wish to hurt the innocent we expect that themselves will Kill the remainder of the Murderers of our people." McLoughlin considered extermination as the next possible step, "if they do not [kill the murderers of Kakarquion and Canasawrette] we will return and will not spare one of the tribe." He confided to one of his clerks that "I desired [LaFramboise] to Kill a few men only of the first party of that tribe that he fell in with and tell those he allowed to escape that we did this to let them see what we could do . . . and that they themselves must Kill those who had been concerned in the murder of our people." He concluded, "[W]e wished to be on good terms with them—we never allowed any of our men do them the least harm—and it is they who brought this punishment on themselves."[56]

The introduction of extermination as a means of colonialist retribution was still some years off, but McLoughlin's comments suggest its growing appeal. Earlier in the 1827–1828 Snake River expedition, Ogden was clearly becoming frustrated with the decreasingly productive duty of creating a "fur desert" and advocated the extermination of the local Shoshone Indians, not the beaver. He wrote in his journal that, if it were his decision, "I would willingly sacrifice a year or two to exterminate the whole Snake tribe, women and children excepted. In so doing I could fully justify myself before God and man." Ogden conceded that "[t]hose who live at a distance are of a different opinion. My reply to them is this: Come out and suffer and judge for yourselves if forbearance has not been carried beyond bounds ordained by Scripture and surely this is the only guide a Christian sh'd follow."[57] He did, however, merely vent in his journal. Historian Lewis Saum took Ogden's self-justification to mean that he did not truly believe his own tirade. Perhaps, but Saum's seems an overly generous reading.[58] Ogden would not be the last colonial to advocate extermination of Oregon Indians in frustration with economic pursuits and to offer a similar rationale.

In his 1831 publication, Ross Cox had mused about the differences between Anglo and American colonization of North America. Although Irish, Cox did not espouse much anti-British sentiment in his book and chided Euro-Americans for their "unnatural and acrimonious hatred to the land of their forefathers." He considered himself British, but he did reserve some criticism for the English who had colonized his native land. He regretted that the English and Americans only paid attention to the Indians during wars with each other, and, with the growing power of the United States, Christianization seemed to have fallen from the ideals of colonialism: the spread of Westernism and Christianity. Indeed, he considered the United States' "anti-republican love of aggrandizement, by the continual extension of their territorial possessions" un-American. Like some Euro-American critics of Jeffersonian political theory, he felt that imperial expansion "must sooner or later destroy the unity of their confederation." Yet, the Euro-American settler colonists' treatment of the indigenous people was the "subject deeply to be lamented." With the "gradual encroachments on the Indian lands," Cox credited Euro-Americans with expounding "extermination, instead of regeneration . . . [as] their motto."[59] With the decline of the fur trade in the lower Oregon Country and the arrival of the Methodist missionaries and Euro-American settler colonialism, one has an opportunity to view the merits of Cox's thesis in the next chapters.

Epidemics and Catastrophe in *Illahee*

Although the violence of 1830 was significant, it paled in comparison with the inadvertent introduction of the epidemic disease malaria. Between 1830 and 1834, malaria reduced *Illahee* in the Greater Lower Columbia region to being a part of colonial Oregon rather than the reverse for the first time. Anthropologist Robert Boyd, who has done the most extensive epidemiological and demographic work on the subject, has provided a probable scenario for the malaria outbreaks. A human carrier of a malarial parasite arrived in 1830 at Fort Vancouver, which was linked to the trans-Pacific trade routes, and was bitten by a local mosquito. The newly infected mosquito then spread the disease to the blood of other people through previously innocent bites; the Indians had no exposure to or knowledge of malaria before 1830.

For the next four years, during the mosquito-breeding season in the late summer, when Indians gathered at seasonal lakes and wetlands to collect wapato and other edible roots, the survivors of the last year became the infectious carriers of the new year, as mosquitoes mingled the blood of unsuspecting victims. As one company officer recalled, "it affected us all from the root eating Indian to the carniverous English seamen."[60] The crucial difference, however, was that the Europeans and Euro-Americans recognized the "fever and ague" as malaria and administered an apparently short supply of quinine among themselves, sending to Hawai'i for as much as the posts there could spare. Citing insufficient supplies in the early 1830s, the traders administered quinine treatment to only the Indian peoples in closest proximity to the fort, such as wives and family of company men. In 1830, the Company lost one Iroquois trapper and "nine women, two children, and several of the Indians about the place," but no more personnel then or in succeeding years.[61] Among the Indians, according to Boyd, a depleted supply of victims largely ended the annual death cycle.[62]

Anthropologist Yvonne Hajda notes that worst damage was done within the first four years on the lower Columbia. She credits the epidemics of 1830–34 with breaking the power of Indians vis-à-vis the HBC in the region.[63] Many contemporaries described the gruesome toll on the Native peoples of the lower country, noting abandoned villages that had bustled with human activity shortly before and bodies being piled high on the isles of the dead, or *memoloose illahee*, on the middle Columbia River. One mission layman claimed that "[i]n one day's ascent of the Willamette in a canoe, I have counted nine depopulated villages: in some instances whole tribes were nearly annihilated, and the few desolate survivors fled from the abodes of death, and identified themselves with their less unfortunate neighbors."[64]

Thanks in large measure to John Work's trapping expedition of 1832–33, the malaria epidemic spread up the Columbia River, across the Plateau, into the Great Basin, across the Sierra to the Sacramento Valley and California's north coast, then northward through southwest Oregon back to the Willamette Valley. Work left Fort Vancouver while the fever was raging. When he reached Fort Nez Perce, near the confluence of the Columbia and Snake rivers, he left some trappers who were too sick to continue. He then continued on his circuit to Alta California and back northward to the Willamette Valley, unwittingly spreading death by the tens of thousands throughout the Oregon Country and neighboring northern California.[65]

Together with previous epidemics, Boyd estimates that from 1805 to 1841 the lower Chinookan and Kalapuyan peoples declined from approximately 15,545 people to 1,932 (by 88 percent).[66] Demographic information for Indians who lived south of the lower Willamette centers of Fort Vancouver, the

Willamette Mission, and the settlements, as well as those of the Coast Range Mountains, is much less reliable. For example, the Tillamooks were said to have numbered anywhere from 200 to 1,500 in the 1840s.[67] Subsequent epidemics of smallpox, measles, and influenza similarly followed the trade routes in the late 1830s and were evidenced among the peoples of northern California and the Umpqua. It seems doubtful that the peoples in between in southwest Oregon were not similarly ravaged. Indeed, on Oregon's south coast, the Port Orford Indian agent noted pocked facial scars on many adult Tututnis years later in 1854, and the Indians advised him that they had twice been ravaged within a generation.[68]

As happened elsewhere, Native curative practices often unwittingly helped along the so-called virgin soil epidemics, in which human populations with no exposure to certain microbes consequently develop no immunities to them and suffer enormously when finally exposed. For example, sweats followed by plunges into cold water further weakened or drowned fevered victims. Malaria carried off many elders and traditional leadership—having both short- and long-term consequences for Native communities.[69] Furthermore, throughout the Oregon Country, Indians suspected unrecognized or inexplicable illnesses of being human caused, and this suspicion created distrust and friction. Such is not surprising.

Without historical experience with large-scale deaths from epidemics, the Native peoples of Oregon made sense of death on an individual basis. For lower Chinookans, for example, inexplicable illnesses resulted from "the intrusion of a foreign object . . . the agency of a malignant shaman, [or] soul loss."[70] Certain individuals were credited with spiritual powers that could conjure and project illness-causing agents, and similarly empowered individuals could remedy the sick person. By failing, however, a medicine person risked retribution, fines, or even death from aggrieved kinfolk.

Indeed, the Indians often fixed the blame for disease on Europeans and Euro-Americans. One widely disseminated story among the Indians blamed the American coaster, the *Owyhee*, which had plagued Fort Vancouver's business, for initiating the "fever and ague," or malaria, in 1830.[71] Notably, the Indians' explanation for the epidemic's beginning does not differ substantially from Boyd's epidemiological scenario. Indians claimed to have seen Captain Dominus of the *Owyhee* release the pathogens from a vial in a pouch that he wore around his neck because he was upset with the trade.

Others claimed that trade beads or "power sticks" (survey markers) produced the disease. The story has several versions, recorded by different European and Euro-American contemporaries, but the core elements remain consistent. The survey markers may have become part of the explanation in subsequent years when Euro-Americans dispossessed Indians through forced land cessions. In 1854, an Indian agent recorded a Chinook version in which a Euro-American captain bewitched a channel marker. Although "medicine men and prophets" determined the stick's guilt and ritually defeated it, the malevolent spirit had already left and gained a foothold among the people.

Boyd notes that the theme of the non-Indians' ability to produce disease from a bottle dates back to 1811, when McDougall supposedly threatened to unleash smallpox from a vial among the Clatsops and Chinooks.[72] However, this story of McDougall as the "smallpox chief" is from Washington Irving (who never visited Oregon); no contemporary records of Astoria support it. Ross Cox's narrative may have been the source, but he seems to have slurred events that he did not witness: namely, the brief stay of the transgendered prophet Kauxima-nupika and the smallpox scare in the summer of 1811.[73] In the 1830s, Dominus and other American sailors apparently relayed the tale of their smallpox powers northward to intimidate Makah traders at Cape Flattery, and it was commonly retold around Puget Sound.[74]

The pervasiveness of the tale is further evidenced by the Kalawatsets of the lower Umpqua in 1840 and their concern regarding missionary Jason Lee's shot pouch, which he wore around his neck. According to the missionaries' translator, the Kalawatset wife of Company trader Jean Garnier, the Indians thought that he bore deadly magic. Still, the Kalawatsets refrained from their supposed plot to kill the missionaries preemptively.[75] The Native peoples generally opted not to take traditionally justified retribution until 1847, when, as discussed later, a handful of Wallawalla and Cayuse men took revenge in the infamous Whitman Massacre.

By 1834, malaria's devastation of the Native population slowed, and that same year a new population began to arise in the lower country, harbingers of a new Oregon. Retiring trappers sought lands to cultivate in the Willamette Valley, and Euro-American Nathaniel Wyeth led a group of his countrymen to attempt a salmon-export business and to settle in the area where until recently Kalapuyas had thrived. McLoughlin, whose promising career as a wintering partner had been terminated by the rise of the Red River Colony west of Lake Superior, feared what settler colonialism would do to the fur trade. Initially, he resisted efforts by retiring Company trappers to remain in the region as farmers, but they pressed and he gradually acquiesced. Because of the joint-occupation treaty, McLoughlin could not prevent Wyeth and his group of "Rocky Mountain men" from settling, but he could refrain from helping them—which would likely doom their enterprise. Significantly, however, he befriended Wyeth and established a commitment to helping Euro-Americans. Later, when Wyeth led the Methodist missionaries overland, and the increasing stream of "pioneers" followed in their wake in the 1840s, McLoughlin continued to help.[76]

Those Euro-American trappers who began to arrive in 1834 joined a changing colonial society already established in and around Fort Vancouver. By the 1820s, families among male Company employees and Native and mixed-blood women further developed relations between lower Columbian peoples and colonials. Still, not all colonial families were comprised of Chinookan women and Western men. Native Hawaiian women (Wahines) began to arrive as early as 1812.[77] Subsequently, other Wahines accompanied their Kanaka husbands as HBC employees through the 1830s.[78] Together with the Nipissings, Iroquois, and others, transplanted indigenous peoples accounted for the earliest colonized families in the Oregon Country, predating the Euro-American "hardy pioneers" and the Red River Metis by decades. Fur-trade economics in the 1810s and 1820s explained these initial population shifts, but in the next decade disease obviously caused the greatest changes.

After the forced merger with the Northwest Company in 1821, the HBC undertook more than just economic reforms to meet the imperial competition of the Americans; colonial social life also came under scrutiny. As discussed in the next chapter, American Methodists founded a mission to the Indians in 1834. Not surprisingly, the London board of HBC subsequently dispatched Anglican Rev. Herbert Beaver to see to their colony's moral, social, and spiritual character in 1837. Beaver complained that the lack of a "civilized population" was no way for England to conduct its "infant colony" and to establish "perhaps a future London" on the Pacific. Rather, the board must send "hither a few respectable English families of the labouring class." American missionaries reacted similarly to Beaver, although they, of course, favored colonization by white, Christian families from the United States, not England. Amid the economic upheaval of the late 1830s and 1840s that fueled the migration of "hardy pioneers" to Oregon, England did export part of its "surplus" population. However, their destinations were the "white colonies" of Australia and New Zealand, where British imperial claims were unchallenged.[79]

At Fort Vancouver on the lower Columbia in 1837 and 1838, Anglican missionary Beaver did his best to undermine the familial relationships that he neither understood nor desired to. As noted, Gov. George Simpson was upset with colonial life in 1824 at Fort George. In addition to the "air of . . . grandeur," he had complained that the Native wives of Company men kept prostitutes whom they hired out to trappers.[80] A decade later at Fort Vancouver (supposedly the embodiment of HBC reforms), Beaver was equally concerned with the similar colonial life that developed as the fur trade declined, and Chief Factor John McLoughlin began shifting the trade settlement into a colonial center in which ploughs and livestock replaced traps and pelts. Reverend Beaver attempted to direct this changing colonial culture.

In particular, Beaver felt that, without a formal Christian ceremony, the relationships between Company men and Native women in the huts surrounding the fort were "concubinage." Totally inexperienced with the North American fur trade or the type of human relations it engendered, Beaver had had overseas experience as garrison chaplain on Saint Lucia, and his stay was marked by complaints that Oregon was not "civilized" like Britain's racially segregated Caribbean "black colonies." To counter "the beastly state of fornication," Beaver wanted the men bunked within the fort in a proposed bachelor's quarters and the "the native females, whether of pure or mixed breed" barred from residence, provisions, and medical attention. Beaver was not terribly popular among the HBC men, not surprisingly because he considered their Native wives to be "the very excrement" on the "scale of humanity." He refused to marry A. C. Anderson to the mixed-blood daughter of James Birnie (a clerk at Fort George) and his Clatsop wife. Having conducted "one marriage between two persons of the lower order, the man being Canadian, and the woman half-bred between an Iroquis [sic] and native woman . . . in the present deplorable and almost hopeless state of female vice and ignorance, I have no desire to unite more couples." He deemed intermarriages on the lower Columbia "both irreligious and illegal."

The following year, in 1838, however, Beaver changed his mind and his tactics, recommending corporal punishment for all men who refused to marry officially their Native "concubines." Beaver left later that year, bound for a garrison chaplaincy in South Africa and frustrated that his many recommendations for Westernizing Native women in lower Oregon were ignored. The regimented racial lines between indigenous South Africans and European colonists better suited Beaver, and he remained there until his death in 1857.[81]

As Beaver made his various complaints and recommendations directly to London, Chief Trader James Douglas responded and, in so doing, provided information on custom-of-the-country marriages and prostitution on the lower Columbia during the late fur trade. Regarding the withholding of medicine and provisions as inducement to marriage, "our own people . . . would absolutely redicule us." Besides, he noted, only five wives receive Company rations and all "have claims to consideration." Regarding charges of prostitution, Douglas firmly stated that "no person is permitted to make fancy visits, and I neither have nor would suffer any person, of whatever rank, to introduce loose women into this Fort."

This was a marked change from Fort George, 1814–1825, a change in which a fort domestic realm had become distinct from other sexual relations that could be considered prostitution. Rather, Douglas continued, the Native women live "in a state of approval by friends and sanctioned by immemorial custom, which she believes strictly honourable." A woman married by custom-of-the-country form, "a perfect contrast to the degraded creature who has sacrificed the great principle which from infancy she is taught to rever as the ground work of female virtue; who lives in a disgrace to friends and an outcast from society."[82]

Thus, Douglas acknowledged prostitution on the lower Columbia but, unlike other writers, he differentiated it from the informal, monogamous unions and stated that prostitutes lacked social status and communal ties. What Douglas left unchallenged was Beaver's assertion that slaves acted as prostitutes at the behest of the Native wives of Company men, a practice that existed at least since Governor Simpson's complaint in 1824. Douglas assured the board, however, that such activities were not allowed within the fort and were not part of the colonial society. The sex trade, such as it was, had clearly declined. Prostitution, whether by "outcast" women or slaves, became a marginal activity by the 1830s. In the 1810s, Native leaders such as Delashelwilt, Coalpo, and their wives had prostituted slaves, and custom-of-the-country wives, in the 1820s, acted similarly.

Whereas prostitution in this manner did not cease, new conditions greatly curbed it, such as diseases that decimated the Native population. Colonization contemporaneously increased the predominantly male Western population that sought intermarriages with survivors. Trappers who became homesteaders needed fellow agricultural laborers, not prostitutes, and Chinookans needed to rebuild shattered kin relations. Demonstrating his ignorance of fur-trade culture, Reverend Beaver termed Chinookan women concubines, but these survivors of a microbial holocaust who took up with colonials were the next generation of custom-of-the-country wives. Ultimately, they and other Chinookan people continued their heritage.

Cataclysmic change shook the foundations of the Native Northwest, beginning with the smallpox epidemic of the early 1780s, continuing with the maritime trade that followed, and continuing through the land-based fur trade and the advent of settler colonialism in the mid-1830s. On the lower

Columbia River, Chinookans altered their society to meet these new, unprecedented challenges. No state existed to direct and implement change. Individual men and women from villages such as Clatsop, Chinook, and Clatskanie competed with one another and with colonials.

The creation of colonial Oregon on the lower Columbia was more than a one-sided, Western economic pursuit. Inadvertently and sometimes purposely, the trade created a field of interpersonal and cultural relations that both created and destroyed. *Illahee* and Oregon shaped each other, although malaria tipped the scales toward the latter. Together with the extermination of the beaver, the decline of the fur trade, problematic relations among Indians and colonials on the margins of the trade, and the renewed American presence, life on the lower Columbia forever changed between 1821 and 1834.

CHAPTER FOUR

A Vital Experimental Religion

The Methodist Mission Colony of Lower Oregon, 1834–1844

Hiyack wah-wah Sakalatie. (Quick speak to God.)
—MARGARET SMITH, Oregon Mission

Evangelical Empire

In 1834 a band of Methodists led by Rev. Jason Lee came to bring salvation to the Native people and the diverse population of fur-trade colonials. Lee and his band of Methodists entered a world in flux. Malaria devastated Native villages; social structures adapted to meet the challenges of the fur trade were collapsing under the demographic pressures. The Hudson's Bay Company searched for a colonial economy less dependent on furs and better able to meet the growing threat of Euro-American colonization. Lee believed that the Methodists would prove critical in reshaping this unstable environment, and he had faith that he would figure out how. His was "a vital experimental religion."[1] Antebellum Methodism, particularly the Oregon Mission of 1834–44, is perhaps best understood in terms of the attempts to find a tenable balance between the ideals of Christian mission and the realities of everyday existence.[2]

To "save" Indians, evangelical missionaries felt that they had to repudiate and completely alter the Native economies and the cultures that gave them meaning. Religious scholar Antonio Gualtieri termed this exclusivist mode of religious conversion "theological imperialism."[3] In his landmark study, historian Robert Berkhofer similarly explained that religion is partly "a system for ranking basic values, and thus a new religion implies new behavior . . . true Indian conversion meant nothing less than a total transformation of native existence."[4] People had to accept the Gospel (the canon of apostolic writings of Christ's life and teachings) as the Truth and maintain a spiritual, civilized life of temperate, honest farming or business. Rev. Henry Perkins railed: "I insist on *holiness*—. . . holiness is something different from common religion. . . . [which] is a *mixture*, & all common christians may say in truth 'To good & evil equal bent, I'm *half* a devil, *half* a saint.'"[5] A minister's duty was to prevent such "backsliding" and save erstwhile Christians from Hell through regular Bible meetings and other participatory observances.[6] Rev. Alvan Waller would extend such doctrine to Indian people at the Wascopam station, preventing them from trading horses on the Sabbath, and making some "quite angry." That the Native traders complied with the wildly gesticulating missionary demonstrated to Waller that he was doing God's work.[7]

Theologically Arminian, Methodism, as exemplified by English founder John Wesley, taught that humans were religious free agents—salvation was a personal choice—unlike Calvinism, in which God predetermined one's fate after death. Evangelical Christianity was supposed to be an intimate, life-shaping relationship between an individual and God, which then produced a community of the saved, a "social church" to reinforce individual spirituality and piety. Believers followed the example of Christ and his disciples—the original evangelists—to spread the Word.

Methodism and other evangelical beliefs found fertile soil among Euro-Americans and African Americans, with periodic upsurges or "awakenings," particularly in the 1760s and the 1820s.[8] The crises that fueled such awakenings also were evident among Native peoples east of the Mississippi, such as the Red Stick Creeks and the followers of Neolin, Tenskwatawa, and Handsome Lake. These "nativist" movements, however, mostly drew on Christianity to repudiate it, effectively countering many missionaries.[9] Evangelicals had to be creative to meet fundamental challenges in the field.

The epic of Jason Lee, the superintendent of the Oregon Mission, is a staple of Oregon historiography, because many contemporaries and historians credited him with "saving" Oregon from British claims by fostering Euro-American colonization.[10] For this action, he is either praised or condemned.[11] This well-trodden historiographical debate misses the larger point, however. Lee sought to create a mission that could cater to both Indians and colonials, and to make the Oregon Country a seat of Christian American civilization, a place dominated by the power of the Gospel, not the undesirable, profane realities of the United States. In short, Lee and his faithful pursued a utopian colony, as did many of their contemporaries and forebears. Lee distanced his sense of mission from other, avaricious forms of imperialism: "I would not abandon the enterprise and return home for all the honors of Cesar, Alexander, and Bonaparte united, and all the temporal pleasures of the civilized world . . . great good will yet be done in this benighted land, that my motto is Onward, come what will."[12] Lee did confront many problems. Indeed, problems defined the Oregon Mission, but returning home as a victorious, enriched conqueror was never one of them.

The Methodists carried a new vision of place alien to both *Illahee* and the Oregon of the fur trade. They colonized parts of the lower Willamette Valley during the period of joint occupation between the United States and Great Britain in the 1830s and early 1840s. These so-called temporal, or secular, efforts have overshadowed Lee's project of Christian mission largely because contemporary critics and historians have generally misunderstood the connection between mission and colony. Antebellum Protestants considered the two enterprises to be complementary.

Politics and religion often reinforced each other in the historical phenomenon known as the American Mission.[13] The Mission Society of the Methodist Episcopal Church (MEC) was a leader among American mission societies. They, unlike the transnational Jesuits with whom evangelicals felt themselves locked in a millennial struggle, could never separate their divine purpose from Euro-American colonization of the West and the Pacific Rim. As Oregon missionary Rev. David Leslie put it: "The New Church and the New Nation starting together . . . having a providential work to do . . . in the cause of God and humanity . . . [have established] the ordinances of Religion coextinsively with the laws of the government to meet the emergent moral necessities of the opening continent." Examples supporting Leslie abound through the nineteenth century, in which the MEC (and they were certainly not alone) fostered both mission and colonialism across the continent and around the Pacific Rim in the name of God and country.[14]

Indeed, Thomas Paine's millennial rhetoric that "we have it in our power to begin the world again" gained new credence decades after the Revolution with the so-called Second Great Awakening of the 1820s and 1830s. The religious fervor led the devout to open their purse strings, allowing evangelical societies to dispatch mission families to Indian Territory, Hawai'i, Africa, China, California, and Oregon. In some cases, Congress also contributed through its so-called Civilization Fund, but the diplomatic complexities of Oregon's joint occupation between the United States and Great Britain prevented any official federal aid to the Oregon Mission. Still, as the missionaries knew, God commanded: "Go ye & teach all nations."

Importantly, for American evangelicals, teaching included the twin powers of the Gospel and the Constitution. Leslie penned: "It is remarkable that American Methodism and American Independence were contemporaneous. . . . [And that the] peculiar organism of Methodism at the Christmass [*sic*] Conference [1784] seemed to anticipate the national organization under the Constitution."[15] This "remarkable" relationship linked the American evangelist's duty to spread both Truths. Just what the relationship between mission and colonialism meant in practice was contingent on particular circumstances. Still, the broad impulses of American Mission and Manifest Destiny were often inseparable.[16] The small but growing expansion into the Pacific trade further complicated the situation.[17] As the entanglements in the Franco-British wars consistently evidenced, the transoceanic trade put American citizens directly into the realm of European imperialism, effectively pitting republican empire against competing European models.

Where American merchants established beachheads, American evangelicals tended to follow, whether to convert indigenous "heathens," combat Islam, or regenerate Catholic Europe.[18] Because so many American citizens supported these pursuits, a kind of "folk imperialism" made the limited formal involvement in missionization by the United States largely irrelevant. In lieu of boards of trade and colonial councils, there were merchant capitalists such as John Jacob Astor bending the ears of politicians such as Thomas Jefferson. Instead of a state church, there were evangelical mission societies funded mostly by private sources but with some congressional assistance. It was a democratic-republican system, to be certain, but it was nevertheless imperialist, with much in common with the European powers, particularly from the point of view of colonized peoples. Traveling overland in 1834, Jason Lee recommended mission stations for the Plains trading posts and advised the Mission Board to keep up the work until its missions spread "from your own highly favored Union to the far off Pacific." An evangelical mission of the American Board of Commissioners for Foreign Missions (ABCFM) already extended into the Pacific at Oahu in 1820, but none yet existed on the Pacific American coast.[19]

A New Plymouth in *Illahee*

New England evangelicals followed the wake of Yankee whalers to the so-called Sandwich Islands to convert the Native Hawaiians. From their Oahu mission, established in April 1820, evangelicals became increasingly curious about the possibilities of "the Oregon," a country linked to the South Pacific Islands by the shipping routes of the fur trade. In September 1821, the *Missionary Herald* attempted to stir up the mission spirit among its northeastern readership. It published a report from two American ship captains who traded along the Northwest Coast and subsequently visited the Oahu Mission, claiming that "[s]ome of the savages when they heard of missionaries being sent to teach the Sandwich Islanders, inquired why they were not sent to *them*." The *Herald* attempted to counter a prior anonymous claim that "it is impossible to propagate the Gospel there." Citing the universal applicability of the Gospel, the paper noted that it is "for every heathen nation, however barbarous and inaccessible. . . . The energy of the Holy Spirit is irresistible, and can . . . easily transform the roaming savage of the north into a humble child of God." The *Herald* prophesied that "[t]he Gospel can be propagated on the N.W. Coast. It *must* be; it *will* be."[20] Similar notices appeared intermittently over the next few years concerning the northern Northwest Coast of modern-day coastal British Columbia and southeast Alaska, emphasizing the expected welcome of evangelists by Russian traders and Native headmen.

By the mid-1820s, the Prudential Committee of the ABCFM, like the Methodists and an increasing number of other Americans, sought a foothold in the Far Northwest. By July 1827 the Prudential Committee began planning for a Northwest mission, seen as a logical extension of the Oahu Mission.[21] Yet, the committee spoke of the inevitability of the westward "tide of emigration" and worried about the influence of "dissolute" settlers who would prejudice "the natives of the wilderness" against the Gospel. The committee proposed a solution in the form of a mission colony "to convey the inestimable treasure of divine truth to pagan tribes . . . and to prepare the way for future settlers from the Atlantic coast and the valley of the Mississippi." The committee members wanted to provide a moral base for the inevitable colonization of the Oregon Country by the chosen nation, the United States. "In a word, thus may be sent forth *another Plymouth Colony* . . . with all the advantages, which two centuries of unexampled progress in arts and knowledge have put into the possession of the church, and with all the encouragements which can be derived from the Providence of God, as displayed before our admiring eyes with the last thirty years."

Despite conjuring the Pilgrim spirit, the committee apparently did not desire a theocracy or wish to bear the expense of the colony: "[S]uch a colony . . . would be founded in religious principles and undertaken from religious motives, yet it would be a secular establishment, governed by its own constitution, and not under the direction, or at the expense, of any Missionary Society." The committee members were well aware of the need for a degree of separation of their dual operations: "The mission to the natives, closely united with the colony in affection and motive, would derive essential aid from it; and thus both enterprises would strengthen and encourage each other."[22] According to the initial vision, secular colony and mission were to be linked into one divine national purpose but exist as separate, complementary institutions.

The ABCFM sent Rev. Jonathan Green from Hawai'i to investigate the Northwest Coast in 1829 for a possible mission-colony site. Green visited San Francisco, Puget Sound, and modern-day coastal British Columbia and southeast Alaska. The weather prevented his venturing up the Columbia River or anywhere in modern-day Oregon. Green disappointed the Prudential Committee by reporting that the Indians were already corrupted: "Indeed, to seek a place on the coast where the Indians have not suffered in consequence of their intercourse with foreigners, will be, I am persuaded, a fruitless attempt." Still, "a counteracting influence might and should be exerted."

Throughout Green's report, he provided information regarding arable lands for possible small-scale colonization to support the mission, but he clearly desired an area that was marginal enough to discourage "land speculation" and Euro-American settlers.[23] For the most part, the northern Northwest Coast was too wet and too rugged. Without firsthand exploration, Green stated that, instead, the lower Columbia would be "desirable" for a centralized mission and a colony. However, he still awaited news of the ill-fated Jedediah Smith exploration of the Umpqua River, where the environs were rumored to be better than the Columbia. He noted that an Oregon mission colony would aid the "Sandwich Islands mission," supplying it with "[t]imber, fish, and other necessaries," as well as providing a respite for missionaries "whose strength had withered beneath the influence of a tropical sun."[24] (The sniffling, shivering missionaries who would later flee the soggy bluster of western Oregon winters for the sun of Oahu would have found this notion amusing.)

Despite the apparent promise for a mission colony, the ABCFM did not take action, probably because of the expense and distance from settlements. Cost seems rightly to have been foremost in Green's and the committee's decisions, but, if it were to be attempted, the lower Columbia region seemed best suited for its ability to support a cost-saving colony. Still, the monetary investment would require extensive fund-raising from the Christian citizenry of the Northeast. Such donations needed a tremendous spark. That spark would come in 1834 with the reports of the Flathead visit three years earlier, although the false sense of wealth from the era's notorious land-speculation schemes probably helped loosen a number of purse strings as well. In March 1833, the *Christian Advocate and Journal* published a letter from William Walker, a Christian Wyandot Indian, to the Methodist Mission Board. In it Walker spread word of the 1831 visit and proclaimed that the

"Flathead" Indians had requested knowledge of the Bible. This letter and the subsequent missionary fervor explain the timing of the Oregon Mission.

Like many evangelicals, Wilbur Fisk was excited by the news, but, as president of Wesleyan University, he was actually positioned to urge the Mission Board to action. Still, neither the board nor any northeastern Methodists knew who the Flatheads were or where they lived. After consultation with officials in Washington, D.C., the board members determined that the War Department, in charge of Indian affairs, was equally ignorant. Regardless, the board created a sufficiently vague "Aboriginal Mission west of the Rocky Mountains" and wrote to the adventurer-turned-bureaucrat William Clark, formerly of the Corps of Discovery, for more information.

By July 1833, the Rev. Jason Lee was appointed missionary to the Flatheads, whoever they were.[25] Drawing on prior Methodist mission experiences, Nathan Bangs of the board immediately recognized the need for "building houses and cultivating land; and in establishing a school."[26] The board appropriated $3,000 to be spent at Lee's discretion; initially, his only required accounting seems to have been a diary of his overland travels and the expectation that he would subsequently send letters with updates. Such writings were presented to the Missionary Society and typically published in Christian publications such as the *Christian Advocate and Journal*, the *Zion's Herald*, and the *Missionary Herald*. Importantly, these newspapers allowed missionaries and the donating lay public to stay abreast of recent developments throughout the increasingly far-flung American Mission. Lee spent the remainder of the year in preparation for his mission and exhibiting his legendary fund-raising abilities. By the late spring of 1834, Lee embarked "to plant the standard of the cross in that barbarous land."[27]

Per his instructions, Lee traveled to the Shawnee mission in modern-day Kansas after departing St. Louis, and, as he moved westward, he surveyed the Great Plains for future mission stations. The board's plan was to establish "a line of missionary operations among the several tribes who inhabit the intermediate places between the frontier white settlements and the Rocky Mountains."[28] Lee and the board were painfully aware of the difficulties of communication and supply that would result from locating their Oregon Mission 2,000 miles overland from St. Louis or nearly 10,000 by sea from the Northeastern coast, the missionaries' base. The interim plan was for Lee to establish a sustainable mission, which could at some point exist free of monetary support from the society.[29]

The first contacts between the Methodist missionaries and the Indians of Oregon had begun late in the summer of 1834. Wailaptulikt, a Cayuse man, was returning with a hunting party from the bison country when he met Lee and his small band of Methodists on their way to the HBC's Fort Vancouver on the lower Columbia River. Wailaptulikt and his fellow Cayuse and Wallawalla hunters accompanied the mission party to their home on the Columbia Plateau. According to Lee, Thomas McKay, a mixed-blood Iroquois and HBC trapper, explained to the Indians "what we are and our object in coming to this country and they were very much pleased . . . more so when told there was a prospect of our locating at [the HBC Fort] WallahWallah."[30]

That night Indians visited Lee with "an interpreter who could speak but little of their language and told us they wanted to give us two horses." McKay told Lee to be wary, because the Indians might want an exorbitant price, so Lee explained that he had nothing to offer. The Native men left the horses with Lee, apparently a gift. The following day, two more men presented Lee with horses. For Lee, this action seemed to indicate "the hand of Providence" and augured "well for our ultimate success among these generous red men."

Soon after, at the Grande Ronde Valley, Wailaptulikt's and his fellow Cayuse "informed the chief [Tawatoy] that we were there and our object in coming to this country." The missionaries met with Tawatoy, "but we were sadly puzzled to understand each other." Lee states that the chief of the Wallawallas, Piupiumaksmaks (Yellow Serpent), joined the group and presented Lee with "some old papers with scraps of writing on them . . . I then, in red ink, wrote my name and Daniel's [Lee's nephew and fellow missionary], stating what we were, dated it and gave it to him and he seemed pleased with it." Contract in hand, the veteran fur trader Piupiumaksmaks then led Lee outside and presented him with "an elegant horse and one of the Kioos presented Daniel a fine horse." The missionaries invited Piupiumaksmaks and Tawatoy to their tent, presented them with tools and fishing gear of no "great value," and "smoked with them, sang a hymn, and commended them to God." Later Piupiumaksmaks took Lee into his lodge, fed him, and presented a sick girl to him. "He wished to try my skill in medicine . . . I gave him some camphor, with directions how to use it." Indians' testing of missionaries' healing powers—their spiritual powers—was a common form of early interaction; Lee, however, did not seem aware that he had just been tested.[31]

Leaving the Grande Ronde Valley, Lee ruminated about the seemingly Providential exchanges. "Who would have supposed that these Indians would have shown such kindness and generosity towards strangers on account of their religion? And yet this is the cause of their taking so much interest more in us than in others," presumably McKay's mixed-blood and Indian trappers.[32] Of course, Lee chose the Willamette Valley over the "upper country" for the Methodists' principal station, but that choice did not end contact with his new friends from the Plateau. The Cayuse and Wallawallas had been impressed with Lee's healing abilities, his emotional (if incomprehensible) sermons, and his gifts. They bestowed on him a few prized horses and considered the Methodists important new players in the region. They even had Lee sign a contract of sorts, and this promising initial encounter likely explains their subsequent arrival at the Willamette Mission in 1836.[33]

The Willamette Mission Colony

Why should the missionaries locate in the Willamette Valley when it had been the Flatheads and Nez Perce of the upper country who had called for a missionary? Jason Lee, his nephew and fellow missionary Daniel Lee, and lay mission-school-teacher Cyrus Shepard all offered similar responses. Lee explained that he had decided to locate among the "real Flat Heads," as he termed the Chinookan, Salishan, and Kalapuyan Indians of the lower country. As he carefully explained, they actually practiced head flattening, unlike the misnamed northern-interior tribe to which he had been dispatched. "Besides," he reminded them in self-defense, "it was left with us to locate where, in our opinion, after having surveyed the ground, we could do the most good." Hundreds of miles from the Flathead homelands, the lower country, with its "beautiful river . . . delightful valley . . . beautiful groves of timber," mild climate, and fertile ground, was "a central situation, advantageous for a principal station."[34] Daniel Lee similarly praised the geography of the lower country, and he went further in condemning the inhospitable upper country and claiming that the Flatheads did not desire missionaries. Apparently William Walker had erred in his representation of the famed St. Louis visit, or the Flatheads had changed their minds. He further explained that the Flatheads were too few for missionaries to bother with and that they were quickly disappearing—a claim that Methodist missionaries would later make regarding the Clatsops, Chinooks, Kalawatsets, Umpquas, and Kalapuyas to explain their lack of conversion efforts in western Oregon.[35]

The Flathead mission would have been unwanted, unnecessary, and doomed to fail, whereas the Willamette Mission was full of promise and, importantly, more suitable for a colony. Cyrus Shepard added the planned agricultural boarding school to the mix: "in order effectually to benefit the rising generation among the natives, a location must be made where a large school can be supported by the produce of the soil; and the place which has been selected appears to be the most favorable for that purpose." From the

Willamette station, "we trust the mission will hereafter be extended to other places, and much good done among the poor natives in the name of Jesus."[36] Quite simply, the lower country offered a better site for a central mission colony from which to establish satellite missions and a manual-labor agricultural school.

Colonial development proceeded quickly. In September 1834 the Methodists arrived at Fort Vancouver, selected their site up the Willamette River in October, began building, and by late 1835 the board was able to boast that the Oregon Mission included a farm and a school for "reclaiming these wandering savages, who are in a very degraded state, to the blessings of Christianity and civilized life." The board reported favorably on Lee's decision to locate centrally in the lower Willamette Valley and then presumably to establish an evangelical circuit among the Oregon Indians "and those emigrants who may hereafter settle in that vast and fertile territory."[37]

Additionally, the board responded favorably to an increased outlay of $1,000 and to send a reinforcement of additional missionaries, who sailed from Boston in the summer of 1836.[38] Two more Methodist preachers, their families, and a teacher sailed in early January 1837, making the "mission family" total twenty-three members. The board reported that "[t]his mission promises great usefulness to the rising colony in that part of the country, and therefore demands the vigorous support of the Society."[39] This increased support, however, did not solve the initial problems of the Oregon Mission: distance, the debate over whether to Westernize or Christianize first, and the language gap.

Regarding distance, the mission obviously had to establish a colony to support itself; however, the nature and size of that colony was less clear—it would have to be worked out in the field by first-time missionary Jason Lee. Under Lee, the mission built and operated mills, cultivated significant acreage (and to the chagrin of emigrating settlers claimed significantly more without occupation or improvements), constructed dwellings and schoolhouses, and possessed substantial livestock. As Lee stated, the mission introduced "all the necessaries . . . of a civilized colony."[40]

The mission-colony experiment had to demonstrate and teach Christian civilization (agricultural settlement) to the indigenous population, bridge the language gap to spread the Gospel, foster an orderly Christian community, and awaken the Holy Spirit within the fur-trade colonials. Many of the latter were "idolatrous" Catholics under the sway of this "formal" rather than "spiritual religion."[41] Also, the "abandoned and disaffected traders and trappers" had arrived earlier than the mission. Faced with these various dilem-

The Willamette Mission, ca. 1841 (Wilkes, *Narrative of the United States Exploring Expedition*; image courtesy of the Oregon Historical Society)

mas, the Methodists confronted the question of whether to Westernize or Christianize first.

Agricultural instruction, or, more accurately, instruction in manual labor, had been a technique employed by Protestant missionaries among the Cherokees, Choctaws, and other eastern Indians since the turn of the century. According to historian Clara Sue Kidwell, the southern Methodists had rejected the schools in favor of camp revivals among the Choctaws in the 1820s, only to have the Choctaws insist on reversing the priorities. The Oregon missionaries would similarly have to work out the issue in the field, although, without a history of agriculture like the Choctaws, Oregon Indians were less interested. They had to be convinced, or the mission to save them would fail. As Henry Spaulding of the ABCFM put it, "no savage people, to my knowledge, have ever been Christianized upon the wing."[42] On the other side of the debate, Gustuvas Hines favored the power of the Gospel and described the children's agricultural "education" in 1837 in unfavorable terms, lamenting that "the amount of labor to be done took many of them away from their studies much of the time."[43] Although the Anglican Herbert Beaver at Fort Vancouver considered the Americans' conversion efforts among the Indians largely wasted, he also believed it "erroneous" to think that Christianity could precede Westernization. He conceded, however, that a civilizing school for Indian children might make "some slow progress."[44]

Ultimately, the practical demands of colonization rather than intellectual debate answered the question. The work of creating a colony occupied the majority of the time and efforts of missionaries, laypersons, and potential Indian converts. As Reverend Hines lamented above, such work came at the expense of evangelizing and Bible study. Cyrus Shepard noted that "[o]ur elder boys plough, harrow, split rails lay fence chop wood &c." Because, as Jason Lee explained, "Ours is . . . a manual labor school . . . we cannot devote the whole day to teaching; we therefore have the pupils labor and study alternatively."

However, the plan to have the boys split time between work and school fell to such realities as "getting in spring grain." Similarly, "The girls . . . learn in addition to reading, spelling &c. sewing, knitting making straw hats housework &c." Any adult Indians who joined the mission family also received "instruction in agriculture, morality and the like." Still, there never seemed to be enough hands, particularly skilled ones. The limited number of artisans and agriculturalists among the mission family led layperson Susan Shepard to quip that useful people should be sent instead of missionaries.[45]

Despite the apparent limitations, the Methodist Mission in the lower Willamette Valley emerged as the first American colonial institution since Fort Astoria to challenge the regional power of the British. In an official mission survey in the winter of 1836–37, Lt. William Slacum of the U.S. Navy commended Lee's successes at converting "children, who, two years ago, were roaming their own native wilds in a state of savage barbarism, [and] now . . . [were] becoming useful members of society, by being taught the most useful of all arts, agriculture." The missionaries were grooming the Native children for their eventual attachment to "the civilized parts of our country."[46]

Lieutenant Slacum backed his praise of the mission colony with a $500 donation and free passage aboard the USS Loriot to San Francisco for representatives of the "California Cattle Company." This Euro-American venture sought Mexican cattle to break their dependence on the HBC and to stabilize the colony's economy. Representing the coalition of Euro-American investors, P. L. Edwards, a mission layman, and Ewing Young, a colonial entrepreneur, embarked and returned together with their jointly purchased herd in 1837. Jason Lee had added $600 of the Mission Board's funds to the total cost of $2,480 for the 800 cattle and forty horses. In microcosm, the cattle venture signified the relationship among the Methodist missionaries, Euro-American colonists, and a facilitating U.S. government. The limited official actions of the United States can be explained by the cloudy diplomatic climate of the Oregon Question. Congress did not openly support the Oregon Mission, although its members had been distributing the general "civilization fund" for decades and contributed directly to other Methodist missions. Slacum's personal donation was quite large, and it seems likely that it may have been unofficially endorsed or reimbursed.[47]

With official aid limited, the practical problems and contingencies of colonization were for the missionaries to confront, not the federal government. Indeed, Lee called for folks, not feds. In addition to the earlier reinforcements, he called for the Great Reinforcement of 1840 to buttress the Oregon Mission. According to Lee, the board's practice of dispersing a few, unmarried missionaries would only lull Christian civilization to sleep like an "opiate," continuing the "delusion" that world conversion can result from the "small means" of scattered, underpopulated missions. Instead, pious Christian families would convert the world by moral-agricultural education, hard work, and example, such as the ever-increasing acreage under cultivation by the Oregon Mission.[48]

In 1834, Lee had chosen the Willamette Valley for its fertile potential for the equally important seeds of conversion, crops, and Christian American civilization. Native conversion was only one aspect of his and God's work and, it appears, not necessarily the most important. Addressing the issue of why the Methodists expended most of their energy creating a Christian community among the approximately fifty Euro-American men and their Native wives in the lower Willamette Valley, Lee explained that such was a necessary first step to converting the surrounding Indians.

Lee boasted of his work among the former mountain men of the short-lived American entrepreneurial period of the late fur trade in the 1820s and 1830s. Lee did not include the Metis trappers-turned-colonists from the British Red River settlement; they mostly emigrated to the Willamette Valley after 1842 and preferred the Catholic Mission established in 1838. As well, because of the language gap, Lee had mostly given up trying to convert the French-Canadian and Metis "Papists" who had earlier settled in the lower Willamette Valley. Of the Oregon Mission's success with the Euro-American trappers, who were among the first non-Native settlers of the Willamette Valley, he trumpeted, "[W]e have thrown a moral influence around that settlement of white people" and kept them from being "a bad influence" on the

Indians.[49] In short, the colony proceeded well. What happened to the mission to the Indians?

Communicating a Christian Oregon to *Illahee*

The problem of the language gap asserted itself almost immediately. On his initial arrival at Fort Vancouver in 1834, Jason Lee preached to "a mixed congregation," which introduced him to the notable diversity of people already living in the lower country. His first "hearers" were "English, French, Scotch, Irish, Indians, Americans, half breeds, Japanese, etc., some of whom did not understand five words of English." (The Japanese were fishermen who had been blown across the Pacific by a storm. Having survived their miraculous voyage and come ashore, they were promptly enslaved by Makah Indians near Cape Flattery on the tip of the Olympic Peninsula. The HBC took pity on them or, more likely, saw them as a diplomatic opportunity, purchased their freedom, and tried to get them home via England. Japan, however, refused to accept them, and they spent their lives exiled in China.)

Lee's frustration with the language gap between his delivery of the Gospel and his hearers had been obvious since first entering the Oregon Country, when he lamented, "O, that I could address the Indians in their language." His complaints about language extended to the mostly French-speaking settlers of the Willamette as well, "few of whom understood what I said." Nonetheless, he assured himself and his readers, "God is able to speak to the heart." He looked forward to more preaching, "though the congregation will consist mostly of persons who will not understand the discourse."[50]

The Indian people of lower Oregon spoke several languages with many dialects, grouped principally as Chinookan (lower and upper), Kalapuyan, Athabascan, Sahaptian, and Salishan. None of the missionaries mastered a dialect in any of these languages in the first decade. Indeed, few tried. As Lee explained, the recent malarial epidemics made the linguistic diversity that much more difficult: "There are no competent interpreters of these Indian dialects, and there are few Indians who speak any of them that we have not as yet thought it best to attempt learning them." Layperson Susan Shepard similarly complained that "there are such a variety of dialects among them that it is very discouraging trying to preach to them." Still, some individual effort was made, in part because, as one missionary put it, "It is a dreadful thing to talk nonsense in the name of the Lord."[51]

The potential problem of the language gap was actually acknowledged before the missionaries even arrived in Oregon. On the overland journey in the spring of 1834, Layman Cyrus Shepard bemoaned the condition of a group of "Kansas" Plains Indians. He stated that no missionaries "understand their language and therefore there is no prospect of doing them good."[52] As Shepard suggested, language was a common problem for missionaries, but linguistic diversity made the problem especially acute in Oregon. Their contemporaries at the Oahu mission did not face the same situation. The Oregon and Oahu missions maintained a regular correspondence, updating one another about their prospects, the evolving political situations, and other news. The Oregon missionaries clearly recognized that their Hawaiian counterparts had an important advantage over their efforts by having to learn only one language.[53]

The Oregon missionaries had to rely on Chinook Jargon, the trade lingo. However, if it contained the linguistic subtleties necessary for discussing theology, the missionaries (and Euro-Americans generally) were ignorant of them. Although Lee, in defense of the Oregon Mission, claimed that the Jargon was serviceable for sermons, Rev. John Frost expressed the more popular sentiment when he described it as "altogether insufficient, by which to make known to [Indians] religious truths."[54] Herbert Beaver, the Anglican missionary at Fort Vancouver from 1836 to 1838, felt similarly that "it is too defective for the conveyance of Christian ideas."[55]

The Euro-Americans' few remaining examples of Chinook Jargon sermons would seem to support the criticisms expressed by Frost and Beaver. Margaret Smith, the girls' teacher at the mission's Indian school in 1838, related the following "sermon I sometimes preach to one or more [adults] when they happen in my path.

> Mican tum-tum Cloosh? (Your heart good?) Mican tum-tum wake cloosh. (Your heart no good.) Alaka mican ma-ma lose. (Bye-and-bye you die.) Mican tum-tum cloosh mican clatamy Sakalatie. (Your heart good you go to God.) Sakalatie mamoke hiyas cloosh mican tum-tum. (God make very good your heart.) Hiyack wah-wah Sakalatie. (Quick speak to God.)[56]

Smith's reductionist sermon suggests the obvious limitations of conveying Christianity's core beliefs regarding death and the afterlife. Notably, although she may have intended for "hiyack" to confer a sense of suddenness as with euphoric revelation, the word commonly connoted speed or haste.[57] Her insistence on haste reflected the colonial climate of disease and depopulation, which would have affected Native comprehension of the sermons.

Translation is inherently an act of interpretation, an imprecise endeavor to match words to concepts that may not exist in the other language. Rev. Henry

Perkins understood that "The Holy Scriptures in the native tongue of any people I conceive to be of the first importance if we would give them the means of rising to holiness or happiness." Ten years into the Methodist mission, he believed that this consistent failing explains why "so little has been done to purpose as yet among Indians generally & especially in Oregon."[58] Yet, the missionaries could evince an almost mystical belief in the power of the Word (despite prior interpretations from Aramaic to ancient Greek to competing versions in English), believing that the Gospel was powerful enough to overcome language barriers and Native recalcitrance.[59] For some, particularly of the 1840 reinforcement, the failure of this power led to frustration, personal anguish, hostility, and calls for abandonment of the mission. Rev. Gustavus Hines, after resigning from the Oregon Mission, traveled to Protestant missions in Hawai'i, the Philippines, China (Canton and Hong Kong), and South Africa. He used his experiences to plead with the Methodist Mission Board to tell the truth to their evangelical donors: the Bible's inherent power was insufficient to change the beliefs and behaviors of non-Western heathens.[60]

According to Hines, the Kalawatsets of the lower Umpua River thought the missionaries talked to God, an ill-understood display that they eagerly anticipated and crowded around to witness.[61] Some Clatsops, according to Rev. John Frost, believed that the missionaries were "being[s] of a different sort"[62] who could "pray," an alien practice that the Clatsops did not believe Indians capable of and which had no relevance for them. At one point, the Clatsops dismissed convert Celiast (Helen Smith) and her claims of a praying ability and worried that Christian prayer would offend the crucial Chinook salmon run.[63] Revs. William Kone and Daniel Lee complained that Indian hearers at both Willamette Falls and Wascopam expected payment for prayer and viewed their participation in camp meetings as a service to the missionaries.[64]

The complaint about expected payments, in particular, illustrates the process of indigenization by which Native people incorporated new ideas or technologies without the underlying cultural assumptions of Christianity and the West. Many Native first-fruits and puberty ceremonies necessarily included visitors who helped ensure the success of the various rites. The visitors, often from distant villages and crossing linguistic and ethnic lines, were given gifts for their participation and assistance in dancing and conjuring.[65] Indian people tried to fit the Methodist newcomers and their ways into existing categories of meaning. From the first interaction between Lee and the Cayuse and the Wallawallas in 1834, one sees Native peoples of *Illahee* attempting to work the missionaries into indigenous beliefs and the preexisting colonial relations of the fur trade. The Plateau peoples tested Lee's abilities, then gave him horses and requested that he sign his name to a document, which he did. As discussed earlier, individuals such as Kauxuma-nupika and other prophets incorporated newcomers into forms of indigenous knowledge and modes of understanding.[66]

Native practices of indigenizing and syncretizing new beliefs and practices differed fundamentally from evangelical attempts to persuade people to abandon their beliefs without compromise. In *Illahee*, Indian people had long exchanged beliefs and practices, incorporating different aspects into their existing spiritualities. Such fluidity was anathema to evangelical Christianity. The predominant Protestant denominations, including Methodists and the combined efforts of the Congregationalists and Presbyterians (the ABCFM), mostly rejected compromise regarding their beliefs about God and evangelism.

Local Native customs, on the other hand, joined with neighboring ones to form regional networks such as the guardian-spirit dances of the Greater Lower Columbia, the *Washat* of the Plateau, and the so-called world-renewal cult of the California-Oregon borderlands. When Native people encountered newcomers, they sought to gain from the interaction. Many Native men, women, and children of the Columbia Plateau and in the lower country of western Oregon were interested in the missionaries and solicited their attentions. Most Indian people, however, rejected the totality and radicalism of Christian mission. Later, some accepted Christianity on their own terms, such as the practicing of both Catholicism and the Warm House Dance at Grand Ronde or joining the regional, syncretic Indian Shaker Church.[67]

As well, Indian peoples did not make the same distinctions among spirituality, political economy, and kinship as did Westerners. Hence, one sees the missionaries' frustrations with Native expectations regarding cooperation in prayer meetings. Without fully comprehending what the Methodists espoused, Indian people sought new knowledge and power as additions, not replacements of their beliefs. Conversely, when they did not see any useful benefit forthcoming or the situation seemed too precarious, Native people withdrew.

As in the case of the mission school, parents simply took their children away. One Kalapuya family sent their boy, Lintwa, to the mission in November 1834, to learn from the newcomers. After getting sick, Lintwa returned to his village and was cured there. Subsequently, he rejoined the mission, but he (and probably his family) had lost much respect for the newcomers.

According to Jason Lee, Lintwa "became unsteady & when told that he must either mind or leave the mission he preferred the latter."[68] Many of those who stayed with the mission had few alternatives.

Mission Mortality

Although clashes over evangelical totality versus Native spiritual inclusiveness proved important to the ways in which people negotiated *Illahee* and Oregon, disease and death again played the most crucial roles. Tragedy struck the Oregon Mission quickly and often, undermining both Native and Methodist goals and contributing to the eventual collapse of Native-colonial comity. Of the eighteen Native people who joined the mission family along the Willamette River in 1834 and 1835, eight died by 1838. Mortality improved for the thirty-four who arrived between 1836 and June 1838, with only two deaths, but the mortality rate over the first five years was still 20 percent. These deaths do not include local mixed-blood children who attended the Sabbath School. Partly because of the mission's deadly reputation, six children left, successfully "absconded," or were taken away by their parents by mid-1838.[69]

One of the men who first greeted Lee at Fort Walla Walla in 1834, Wailaptulikt, made a fateful decision to bring his family to the new mission over the Cascade Mountains in the Willamette Valley, arriving in July 1836. Like other Native parents, Wailaptulikt put his five children under the care of Cyrus Shepard. They joined sixteen other Native "mission family" members, including Kalapuyans, Chinookans, Iroquois, mixed bloods, a Tillamook, and a Chehalis. (Five other children had already died, and two had left.) Like Wailaptulikt, Piupiumaksmaks also visited Lee in August 1836 and entrusted the mission with his eldest son, Toayahnu. The Methodists christened him Elijah, indicating both the hope that Native converts would return to their people as evangelists and, likely, their respect for Mission Board director Elijah Hedding. Wailaptulikt's daughter, Tshecooitch, and a son became Clarissa Perkins and James Charponke respectively. Wailaptulikt became John Linsey.

Wailaptulikt, his daughter, and son all received different surnames. This practice seems odd, because it diverged from the fundamental basis of identity, patriarchy, and property ownership in Western civilization and the United States. Instead, naming reflected a more fundamental desire to shed Indians of their individual and familial identities, to break up *Illahee*, and to set the path for their conversion and Westernization. Unlike Piupiumaksmaks, Wailaptulikt stayed at the mission station to help support the mission family, of which his was now a part.[70]

Native motives for bringing children to the mission varied from desperation to the promise of power. Lee arrived four years into the annual cycle of disease that devastated the Indian population of the region. Orphans accounted for several of the initial mission family members, including the three Iroquois children of trapper Shangarati and their slaves, whom the missionaries freed on arrival. Too, a couple of the children were ill when they arrived; indeed, their poor health was the reason that they were given over to the Methodists' care. Thus, in one respect, the Willamette mission house played a similar role for the Native people of Oregon as the Christian orphanages and almshouses did for the poor in the United States.

In the case of Toayahnu, Wailaptulikt's children, Kokallah (a Tillamook boy), and Lintwa (a Kalapuya boy), Indian people also sought some benefit through their children's exposure to the newcomers. Although the written record of Native opinions is sparse, their actions suggest a period of experimentation with the evangelicals, after which they decided whether to remain or leave. Cyrus Sheppard related a representative example: "Another [Indian child] whose [Tillamook] father came here last spring, and desired brother [Lee] to take his son, expressing a strong desire that his son might be educated in the way of the white men, after staying with us two months, and having made laudable progress in learning, that same father came and took him away."[71]

In March 1837, Wailaptulikt's youngest son, "Samuel," died of the "fever and ague." His daughter Tshecooitch ("Clarissa Perkins") lay ill with the same sickness. Wailaptulikt gathered his surviving children and left the Willamette Mission, although Tshecooitch died shortly after arriving downriver at Fort Vancouver.[72] Infamously, in 1847, the Whitman Massacre resulted from a measles epidemic and the gulf of misunderstandings between ABCFM missionaries and a group of Cayuse, Wallawallas, and Shoshones. Piupiumaksmaks played an integral if unintended role. He led the trade excursion to John Sutter's fort that unwittingly brought back the measles, which instigated the massacre. As well, his son and the Methodists' great hope, "Elijah," had been killed in a confrontation at Sutter's fort.

Although Piupiumaksmaks played an intermediary role in the ensuing, so-called Cayuse War, his position changed over the following decade. Both Piupiumaksmaks and Wailaptulikt became important figures in anticolonial campaigns against Euro-Americans in the 1850s. Wailaptulikt emerged as a war leader among the Tygh band of Deschutes River Sahaptins, and

Piupiumaksmaks led hundreds of Plateau Sahaptian warriors in 1855 and 1856. Individuals sought power in a shifting landscape, and some of those who experimented with the missions ultimately found a path that would have probably been unthinkable to them only two decades earlier.[73]

It is unclear to what extent Native beliefs about death and disease affected the actions of the Oregon missionaries before the Whitman Massacre. In 1840, Rev. John Frost cited the common Indian belief that disease was human caused for his refusal to administer medicine among sick Clatsops. He feared retribution if the patient died and claimed that his inaction was an official policy of the Oregon Mission. Jason Lee, however, freely treated Native patients from the time he entered the Oregon Country in 1834 until he left in 1844. Perhaps, Lee distrusted Frost's abilities or had some specific reason for a temporary order, but Frost likely fabricated it to cover his inaction.

Lee's repeated petitions to the Methodist Mission Board for a professional doctor suggest that Frost was wrong or dissembled, and Lee eventually did secure the services of Dr. Ira Babcock for a limited time. Alvan Waller explained that Indians at the Wascopam "indigenized" Western medicine. Without knowledge of the new illnesses afflicting their people, some Native doctors apparently waited until Waller determined whether a person was curable before they tried a cure, or they took the credit, which Waller insisted was owed to Western medicine, not their "juggling."[74] Regardless, the missionaries and laypeople barely succeeded in maintaining their own health, let alone stemming the tide of depopulation among Indians.

The Methodists had to have a certain objectivity regarding death among the Indian people. In fact, the mission maintained what might be termed a "grim ledger" between 1834 and 1839. As with all Methodist missionaries, the board ordered Lee to report his activities regularly and to account for expenditures. Although Lee has earned a reputation among historians as a poor mission accountant, this ledger (probably kept by Cyrus Shepard) of Native mission family members is a notable exception. It contained a balance sheet of expenses (i.e., clothing, board, funeral services, and coffins) and revenue-producing activities (i.e., farming, laboring, hunting, and gathering). For those who died or left, it noted a net loss or gain, a rude cost-benefit analysis for the Mission Board, which funded and oversaw the missions.

For example, Chilapoos ("Charles Morehead"), a Kalapuya boy, admitted on November 29, 1834, cost the mission $23.43 for clothing, board, and tuition, but his nearly six months of labor earned him a credit of $15; and he left behind one shirt and one woolen cap when he ran away on April 19, 1835, rendering his balance a net loss to the mission of $8.10. For others such as Kenoteshia, a Chehalis boy, it noted a total loss. Kenoteshia died of "pulmonary consumption" (tuberculosis) on August 19, 1835, after getting sick within weeks of entering the mission on April 26, 1835. He cost $19 for board, medicine, and a coffin plus $7 to send a messenger to his people: a total expense of $25 with no offsetting labor credits. The Cayuse man, Wailaptulikt, ("John Linsey") earned substantial credit for his labors and contributions between the summer of 1836 and his departure with his family the following spring. His credits came from hunting, primarily: beaver, otter, two bales of dried salmon, one elk, twenty-one deer, seventy ducks, fourteen geese, two cranes, and two partridges, as well as the payments of dressed elk skins for $23.50 and two horses for $26. His credits totaled $78.08. Still, Wailaptulikt's account was charged for items such as ammunition, fish hooks, and knives, as well as $220.56 for the family's clothing, their "sickness, tuition, & funeral ex for children." When Wailaptulikt left with his surviving children, his mission account was "142.48 due." In the cold accounting of the grim ledger, death took a heavy toll on mission finances.[75]

Like Indian people who experimented with the mission, the Methodists fit their observations into existing categories of understanding. Before the significant arrival of settler colonists who brought racialism to the forefront, the Methodists interpreted Native deaths in light of evangelical Christianity. Waller became indignant when the relatives of a deceased man of the Wascopam refused Christian burial, instead taking the body to "a rock island in the midst of the Dalls." He complained that they were too distracted arranging the property of the dead to attend his service. They were not persuaded that they were dooming the soul of the deceased. Indeed, with so few healthy Native converts, the missionaries instead lauded "happy deaths," in Daniel Lee's words. That is, they applauded deaths when Indian victims exhibited signs of conversion on their deathbeds. Teacher Hamilton Campbell praised the death of an Indian girl named Harriet thusly: "she died a bright ornament of our holy Religion—she died shouting glory to god." Layperson Chloe Clark explained that dying a convert would "reserve these poor degraded souls, from the death which never dies." The "happy death" mentality was widespread; indeed, it was a common reaction to mortality among evangelicals. The *North American*, a Philadelphia newspaper, provided the following eulogy of one of Oregon's few celebrated converts, William Brooks, a young Chinook man. The obituary described his favorable attributes, "[b]ut best of all is, he died an experienced Christian. . . . One native Indian, at least, of Oregon, is saved, as the fruit of missionary labor."[76]

The use of "happy death" rhetoric in Oregon can be explained by historical context: the millennial movement of which the Methodists' mission was a part and the epidemics decimating the Native population. Rev. David Leslie of the 1840 reinforcement penned a history of the Methodist Episcopal Church, which demonstrated his understanding of the so-called Great Awakening, or Holiness Movement. He credits sect founder John Wesley with countering the demise of "True Evangelism" in the 1760s. The Methodists took up the "standard" against "the Enemy" and under God's "divine tuition [became] the chosen instruments by whom he would turn away ungodlyness from Jacob resusitate the Church and evangelize the World." Between the 1820s and the 1840s, their global crusade against "Satan's Empire" was reinvigorated. The movement compelled the missionaries to seek conversion when possible and, as layperson Almira David Raymond expressed it, "[i]f souls are not converted [then, at least] souls are strengthened and blessed. . . . [M]y only object is to glorify God and win souls." Although Leslie was dubious of the new prophet movements catching fire in the United States, he agreed that the millennium was approaching imminently: "[A]ll agree that it is our duty to send the gospel & the Bible to as many heathen as we can *Now*." Indeed, as Mrs. Raymond expressed it, the Indians "are dying off very fast and all we do for them must be done shortly."[77]

Chinook convert William Brooks incorporated the "happy death" mentality into his understanding of Christianity. While fund-raising in Baltimore with Jason Lee in 1839, Brooks pondered the condition of a blind African American man and expressed an affinity with him that hints at Brooks's conception of race, Christianity, and death. Apparently, his fellow Baltimore Methodists referred to the man as "miserable." Brooks took exception and presented a revealing reflection:

> A great many men saucy to me, and I go on. My heart says, I not come here to see that kind [of] men. . . . These don't care what say God in Bible. If they die, that old man go in heaven; and these rich men— where they go to? You see children, how much more better if he die and go in heaven. I shall never forget him again.[78]

The speech is mediated through Chinook Jargon, Lee's translation, and the whimsy of the *Christian Advocate and Journal*'s correspondent who is responsible for the "pidginy" nature of Brooks's voice. Still, Brooks clearly recognized racial and economic stratification among Americans and rebuked them, associating himself with the blind African American man. His affinity with the man was based on infirmity and condemnation. Brooks connected

Stum-Ma-Nu, a Flathead boy, 1836 (William Brooks [Chinook]; image courtesy of the Oregon Historical Society)

with Christianity through physical suffering and death, not surprising, given the nature of the religion and the realities of his disease-ravaged homeland. Never really knowing a time without pathogenic horror, the young man internalized the rhetoric of the "happy death" to which his mentors condemned his "doomed race."

The display of race, particularly Brooks's physical exoticism, was a purposeful component of his inclusion on Lee's trip. His flattened head constantly drew notice, as Lee undoubtedly intended. Similar to his Baltimore visit, in Massachusetts Brooks stated that "he had been insulted while passing through the streets, and his ears pained with oaths."[79] Indeed Lee described the "barbarous custom" as part of his standard stump sermon, pointing at Brooks and explaining that Kalapuya Thomas Adams, stranded and convalescing in Peoria, was even more deformed.[80] In Albany, New York, the *Christian Advocate and Journal* reported, "[I]f ever a congregation of professing Christians had their duty to the heathen portrayed before them . . . it was acknowledged and felt on the present occasion."[81] Lee's venture had begun with drama, or at least the appearance of drama, with the Flathead's call from the heathen wilderness. Brooks and Adams were likely meant to renew the spark of Christian fervor; the young men blatantly bore their marks of savagery on their skulls yet evidenced the power of Christ in their conversion.

During the trip, Brooks's English reportedly improved, and with time he likely could have produced some revealing unmediated insights into his sense of Christianity and colonialism in the manner of fellow Indian Methodists with "tutor'd minds," William Apess (Pequot) and George Copway (Missis-sagua Anishinaabe). In a recent study, Bernd Peyer analyzed such "transcul-tural" Indian writers of the antebellum era, or what he terms the "salvation-ist period," dominated by missionaries and largely independent of federal bureaucracy, which developed after the Civil War. Peyer explains that these Indian writers "reflect their own overall acceptance of Protestant ideals and their sincere belief in the need for all Indians to adapt to the dominant soci-ety in order to survive." Yet, these mission writers also leveled fundamental criticisms against colonialism.[82] Whereas Brooks's voice was extensively me-diated, Peyer's analysis does contribute to an understanding of his messages.

Brooks confronted the colony-mission relationship and Eastern mission-aries, whom he deemed more interested in creature comforts and the eco-nomic resources of Oregon than in the welfare of the Indians. "Great many ministers, when he ask me, 'You got everything good in your country?' I tell him, 'No, sir.' He ask me, 'You got plenty good houses in your country?' I say, 'No, sir.' Then he say, 'I not go in your country.' Now I don't call that Christian at all: I say, 'You stay *home*, sir.'"[83] Brooks's analysis of the Oregon Mission, complicated as it was by its relation to colonization, suggests that he could have emerged as a compelling critic even as he devoted himself to saving his people through Christian American civilization. Like so many of his fellow Chinooks at this time, however, Brooks died while on the Eastern fund-raising tour in 1839. He was buried in Philadelphia, and the local Christian media noted his "happy death."[84]

The differences between the ideals of Jason Lee's mission in 1833 and the realities of the early 1840s were striking. In 1833, during his original fund-raising tour, Jason Lee harangued the congregation to use their prayers and money to send the Indians "a better religion" than their current one, which caused them to seek vengeance for deaths and made them a violent people. He requested support to preserve "one of the many remnants of tribes of the Indians in the distant west, from utter extinction."[85]

A few years later, hope for saving the Indians from extinction had been replaced by praise of happy deaths. Similarly, en route to Oregon, Lee had scoffed at a substantial colony. In response to a query from the so-called

Western Colonization Society, he dismissed establishing a substantial colony because of the time entailed and because it would attract "abandoned and disaffected traders and trappers; and, like every other colony that has been planted among the Indians, would ultimately scatter and cause to become extinct the very tribes which they designated to save." Moreover, he said that, "everything else apart, I think the difficulty of establishing a colony at present is almost unsuperable" and too expensive.[86]

As Lee found, however, substantial colonization not only was feasible, but he found it necessary to his mission because of the distance and lack of formal imperial support from the United States. The Methodists were in a similar position to the Rocky Mountain trappers turned settlers. They had to initiate colonization on their own and subsequently press for assistance from and eventually acquisition by the empire republic. As with much of the American West, Euro-American colonization featured a folk imperialism where citizens imported institutions, directed change, and pressed for the formal imperial sanction of territorial status. This push from the colony determined much of the history of creating an American Oregon over the next decade.

CHAPTER FIVE

Trophies for God

From Mission Colony to American Colony, 1840–1845

Ask of Me and I will give thee the heathen for thine inheritance and the uttermost parts of the earth for thy possessions.—Psalms 2:8

Colonial Quandaries

The Methodists' experiment in Oregon would ultimately fall to the politics of mission and colony. By the early 1840s, emigrants, missionaries (Catholics and Methodists), and John McLoughlin of the HBC bickered over various matters, including religion, land claims, national sovereignty, and a provisional government. The following case illustrates the pattern. In 1827, McLoughlin filed a land claim in London for the area surrounding Willamette Falls, an obvious town site because it had excellent potential for hydropowered mills, was the terminal point on the Willamette River for direct shipping to the Pacific, and was a productive fishery. McLoughlin rightly foresaw that the sale of town lots in what became Oregon City to the predicted Euro-American hordes would be lucrative. He planned to build his own home there following his retirement from the HBC. However, in 1840, Rev. Alvan Waller of the Oregon Mission claimed 640 acres, almost the entirety of McLoughlin's proposed town site. Waller lived there "in a farmlike manner" and sold, traded, or rented other lots. Other Euro-Americans operated a gristmill on an island near "the colony," also within McLoughlin's 1827 claim. In 1842, with Euro-Americans beginning to arrive in larger numbers, McLoughlin tried to assert his prior claim against Waller's and resurveyed the land without accounting for the squatters. By 1843 the case threatened to enflame Anglo-American relations, as Waller petitioned the U.S. Supreme Court over what he deemed McLoughlin's violations of the Treaty of Joint-Occupation.[1]

Reverend Waller positioned the case as a clash between good and evil empires, Jeffersonian yeomen versus monarchical hirelings. Waller did not dispute that his was the second claim; indeed, he disposed of lots using McLoughlin's survey. Instead, he petitioned Chief Justice Roger Taney that a hireling "of a foreign monopoly" had no constitutional right to American land. He conceded that Congress had not yet acquired Oregon as a territory despite an 1843 petition from several Oregon colonists to do so. Still, Waller argued that his land claim was superior because the "People of Oregon" created a provisional government and land office (discussed in the next chapter), which he claimed "has power de facto to perform all such temporary acts of necessity, as conduce to the rights of Citizens of the United States" based on precedents such as Florida. Several other members of the Methodist Mission family became involved in the promotion of territorial acquisition and land development and agreed with Waller's petition. Opposition to McLoughlin became Oregon Mission policy when Jason Lee signed the petition and forwarded it to the U.S. consul in Oahu.[2] However, the small colonial Oregon community split between backers of McLoughlin and Waller, and complaints against the missionaries for this and other land claims ignited controversy among the Mission Society and its donors back east.[3]

McLoughlin and Waller settled their dispute in 1844, but the case highlights three important changes in the lower Oregon Country: the increased importance of land claims, criticism and scrutiny of the Oregon Mission, and the dwindling importance of Native people to either the erstwhile fur traders or the supposed saviors of Indian souls. American settler colonialism had arrived in lower Oregon. As one mission layperson expressed it, "Oregon is our adopted country and wee [sic] have no longing desires for our former home." They petitioned for acquisition by the United States as early as 1838, and they saw themselves as setting the groundwork for further colonization.[4] In 1845 mission layman turned colonial entrepreneur George Abernethy was "elected Governor of the Colony."[5]

The idea of colonization had gone hand in hand with the idea of an Oregon mission since the 1820s. Before Reverend Lee left on his initial overland journey, his fund-raising speeches had excited "the spirit of Christian enterprise" among many in the Northeast. In the hearth of the "burned over district," the 1834 Genesee conference of the Methodist Episcopal Church met in Rochester, New York, and discussed "the propriety of establishing colonies in heathen countries, for the introduction and more general diffusion of Christianity," particularly in "Africa and the Oregon." The conference failed to produce a colony, but, like the earlier meeting of the Prudential Committee of the ABCFM, it pointed to the direction of evangelical Protestant thinking: colonization. A few years later, the short-lived publication

The Oregonian and Indian Advocate went into print from October 1838 to August 1839. The Oregon Provisional Emigration Society, founded by Methodist ministers and laypersons, published the tract from their base in Lynn, Massachusetts, in a failed attempt to organize and send Methodist colonists overland. The emigrants were to found settlements that would have a Westernizing effect on surrounding Native populations. The editor emphasized that six white women (of the ABCFM's Whitman-Spaulding party) had already made the arduous overland trek safely; thus, families could go together. Critics charged that they planned to overwhelm the Oregon Country with thousands of Northeastern Methodists. The quick collapse of the venture prevents our knowing their true intent, but the proposals of these evangelical groups demonstrate that Lee and his missionaries were hardly alone in their mix of colonization and Christianization.[6]

Moreover, the Methodists were not the only evangelical Protestant denomination in the Oregon Country that favored the mission-colony relationship. Although they were rarely condemned by historians, as was Jason Lee, Henry Spaulding and Marcus Whitman of the ABCFM also called for colonists to support their missions on the Columbia Plateau. Contemporaneously with Lee's initial call for the Great Reinforcement in 1838, Spaulding wrote to the ABCFM requesting a massive reinforcement of 220 people: "30 ordained missionaries, 30 farmers, 30 school teachers, 10 physicians & 10 mechanics, with their wives."[7] As well, during his first trip back east in 1838–39, Lee exchanged letters with David Greene of the ABCFM, in which Greene tacitly condoned the Willamette mission-colony and requested Lee's recommendations on mill designs for the expansion of the Columbia Plateau missions.[8] Moreover, Whitman actually lobbied for acquisition in 1842 in Washington, D.C., and led a huge train of nearly 900 Euro-American emigrants on his return in 1843. This party dwarfed the HBC-instigated emigration of Metis from Red River, maintaining the demographic balance of power in favor of U.S. citizens and "whites." Finally, Whitman's mission assisted numerous other Euro-American emigrants when they reached the Columbia Plateau through the mid-1840s.[9] Whitman's actions could be seen as a desire for the emigrants' safety rather than American colonization. Still, the historiographical tendency either to praise or vilify Lee for his mission colony ignores the intellectual climate of antebellum evangelism, which clearly included colonization as a matter of course. As ever, however, the degree and nature of colonization would be contested.

The Methodist Mission Board occasionally wavered in support of Lee's colonial activities but always renewed their support after he lobbied them.

In 1835, 1836, and 1838 the board agreed with Lee in increasing both the Mission Society's expenditures and Methodist personnel. However, between 1837 and 1839, the society had heard sufficient evidence of the lack of conversions among the Indians to begin to doubt the usefulness of the Oregon Mission. Lee and fellow staunch-believer Henry Perkins (of the 1837 reinforcement) broadcast the large attendance at a revival among the middle Columbia Indians at the Wascopam in 1839. Despite the expense and the continuing failure of Lee to account for his expenditures, the society celebrated the unprecedented revival, prayed for numerous conversions, and backed off temporarily. Lee visited the East in 1838–39 and succeeded in getting the society excited enough to back a huge investment of money and people known as the Great Reinforcement of 1840.

Border Maintenance between Oregon and *Illahee*

Since the arrival of the 1840 reinforcement, the Oregon Mission had a decidedly defeatist demeanor. The Clatsop mission was emblematic of the missionaries' conflicted attitudes toward their potential Native converts. Near the Columbia's mouth, the Methodists claimed the Clatsop Plains, a thin valley proximate to the coast; contemporaries were certain that a commercial center would arise there at the gateway to the Oregon interior. The mission entertained a few Indians who were mostly disinterested in learning the Gospel, but the missionaries made little attempt at active recruiting; the "stupid and superstitious" Clatsops were degraded and disappearing, according to their missionaries William W. Kone and John Frost.[10] Still, one Clatsop family did move into a mission house, built for Indian occupants, next to the Frost family abode, but these Clatsops did not convert either. Frost and Kone had constructed the house because visiting Indians sometimes overstayed their welcome and bunked with the mission family—which the missionaries found both frightening and distasteful.

Ironically, the missionaries built the Indian house at the Clatsop mission to retain a degree of separation between the races, thus discouraging contact and hence conversion and Westernization. As Frost put it, "[t]his we deemed to be the most prudent way as by turning them out of doors might have offended them, and then our lives and property would have been in danger."[11] Frost complained when the Clatsop family took up residence there during the spring and remained through the winter; the rest of the nation had retreated to their winter village in the southern part of the valley. Frost endeavored to teach the father something of Westernism and offered food for work, but the effort devolved into a power struggle over the men's social status. After a few days of the arrangement, the Clatsop man complained that Frost was making a slave of him. Frost asked "if I was not rather the slave, having furnished him the boards that covered him and his family, and Mrs. Frost had carried them food almost every day during the winter." The Clatsop man reportedly answered, "What of the boards? [W]hat do [you] do with them? [T]hey simply lie there!!"[12] If the men had a more fruitful discussion—about the Gospel perhaps—Frost did not record it.

Frost seldom evangelized among the Clatsops. Frequently, he blamed the distractions of manual labor, foisted unexpectedly on him by the Mission Society's apparent shortsightedness in sending too few skilled laypersons. Predictably, however, he saved his worst condemnations for the Clatsops, whom he saw as often polite though noncommittal listeners. During one of his rare attempts at conversion, Frost asked "the oldest man among them where he thought he would go after death." With apparent frustration, Frost related that the Clatsop elder replied that "he did not know, and when I asked him if he did not want to know, he said no, and soon very deliberately filled his pipe for a smoke." Frost proceeded to tell him "what would be the condition of different characters of men in a future state," but the Clatsops seemed uninterested in the supposed fate of Indians in heaven.[13]

On another occasion, Frost claimed that one of the few Christian Clatsops, Celiast, had a religious debate of sorts with other Clatsops.[14] Supposedly, she was trying to prevent the live burial of a dying Clatsop man. The Clatsops were intent on abiding a "custom" related by Frost whereby a death above ground would offend the salmon and cause them not to return. Smith said "that if they would leave him until morning she would pray with him and if he died, they would bury him in a proper manner; but they told her that she [k]new nothing about praying, a minister could pray, but she could not, and scolded her for being so heedless with refference [sic] to their obtaining a supply of salmon." Frost stated, "The man was buried alive and no doubt, as they had a great abundance of salmon, they felt satisfied that they had a good work."[15]

I have not found any information that corroborates such live burials among the lower Chinookan peoples in relation to salmon taboos or otherwise. Indeed, only slaves were said to have been buried in the ground and then only if they were killed and placed beneath the elaborate above-ground interment of their master's corpse.[16] Frost may have misunderstood or embellished the tale for effect, but his point remained that Christianity was not reaching the Clatsops. Frost insisted that they regarded him and other whites as "being altogether different from themselves, and all they expect from his being among them is temporal benefit. . . . They . . . consider a white man as a being of a different order."[17] In their dismissal of Celiast's ability to access the Christian God through prayer, the Clatsops may have regarded the Gospel as inapplicable to themselves and not particularly valuable. Their treatment of Frost and their apparent assessment of "whites" suggest that, although the Clatsops welcomed change, they were not interested in fundamentally altering their beliefs or identity—that is, converting.

The Clatsops' dismissals and the soggy western Oregon winters soon drained Frost of his missionary fervor. "To be housed up through such a gloomy season is exceedingly trying," he complained in his journal. "And the prospect with regard to christianizing these few Indians is so exceeding unpromising that it is difficult not to murmur." Not even early spring with the renewal of "the vegetable kingdom," and the spring run of Chinook salmon, which Frost put against any Manhattan culinary delight, could alter the missionary's perception. "The Indians are beginning to take a few salmon, they will soon be supplied with enough to eat. But alas for them, they feel no need of the bread of life."

On his 37th birthday, Frost drearily summed up his feelings about the Oregon Mission. The missionaries worked hard, the Gospel was sufficiently powerful, but the Methodist Church expected too much "because of the material to operate upon." He rattled off a litany of increasingly common complaints about the Indians of western Oregon. "These . . . mere dregs of former tribes, so much dispersed and so migratory in their habits, and so much diseased and withal having so many different languages, which are so imperfect as a medium of communication, that nothing encouraging can be expected."[18] Frost, it seems, began to panic about his failing service to God. On one occasion, he wailed, "O! what degradation do we witness every day. What wretchedness have we seen since we have sojourned in this wilderness! O Lord hasten to come and take possession of the purchase of thy blood. Turn and overturn, until the wickedness of the wicked shall come to an end, and when righteousness and truth shall universally prevail."[19]

Frost also was worried about the health and safety of himself and his family. Indeed many individuals associated with the Oregon Mission had been injured or killed in various accidents, often by drowning in the infamous rapids of the lower Columbia and Willamette rivers. There were other worries as well. Frost's young son, although "in very good health and spirits," displayed a disconcerting affinity for Chinook Jargon, "which he acquires much more readily than I could wish."[20] Not only was his mission a bust, but his son appeared to be going Native![21] Frost pressed Lee for reassignment to his home conference, "[t]he name of the Lord be praised that I am yet alive, and that my family are still with me."[22]

As with the Clatsops, other western Oregon Indians similarly rejected the missionaries' overtures at Christianization. Westernization efforts fared no better among the Kalapuyas of the lower Willamette Valley. They preferred their own housing technology to Western abodes built for them by the mission, and their proposed educational farm reverted to Euro-American colonists. Visiting the HBC's Fort Umpqua, Jason Lee and his peers determined that the Kalawatsets also were too few and supposedly too degraded. This determination came despite the claim from Kalawatset headmen that their people would welcome the missionaries. One Kalawatset headman actually seemed interested in forging a relationship with the missionaries to improve his peoples' image in the minds of Euro-Americans in the years following their clash with Jedediah Smith and his trapping party.[23]

Even individual converts were hard to come by, however. In 1836, after a year in Oregon Country, Lee explained that "[t]he truth is, we have no evidence that we have been instrumental in the conversion of one soul."[24] In his 1839 sermon-report, he railed against the Native practices of slavery, gambling, vengeance killings of accused witches, and infanticide; and although he described such behavior, the missionary affectedly exclaimed, "I cannot describe the wretchedness of these Indians. They are poor and miserable, blind and naked."[25]

Still, conversion would save their souls if not their lives, and for the effort Lee claimed to need more Euro-American families to act as laypersons. During his trip to the Northeast, Lee delivered several promotional devotionals, seeking donations and encouraging the emigration of upright, Christian families as missionaries and laypeople. Notably on one occasion, he invited Lieutenant Slacum, returned from his exploration of the coastal Far West, on stage to share the pulpit and offer his scientific appraisal of the Oregon Mission and the agricultural promise of the land. (Lee also delivered a petition for territorial acquisition that both men had helped draft, but for appearances did not sign, to Oregon-booster Sen. Lewis Linn on this trip.) The recruitment effort worked, and the ranks of the missionaries swelled after 1840.

Yet, the number of Indian students ranged from only ten to thirty, thanks to a combination of ill health at the mission, runaways, and the recalcitrance of Native parents, undoubtedly due to the missions' high mortality rate. Disease spread easily at the Willamette Mission, with the "mission family"— missionaries, laypersons, their families and the Indians—crowded together in tight quarters. Although the Willamette Mission's Methodist colleagues at the Wascopam could occasionally gather large Native congregations, especially during exciting camp revival meetings, the western Oregon missions could not claim as many successes. Indeed, the large gatherings on the middle Columbia probably owed more to the bountiful and accessible salmon runs and seasonal trade fairs of the Indians, who had been gathering there for 10,000 years, than the appeal of the Gospel.

Mission and Money

By 1840, Lee's recalcitrance in accounting for mission expenditures was becoming a problem again, and the board was forced to make excuses to the society. The board assured the members that "thousands and tens of thousands of Indians [would be] gathered into the fold of Christ, when the fires of civilization and the lights of Christianity shall everywhere illuminate the shores of the Pacific Ocean and reflect their holy beamings until the darkness of heathenism shall be driven from that portion of our western continent." In 1842, still with no details of Lee's growing expenditures and amid rumors of his colonial activities, the board expressed "regret [for] the want of specific information" but continued to make excuses for Lee and looked "forward to no distant period when that wilderness land shall 'bud and blossom as the rose.'"

In 1843, instead of an accounting, the board received a letter from Lee assuring them that "the day of eternity will reveal that the good effected here in Oregon will ten thousand times repay the labor and expense of this mission." To buttress the society's zeal, he quoted from a letter from Henry Perkins of the Wascopam station. Perkins's impassioned exclamations called for the continuation of the mission regardless of rumors of secularization and speculation: "Oregon will be saved," he cried. Perkins quoted from the second Psalm to express the mission's purpose, "Ask of Me and I will give thee the heathen for thine inheritance and the uttermost parts of the earth for thy possessions." Perkins excluded the Psalm's subsequent martial line: "Thou shalt break them with a rod of iron, thou shalt dash them in pieces like a pottery vessel." He apparently wanted to make clear with whom he was at war. Drawing instead on Exodus, "Satan will doubtless try to hold on to these old possessions; but the Lord is a man of war; the Lord is his name." Lee concluded with a tone to match Perkins: "we must not cease to labor and pray for the salvation of Oregon, until the conquests already won shall be repeated." Despite the pleas of the two Oregon crusaders, in 1844 the board had had enough and appointed Rev. George Gary as special agent for "a thorough and impartial investigation of [the Oregon Mission's] conditions and prospects."[26]

Gary's appointment came on the heels of critical testimony and condemning letters from Revs. Gustavus Hines, William Kone, John Richmond, and John Frost, as well as Euro-American laypersons and colonial emigrants to the Willamette Valley. The colonists cumulatively owed $30,000 to Lee for start-up costs on their homesteads.[27] Loans to emigrants had not been part of the mission instructions, and the members of the Mission Society were likely surprised to learn of their role as colonial investors. Gary took his charge quite seriously, wanting to dispose of all secular investments promptly and then return to the comforts of New York. He personally rejected the idea that missionaries should own colonial properties, and he instead favored a metaphorical link between mission and agriculture, "toiling to cultivate Immanuels land . . . to be found ready for the allotments of Divine Providence."[28] Lee, having received word of the pending investigation, left for the East to disarm it.

An important factor in investigating the Oregon Mission was the image of the mission to arriving emigrants, "that it presented more the appearance of a design to establish a colony than of an associated effort to promote true Christian evangelization."[29] Reverend Hines had complained of this image to the board the year before: "it is exceedingly difficult from the multiplicity of business among us to convince the Oregon public that our object here is not principally of a pecuniary character."[30] Gary claimed that "[t]he emigrants of 1843 brought with them a strong prejudice against the Mission as a powerful monopoly, especially in view of the number and location of sections of land to which it had already laid claim." The aforementioned land dispute between Reverend Waller and Chief Factor McLoughlin accentuated the "jealousy and prejudice." "In this state of affairs our claims in some places are being 'jumped,' as it is called." Moreover, in this climate, "the public feeling will sustain the jumpers."[31]

The board considered Gary's report and stated that "it will be the policy of the Board, in future, to confine ourselves strictly to their proper calling." They would continue to defend the piety of their intentions for years, admitting only that the "great reinforcement of 1840" and additional appropriations had been mistakes. The mission-colony relationship had tilted too far toward the latter, but the results were nevertheless laudable. The board reassured the society that, "[w]hether we regard its colonization, civilization or evangelization, the Methodist missionaries have been its most influential and successful pioneers." In time, "the indebtedness of the colony to our mission, we doubt not, [will] be generally acknowledged."[32]

The worrisome image of Methodist colonization indicated that the real issues were land ownership and speculation. Emigrants of the 1840s came for the "free land" of the Oregon Country; instead, they found potentially valuable and unoccupied farmland to be unfairly locked up by mission claims in the lower Willamette Valley. Indeed, the mission claimed an entire township of 23,040 acres or six square miles in the heart of Willamette Valley farmland (modern Salem) in the initial provisional government's land law of 1843.[33] As detailed in subsequent chapters, emigrants wielded charges of speculation with the force of two centuries' worth of westward colonial expansion to legitimate their claims to the land. The board clearly took such charges seriously and questioned returning missionaries and laypersons, including Jason Lee, about the accusations of speculation. Joseph Whitcomb, Oregon Mission farmer from 1837 to 1843, testified that, although Lee never speculated in land or cattle, such was not necessarily true of other missionaries. Susan Whitcomb, his wife and fellow mission layperson, testified of Rev. David Leslie: "I should think it might be better for himself, as well as for the mission, if he were less taken up with world[ly] things."[34] Indeed, the charge was not that the missionaries and laypeople had broken laws but that "the circumstances giving occasion to these complaints . . . arise more from what is expedient in a minister, than from what may be right, in a citizen."[35]

For his part, as early as January 1839, Lee formally declared to Nathan Bangs and Orrin Howard of the Board that his land claims were taken "in the name of the Missionary Society of the Methodist Episcopal Church . . . with a view to aid it in spreading the Gospel among the Aboriginies [sic] of that country, and others who have settled there or may hereafter settle there." He disavowed any personal ambition and was holding the claims in trust until the United States gave him title, and he "hereby . . . relinquish[ed] all title to said property." Bangs and Howard were apparently pleased, and, in June 1839, the Mission Society took legal steps to make preemption claims to the mission lands.[36] Following the financial Panic of 1837 and the consequent collapse of the stock market, mission funds became increasingly difficult to obtain, and by 1840 the board felt the pinch. However, Lee attempted to dispel the Missionary Society's "unbelief which seemed to pervade many minds in relation to the expediency of the large appropriation necessary for founding this expensive mission in view of our embarrassed treasury."[37] In 1843, Lee again appeared before the board, this time defending himself from criticisms "that our object is principally money," and his failure to account for mission expenditures, which by then exceeded $100,000.[38] Lee could not , however, undo the investigation that was proceeding back in Oregon. The complaints against missionary land ownership were not limited to Lee, although he bore the brunt of the attacks. William Kone testified to the board that "Some of the missionaries [himself included] had taken up land in their own name, while others have purchased improvements of settlers." He assured them that "the land, stock, &c. in the possession of the Members of the Mission family was purchased out of money saved from their salaries."[39]

The board responded directly with its instructions to its agent, Reverend Gary. It directed him to determine whether mission funds were being used by missionaries and laypersons and to cut their salaries to discourage the use of their own funds for "their own personal emolument." Similarly, the board instructed Gary to "dispose of any property belonging to the Missionary Society, which in his judgement . . . is useless to the Mission."[40] The board's reversal from 1839 when it sought to legitimize their claims reflected its attempt to protect its public image. All the letters of complaint and testimonies were forwarded to Gary in November 1843, along with final instructions to give "to our Mission as far as practicable, a strictly spiritual character."[41] Faced with public outcries about land claims, a cadre of disaffected missionaries and laypersons, and the apparent decline, degradation, and disinterest of the Native population, Gary rid the board of the headaches of a mission colony and disposed of the society's real property in Oregon. Without Lee present to challenge him, Gary sold off the mills, cattle, farms, thirty-six sections of unoccupied land claims, and sundry improvements.[42] As much as possible, he used these holdings as severance in dismissing the numerous mission laypersons and a number of missionaries. Mission Clerk and future Provincial Governor George Abernethy became Oregon's first loan shark when he purchased the society's outstanding loans from Gary at a profitable discount, a deal that paved the way for his subsequent wealth and power.[43]

The Methodists witnessed their lofty experiment collapse after scarcely a decade. They had founded a mission based on suppositions, faith, and millennial aims, only to have the realities of disease, Native resistance, and colonization undermine these aims. In the 1830s, Lee and company dreamed of converting the world, with the Oregon Country as their particular garden to cultivate Christian souls. Although doubts had existed for years, the missionaries fought to overcome them. Daniel Lee rhetorically asked David Leslie, "Are the poor Indians more *dark* and *ignorant* than I can conceive?" He answered that he could not allow himself to think that way, "for this would destroy my own faith, and . . . hinder my efforts for their Salvation." By the early 1840s, however, critics of the mission cited, in addition to colonization, the diminishing Native population as a reason to close the mission. Remaining loyal to the mission, Lee sought to save "a remnant, as trophies . . . to serve" God, although he conceded, as a "race," the Native Oregonians were destined to extinction.[44]

The Ascension of Racialism

The idea of the vanishing Indian was of course not new in 1843, and whereas Jason Lee came to favor the idea that Indians were naturally disappearing and making way for Anglo-Saxons, other missionaries suggested more forceful means. In his scouting tour of the Far West in 1835–36, Rev. Samuel Parker of the ABCFM used the old colonial argument that the indigenous "claim [to their lands] is laboriously, extensively, and practically denied . . . and that nations who inhabit fertile countries and disdain or refuse to cultivate them, *deserve to be extirpated.*'" (The italics are mine.) By *extirpated*, did Parker mean exterminated? He did not mean removal, because he also stated that, "there being no further west to which [the Oregon Indians] can be removed, the Indian race must expire."[45] He clearly thought Indian extinction inevitable and removal impractical, and his use of the agricultural term *extirpation* connotes his desire for the land to be cultivated by "whites," not Indians. Methodists Daniel Lee and John Frost felt similarly about these "most degraded human beings . . . [who] are rapidly wasting away, and the time is not far distant when the last deathwail will proclaim their universal extermination."[46] Still, Parker, Jason Lee, and other Protestant missionaries who flocked to Oregon between 1834 and 1840 made an exception for the survival of individual, acculturated Indians. The future, however, lay with the American colony and the ascending "white" race.[47] The racial logic of settler colonialism left no other alternatives.

The concept of race drew heavily on beliefs about nature, although it could have aspects of divinity when used to explain Native depopulation or to excuse human-induced inequalities such as slavery as sanctioned by God's will. Recently, historians have been mining the depths of racial ideology to understand how and why it displaced earlier explanations of human difference, particularly within the context of colonization, of which Christian mission was an essential part. For example, despite the famously heroic efforts of Catholic missionaries, French colonialism is often misunderstood as featuring an acceptance of Native peoples and cultures in North America. This view is particularly strong in contrast with the cultural separatism espoused by the majority of British North American colonials. Recent studies have shown, however, that French colonialism did promote an active assimilation program in the 1600s. Furthermore, French policy became racialized (based on beliefs about supposedly insurmountable natural differences) in the 1700s after Indian people had successfully resisted a century of *francisation*. Supposedly natural distinctions among humans displaced cultural (and thus changeable) ones in the minds of French colonials after a century of failed *francisation* and imperial competition with Great Britain. This example evidences two common features in the history of racialism: Westerners used racial explanations in specific situations to rationalize either their own failures to force conformity or their need to circumvent beliefs about the acceptable treatment of fellow humans. British (then American) colonialism racialized African Americans only after plantation labor economics and republican government collided and created the need to legitimize the enslavement of "blacks" while "whites" were being liberated from alleged tyranny. More to the point for Oregon, in the North American backcountry, frontier British (then American) homesteaders racialized Native peoples as irredeemable "savages," deserving death or removal, only when they competed for the same land and resources. In other instances, such as when Indians allied with Anglos against the French, colonials often deemed Indians noble and brave. So-called Indian hating was an historical phenomenon that arose from the practical challenges of colonization and became particularly acute when Anglos saw Indians only as obstacles.[48]

Racial ideology grew from ground-level colonial decisions about political economy, not from an imposition by high-level officials, philosophers, and scientists. Racialism was a "grassroots" movement in which colonial thoughts and actions came to shape policy and the accepted wisdom of society, or "common sense." It never had a neat trajectory, because racialism was so contingent on particular circumstances. Euro-Americans employed race to fit myriad different situations, and competition among themselves further complicated the picture. Different people contested, defined, and redefined race and fought equally hard to give it practical meaning. Through racialism, Euro-Americans rationalized actions that, if perpetrated against other "whites," would have been unacceptable; it was ideology in its most terrible form. Christian missionaries were not above the fray, because they had to make their ways through a world that included painful realities such as epidemic diseases, slavery, and Native dispossession, as well as the contradictory explanations for these phenomena. Famously, slavery caused the Methodists to split into northern and southern episcopacies.[49] One should not expect the complications and challenges posed by colonization on the Oregon Mission to have been any less divisive among missionaries in the field.

Colonization shared a close relationship with Christian mission in the history of American expansion; yet, the two endeavors often clashed. Such was evident in the original plans for a Northwest Coast mission in which the ideal site would not attract "dissolute" settlers who would corrupt the potential Native converts. As well, colonization left no room for the Indians, whom the missionaries committed themselves to save. Lee demonstrated his awareness when he criticized a group of colonial speculators and emigrants called the Western Colonization Society for "[t]heir first object . . . to get a title to land, and hence circumscribe the boundary of the Indian." This object he knew would eventually cause the Indians to "scatter and . . . become extinct" and undermine the Oregon Mission.[50] Generally, the opinions of missionaries such as Frost, Hines, and Parker regarding Oregon Indians and their potential for conversion were a curious mix of fatalism and optimism: the Native majority, supposedly degraded and disappearing, was a lost cause, but individuals could be saved in soul and perhaps in body. The missionaries were obviously not ghouls, but they could not escape the conventional wisdom of their culture, a "common sense" derived from two centuries of Native death and dispossession.

Jason Lee actually tried to flip the idea of the vanishing Indian on its head as a reason to save the Oregon Mission. Lee turned criticism of the mission to a discussion of his great success among the "Rocky Mountain men" whom he saved from liquor by closing Oregon's first distillery, from sinful sexual relations with Native women by encouraging marriage, and from poverty by assisting nascent homesteads. Indeed, he exclaimed with his trademark bombast, "[n]ever, never since the world commenced has a Settlement of such men been so benefited by Christian influence as the Oregon Settlement." The colonial activities of the mission were simply part of converting the world.[51] Indeed, early Willamette settlers did contribute funds to the mission for the local Kalapuyas on Christmas 1837.[52] Importantly, in his colonial project, Lee dabbled with the notion of race in his "vital experimental religion," promoting what he termed "amalgamation" of the races to create a solid Methodist base in the Oregon Country.[53]

To Lee intermarriages provided the same fundamental basis of Westernization as racially endogamous marriages. On reaching the Snake River in 1834, Lee witnessed an unofficial, or custom-of-the-country, marriage between trapper Thomas McKay and a "Snake . . . digger" woman (probably Shoshone or Northern Paiute). McKay reportedly told her uncles (the arbiters in marriage) that whites "gained the consent of the lady then the relatives gave their consent and did not sell their females like their horses. The uncles did not object and they were man and wife." Lee took as a portent that her uncles conceded to their niece's decision and did not demand a bride price. "Surely these Indians must be very desirous to adapt the customs of the white people when they so readily yield [in] a matter of so much interest for a female sells for a pretty large sum."[54] Notably for a Christian missionary, Lee did not comment on the lack of officiation or ceremony, although he seems to have preferred a tighter marital institution. In 1839 he exhorted his successes of marrying the "Rocky Mountain men" and their Native wives and sanctioned intermarriage between his single Methodist laymen and Indian women of the mission.[55]

Lee was convincing enough regarding "amalgamation" that the Mission Board related intermarriage among Lee's successes to the Mission Society in its annual report in May 1841. "The wives of all these working men [mission laymen and unaffiliated emigrants], by their example and influence, with the Indian women, are training them in the habits of domestic comfort and economy and preparing them for civilized life, to which the Gospel is destined to introduce them."[56] The board could have related the example of Celiast, or "Helen Smith," the Clatsop woman who married the Euro-American farmer Solomon Smith and actively though unsuccessfully proselytized among her people.

By 1844, the waves of disease among the Native population of the lower country tempered Jason Lee's hopes for the Indians' future, but he still saw "amalgamation" and the resulting mixed-blood children as an avenue of salvation. Testifying before the board, he explained that "the Indians on the Walamette, will become, as a distinct race, extinct." However, intermarriages performed by missionaries would keep "more Indian blood . . . running in the veins of white men a hundred years hence than would have been running in the veins of the Indians."[57]

Yet, amalgamation ran into problems among the Indians and other Euro-Americans. Mary Sargeant, a Molala woman who resided for a time at the Willamette Mission, repeatedly left her husband, Euro-American emigrant Felix Hathaway, during their two-year marriage. Hathaway petitioned the Oregon Provisional Government for divorce in 1845, reportedly after learning that "Mary was constrained to give her consent . . . to marriage through fear of those persons having controll of her at that time."[58] An independent missionary from Connecticut, Congregationalist John Griffin, refused to recognize the sanctity of the interracial marriages and accused the Methodists of "taking sides in favor of adultery." At Fort Vancouver, the Anglican missionary, Rev. Herbert Beaver, reacted similarly, condemning "the state of concubinage" and "fornication" because the Native wives were not properly instructed in and converted to the "truth" and thus could not be considered to have been legally and religiously married.[59] As historian Robert Loewenberg put it, "Methodists, seeking in their dilemmas to erect bridges from what were essentially barriers, were open to such criticism."[60]

Indeed, early emigrant John Minto recalled the change during the mid-1840s with the influx of Euro-American settlers that "some of them who had Indian families were rather exiled in civilized society afterwards. Some of them found it more agreeable to go . . . to their wives' people."[61] Lee's experiment of amalgamation fell to more widely accepted contemporary folk beliefs about racial exclusion, but mixed-blood children were a substantial part of the colonial population, and their position was as yet undetermined.

Lee held particular hope for the roles of mixed-blood children, recognizing their potential as culture brokers, a role such individuals had filled for fur traders, colonists, and missionaries for centuries. Before his initial departure from Philadelphia for St. Louis in February 1834, Lee met Nathaniel Wyeth's thirteen-year-old Canadian-Chinook servant and announced: "I have seldom seen a more interesting lad. He can speak the Flat Head [Chinook] and French languages, and has made astonishing proficiency in the English, and can converse considerably with the other Indians of whose tongue he knew nothing a few months ago."[62] In 1836, Lee felt that the mixed-blood children would be the future of Oregon Christianity, although he clearly held the racialist position that Euro-American children would eclipse them if both were present in Oregon. The mixed-blood children would be "the future of the country, they *will*, they *must* have the influence, unless a colony be introduced from the civilized world." Mixed-blood and converted Indian children would solve the language problem as well. Learning "english," these "Native Elisha's shall go forth declaring to their Red Brethren in all things ye are too superstitious" and proclaiming the Gospel.[63] Lee could draw on a long line of converted Indians to support his hopes, most obviously his Methodist contemporary William Apess, the Pequot missionary and moral reformer.

Native Elishas could serve another important purpose as well fundraising, the real lifeblood of the effort to convert the world. When Lee brought William Brooks and Thomas Adams, Chinook and Kalapuya respectively, back east in 1838, he was basically following a pattern established by

Christopher Columbus of taking indigenous people back to the metropole to impress both the Native people and the colonizing population. Indeed, the practice was established so well and so early that Harald Prins has estimated that 2,000 Indians went to Europe before the Pilgrims landed at Plymouth Rock in 1620.[64] Brooks, Adams, and three mixed-blood sons of Thomas McKay proved their worth at Lee's first stop in Illinois, when their hymnal produced a $50 donation for the Oregon Mission from a delighted Baptist congregation.[65] With the help of the Indian boys, Lee would collect thousands of dollars on his eastern tour. Yet, like his dream for intermarriages, colonial realities also preempted his vision of mixed-blood evangelists saving their Native kin. Similarly, over time, as the number of "whites" increased, people of mixed heritage found themselves a distinct minority whose rights were protected by law but not necessarily in practice. In the short term, the fate of the mission presaged that route.

As a result of his investigation, Gary divested the Methodist Episcopal Church (MEC) of most of its holdings in Oregon and largely ended the mission to the Indians, whom he deemed a lost cause. By 1843, the mission cost $6,334 annually, and the new school was the most expensive operation, with the building alone costing $10,000 to construct. The cost of room and board for the Indian children was more than $3,400, and it was to the Native students that Gary directed much of his criticism. With a touch of sarcasm and the evangelical rhetoric of "happy deaths," he noted that "nearly all the good" done for the "scholars" was that some "had experienced religion here and died when in school and hopefully had gone to heaven." In the previous winter, four children had died among the twenty-five to thirty students who resided there semiregularly. Yet, for the most part, according to Gary, "[i]f they have distinguished themselves in any way it is for their depravity." Former headmaster Rev. Gustavus Hines had painted an awful picture of the students before he left Oregon, which greatly influenced Gary. Gary cited the students' supposed "criminal intercourse," likening their sexual behavior to "pigs in the street." Such sexuality may have been a result of the shattered Native social norms from the demographic collapse or merely overstatements, as headmaster Hamilton Campbell insisted. Critics of the mission effectively silenced Campbell on the matter, however, when it was rumored that he had personally had an inappropriate relationship with a student.[66]

Gary also blamed the boys for destroying their tools through neglect, thus wasting the society's funds.[67] Worse, the girls and a male laborer gave away mission supplies as gifts to visiting Indians; the latter charge further evidenced their retention of "savage" ways despite the lessons of Western-ization. In redistributing mission supplies, the girls were apparently chang-ing the school for Indians into an Indians' school, and this was clearly unacceptable.[68]

Gary's assessments are in stark contrast to Hamilton Campbell's, who would be out of a job if Gary followed Hines's advice to close the Indian school. Campbell claimed that "[t]he children of the school are, and have been doing better than they have done at any other time, in Religion." All but one of the children, "Frank," had converted. However, the Methodists had differing opinions regarding what it meant to be converted, and Campbell's view was not necessarily shared. He had earlier claimed 1,000 converts in 1840, a vastly exaggerated figure that no other Methodist would corroborate for western Oregon. He may have referred to the 1839 Wascopam revival. Reverend Waller of the Willamette Mission had reported only that some chil-dren had "recently professed religion and gave good evidence of a change of heart."

Still, Jason Lee's dream of Native Elijahs going forth to convert their people was approaching some degree of realization. According to Campbell, "Joseph and Thomas have become exhorters—both of them are ecceedingly anxious to qualify themselves to go out and preache to the Indians." Campbell praised Piupiumaksmaks's son, who was supposedly fulfilling the missionar-ies' dream: "Eligah [sic] is now trying to teach his [Wallawalla] people the principals of Religion as well as can. He Reads the Bible to them twice a day and explains it to them. A greate many comes to him from a distance to hear him explain the scriptures." (Elijah would die the following year at Sutter's Fort in California during a horse trade gone awry.) Campbell hoped that he was only the first, as "[e]verything bids fair for many other to go out as her-alds of the cross."[69] Not surprisingly, Campbell bitterly opposed Gary's plan to close the school. The Indians could both survive and convert.

With Gary, the fixed biological notions of race became increasingly ap-parent. Gary attributed the high mortality rate and generally poor health of the children to "venereal scrofula," a lymphatic condition supposedly inher-ited from "their degraded and [sexually] depraved ancestors."[70] Neither he nor any contemporary offered any evidence that the children's chronically swollen lymph glands resulted from venereal disease or that it had become a racial inheritance. The scourge of syphilis had been assailing the colonial and indigenous populations since the introduction of the Pacific fur trade, but the descriptions do not indicate it here. Like the dreaded "fever and ague," scrofula was vague, antebellum medical terminology. The tubercular bacillus was eventually isolated in the 1880s, and *scrofula* became the term for the lymphatic form of tuberculosis (as opposed to the lung form, or "consumption.") In the 1840s, however, scrofula was still mysterious and referred to any number of medical problems displaying swelling of the neck, particularly among children, and could result from numerous factors associated with poor standards of living or crowded conditions; various contagious infections easily passed in the dormitory.

As well, Jason Lee who had lived among sick Indian children in Oregon for ten years disputed that the swelling was accompanied by "sores" or that scrofula was so extensive. Lee denied seeing any scrofula or venereal disease among the "several hundred" Kalapuyas of the upper Willamette Valley and Umpquas above and below Gagnier's fort. Among the Indians of the lower Willamette and Columbia rivers, scrofula prevailed "to a great extent . . . [but] it is very far from the truth that scarcely an exception is found."[71]

Indeed, Lee seemed to take great exception to the conclusion of inherited venereal disease held by Gary, Frost, and Hines. Each of these missionaries, he explained, wanted to leave Oregon as soon as possible and readily cited the supposedly hopeless condition of Indian health to buttress their appeals for reassignment to Euro-American conferences in the northeastern United States. Similarly, Waller stated: "I have little sympathy with runaway missionaries, possibly too little. . . . Our prospects among the natives are not as favorable as we desire, but we yet hope to do something for them."[72]

The children's condition could just as likely have been an infection that spread easily into the respiratory system, given a subsequent description that noted that the disease often spread from the neck to the lungs, at which point the children rarely recovered.[73] There was a more likely cause of this common condition among the children. The children spent a large amount of time being "educated" in manual labor at the agricultural school throughout the long, wet, chilly western Oregon winters, although Gary's condemnation of the harsh treatment of students was in stark contrast to other Methodists' views.[74]

Layperson Susan Shepard claimed that "we dont make servants of the children we are rather there servants we try to treat them like brothers and sisters and we love them very much." She labored for years trying to keep the children in warm clothes; however, homespun was notorious for its chilling dampness once wet. The Willamette Valley's rainy season can stretch from September through June many years, and, when combined with persistent illnesses and outdoor labor, it was a deadly mix. In the early years, Jason Lee had complained that several Native parents allowed their children to attend the mission school only during the summer.[75] Regardless of other possible causes, Gary and other critics faulted the Indians' supposed biologically inherited depravity; the mission could not change the physical nature of the children.

The ambiguities of the Methodist mission project in Oregon—whether to Westernize or Christianize, how much colonization was necessary versus distracting, and was the number of Indians worth the effort, indeed how to measure success—were resolved through the racialization of the Indians and the termination of the mission. Since the 1820s, there had been two prominent discourses evident among the Protestant missionaries' perceptions of the Native peoples, one racial and one ethnic: Indians, the dying race of savages, and Indians, the salvageable heathens. Racial definitions were biologically and divinely fixed and left no room for human agency to alter them; Indians were irrevocably savages and they were destined to vanish. Ethnic definitions, the older and receding set of meanings used to explain human difference, were more fluid, assumed monogenesis and universality, and thus allowed for change.[76] Inherently, it would seem, evangelism and missionization occupied the intellectual realm of ethnicity: convert the heathen—also God's children—to the Truth. The *Missionary Herald* expressed the notion well in an 1821 appeal for a Northwest mission: "God has made of one blood all nations, and provided a Savior for all, and designed his Gospel for every heathen nation, however barbarous or inaccessible."[77] However, such views had competition from racialism and nascent race science.

Readers should not be surprised to see Jacksonian Americans employing pseudoscientific racial beliefs in the 1840s. By 1830, according Reginald Horsman, pessimistic racialist thinking began to dominate Euro-American views of Indians.[78] Earlier, during the Enlightenment of the late 1700s, popular beliefs about human differences fueled an incipient scientific racism, which, in turn, gave apparent support to the folk beliefs that generated it. It was a cycle of mutually reinforcing suppositions based on the ever-faulty "common sense" and the need to rationalize Western behavior such as conquest and dispossession of indigenous peoples, imperialism, and slavery.

In 1799, Englishman Charles White combined Christian doctrine with folk beliefs to begin a new era of pseudoscientific beliefs about human differences. White argued that, just as God ordered nature with humans above all living things in the Great Chain of Being, he also created a hierarchy among humans. In a pattern that would be a hallmark of scientific racism, he cast popular perceptions about human-made inequalities as both natural and divine. Europeans, masters of the imperial food chain, were closest to God. In

White's hierarchy and subsequent versions by other "scientists," American Indians were not of the lowest rank, which was reserved for sub-Saharan Africans, thus conveniently rationalizing their enslavement. Nevertheless, Indians occupied a low position, which was evidenced by their supposed lack of civilization and, notably, their diminishing numbers. Scientific racism grew throughout the nineteenth century, infamously reaching its height with American eugenics and Nazi science in the 1940s. However, we must not lose sight of its origins: it sprouted from popular folk beliefs of the eighteenth and nineteenth centuries. Race science was an effort to grant a self-serving ideology the legitimacy of fact; it followed rather than led commonly held beliefs about European and Euro-American domination.[79]

Racial folk beliefs purporting to explain human inequalities were endemic by the 1840s, although the "science" was only then emerging to support the common wisdom. Not all the Methodist missionaries would have agreed with Rev. John Frost's use of the fledgling pseudoscience of craniometry. (Beginning his skull studies in the 1820s, Samuel Morton concluded, among other convenient nonsense, that Indians were racially predetermined to extinction and that both Indians and African Americans were physically incapable of republican citizenship.) Frost explained that the Tillamooks' supposed greed was evident in the shape of their skulls, their "bump of avariciousness being very prominent."[80] Yet, the idea that the Tillamooks and Indians generally were a vanishing race was widely accepted well into the twentieth century. As well, Frost evidences the incipient nature of race science. He incorporated the older idea of ethnic (or changeable) human difference by blaming the Tillamooks' supposed pecuniary bump on their custom of head flattening—culture, behavior, and physicality were linked. In the larger framework of the United States, Frost would have found many like-minded people.

Indeed, famous Oregon booster Sen. Thomas Hart Benton issued his famous "Destiny of the Race" speech only four years later, drawing on the common wisdom of Indian extinction, when he proclaimed that "the White race will take the ascendant [position]. . . . The Red race has disappeared from the Atlantic coast" because its members refused to assimilate. Leaving aside the historical inaccuracy of his statement, Benton believed that history on the Pacific Coast would necessarily be similar: divinely blessed, the "superior race" was the new vanguard of the world.[81] In the Oregon Country, racial thinking did not determine the fate of the mission, but it did inform the decisions of missionaries who negotiated the maze of their own perceptions regarding the Indians, competition from Catholics, and the growing emigrant population's challenges to their property.

In closing the mission, Gary cited the actual numbers of the apparently vanishing Indians within the Oregon Mission's claimed boundaries of modern western Oregon and Washington.[82] The Indian population in the lower country had been a point of concern since the Protestants' initial arrival; indeed the "vanishing Indian" was a mainstay of any discourse concerning Native peoples in the nineteenth century. John Richmond, a missionary of the 1840 reinforcement and an avid critic of Jason Lee, wrote to the board in 1841 that "I have been most disappointed . . . in the number of Indians. . . . Instead of thousands I have found but a few hundreds belong to [the Nisqually station on Puget Sound] and these are fast sinking to the grave."[83] William Kone, also a disillusioned 1840 recruit and vocal Lee critic, wrote from the Clatsop station a few weeks later, "there are too many [missionaries] . . . [while] the Indians are few in number, and *not prepared to receive the Gospel.*"[84]

Numbers continued to be an issue of complaint by missionaries critical of the Oregon Mission such as Hines and Frost, although demographics were not necessarily the most important "failing" to them, as evidenced by Kone's italicized editorial above. "Migratory habits," "degraded" behavior, savage customs, and language were commonly cited. Frost, for example, complained about the number of the Indians of the lower Columbia in relation to learning their dialects. There were too few people per dialect to make gaining sufficient proficiency for evangelizing worthwhile.[85] Hines authored a similar complaint to the board, although Lee subsequently disputed such claims.[86] Also, missionaries complained about the difficulty in getting enough Indians together at any one place because of their seasonally peripatetic way of life.[87] Venturing outdoors to the Indians' sedentary winter villages in western Oregon was apparently too burdensome.

Rev. Josiah Parrish, one of the only members of the 1840 reinforcement to continue to support the mission, noted the role of racial exclusion. Regarding the Indian school, he explained that the newly arrived Euro-Americans decided "to have our children educated separate and apart rather from the Indians." Gary closed the Indian school in 1844 because "it was not productive [of] very much good."[88] As Parrish suggested, the Oregon Institute, which replaced the Indian school, was only nominally racially inclusive. Article III of its constitution included nonwhites but allowed the committee to exclude Indians in practice.[89] The Mission Society concluded that "this institution is destined to wield a powerful influence in molding the mind and heart of the medley mass with which the Valley of the Columbia is so rapidly filling up."[90] As early as 1841, prior to its construction, the idea for the school had begun to shift from Westernizing Indians to "the prospective political and national interests of Oregon [that] depend upon the instruction of the rising youth." The latter referred, of course, to the children of colonists who could use an "elivation [sic] of character."[91] Noting the role of racism, Parrish explained to historian Hubert Bancroft, "[y]ou know many of our people do not think there is a good Indian without he is dead. After the arrival of the [Reverend Gary] in 1844 . . . the mission work was principally to the whites."[92] Although he did not overtly accuse the other missionaries or the colonists of any wrongdoing or misrepresentation of demographics, he pointedly claimed that he had maintained an ever-increasing number of Indian converts at the Clatsop mission. Still, an increasing number of converts does not mean an increasing or even stable population of Indians even if, as is likely, missionaries such as Hines and Frost misrepresented Native demographics to further their cause to go home.

Granting that diseases annihilated thousands of Indian people, the question remains, how many Indians had to be alive to be worth "saving"? The reason for closing the mission and transferring the school to Euro-American children was not as simple as often presented. In fact, as late as 1843, the Methodist missionaries resolved "[t]hat we are yet Deeply impressed with the importance of our missionary operations in this country, and that this mission presents Strong claims on us and the church for our prayers confidence and support." They even considered increasing the number of their mission stations in the Oregon Country.[93]

Despite "destiny" and propaganda, the Indians had not disappeared. In recognition of this fact and uncharacteristic of his peers, Parrish returned to Methodist tradition in 1845 and became an itinerant preacher "to the indians and to the whites." Indeed, "The Indians were moving aboutt [sic] hither and yon, as they always had done," although he granted that "there were more than 500 Indians that died in this valley, with chills and fever and typhoid fever."[94] Similarly, Hamilton Campbell claimed in 1843 that "more children are brought to the school than we can take care of. I could get 200 children during this winter if I had the means to take care of them." Like Parrish, he declared, "I have not yet Forsaken the poor Calapooa [sic] Indians nor do I ever intend to." He countered the prevailing idea of the vanishing Indian, decrying that Hines was leaving despite the significant amount of mission work to do among "the poor calapooa Indians all around him, and not a few in number, as I have been about one hundred miles South of this, and know for myself that there is doubtless over a thousand of these Redskin brethren." Again like Parrish, Campbell blamed Hines, who only cares about going home, and his wife, who "is all most crazy to get home."[95] Importantly, such eastward migrations of mission family members encouraged the westward migration of settler colonists, because some turned to writing about their experiences in Oregon.

Overwriting *Illahee*

They had practice in writing, as evidenced by their letters to the board and articles in Christian newspapers, which 1844 emigrant John Minto credited with first attracting him to Oregon. He claimed that such was true generally; although few read the accounts, they "were kept in circulation by verbal communication . . . and did not diminish in attractiveness amongst a restless enterprising people."[96] As has been noted by many historians from Bancroft onward, Lee's numerous stops in Illinois also contributed to Oregon Fever among likely emigrants. Thomas Adams apparently contributed as well, despite his inability to speak English. Falling ill, "Indian Tom" remained in Peoria, Illinois, from the fall of 1838 until the spring of 1839, became a local celebrity, and apparently used signs and gestures to describe his homeland. Joseph Holman of "The Peoria Party," one of the trickling emigrant parties that would become a deluge within a few years, credited Adams's descriptions of massive Columbia salmon runs with encouraging his 1839 emigration. Holman, a cooper, planned to pickle and pack the salmon and make a fortune.[97]

Philip Edwards, a mission layman from 1834 to 1838, contributed to the growing body of "knowledge," with his emigrant guidebook published in 1842. He made the connection between racialized Indians and the land very explicit. Edwards described the arid eastern Oregon country as "entirely unavailing to any of the purposes of civilization." Of the local Native population, the "gaunt and dirty Diggers, a sort of half human, half vegetable race, indolently plodding along the margin of the river, or gravely loitering around fisheries, as if they considered the country which the beasts have forsaken, as amply good enough for them."[98] He was typically enthusiastic about the Willamette Valley, although it was "by many greatly overrated . . . [and] not . . . on the whole superior to Missouri." Further, Easterners tended to be more impressed than Westerners who were actually "better adapted to the country." Regarding the Indians of the lower country, he stated, they "are generally mild and indolent. . . . Settlers in the Wallamette need entertain little apprehension of hostilities, and if death continues his annual harvests, there will in a few years be few in the valley. I should feel as safe there as I do here [in Richmond, Missouri]."[99] The knowledge produced by the published texts of the mission family are reflected in colonist John Minto's being "astonished ... that such a degraded race as the Indians were, could grow out of such rich ground as this was."[100] The mission narratives deserve some commentary, because they were important to the overall impact of the Oregon Mission on American colonization.

The published texts of the mission family of the 1840s and early 1850s stressed the ongoing disappearance of the Indians and promoted the settlement of their homelands. The effects probably contributed to the subjugation of the Native people more than Christianization could have, had it been attempted in earnest and had the Indians cooperated and not been decimated by disease. The 1844 narrative of Daniel Lee and John Frost explained the futility of efforts among the Chinooks, Kalapuyas, and Clatsops. They compared these groups with the Umpquas to the south, the "miserable fish-eaters, who were as savage as the bears." The coauthors donated much space to explanations of why they, as missionaries, spent so little time evangelizing among the Indians other than scattered camp revivals during the warm, dry summer months. Had the missionaries been more active in the winter when the Indians tended to keep to their home villages, they would have had more of an audience. Instead, they merely complained about the savagery of seasonal migration patterns that took Native people away from the mission stations. Lee and Frost further explained that the Indians of the "lower country" were "both *thieves* and *liars*," mocking Reverend Parker's assessment of them in the mid-1830s and adding, "in two instances attempts were made upon *white* ladies who resided among them." They remarked sarcastically, "Surely these are virtuous Indians."

Yet, the dangers the Indians posed were only temporary, for these "most degraded human beings" would soon be universally exterminated. In the missionaries' opinions, the Indians were responsible for their own demise and were beyond salvation. Although Daniel Lee remarked that the Wascopam mission had occasionally been successful in attracting Native congregations, he concluded by 1843 that they were not serious, easily backsliding into heathenism and treating the Christians as sport. At the last camp meeting that he attended before heading home to the Northeast, he claimed that three-fourths of the Indians "arose to laugh, and ridicule, and mock." He concluded, "Such was the state of the people at the time the writer left the country, in regard to the direct tendencies of missionary labour among them." Lee, however, did note the success of the first camp meeting for colonials in Oregon in the Willamette Valley in July 1843. Indeed, throughout, Daniel Lee and Frost made much of their conversion of colonials as had Jason Lee some years earlier.[101] The Mission Board also noted the event with adulation to the Missionary Society.[102]

Like the overland guidebooks that became common in the 1840s, the missionary tales often included helpful information for colonization, such as descriptions of promising places for settlement and advice on dealing with the "wretched" Indians, particularly useful language for communication. By the late 1840s and 1850s, the brief glossaries of words and phrases (usually Chinook Jargon and Nez Perce for the lower and upper countries, respectively) provided emigrants with an ability to communicate specific needs. Traveling overland from the Snake River country to the Columbia River and then down to the Willamette Valley required aid from Indians on the Plateau and at Wascopam. Horses could be fed, purchased, bartered, or exchanged. Canoes could be obtained to cross and navigate the Columbia River and the mouths of its tributaries. Labor was critical as well; usually emigrants required a crew of Native people experienced with the brutal rapids of the Columbia River to avoid an unfortunately common fate of drowning.

Lee and Frost, among the earliest producers of the literature, included a Tillamook and Chehalis glossary, reflecting their thinking that the mouth of the Columbia River would inevitably be an important colonial center. Their glossary included phrases, which they must have found useful, such as "Whose canoe is that?" "Make a canoe, you." "Whose is that boy?" Although most were abolitionists and repeatedly complained about Native slavery, the missionaries, like other non-Indians in the region, commonly retained Indians, particularly children, as personal valets. "Make a fire." "Give me salmon." "I am hungry."

Father Blanchet of the Catholic Mission, generally far less concerned with colonization than his Protestant counterparts, nevertheless provided useful examples of "Conversations" in the Chinook Jargon. The exchanges that he selected entailed contracting Indian labor for chopping wood, cooking, cleaning, portering, borrowing a canoe, and dickering for payment (trading shoes, coats, pantaloons, or money). Although Washington Irving's semifictional account had long since established the Indians of lower Oregon Country as shrewd traders, Blanchet apparently felt the need to stress the point again: always haggle the price.

Early colonist Joel Palmer authored a popular guidebook that similarly included helpful Chinook Jargon words as well as examples of Nez Perce. The latter section particularly reflected the types of interaction emigrants would likely need: words about different types of horses; river activity; crossing, sleeping, and eating, in addition to some kin terms, food items, and animals.

Far from creating a new body of literature, Palmer and other guidebook writers capitalized on a genre initiated by the mission family, adding advice about supplies, fort locations, and water availability.[103]

Crucial information regarding the borderland between the Willamette Valley and Mexican California slowly took shape also. The demographic realities of the Willamette Valley, particularly the large influx of colonists and the massive Native depopulation, contributed to a colonization that did not require violent conquest, but such was not to be true of southwestern Oregon. The borderland between the Oregon settlements and those of northern California's Sacramento Valley was largely a mystery to Euro-Americans, and contact with the Indians was slight. The northernmost people of the borderland, the "Umbaquah Indians," called on the missionaries in their first year of operation, leaving a boy for instruction. Like many of his schoolmates, he became gravely ill the following summer. His relatives visited when beckoned, but he died before they arrived. A fearful Lee was much relieved that they seemed to accept the death and "left after a friendly parting." That summer a party had arrived from California that had been assaulted by "the Indians who live south of the Umbaquahs."[104] The mission family wrote only one detailed narrative of southwestern Oregon, at least the northern perimeter, which was as far as any missionary would travel.

When Gustavus Hines arrived with the 1840 reinforcement, Lee assigned him to establish the Umpqua mission, a task that neither he nor any missionary ever fulfilled. Hines described his one-time encounter with the Kalawatsets in 1840 in terrifying terms: "[W]e were lying at the mercy of those who had proved themselves to be among the most treacherous of savages." Hines was much more content to remain at the Willamette Mission and preach the Gospel, and later did become headmaster at the school. On his canoe trip down the Umpqua River, while "contemplating the barbarous appearance of both animate and inanimate nature around us," "[w]e found little land along the river which holds out any inducements to emigrants . . . it is certain that along the stream it can never sustain much of a population." Hines, of course, was referring to future Euro-American colonists and excluded the four Kalawatset villages below Fort Umpqua from his assessment. The first village, which he put at fifteen miles below the fort, was home to approximately 100 Indians "crowded" into four houses and "exceedingly squalid in their appearance, and subsisting entirely on fish." As Elizabeth Vibert has argued, many Europeans and Euro-Americans denigrated Indians who subsisted on fish instead of "the hunt"; fish was a poor man's food. Two hundred more Kalawatsets dwelled in three closely situated villages on opposite sides of the Umpqua near the mouth. Hines again derided the Kalawatsets for their dinner of fresh roasted salmon and hazelnuts, although he seemed impressed with the ingenious preparation without benefit of a stove or identifiable cookware. With typical missionary prose, Hines judged the Kalawatsets as being genuinely jovial "sons of nature," but he claimed that "[t]he sombre shades of moral darkness, which had ever cast a melancholy gloom upon the people, had never been penetrated by the rays of gospel light." He credited the Kalawatsets with intelligence and good spirits but was careful to point out that they lived in Satan's empire, a land of savages and ill suited for agriculture.[105]

Their Kalawatset guide and interpreter, the Native wife of trader Jean Gagnier of Fort Umpqua who had agreed to accompany Lee and Hines, advised the party to camp outside the largest village to await the headmen. On their arrival, Lee attempted to explain the United States, the missions, and Christianity through the multilingual Kalawatset woman. In his narrative, Hines conflated their replies, "there being little difference in their speeches." His rendition was: "'Great chief! We are very much pleased with our lands. We love this world. We wish to live a great while. We very much desire to become old men before we die." The intimation of possible land loss and premature death suggests a strong familiarity with events to the north along the lower Willamette and Columbia rivers, and one man did subsequently reveal that they had been warned about the Methodists. Such knowledge was not surprising, because the missionaries had themselves encountered a dozen Kalapuyas from the upper Willamette Valley at Fort Umpqua two days earlier.

Still, the rhetoric of the vanishing Indian may have been a flourish added by Hines for his mid-century readers. The compilation speech continued: "It is true, we have killed many people, but we have never killed any but bad people. Many lies have been told about us. We have been called a bad people, and we are glad that you have come to see us for yourselves. We have seen white people before, but they came to get our beaver." The latter reference was almost certainly to the ill-fated Smith party. "None ever came before to instruct us. We are glad to see you; we want to learn; we wish to throw away our bad things, and become good.'" The reputation to which he referred was indeed commonly held; even Gagnier had warned the missionaries, according to Hines. The Jedediah Smith massacre of 1828 was apparently still fresh in the minds of Indians and colonials.[106]

In his narrative, Hines was careful not to make the Kalawatsets seem too sympathetic, and so he built up the savage image. Of the headmen's demeanor, he wrote that "[t]hey spoke very loud, and their gestures were remarkably violent. Sometimes they would rise upon tiptoe, with both hands stretched high above their heads, and then throw themselves forward until their faces almost touched the ground." Thus, even when pleading for peaceful understanding and Christian instruction (what they understood of it anyway), Hines cast them as savage and dangerous. The headmen left but were excited to return after dinner to hear the missionaries "talk to God." Unable to sleep for fear that the Kalawatsets would "molest us during the night," Hines looked forward to leaving as soon as the incoming tide covered the sandbar upriver from the villages. One headman explained that he felt that he had been misinformed about the missionaries just as they had been misinformed about the Kalawatsets, and the safely departing Methodists were given a beaver hide and a cedar-bark dress. Hines noted that all the women wore such garments except for two who were dressed like "Swiss peasants," referring to a woman who had escaped enslavement from a French-Canadian "master," and Gagnier's wife. Unfortunately, he did not offer any insight into why the Kalawatset headmen gave the missionaries a woman's garment. Perhaps it was a wealth item, or it signified their desire to establish kin relations.

Hines's assessment of the Kalawatset country did not improve near the mouth of the Umpqua near modern-day Reedsport, Oregon. He condemned the place as destined to be unimportant "with reference to either agricultural or commercial pursuits," although the river mouth would be useful as an outlet for crops grown in the interior valleys of the upper Umpqua. After "[c]ontemplating the probable period when the barbarism of both animate and inanimate nature along this river shall give place to civilization and christianity [sic], we turned our backs," and headed upriver to Fort Umpqua. Despite the exchanges between the Kalawatset headmen and the missionaries, Hines claims that he received a shocking report from Gagnier on their return. Supposedly, one of the headmen had been at the fort when the missionaries had first arrived and, alarmed by Lee's shot pouch around his neck, had fled to warn his clan that Lee carried evil medicine. According to the tale, the Kalawatsets had intended to kill the Euro-Americans, but the careful watch of Gagnier's wife and her brother had saved them. It would seem equally probable that Gagnier, a Hudson's Bay trader, would not have wanted the competition and headaches of a local American mission and a colony that tended to accompany them. Hines did not question Gagnier's motives but instead explained that these "most treacherous of savages . . . are capable of practising the most consummate duplicity." He backed his interpretation by recounting a version of the Smith party massacre as evidence.[107]

Guided by "We-We," an Umpqua Indian employed by Gagnier, the two missionaries traveled some distance upriver from the fort to visit the "Umpqua Indians" and prospect their potential for conversion. The party soon reached their first of two brief stops on their journey into the upper reaches of southwestern Oregon's interior. Considering the relatively short, one-day travel distance, the Native village of forty-five people was likely Kalapuyan Yoncalla or Athapaskans; the Takelman Umpquas of the Cow Creek area would have taken longer to reach on foot. Hines, like his Euro-American contemporaries, lumped the peoples of the lower, upper, and southern forks of the complex Umpqua River system together as Umpquas, or "Umbaquahs," although the four principal Native groups differed significantly linguistically and culturally. The Kalawatset people downriver were related to other Penutian speakers from the Siuslaw River, northward on the central coast, down to the environs of the Coos River of the southern Oregon coast. The "Umpqua Indians" of the upper sections of the river were Kalapuyan and Athapaskans, descendants of the most recent Native emigration to the Oregon Country. Finally, to the south, the Cow Creek band had their closest kin among other Takelman speakers of the middle and upper Rogue River in interior southwestern Oregon. Lee and Hines did not spend enough time in southwestern Oregon to make such distinctions, however, and they never ventured south of the upper Umpqua Valley.

According to Hines's account, on arrival at the Umpqua village the headman "harangued" the missionaries with a story about how he had recently killed one of his wives over alleged infidelity. During the headman's speech, a violent altercation erupted between two Native women, offending Hines's sensibilities about proper female behavior. Although the headman expressed his gratitude that the missionaries had come to his village, his "murderous" act and the "savagery" of the women frightened the ethnocentric missionaries into leaving or, at least, provided sufficient excuse. A short day's travel brought them to a small village of thirty people who welcomed the Methodists, listened to their preaching, expressed "great attachment," and asked the missionaries to stay and teach them more of the Gospel. The ever-wary Hines refused the offer: "[We] concluded that their love was not so ardent as to render it desirable . . . we decided to set our faces towards the Wallamette [sic] Valley." Of his trip northward from the Umpqua to the Willamette, Hines recounted the beauty and potential of the arable, well-watered land. He mused, "[t]hough the country is now destitute of inhabitants, except the wild beasts, and a few savages as wild as they, yet the day is not far distant, when it will be teeming with a civilized and christian [sic] people."[108]

Hines included a summary description of the Umpqua River region and its Indian inhabitants, maintaining that the Umpquas were too few—375 by his count, which made no allowance for the brevity and limited scope of his visit—to bother missionizing. Worse, he doubted the Indians' sincerity to learn the Gospel. He maintained that their interest in Christianity was merely pecuniary; it would help them obtain greater prices for their furs, apparently considering the American missionaries' potential trading partners and desiring to play them off Gagnier and the HBC at Fort Umpqua. His assessment may not have been far off in this regard, if the missionaries' reputation for commercial interests had preceded them, which it likely had, given the active communication among the lower Oregon Indians. Finally, Hines concluded that missions among the Umpqua peoples would be a wasted effort, because, as he informed his eastern readership, "the doom of extinction is suspended over this wretched race, and . . . the hand of Providence is removing them to give place to a people more worthy of this beautiful and fertile country."[109]

The return trip to the mission brought the Methodists through a Kalapuya village in the upper Willamette Valley, consisting of approximately 100 people, many of whom were sick. "Our bowels of compassion yearned over them [during a four-hour visit and feast of roast duck], but it was not in our power to help them." Yearning bowels in tow, the missionaries "commended them to God" and left. Typically, although Hines mentioned no intention of establishing a mission among such ill-fated people, he marveled at the "good water" and the "country of unsurpassing loveliness . . . and amazing fertility. Surely, . . . [the] country . . . requires nothing more than a population under the influence of the religion of Christ, to render it a perfect paradise."[110] Obviously, he did not consider these Kalapuyas, anymore than the Umpquas, the ideal population for the promised land.

Hines's narrative, based on his journals from a decade earlier, employed a literary device, well-worn by Anglo-American writers and hackneyed by 1851, in which he described the Indians as irredeemably "wretched" in direct contrast to the commercial usefulness of their surroundings, which they squandered and thus did not deserve. An erstwhile savior of Indian souls, he then provided an excuse or two to explain why a mission effort was implausible or unwarranted. In his discussion of the Kalawatsets, he had related the Smith Massacre tale and the thwarted assassination attempt on his own party. The Athapaskan Umpquas were embroiled in their savagery before his eyes at the first village, whereas the second village was guilty by association, their overtures duplicitous. Written for an eastern audience of potential emigrants, Hines's text now seems constructed as a justification for his decision to forsake their duties as missionaries and to promote the colonization of Oregon. Yet, for Hines, perhaps the narrative better reflected his inability to distinguish between mission and colony during an era of Native depopulation and aggressive colonial expansion.

Mission and Empire

The Methodist experiment and the paradox of mission and colony reflected the Euro-Americans' refusal to see the United States and themselves as imperialists. This myopia stands in stark contrast with their British competitors. In 1835, in response to Lee's mission, Gov. George Simpson of the HBC selected Herbert Beaver of the Church of England as chaplain for Fort Vancouver, seeking to model the lower Columbia establishment after the successful Red River colony south of Lake Winnipeg. Beaver's brief tenure, September 1836 to November 1838, demonstrated few of the intellectual conflicts so evident among the Euro-Americans. He considered Fort Vancouver an "infant colony" of the "Mother Country" and called for better administration to improve the Crown's position vis-à-vis the Americans' "fast increasing and thriving colony," which will otherwise "become a thorn in our side." Beaver criticized Chief Factor McLoughlin for assisting the Euro-American colonists and thus undermining "the interests of the company." Like the Methodists, Beaver called for settlers, "a few respectable English families of the labouring class," to build a Christian community. Unlike Lee, however, Beaver unapologetically confined his missionizing to the European men and the mixed-blood children of the fort, considering Indian conversion a wasted effort among adults because they were too "migratory and erratic" and arguing that children would have to be confined in a boarding school, to which he doubted Native parents would consent. He did hold out some hope for the Klikitats, whom he believed were religiously "an unprejudiced blank" and could perhaps be converted if given their own agricultural settlement away from the colonials, where gradually "civilization would become the handmaid of Christianity, and both would mutually advance each other."[111]

One commonality between Beaver and the American Methodists was his hatred of Catholicism and the competition of Catholic missionaries. Although the HBC was a royal company and the evangelical Anglicans known as the Clapham Sect had a powerful member on the London board of directors in Benjamin Harrison, the colonial workforce was largely Franco-Canadian and Catholic. Thus, both Catholic and Anglican priests were represented at Company establishments.[112] Beaver's brief tenure was marked by a constant battle with the Catholic Chief Factor McLoughlin, culminating in a violent episode in which the larger McLoughlin physically assaulted Beaver. Beaver, an imperial representative, expected to enact reforms decided on by individuals outside of the Oregon Country. McLoughlin, by contrast, was a colonial who made decisions on the ground level, balancing imperial policies with local and regional circumstances. As well, his personal preferences and sensibilities played a role, as a degree of autonomy certainly came with distance. The men's mutual enmity resulted in Beaver's departure in late 1838, after which McLoughlin succeeded in replacing him with a Catholic contingent from Red River. Denominational jealousies aside, the Anglican and American Methodist missions differed significantly.

As an agent of empire, Beaver never attempted to hide the naked imperialism of Great Britain as the reason for his presence in Oregon. He had earlier been garrison chaplain at the African-slave colony of Saint Lucia in the British West Indies and would later occupy a similar office in South Africa until his death in 1858. He did not conceive of his position at Fort Vancouver any differently. Whereas diversity and complexity certainly played a role in shaping mission in the British Empire, the creation of a paradox between Christianity and colony was more of an American dilemma. Even as they openly competed with Great Britain for dominion in lower Oregon, Euro-Americans preferred protracted delusions about the hand of Providence to viewing themselves as imperialists.

Although their influence declined rapidly in the late 1840s, the Methodists of the Willamette Valley created three crucial legacies for western Oregon. First, they legitimated Euro-American colonization through a divinely sanctioned, nationalist mission that readily usurped the land and resources of a Native population reeling from disease and dislocation. Second, they fostered early Euro-American colonization through their mills, credit, and appeals for territorial acquisition. Third, by officially ending their mission to convert and Westernize the Indians of the lower country, they reproduced and popularized the image that Indians were destined to vanish as a consequence of divinely appointed historical processes. Taking stock of their Oregon enterprise in mid-1848, the MEC Mission Board recounted their successes and mistakes, concluding with the rhetorical question, "who will dare to pronounce the Oregon Mission a failure?"[113] Indeed, considered as emblematic of the relationship between colony and mission, divinely sanctioned conquest and colonization, the Oregon Mission succeeded even as it collapsed under the weight of competing visions of republican empire. For the next several decades, Euro-Americans, asserting their rights to property, would seek the removal of the Indians from the colonial equation.

Euro-American contemporaries believed that the Native people degraded and withered on the evolutionary vine and had no right to the land they occupied. Whether by divine intervention, disease, racial nature, or the "bad influence" of whites of poor character and their liquor, Indian extinction was generally considered inevitable. Although the missionaries' brief visits to the Native peoples of the Umpqua River in 1838 and 1840 seemed to confirm that the same future awaited the Natives of the constricted but fertile river canyons of the southern valleys, the Indians of the Oregon-California borderland had different ideas about their fate. The failure of southwestern Oregon Natives to comply with divine, nationalist, and scientific logic contributed to their roguish image as irredeemable savages who must be forcibly extirpated. The imperial ideology and imagery of the land and Indians fostered by Methodists and early colonists rooted and grew strong during the subsequent international boundary disputes, legally unprotected land claims, and political factionalism. The central government of the United States would haltingly provide solutions and halfheartedly administer them, leaving much to local machinations and imaginations.

In the Oregon Country, Methodists both instigated colonization by United States citizenry and became ensnared in the colonial politics of property and race that eventually undermined their moral authority and destroyed their mission experiment. In the 1820s and 1830s, Protestant missionaries had imagined themselves in a race with time to convert and Westernize the dying remnants of once powerful Indian tribes of the lower country before they were overrun and hopelessly corrupted by Euro-American colonists. Two centuries of Anglo-American conquest and expansion made the prediction seem an inviolable natural law. By the early 1840s, the Oregon Mission faced property disputes with emigrants and HBC personnel and internal strife among disgruntled missionaries and laypersons of the last and largest mission reinforcement of 1840. In 1844, the Mission Society of the MEC conceded defeat and set its sights on converting the people of Manifest Destiny, closing its doors on the Indians.

As late as 1845, one mission society in the East disagreed with the Methodists, sought to save the Oregon Mission, and contested the racial discourse. The American Indian Mission Association explained to Congress the "lamentable decline" of Native peoples in explicitly nonracialized terms. Rather than "any constitutional defect peculiar to the race," the various causes of depopulation "emanated from their conquerors."[114] They advocated removal from the corrupting influences of the "settlements," international disputes, and the fur trade: the Oregon Indians could still be saved. However, the memorial was issued from Louisville, Kentucky, far removed from the local realities of western Oregon and came to nothing.

The racial discourse of the "doomed race" became dominant in Oregon in 1844 with Gary's replacement of Lee and the emigrants' challenges regarding mission property. The racial determination of "vanishing Indians" became fixed despite the increased Klikitat presence and the continued, if diminished, indigenous presence. Racial ideology made the actual Indian population irrelevant and allowed colonists to focus on competition among each other for property ownership, eliminating Native sovereignty from the equation. American settler colonialism used race as the prime indicator of human difference, a fixed pseudobiological construction legitimizing the conquest of property through the dehumanization of the Indians. Racializing Indians denied their rights to the land; indeed, it denied their continued existence. The timing of the missionaries' abandonment of conversion at the moment when mission property was challenged reflects their confronting the reality of Oregon colonization; settlers were advancing westward and making claims of occupancy. Time was running out for the Methodist mission-colony experiment. Euro-American emigrants brought the folk belief of race—the determinant of who can possess the land and who has a right to exist if that "right" is challenged—to the Oregon country, forcing the missionaries to play the land-title game and abandon their evangelical efforts.

The Mission Society had established the Oregon Mission and had donated huge sums of money to affect Native conversion, although the image of the "degraded and disappearing Indian" was well understood and widely accepted at home and in the field. Lee established his mission with the long-term view of an American colony in Oregon in mind: save remnants of the fading Indians to obtain trophies for God and convert the settlers to the Truth. Still, Lee and the board had to justify the massive expenditures of donated money in terms of Indian converts, but they could not. Among the missionaries and laypeople, disagreements raged over the value of the mission, particularly regarding Native mortality. Their disagreements weakened support for the mission at a time when unity was most needed to meet the challenges of colonization.

For the most part, the Indians of western Oregon did not fully embrace Christian civilization in the 1830s and 1840s. When some Indian people of Oregon did later accept Christianity, they did so on their own terms, and many continued to associate the Methodist experiment with death and destruction, not salvation. In 1857, Mary C. Ostrander, a teacher at the Grand Ronde reservation, complained about the "Indian prejudice" against attending the reservation school: "It seems that most of the children of the mission school died."[115] Indeed, epidemic disease and Native mortality were the inescapable realities of the time, and their legacies continued to shape attitudes among Indians and Euro-Americans well into the future.

In effect, both Jason Lee and his opponents within the mission employed racial beliefs. With the exception of a few "trophies," Lee viewed race mixing or "amalgamation" with the apparently stronger white population as the only means for Indian survival. However, Revs. John Frost, Gustavus Hines, and other opponents of the Oregon Mission used racial beliefs to negate an Indian future entirely and were far more critical of Native people generally. Their condemnations of Native cultures and languages neatly coincided with their beliefs that Indians were a vanishing race. Race was a manipulable tool usable in a variety of situations and in seemingly contradictory ways—hence its appeal, staying power, and growth over time. Racialism released its wielders from the responsibility of their actions, actions that would otherwise have been repellent and unacceptable. Methodist missionaries who favored terminating the Oregon Mission relied on race to excuse their abandonment of what they deemed God's work—a powerful ideology, indeed. Race, as ideology, did not have to make complete sense (although so-called race scientists tried for more than a century) or to require total adherence from the dominant Euro-American population. There was always a Josiah Parrish to question "common sense," and reformers in the late 1800s reinvigorated the cause of assimilating Indians into Christian America following the Civil War, only to again see their efforts fall to racial pessimism in the early 1900s.[116] In Jacksonian America, the "Gustavus Hineses" outnumbered the "Josiah Parrishes," and racialists would only increase their majority in the United States, limiting competing discourses and actions.

CHAPTER SIX

The Colonization of *Illahee*, 1843–1851

The Euro-American emigrants of the 1840s who survived the Oregon Trail were not plagued by the subtleties of balancing Christian mission and colony. Indeed, the missionaries' reports of "vanishing Indians" encouraged their colonial migration, as did faith that the United States would achieve sovereignty over Oregon and grant them the lands of the "doomed race." More than 10,000 migratory Euro-Americans left their homes in the Northeast, Midwest, and Southeast to speculate and cultivate the famed "open" land of the Willamette Valley between 1843 and 1851, quickly claiming full sections of 640 acres, or one square mile, of Indian land in the lower Oregon Country.[1] Too large for individual farms, the mammoth land claims, some as large as 1,920 acres (three square miles), were speculative ventures in which ordinary citizens stood to profit from future land sales to the expected hordes of future emigrants.[2] Earlier eastern colonization had featured the exploits of moneyed land speculators and corporate enterprise, as these veteran settlers and survivors of the Panic of 1837 well knew and feared. They fled their mortgages and property taxes imposed by revenue-starved governments during the depression and headed west to the supposed Jeffersonian promised land. If the colonists achieved their goal, western Oregon would feature settler-speculators with claims based on physical occupation rather than capital.[3]

Before 1846, the Oregon Question was still unresolved—both the United States and Great Britain continued to share imperial sovereignty, creating a vacuum in which the growing body of Euro-American colonists shaped their desired system of land tenure.[4] In 1845, the colonists established an idiosyncratic, provisional land office in Oregon City to record claims and sales, as well as sundry property-related business deals, marriage contracts, and wills.[5] Officially, the colonists adopted the United States' formal position of "utmost good faith" toward the Native population and pledged not to seize Indian lands without consent and compensation.[6] In practice, however, they ignored the legal notion of "Indian Country," which recognized Native sovereignty over aboriginal lands until "extinguished" by treaty with the U.S. Senate. To Euro-American colonists, the Oregon Country was "unsurveyed public domain," not "Indian Country."[7] In fact, colonists sometimes used Native villages and resource sites to mark their private claims in the absence of the formal surveys for which they lacked the equipment and expertise; or, at least, most refused to pay for such functions that were deemed the responsibility of the central government. Others simply included Native villages within their land claims, figuring that a combination of violence, threats, and official "Indian removal" would eventually clear away the Indians.[8] Rarely did Native peoples appear in the provisional claims records, other than having their villages and fishing sites serve as boundary markers. One Klikitat man did manage to have his claim to a lower Willamette prairie recognized in name at least—"Clickita Indian Jacque Prairie"—although it is unclear from the land office records whether the colonists who settled on his land paid him.[9]

Historical precedent in the East strongly suggested that the colonists would eventually gain title to their land claims, and there was little in western Oregon to suggest otherwise except for the limited British presence, widely considered temporary.[10] Vicious disease epidemics, primarily malaria, smallpox, and measles, had decimated the several autonomous bands of Kalapuyas, Molalas, Clackamas, and Chinooks between 1830 and the mid-1840s, reducing their numbers from conservatively 15,000 to fewer than 2,000 in the Willamette Valley.[11] Meanwhile, the Euro-American population grew from approximately 160 men in 1843 to 2,100 men and women in 1844. It continued to explode annually, reaching between 9,000 and 12,000 by 1848 and over 23,000 by 1850.[12] Demographically, there was no question as to the balance of power by the late 1840s. Ecologically, pigs and tilling quickly destroyed camas fields, and wild game diminished from the pressures of overhunting and lost habitat.[13] The environmental changes noted earlier by fur traders increased in pace with demographics. The Euro-Americans commonly referred to the lower Willamette domain as "the settlements," and, indeed, they were transforming the environment of *Illahee* into a colonial landscape of Oregon.[14]

Indian People in Oregon

Although the fur traders had been employing Native people for decades, Indians of the lower Columbia and the Willamette Valley soon came to depend on wage work to supplement their seasonal food procurement by the late

1840s.[15] Colonists readily employed local Indians as cheap laborers on their farms and businesses. Sometimes calling them "pets," the newcomers obviously did not much fear Native laborers, particularly the young boys and girls, whose positions on colonial homesteads more closely resembled slaves than employees.[16] Still, adult Indians were not passive laborers, and some reportedly took advantage of the increased colonization to double their wages from the early 1840s.[17] Euro-Americans were more ambivalent about the northern Molalas, who lived along the Willamette tributaries in the Cascades foothills and maintained ties with the more numerous and feared Klamaths and Wascos from the south and east, respectively, who traveled to the Willamette Valley annually for trade, hunting, and gathering. Still, whatever the colonists' trepidations, no conflicts with the Molalas or their friends occurred before 1848. The newcomers also welcomed the labor of the 500-600 Klikitats who remained in the valley after being attracted from the northeastern Cascades foothills by the fur trade centered at Fort Vancouver. Large numbers of Columbia Plateau Indians such as Yakamas and Spokans similarly came to work each winter on the farms of the Willamette and Cowlitz valleys and in the burgeoning communities of Fort Vancouver and Portland. The understanding was, however, that these Indians should leave in the spring and return to the distant lands where they "belonged."[18] The Euro-Americans would later force the Klikitats, the largest Native ethnic group in the area, from their occupation of parts of the Willamette, Umpqua, and Coquille valleys and would target the Willamette tribes for removal east of the Cascades.

Creating official designations and an enumeration of Indians in the Willamette Valley was an essential part of colonization, because it created an aura of legitimacy for the occupation of Indian Country. The Indians officially numbered approximately 2,000—the tally of local Kalapuyan, Chinookan, and Sahaptian bands—although at any given time there were probably closer to 3,000 or more Native people actually in and around the "settlements." Some Indians, particularly Klikitats, were not so willing to concede the bountiful western valleys to Euro-American colonization. The colonialists' trick, which would emerge most clearly with the 1851 treaty commissions, was to exclude the Klikitats and others from treaties, effectively deeming them nonindigenous Indians, denying that recently emigrated Native peoples had the right to be there.[19] Colonization was not a "color-blind" act; only "whites" could move into the valley and legitimately claim territory. Euro-Americans considered only the so-called remnants of local Native populations as aboriginal sovereigns, people whom they could conceivably bully into illicit land cessions with vague promises of future compensation.[20]

WILLAMETTE FALLS

Willamette Falls, ca. 1841 (Wilkes, *Narrative of the United States Exploring Expedition*; image courtesy of the Oregon Historical Society). Note the Western garb of the Native fishermen.

Still, the Klikitats had their champion in Rev. Josiah Parrish, an evangelist who had not given up on the Methodist mission in western Oregon even if the Mission Society had. Parrish may have considered his work divine, but his methods were generally secular, using the courts and government administration. In two court cases in Washington County, Parrish persuaded a district court judge to rule in favor of one band of Klikitats, which had laid claim to small tracts in the agriculturally valuable lower Willamette Valley. In the first case, Donald McLeod brought action for trespass against the Klikitats who had destroyed timber, which he had cut for his house in 1851. Unfortunately for McLeod, the judge ruled that he was the trespasser, not the Klikitats, and that he had received prior warning from them not to occupy the claim. Indeed, the judge ruled that the Klikitats held "right of conquest" over the previous Native occupants, a questionable if effective reading of the impact of disease and migration among the Indians. In the second case, the

Klikitats removed and destroyed fencing, and the judge again ruled that the Euro-American farmer, who had brought action of trespass, was at fault.[21] The unlikely decisions legitimized Klikitat emigration and granted them an aboriginal land title, at least temporarily.

The court did not represent popular opinion, as evident in the settlers' actions and subsequent clashes. Successive treaty commissioners better reflected settler-colonial zeitgeist by placing the Willamette Klikitats under the purview of an imposed identity, the Yakama Nation of the southwestern Columbia Plateau, and insisting on their removal to that region.[22] The missionaries too had played a numbers game when they had dismissed the few thousand Indians in western Oregon as vanishing, but the colonists were not looking for reasons to abandon a frustrated project. Rather, they sought to legitimize and advance one. By limiting the reporting of Indians, Euro-Americans perpetuated the idea that extinguishing Indian title and granting donation lands should be cursory endeavors.

Speculating *Illahee*

The speculative newcomers began dividing and selling their land claims soon after recording them with the provisional land office, as new emigrants arrived seeking farmland in a region increasingly checkered with the sprawling claims. Colonists completed thousands of transactions between 1845 and 1848, before the United States had sole sovereignty or had granted land titles.[23] Many transactions were vague, using phrasing such as "abandoned by request of [original claimant] in favor of" without disclosing terms, or noted only "valuable consideration," whereas others spelled out formal indentures and crop liens.[24] Often "fractions of land" were sold, sometimes with pre-built cabins likely constructed by inexpensive Indian and Kanaka laborers.[25] Profits could be considerable, given that Euro-Americans had not paid for the land yet sold it for prices as high as $2.50 to $35 per acre, and farms on the Clatsop Plains fetched $2,000 to $6,000.[26]

Not surprisingly, politics was not far removed from profits. The "founding fathers" of the United States had been among the great land speculators of the eighteenth and early nineteenth centuries, and so too were the leading lights of Oregon.[27] Future provisional and territorial Oregon governors George Abernethy and George Curry and Supreme Court Justice John Q. Thornton were well represented in several lucrative transactions. Judge Thornton held some expensive town-site lots in Oregon City, once pledging the same lots simultaneously as collateral to three different creditors.[28] He also certified some remarkable deals in which his wife was listed as the official owner, including a claim adjacent to Salem center obtained from Reverend Gary for only $1 during the latter's dash to divest the Methodists of their holdings.[29] Thornton may have been ahead of his time in supporting the cause for married women's property laws, but, more likely, he was hiding assets from creditors using a common method of his day.[30]

By the late 1840s, Oregon City lots were arguably the hottest investment in the Willamette Valley, going for $70 to $2,000, depending on their location, and, presumably, the gullibility of the buyer.[31] Entrepreneurs staked out other less successful town sites, as far away as William Tichenor's lonely Port Orford on the southern Oregon coast, which was supposed to compete with San Francisco as the major West Coast port; it was a time for dreams and schemes.

Euro-Americans saw potential profits in the land both for agriculture and for sale, but also in the massive timber stands, mineral deposits, abundant salmon runs, and coastal shellfish stocks. Two partners in a land claim who took 1,280 acres formally pledged to leave the timber for future value determination, rightly figuring that the towering conifers would become an important commodity milled and exported from the Willamette Valley via the Columbia River.[32] Others filed claims, clear-cut the timber, and moved on to the next claim, a practice facilitated by an 1844 clause that allowed for nonadjoining acreage, specifically 600 acres of farmland and a separate 40 acres of timber.[33] Although felling a 300-foot-tall fir with a 7-foot-diameter base was no minor task, the colonists were successful in bringing the ancient giants down.[34] As early as 1852, James Swan described the forestry detritus evident well offshore in the Pacific "about thirty miles to the westward of the Columbia River . . . [which carried] in its course great quantities of drift-logs, boards, chips, and saw-dust, with which the whole water around us was covered."[35]

Minerals were, of course, another important commodity; and after colonists "discovered" the coal deposits along the upper Siletz River, they were careful to note that claims included the ore.[36] After the land claims spread southward across the Umpqua-Calapooya divide into the Rogue River Valley in 1851, James Cluggage would profit hugely through his claim to the Jacksonville town site. Although mineral claims were not yet protected by the central government administration, the Jacksonville goldfields, which brought the California Rush to Oregon, were located within Cluggage's land claim, bringing him a huge payoff in an 1858 lawsuit against townspeople and local miners.[37] The colonists were well aware of the multiple ways in which they could profit from the lands of western Oregon without necessarily breaking a sweat behind a plow.

With the fur trade dwindling, the HBC had experimented with commodifying nonfurbearing animals, and Euro-American colonists aspired to do the same, relying on Native labor to harvest the salmon and shellfish. Employing Chinook, Chehalis, and Quinalt laborers at Shoalwater Bay (later renamed Willapa) north of the Columbia's mouth, Charles J. W. Russell began an oyster trade to California in 1851 in which he exported as much as 20 tons of oysters in a single shipment.[38] Ethnically diverse Native people traveled to the bay for oysters, clams, and crabs for subsistence and for trade with colonists, working their labors for Russell into their regular gathering rounds.[39] Aided by his English-speaking Native wife, Suis, Russell also employed Indians, mostly Chinooks, to procure salmon and clean, salt, and package them in crates. James Swan, who wrote of Russell's business and recorded numerous daily interactions with "our copper colored attendants," did not note any resistance to treating the salmon thusly, although the Indians balked at taking too many salmon in any one location.[40] After taking hundreds at a single camp in one day, hired Chinooks explained that a dead person had spoken during the night, telling them to leave and to take no more. When Russell complained that the sound had been a plover's whistle and not a talking spirit, one man reportedly retorted: "You are a white man, and don't understand what [the dead] say; but Indians know, and they told us not to catch any more salmon."[41] A frustrated Russell had no choice but to oblige and move on. Catching extra salmon for trade was a long-established practice among the Native peoples of the Oregon Country and one that necessarily depended on maintaining a sustainable harvest. Russell could find a new commodity to exploit; the Chinooks could not so easily replace the heart of their economic and spiritual world.[42] Suis, "a most remarkable woman, possessing a fund of information in all matters relative to incidents and traditions relating to the Bay," may also have tried to influence Russell, but he seemed little impressed: the colonial mission was to profit while the getting was good.[43]

Indeed, when the going got tough during a smallpox outbreak originating at Clatsop, Russell left for San Francisco, although he (unlike his Native workforce and presumably his wife) was vaccinated against "that most disgusting and contagious disease."[44] By the mid-1850s, Euro-American colonization was increasing on Shoalwater Bay and elsewhere in the environs of the Greater Lower Columbia River. Consequently, although Native labor would still play an important role in the economy for decades as a cheap and easily exploited workforce, it would be less crucial with the influx of thousands of young Euro-American men.[45]

As evident in the mission-colony disputes, these arriving settler colonials saw unity in their perceived race, a unity undergirded by their legal status as enfranchised citizens of the republic.[46] Even non-Native born "white" males could claim this supposed "birthright" through naturalization. Their land claims that they both worked and divided for sale, their timber, shellfish, and fish harvesting, and their developing strategies of dealing with the local and regional Native population comprised the western Oregon form of settler colonialism. Their provisional land office, petitions to the federal government, and evolving governmental structure can be considered an American folk imperialism, an attempt at ordering their endeavors based on the institutional and personal memories of colonizing the Old Northwest and Southeast. This folk imperialism reflected the ideals, expectations, and mechanics of antebellum republicanism.

Folk Imperialism

Republican discourse was readily apparent in the writings and debates of early colonists in the Willamette Valley. Drawing on the rhetoric of classical republicanism, they touted yeoman citizenry and the common good and bemoaned wildcat banking and economic speculations that had caused the financial panics of the day. Indeed, David Johnson's influential study of early Oregonians' political rhetoric argues that Oregon settlers put their discourse into practice. According to Johnson, the emigrants to Oregon differed both from the market-oriented Easterners whom they left behind and from their fellow overland emigrants who had flocked to Gold Rush California. They were a self-selected, homogenous group of Midwestern farmers that sought to create a society separate from the major changes brought on by nascent capitalism during the era that historian Charles Sellers has pegged as the "market revolution."[47]

Yet, widely held beliefs in classical republicanism did not displace or necessarily contradict the liberal economics of speculation by individual citizens. The Oregon citizenry definitely wanted to mitigate the painful disruptions of the market revolution, as noted by Johnson: they were against the evils of banks and corporations. Such is not surprising; criticisms of the effects of the early market economy were common. Sean Wilentz, Paul Johnson, and Mary Ryan have shown that attempts to resist and mitigate the social, political, and economic upheavals of the era occurred among groups as diverse as New York City laborers, Rochester merchants, and families of the emerging middle class.

However, although I agree with Johnson that the Oregon colonists meant what they said in their republican language, I disagree that they then differed fundamentally from California colonists or Easterners. Their condemnation of large-scale speculations of corporations and banks did not inhibit individual speculations or suggest that the populace was economically illiberal and thus unique among their generation of Euro-Americans. As will be further evidenced later regarding federal war remunerations, they picked and chose which speculations they deemed appropriate. Put simply, speculation did not necessarily contradict republicanism. As Daniel Feller has observed, citizens of the early republic distrusted excesses but, nevertheless, sought improvement of themselves and society through progress and economic achievement. Importantly, this notion of citizenship was racially exclusive, reserved for "whites," and functioned as a unifying factor among the settler colonists, against Eastern/corporate interests (unsuccessful) and against non-"whites" (more successful).[48]

The race-colonial equation was complicated by the history of the fur trade, however, which had created a relatively cosmopolitan population in the lower Willamette Valley. As explained earlier, the HBC had brought to the Oregon Country Algonkian and Iroquoian Indians from the East, French Canadians who intermarried with Native Oregon women, and Pacific Islanders (mostly Kanakas but also Tahitians, Maoris, and Aleuts). Additionally, the Euro-American "Rocky Mountain men" who had crossed into the Oregon Country in the late 1820s and 1830s had intermarried in Native communities and, like the French Canadians, had produced a number of mixed-blood children. In the colonization of the Oregon Territory, mixed bloods had obtained a conditional inclusion as citizens and were allowed to pass as members of the "white race." The 1846 Oregon Treaty between the United States and Great Britain established the 49th parallel as the boundary, granting modern Washington, Oregon, Idaho, and western Montana and Wyoming to the Americans. Importantly, the treaty protected the property rights of the HBC employees: many were mixed bloods who had established land claims and, together with the French Canadians, equaled the Euro-American population until the massive emigration of 1844.[49] Throughout the West, the increasing number of free African Americans and the slavery question that ran hand in hand with westward expansion complicated the color coding of citizenship, as did the formal inclusion of Tejanos, Californios, and other former Mexicans following the Treaty of Guadalupe-Hidalgo. Still, the distinction between imperial formality and colonial reality was evident in that few Latinos in the Southwest and mixed bloods in the Northwest enjoyed long-lasting protections.[50]

Oregon Territory's definition of whiteness, reflected in the early Organic Laws of Oregon regarding citizenship, was that "Every free male descendent of a white man . . . shall be entitled to vote . . . [and extended] the rights of citizens," thus including mixed bloods.[51] However, as noted in contemporary Oregon Trail guidebooks and governmental reports, the conditional extension of whiteness and citizenship to mixed bloods was not reflected in popular racial thought. Consistently, writers separated mixed bloods from the designation of white when discussing the territory's population.[52] An enduring sentiment, one official baldly explained in 1858 was that "[w]hen I speak of whites I mean Americans." This explanation distinguished what another had called the "mongrel race" of the HBC.[53]

The Euro-American emigrants from the Methodists' Great Reinforcement in 1840 through the massive emigrations between 1843 and 1848 increasingly came as families. Thus, the early high ratio of Indian-white intermarriage among colonists—25 of 36 in 1840—dropped precipitously.[54] Even after the advent of the 1849 California Gold Rush, which attracted thousands of single men to the southwestern Oregon—northern California borderlands in 1851, the intermarriage rates were not very high. At the end of that decade, there were only thirty-two such interracial unions in the six counties of southwestern Oregon, although the sex ratio among Euro-Americans aged fifteen to fifty averaged 3.7 men to 1 woman or 5,268 to 1,428. In the remaining fourteen counties, there were an additional thirty-four intermarriages (including two African-American—Native couples) and the sex ratio among similarly aged Euro-Americans averaged 1.7 men to 1 woman or 12,634 to 7,590.[55] The intermarriage figures account for only official unions, however, and the number of Indian-white cohabitations was likely higher.

Still, there was a compelling reason for Euro-American men to make their marriages to Native women official: the provisional land laws and the subsequent federal version allowed married men to take 640-acre land claims (320 in the name of the wife), whereas single men could take only 320 acres.[56] The Oregon Supreme Court upheld the legality of the doubled acreage in the case of Native wives, finding that, for the purpose of land law, the race of the Native women was subsumed by the racial identity of their "white" husbands. In this instance, white patriarchy altered the legal status of the women from "Indians" to the "wives" of citizens and entitled them to 320 acres by virtue of their "wifeship." To rule otherwise, Justice C. J. Williams reasoned, would effectively make all intermarriages illegal and all the children of such marriages bastards. He opted not to comment on the Native wife's racial status and property rights in the case of widowhood. He regretted that intermarriages had occurred before congressional authority had been extended to Oregon Territory because "it is not to be supposed that Congress would, by law, sanction marriages between" the races.[57]

Illahee in Oregon Society

For Native communities, intermarriage would prove to be a mixed blessing. On the one hand, marriage gifts, or "bride prices," brought much-needed food and wealth items into the village, and Native wives of Euro-Americans were immune to "Indian removal." Eventually, interracially married women became the only connection between some tribes and their former homelands. On the other hand, intermarriages, particularly informal unions and temporary arrangements, wreaked havoc on Native formulations of status and identity. Colonists commodified traditional gift exchanges into so-called bride purchases, undermining communal practices and women's power.[58]

Among southwestern Oregon Indians in the nineteenth century, parents and/or local headmen typically arranged marriages, which involved a reciprocal bride price that, in turn, determined the initial status of the children, and the marriages tended to be village exogamous.[59] Marriages, although monogamous relationships between two individuals, also were, to some extent, communal ventures, in that wealthy individuals (or several village members with pooled wealth) often contributed to bride prices for poor local men.[60] The alternative was to lose such men to the wives' villages, which would gain their labors and future children.[61] Importantly, despite the English term "bride price," Native women were not commodities. Several consultants of early "salvage" ethnographers and linguists (ca. 1880–1940) pointed to the agency of women who could refuse their "purchase," manipulate the terms, and leave relationships if they were unsatisfied or abused.[62] Indeed, bride price had much to do with children. The children's social status, much more than that of their mothers, was closely tied into the supposed marriage by "purchase."

As the bride price was a reciprocal (although not necessarily equal) exchange, the child had an ascribed status from both sides of his or her parentage. Indeed, in some cases, a further payment was owed to the woman's family on her first birth.[63] Children of single mothers ("unpurchased" women) suffered the pains of low status. Nettie West stated that a Coos child born to a single mother was *titasre,* or "nobody's child," a very deprecating stigma for children. The stigma, according to West, was erased only by the "purchase" of the mother; notably, the premarital status of the mother at conception was irrelevant.[64] Agnes Johnson put it succinctly, "If [mothers] not bought, children are bastards."[65] Suggesting the importance of avoiding bastard status, consultant Coquel Thompson told linguist John Harrington, "If a man knocks up my daughter and [is] going to marry her, it is all right with me, I let him go, but if he does not, then . . . I can kill him."[66] Thompson later added that the stigma carried a dangerous correlate when the child became an adult. Just as the Coquille word became the same for bastard as "half-breed," the punishment for killing either people (bastards or mixed bloods) was equally low—a relatively small fine or a haircut. Obviously, the cutting of hair was significant to the people at the time, but Thompson intimated that it was a relatively small punishment, compared with killing someone of "importance."[67] Further demonstrating the connection between bride price and child status, H. G. Barnett's consultant Tom McDonald warned that a divorced man did not necessarily want to recover the bride price immediately because his ex-wife might have been pregnant. Regardless of marital status at the time of conception, "if no money left, [the] child would be a bastard . . . You gave money so people could respect your child."[68] Thus, the husband would doom his child to bastard status by retrieving the bride price. According to Agnes Johnson (Coos), Frank Drew (Coos and Siuslaw) and an anonymous Tolowa consultant, the bride price was partially refunded if the first child died or was stillborn.[69] Indeed, further evidencing the direct connection between bride price and children, a Tolowa man was expected to "buy" his wife "over again" with the money returned to him by her family.

Clearly, other factors, such as women's labor and what might be termed alliances (for trade, warfare, or resource use), also played a role in marriage arrangements, but the main reason for the institution of bride purchases seems to have been children. Perhaps because women were the indirect focus of the bridal purchase system (despite outward appearances), they found a degree of maneuverability evident in refusing to marry or making special arrangements. Evidently, wealthy men could alter this system to fit their needs.[70] Moreover, death customs suggest that bride price represented an emotional link between families, not simply a monetary exchange for the woman. If a woman died, her family sent another woman to the man to prevent him from requesting the return of the bridal price—a deep insult and an endangerment to any children. Lotson stated that the deceased woman's family could become so incensed by the man's request for his "money back" that the "wife's side gets mad—might get after him, might kill him."[71] Finally, throughout the Oregon Country, marriages presupposed continued visiting among newly established kin, and the bride price was predicated on ongoing reciprocal exchanges and obligations.

During Euro-American colonization, the complex traditions of bride gifts, social status, reciprocity, and establishing and maintaining important kin connections mutated into the outright purchase of Indian women.[72] Bride purchases represented a fundamental change in society and the political economy of Oregon and *Illahee*. The choice of Native women and their families consisted of denying a marriage that would bring much-needed supplies (the bride price typically consisting of blankets or food) or accepting white men of questionable intent. One settler, Richard Cannon, recalled that "[m]ost of these squaw wives were bought from the Indian father for a consideration such as: one or more ponies, a blanket, food, or supplies, depending upon how desirable the girl was."[73] Judge Mann stated that the Indian women "could be purchased . . . for a few pairs of blankets." Then, the new couple lived, "clandestinely without any marriage ceremony."[74] Such interracial marriages were arguably the first bride purchases of Indian women in southwestern Oregon, using the English definition of the phrase ("bride price").

Native women became another exploitable resource for procuring berries, eggs, fresh fish, and game for colonists, but also for sexual labor. As one colonist put it, "[w]e were all bachelors . . . [and] there were but few white females in that part of Oregon in 1852. But there used to be a great many Indians . . . and a good many loose squaws would come around the ferry to beg and trade, and they liked whiskey whenever they get it."[75] Early colonists stated that the trade visits of these Indian women were common, because some popular items among Euro-Americans were too difficult to get themselves, such as "Blackberries and Raspberries [that] were scarce in the valley although plentiful in the hills."[76] Furthermore, the Indians commonly stopped for social visits following a long-established custom in southwestern Oregon.

Among the miners, these trade and social visits took on another meaning. Colonist Herman Francis Reinhart stated that some of these women traded sex for whiskey. This trade apparently led to "licentiousness and debauchery," with the tragic results of rapes, alcohol abuse, and widespread venereal disease.[77] Annie Miner Peterson, a Coos woman, related one such story of a fellow Indian woman, Kitty Hayes. (Anthropologist Melville Jacobs added the parenthetical clarifications to his transcriptions.) After her husband and children died, Kitty became a "bad (loose, drunken) woman. She lay drunken all the time. Then she became ill. She did everything (prostituted) for nothing (i.e., for drink). She was just completely drunken all the time. Then she died poor. (She was about forty at her death.)"[78] Although Hayes lived out her tragic life some years after Reinhart's reputed trade arrangements, one can reasonably assume that similar dynamics were involved. The environmental effects of Euro-American agricultural and mining activities exacerbated the inequality between Indian women and Euro-American men. A broad range of colonial activities decimated traditional economic activities such as mining sluices, which clogged and polluted streams, inhibiting fish runs and spawning activity, and raising cattle, which trampled and devoured camas fields. Some Native bands literally faced starvation as a result.[79] In this desperate state, some Indian women prostituted themselves for food and, increasingly, whiskey. Their actions reinforced the stereotype of the "loose squaw." Reinhart provided an excellent example of such a desperate situation in the upper Umpqua region,

> I had got through dinner, and the man, Ashcraft by name, was alone with me, when two squaws and a little girl came to camp. One was an old woman; one about twenty, blind of one eye, and the little girl about seven or eight years old. They were begging for bread, flour, or sugar. Ashcraft for fun asked them some questions, and the old women said the young woman *would* for some bread and a handkerchief or some sugar. They sat by the fire and eat some bread and meat we give them, and Ashcraft went off with the one-eyed one.[80]

Reinhart commented that a "chief" came to their camp requesting that the miners not molest "their squaws."[81] His appeals probably sounded absurd to men who felt that they knew the nature of "squaws" and their uses.[82]

Children of white fathers and Indian mothers created another dilemma for Native communities when they were not born within a marriage, as often occurred. As mentioned, the Coquille used the same word for "half-breed" as "bastard," confirming the low status of the children of these interracial sexual relations.[83] Lottie Evanoff related the parentage of fellow Harrington informant Frank Drew, whose Umpqua mother had gone "home from Yachats [a coastal reservation agency] to visit at Umpqua, and some white man knocked [her] up there, and kept on going. And she returned to Yachats to have her baby."[84] Evanoff explained that Drew's mother and twin brother died during childbirth and that "[t]hey were going to throw [him] in the hole with his mother cause he was a bastard kid."[85] Relatives adopted and raised Drew, however.

Interestingly, Evanoff drew a correlation between these white men and the cultural trickster Coyote: "The early whites here were just like coyote—they would make a baby and then just keep on going. Coyote did this too."[86] Given the devastation and limited control over their lives, a link between the mythical "creation" era of Coyote and Euro-American colonization is not surprising. Such sentiments led to vast overgeneralizations, such as Evanoff's statement that "All people in my country have no father" and her statement that "You know those old half-breeds, none of them know who was their father."[87] Such was likely the derivation of the curious Coos term for Euro-Americans, "moving people," which some scholars have viewed as a reference to their bustling pioneer endeavors but may be instead a derisive comment on their paternity and lack of social commitment.[88]

The place of mixed-heritage individuals was undetermined for Native and colonial societies in the first two decades of colonization; they were in some sense nonentities. They often lacked status within Indian communities, and government officials ignored them in enumerating the Native population. Among the Chinooks, for example, mixed bloods would have doubled their nation's numbers in the treaty census of 1851; but counting them would hardly have benefited the colonial cause.[89]

Race and the Empire Republic

Successive colonial governments from the provisional "wolf" assembly (1843–48) to the federally recognized territorial government (1848–58) to the state constitution of 1859 explicitly used "white" as a criterion for citizenship and thus for holding and protecting property.[90] The Euro-American colonists barred the hundreds of Kanakas from taking claims.[91] The Kanakas were residing in the country as current and former contract laborers for the HBC. Euro-American colonists subsequently employed them as cheap laborers, boarding them or renting them living space instead of allowing them property ownership. Illicit minority-squatter communities such as "Kanaka Flats" outside of Jacksonville—comprised of Native Hawaiians, dispossessed Indians, Chinese, and unrespectable white "squawmen"—provided additional though precarious and temporary homes.[92] The colonists banned African Americans from settlement, as they would the Chinese in the state constitution of 1859. The ban on African Americans was not a means of avoiding the slavery question. As one colonist put it, "poor whites . . . hated slavery, but . . .

hated *free negroes* worse."[93] Indeed, in 1857, Oregon voters cast two separate ballots on slavery (per the "popular sovereignty law" of the 1850 Compromise) and on allowing free African Americans in the territory. Slavery was defeated in all counties 7,727 to 2,645 (by 74 percent), and "free negroes" were banned by a greater majority, 8,594 to 1,081 (by 89 percent).[94]

When Oregon territorial representative Samuel Thurston debated the Donation Land Act of 1850 on the House floor, he carefully explained his Oregon constituents' views on race and settlement. He argued for the phrase "American citizen" in establishing land claims. Otherwise, the land law "would give land to every servant of the Hudson's Bay Company, including some hundreds of Canakers [Kanakas], or Sandwich Islanders, who are a race of men as black as your negroes of the South, and a race, too, that we do not desire to settle in Oregon." Making clear the connection to the 1790 Naturalization Act, which allowed only "whites" to become citizens, he stated, "If we are to give lands, let it be to American citizens by birth and those who will become so by naturalization." Furthermore, "I am not for giving land to Sandwich Islanders or negroes. . . . Our Legislature passed a law at its first session, excluding free negroes; that law I approve, the people there approve it." Thurston then explained a homegrown Oregon racial alchemy in which "the Canakers and negroes, if allowed to come there, will commingle with our Indians, a mixed race will ensue, and the result will be wars and bloodshed in Oregon. The members of our Legislature foresaw this, and, like wise men as they were, they guarded against it."[95] In other words, the supposedly inferior, savage races would naturally combine and form a sort of Super-Rogue, and deny American citizens ("whites") the security of their birthright. He also explained that, at the very least, banning "any free negro . . . [was] a matter of protection to themselves against the injurious influences which are exercised over the Indian race, inclining them against the whites."[96] This latter comment probably referred to the colonization of the Deep South, particularly Florida, where escaped slaves joined with Seminoles to resist Euro-American colonization.

Indeed, the Oregon situation came to resemble Florida, if less by design of the central government than by the practice of the Euro-American colonists. In the case of the "Armed Occupation Act of Florida," Congress went so far as to use Euro-American settlement as a means of exterminating Seminole Indians who refused to "remove" to Indian Territory. During the so-called Second Seminole War of 1835–42, Col. William J. Worth waged a brutal campaign in the summer of 1841, initiating a scorched-earth policy, torching villages and crops and preventing the harvest of wild foods by constantly assailing the Seminoles. By the following spring, only about 250 Seminoles were estimated to have survived the late campaign and the resulting hungry winter. President John Tyler advised Congress that "further pursuit of these miserable beings by a large military force seems to be as injudicious as it is unavailing." Worth proclaimed the war over in August 1842; it had cost the lives of thousands and $20 million.[97] After the official end of the war, Congress found it cheaper to allow settlers to "solve" the remaining "Indian problem" through private wars paid with land bounties: the Armed Occupation Act. The well-established tradition of using land bounties to pay individuals for military service mutated into an outright call for armed occupation by "any [white] man capable of bearing arms." The 1842 law made available 200,000 acres as bounty "to provide for the armed occupation and settlement of the unsettled parts" south of Gainesville. Public land historian Paul W. Gates argued that the Oregon Donation Acts (as well as the related measures regarding Washington and New Mexico territories) were related to the earlier Florida act. All were intended to "help to reduce the Indian menace" while encouraging Euro-American settlement in dangerous areas.[98] The link between Florida and Oregon was not lost on contemporary citizens. Charles Drew, who would emerge as one of the most vehement advocates of Indian extermination among the citizens of southwestern Oregon, twice compared the situation in the Rogue River Valley with the "Seminole Wars" of Florida in one of his infamous diatribes against the Indians "infesting" the region.[99] Drew's Oregon-Florida comparison was matched by articles locally in the *Oregon Statesman* and nationally in the *Army and Navy Journal*.[100]

Land bounties, properties donated to citizens for military service against foreign nations and federally sanctioned wars against Indian nations, were obviously not new in the 1840s. Since the American Revolution, land was the primary means for the central government to pay its soldiers, and, by October 1851, land bounties exceeded a staggering 16 million acres, compared with 3.4 million then reserved for Indians.[101] By the 1840s, land bounties were a crucial imperial apparatus and served the purpose of conquest and "occupation" at little cost to the central government. Similarly, in May 1848, after an appeal from the territorial government of Oregon for military aid, President James Polk recommended that Congress allow the issuance of land bounties to men willing to stake claims in Cayuse country, among a Native people with whom Euro-American Oregon considered itself at war.[102] That particular move was a flop, because most Euro-American men who served in the so-called Cayuse War of 1848 had already staked claims in the arable Willamette Valley through the provisional government's land office.[103] Indeed, the object of the Oregon settlers' campaign against the Cayuse, according to Governor Abernethy, was "to keep the Indians busy in protecting their families and stock in their own country, and by this means keep them out of the [Willamette] valley."[104] As well, the torched and plundered properties of the Protestant missions and neighboring ranches as well as the limited success of the Oregon militia in the war did not bode well for the successful colonization of the Columbia Plateau at that point. Nevertheless, Polk's equation of Oregon colonization and "occupation" land bounties demonstrates the extent to which the central government sanctioned and encouraged private militancy and settler colonialism in Indian Country regardless of its pledge of "utmost good faith."

When news of the Whitman Massacre arrived in Oregon City in November 1847, Oregon's provisional government created its first in a long line of volunteer militias to campaign illicitly in Indian Country without permission or direction from the United States Army. Polk's support was ex post facto. At the time, the regular army, buttressed by several state militias, was busy conquering Mexico, leaving Oregon's provisional government on its own militarily and unwittingly contributing to a tradition of independent militarism that federal officials would later have difficulty stopping. The Willamette Valley militia called its retributive expedition to the Columbia Plateau the Cayuse War.

Early Colonial Wars of Oregon

Euro-American colonists sought vengeance following the Whitman Massacre and subsequent raids, including one on The Dalles, on a mission station (Wascopam), and on a recent extension of colonial settlements of the Willamette Valley. A group of Native men from Cayuse, Wallawalla, and Shoshone bands had killed and captured several Euro-Americans and destroyed mission and colonial property on the Columbia Plateau. By their own admission, the Indians were retaliating for a raging disease epidemic for which many blamed the colonials. The colonists' ensuing six-month campaign failed to achieve the desired vengeance against the perpetrators of the massacre. However, all of the Euro-American captives of Teloukaikt and his colleagues were retrieved, although HBC trader Peter Skene Ogden had affected this success diplomatically on his own before the militia began its campaign of retributive violence. Indeed, the freed captives' salacious accounts of murder, rape, and forced marriage contributed to a public clamor for the extermination of the offending Cayuse instead of an alternative scenario in which the captives' safe return circumvented further bloodshed, which had been the hope of Ogden, Teloukaikt, Five Ravens, and others. The provisional government raised a militia and attempted to get help from Euro-Americans in Alta California and the United States. After two brief fights, successful peace negotiations between several Plateau Sahaptian bands and the provisional government's "Peace Commission" occurred at the HBC's Fort Nez Perce (alternatively Fort Walla Walla) in early March 1848. Satisfied that he would not face a substantial pan-Indian force, Col. Cornelius Gilliam continued his militia campaign to track down the perpetrators of the massacre, fought 400 Palus Indians on the Snake River (a case of mistaken identity), then retreated southward across the Columbia River.

The militia maintained a presence in the Grande Ronde Valley to protect seasonal emigrant parties that typically arrived in late summer.[105] As discussed in the next chapter, this practice would continue through the mid-1850s on the northern emigrant route across the Columbia Plateau and the southern route across the Klamath Basin into the Rogue River Valley, engendering more conflicts than it prevented. After the colonists' "war" had sputtered to a halt, the provisional government declared peace—established on July 5, 1848—and offered bounty lands in Cayuse country to volunteer militiamen if they would remain as guards. Few were interested, as mentioned; the Willamette Valley was still "open," most of the militiamen had claims there, and the Plateau seemed a dangerous place for Euro-American colonization. Thanks to the restraint of numerous Plateau headmen and their bands, the efforts of the peace commissioners of the provisional government, and Ogden, the so-called war did not flare up into a wider conflict more deserving of the name.

The colonial wars of the Willamette Valley, or as one pioneer called them the "contest of races in Western Oregon,"[106] were relatively minor affairs. In midsummer 1846, a band of Chinookan Wascos from the Wascopam had moved into the headwaters of the Santiam River in the foothills east of the Salem settlements. Likely, the Wascos were only in the area on a seasonal hunting and berry-picking excursion, as Plateau peoples had used the lush western valleys and foothills at least since the earliest records of Fort Astoria in 1811; indeed, their seasonal use almost certainly dates back hundreds of years. Euro-Americans nevertheless resisted the incursion into their claimed territory, and a company of "Oregon Rangers" engaged them at what is still known as Battle Creek, although the confrontation barely deserved the moniker. The militia wounded one Wasco man and temporarily lost one of their own when he fainted from the heat and excitement. The "battle" ended with the Euro-Americans paying a horse to the family of the wounded Wasco man in recompense for having shot him; such was the only acceptable alternative to a blood feud in much of *Illahee*. The Wascos had not shot any volunteers. The militia may have gained some sense of accomplishment from the Wasco band's eventual withdrawal back to the Wascopam, although such was probably a planned seasonal move anyway.[107]

During the Cayuse War in early March 1848, another citizen militia attacked a group of Indians in the environs of the lower Willamette, supposedly defending their land claims from invaders. The militia surprised and murdered a number of Koosta's band of Molalas camped on Abiqua Creek in the foothills east of the Euro-American settlements of Oregon City and Molalla. Individual homesteads had recently extended eastward from the Willamette River, as Euro-Americans claimed a number of sprawling 640-acre properties along Abiqua Creek by 1848.[108] Sahaptians, the Molalas had emigrated westward from the Columbia Plateau into the Cascade foothills in the eighteenth century, probably as a result of Shoshone ("Snake") raids. (The Shoshones acquired horses from the Spanish borderlands and brought them to the Oregon Country. The *Illahee* first confronted by Euro-Americans was much affected by their earlier raids.) The Molalas had by the 1840s become middlemen of sorts between Native traders from the Wascopam and Klamath Basin, and, not surprisingly, Koosta had married a Klamath Lake woman. Thus, his band of Molalas commonly hosted Klamaths as well as fellow Sahaptian speakers from the Columbia Plateau. During the war hysteria of 1848, Euro-Americans became convinced that a pan-tribal plot would result in an attack on the Willamette Valley while the main militia was campaigning on the Plateau. Problems with Klamaths, relatives of Koosta's wife, who were visiting the Molala camp on Abiqua Creek, thus took on greater significance than normally would have been the case. Apparently, some of the young Klamath visitors had scared settlers on Abiqua Creek by supposedly taking potshots at cabins, wearing paint and yelling while riding their horses, and killing a cow. As well, "Cayuse emissaries" were rumored to be at Koosta's camp to entice him to attack the settlements. Margaret Hutchins, the daughter of Koosta and his (unfortunately anonymous) Klamath wife, later stated that the "Cayuses" were actually visiting Wascos. At the time, however, no colonists bothered to ask.[109]

In a practice that was becoming increasingly common by 1848, local colonists formed a militia and began shooting indiscriminately at any Indians seen along Abiqua Creek and the surrounding area. Over two days, the militia shot at least ten people, although, as one contemporary stated, "It is impossible to say with certainty how many Indians were killed as the whites were much divided" of opinion. At least three of the dead were women, and "[n]one of [the militiamen] were quite certain whether the Indians killed were of those that should have been killed." Presumably, the ones who "deserved" death were the Klamath visitors and supposed Cayuse emissaries. One colonist explained that "[i]ndeed killing the Indians was not the object, so much, as driving them off to their own country, which was done most effectualy."[110] The Willamette Valley was for Euro-Americans and the few local bands that behaved in an acceptable manner (i.e., furnishing cheap labor and wild foods for trade). Still, as will be seen, the Willamette Valley tribes were not to be permitted to retain even the smallest portion of their homelands.

Ultimately, the larger significance of the Cayuse War for Euro-Americans lay with the nationalist political campaign the colonists waged during and after the hostilities. Waving the Whitman Massacre and their military exploits around like bloody flags, proving both their need for protection and their dedication to United States sovereignty, the colonists urgently pushed a reluctant and divided Congress for territorial recognition. Since 1843, Congress basically had ignored such calls. Now the colonists had a compelling case. In their petitions for territorial status, they consistently used the rhetoric of citizenship to legitimize their claims, to request army forts to protect emigration routes, and to request treaty commissioners to clear away the Indians and their land titles. In a memorial of December 29, 1847, the provisional assembly deemed the Cayuse War a dilemma requiring an immediate solution. The citizens of Oregon demanded absolute possession of western Oregon: such was their Euro-American birthright. Not surprisingly, in the December memorial, they stressed the pressing need for their pet legislation, the Donation Land bill, which would formally grant them the massive landholdings that they had already claimed through their provisional land office. In recommending quick action on behalf of Oregon, President Polk on May 29, 1848, pressed Congress to establish a territorial government, extend land bounties to volunteer militiamen who remained on the Plateau in Cayuse country, and appoint treaty commissioners to extinguish Indian title to western Oregon.[111] After years of ignoring the matter, exaggerated accounts of the "Cayuse War" finally convinced Congress of the urgency to end Oregon's indeterminate governmental status, and it formally created the Oregon Territory on August 14, 1848.

The new territory of Oregon lost no time in pressing Congress and the national treasury for full reimbursement of their war effort. On October 31, 1848, the territorial assembly passed an act creating a claims commission to begin gathering evidence of expenses. In a memorial the following summer, in 1849, the legislature advised Congress that the bill could be as high as $200,000, but it assured that "the most rigid and scrupulous economy" had been followed in the prosecution of a war fought by "citizens . . . in the public cause."[112] The assembly eventually whittled the request down to $87,230.53. Congress generously appropriated an even $100,000 on February 14, 1851, although two more congressional acts in 1852 and 1853 were necessary before Oregon officials could meet the increasingly loosened burden of proof required by the Comptroller's Office of the Treasury Department. The remuneration was finally allocated in March 1853. Soon after receiving these monies, the territorial government discovered more expenses and pressed for another $30,000, which they received in March 1854.[113] With their massive land claims nearing legitimacy, their militia effort well covered financially, and the Native peoples of Oregon vilified nationally, the Willamette Valley colonists had done well by their Cayuse War and the evangelical martyrs of Whitman's Waiilatpu mission.

Negotiating Oregon into Place

The territory also dispatched Rep. Samuel Thurston to Washington, D.C., to secure congressional approval of the colonists' economic speculations. From December 1849 through June 1850, Thurston lobbied, or "electioneered," daily, sometimes until midnight, to gain senatorial approval of an Indian treaty commission and the appointment of Anson Dart as superintendent to conduct the negotiations. Dart was told to effect the extinguishment of Indian land title and the removal of the western Oregon Indians to the more arid Columbia Plateau east of the Cascade Mountains.[114] Dying en route back to Oregon, Thurston did not witness his hard work on Oregon Indian affairs undone by Native negotiators, people whom one senator had dismissed as "inconsequential."[115]

To provide order to colonization and land speculation, the U.S. government had adapted the British imperial policy of "extinguishing Indian title" to aboriginal holdings, a formal-legal termination of indigenous peoples' claims to their homelands. Although the competing imperial powers had divided the region between themselves in 1846, Congress had not yet performed the legalistic alchemy that transformed indigenous homelands into "public domain." Perfected in 1841, the idealistic formula required a three-step process performed in order: a Senate-approved treaty commission to extinguish Indian title, an official survey of the land to translate it into a series of grid lines, and a disposal of the resulting public domain through sales, bounties, and donations.[116] The 1841 reform was meant to address the confusing mess of conflicting claims that had consistently resulted from expansion since the 1780s and to liberalize the disposal process. In practice, the reform accomplished neither very effectively. Euro-American colonists disrupted the ideal by skipping the first two steps of the formula and seizing sprawling land claims, and they had already commenced a lively trade in selling and swapping sections of claims that they legally did not own.

Oregon's Donation Land Act of 1850, then, had to be an exception to the rule of American imperialism. Unlike similar contemporary legislation regarding the disposition of the public lands in the territories of Kansas and Nebraska in 1854, Congress omitted the ordering stipulations of section 10 of the 1841 preemption law from the Oregon legislation, nullifying the chronology of treaties and government surveys before settlement. Indeed, thanks to Thurston's tenacious daily lobbying, Congress acted as if the Indians and their claims were a mere formality to be accounted for on paper. In May 1850, Congress granted preemption rights to settlers and moved onto the donation land law, creating a surveyor general's office. It also provided for a treaty commission for "the negotiation of treaties with the Indian tribes in the Territory of Oregon for the extinguishment of their claims . . . west of the Cascade mountains." The relatively speedy passage of these bills by September 1850 and the manner with which Congress dispensed with section 10 of the 1841 law speaks volumes about how seriously the legislators took issues concerning Native sovereignty.[117] Thurston had to direct his lobbying efforts more toward combating the ambivalence of Eastern senators than overcoming defenses of Indian land rights.

Ratification of the resulting treaties was another matter: When the nineteen treaties arrived back from Oregon in the summer of 1852, the Senate sat on them for two years, failing to ratify them before events in Oregon made them largely irrelevant.[118] There were two reasons for the Senate's inaction. First, the Senate faced a daunting number of treaties in the early 1850s, as the war with Mexico and increased colonization of the prairies and southern plains created a huge expense, although Native people received a pittance of their land's actual value. As of January 1850, the government had paid more than $61 million for land purchased from Indians and foreign nations (the majority of the expense paid to Mexico, Spain, and France), over $6 million for surveying, and nearly $7.5 million for its imperial disposal system—a total cost approaching $75 million. Still, the net profit from disposing of the public domain was more than $60 million.[119] In a contemporary 1850 debate over Indian treaties in Minnesota, one senator worried about busting the Treasury through massive outlays to Indians, while another countered that, "if this Government could buy these lands for ten cents an acre, it would be the most splendid speculation they ever entered into."[120] In the case of Oregon, however, the Donation Land Act meant that the federal government would not profit from its outlay. Thus, the Oregon treaties were not profitable ventures for the Treasury, and there was some question in the capitol as to whether the declining Native population of western Oregon was worth the bother and expense.

Although the Native population figures were indeed considerably smaller than in other parts of the West, the Chinookan and Kalapuyan peoples of western Oregon proved themselves anything but inconsequential. They outmaneuvered the colonists' political machinations and undid six difficult months of Thurston's lobbying by forcing Dart into treaty concessions that were unacceptable to the Oregon citizenry. Demonstrating their grasp of Oregon settler colonialism, the Clatsops explained that the speculative land sales by which Euro-Americans were making "much money"—$2,000 to $6,000 in some transactions, according to the Clatsops—were not benefiting them, although they had allowed this business in their country. They referred specifically to the Clatsop Plains, coastal valley lands enriched with deep topsoil and laden with massive timber stands and streams that ran throughout the summer, land long praised in writings from Lewis and Clark to the Methodist missionaries. Indeed, one of the treaty commissioners, Rev. Josiah Parrish, had a 640-acre claim there (which he subsequently traded for two promising Oregon City lots), as did other former Methodist Mission associates and more recent emigrants who benefited from the missionaries' initial colonization. Before the Clatsops would treat, they demanded that commercial traffic on the Columbia cease and two sawmills be removed because they had "frightened the fish away!"[121] The mills and the salmon depended on the same waters, and the latter were already losing the conflict by 1851.

Dart claims that he had difficulty convincing the Clatsops of the "impossibility of . . . their demands," although it seems more likely that Clatsops were simply bargaining. The Clatsop Plains were already lost to them: colonists had claimed "nearly or quite every acre." The Clatsops' subsequent counteroffer included only their burial grounds and lodges at Point Adams, which would ensure access to their ancestors and to their fishing sites. Although three Euro-American colonists claimed the area, Dart deemed them to be inconsequential, compared with the half-million acres of farmland and timber stands that the Clatsops were prepared to cede. In effect, the Clatsops ceded only what had already been taken from them, and by issuing "impossible" demands they had secured a small core of their homeland and the removal of three troublesome land claims.[122]

The Chinooks agreed to cede much of their homelands to the United States in exchange for annuities, but, like the Clatsops, they negotiated what they wanted. They retained their principal surviving village, usufruct rights to fishing sites, timber stands, grazing lands, cranberry marshes, and even arable lands for future cultivation. Opposing removal, the Chinooks noted their value as laborers. Dart agreed that, because the "Indians make all the [fencing] rails . . . and do the greater part of the labour in farming," the colonial economy would suffer from their removal. Instead, the Chinooks insisted on the removal of a Euro-American colonist named Washington Hall, who claimed their village, damned up their fresh water, and generally acted obnoxiously. Hall's haughtiness was despite his marriage to a slave, a bond that completely undermined his pretensions to high status among the Chinooks. Notably, the Chinooks also flipped the "vanishing Indian" thesis on its head. They acknowledged that their population of 320 (the official figure excluded the equal number of mixed bloods and slaves) was vastly smaller than it had been in 1830 and that the federal government had the power to exterminate them if it chose. Indeed, they used this position of claimed inferiority to push Dart into promising a speedy delivery of the treaty stipulations before they died. The only part of the negotiations in which Dart was successful was preventing the Chinook women, all of whom participated in the negotiations, from signing the treaty.[123]

In his treaties with the Clatsops and the Chinooks, Dart agreed to create a permanent Indian Country on both banks of the lower Columbia and was forced to promise the removal of Euro-American colonists—the complete opposite of what his instructions had been! Treaty commissioners led by John Gaines did not fare any better among the Clackamas or any of the other Willamette Valley peoples, all of whom insisted on retaining small reservations within the hearts of their homelands, which were now largely claimed by colonists.[124]

By forcing commissioners to concede to "colonist removal" instead of Indian removal and securing parcels of Native homelands as permanent reservations, the Indians, knowingly or unknowingly, negotiated treaties that were not passable. The Senate simply would not ratify Indian treaties without extensive lobbying pressure on key senators, men more concerned with the slavery question than with far-western Indians who were generally thought to be disappearing. In the immediate aftermath of the Compromise of 1850, with the entrance of California into statehood, Oregon land legislation (of which Indian treaties were an essential part) threatened to reopen unhealed sectionalist political wounds. Thurston had had to walk a fine line in the winter of 1849–50, assuaging senators from Ohio, Alabama, and Tennessee to achieve his Indian commission. Western colonization consistently shaped and was shaped by the slavery question and would, of course, finally break the uneasy truces ten years later. In 1851, Oregon's territorial government did not support the treaties, and Thurston's tireless lobbying was not repeated. Thus, the second reason that the Senate did not ratify the treaties was that Oregonians did not want them ratified; Native negotiators were too successful. Unfortunately for the Oregon colonists, American empire was too complicated to be easily manipulated from the periphery, and the surviving Native population had several decades of experience dealing with competing empires and had no intention of surrendering the remaining core of their homelands.

The nineteen bands of Chinookan, Kalapuyan, Salishan, Sahaptian, and Athapaskan peoples of the environs of the lower Columbia and Willamette rivers had demonstrated that they were a people of history. They were prepared to change with the times and sought to re-create Indian places within colonial Oregon, *Nesika Illahee* "our land," as the Confederated Tribes of Siletz came to call their piece of Indian Country. The Oregon of the 1850s, however, was not that of the fur trade before the epidemics of the 1830s had decimated the Native population. Indian people caught a glimpse of how far their power to negotiate had slipped when their efforts were simply ignored: the colonists continued to stream into their lands, pushing them farther away from resource sites and giving them no funds in compensation. The pain for the Native peoples was not only economic. Colonization fundamentally undermined interrelated concepts of property, place, and identity.

Imperial Limits on Folk Expansion

To some degree, the Indians were joined in frustration by the colonial population that was unable to orchestrate imperial expansion from the periphery. Because of the Indians' temporary success and the commissioners' failure in the 1851 treaty negotiations, the Donation Land Act went into effect despite the continuance of indigenous title and Native occupation of western Oregon. Ironically, the initial law of 1850 undermined the colonists' speculative efforts, in that it required four years of occupation before title would be granted; thus, land sales had to be suspended. Furthermore, the term of

TABLE 1. Certified Donation Claims, 1853–1856

Year	Number of Claims Filed	Married Filings (% of total)	Single Men (% of total)	Single Women (% of total)	Heirs (% of total)	% Who Took Maximum Acreage*
1853	70	53 (76)	13 (19)	2 (3)	2 (3)	90
1854	159	132 (83)	15 (11)	1 (1)	11 (8)	81
1855	135	82 (61)	49 (36)	0 (0)	4 (3)	65
1856	56	17 (30)	37 (66)	2 (4)	0 (0)	11

Source: Abstracts of Oregon Donation Land Claims, 1852–1903 (Washington, D.C.: National Archives, National Archives and Records Service, General Services Administration), rolls 1–3.

Note: Between 1853 and 1856, the percentage of married filings dropped; the percentage of single men rose; the percentage of single women was small but constant; the percentage of those taking the maximum allowable acreage decreased; and claims recorded dropped precipitously in 1856. See Table 2 for further explanation of the decreased size of claims.

*Includes claims of 600 acres or more for marrieds and 300 acres or more for singles.

occupation did not begin until a new federal claim was filed, which could not be done until after an official survey. The surveys were delayed by logistical and administrative problems, preventing the initial claims from being certified until mid-1853, and inefficiency prevented most claims from being patented until 1862.[125]

Indeed, the imperial land system was much more complicated and economically exclusive than the colonists had hoped. J. R. Preston, the surveyor general, arrived in the spring of 1851 to implement "the national survey system," in which the baseline and meridian were established "as far as practicable," and surveys were free—provided that the land was located within areas with established township and section lines. Thus, most colonists who claimed land outside the principal lower-Willamette Valley townships surrounding Portland and Salem had to pay for their own surveys—$8 per mile—because Preston intended to work backward, using the individual claim surveys to create townships and sections.[126] The effects were obvious: although 1,079 colonists quickly filed "notifications" (statements of occupation and requests for survey) in 1852, by the end of 1856 only 420 claims had been surveyed and certified.[127] (See Table 1.) This was the result despite Preston's claim that "every settler is anxious to receive his patent in order to divide and sell."[128] Preston collected the survey fees from his deputies, and doing so made him the enemy of the Oregonians. By the time the colonists successfully had Preston removed from office in November 1853, he had

TABLE 2. Land Claim Size Exceptions, 1853–1856

Year	Total Exceptions* (% of total claims)	Exceptions: Noncash Donation (% of total claims)	Exceptions: Cash Donation (% of total claims)
1853	7 (10)	7 (10)	n/a**
1854	30 (19)	17 (11)	13 (8)**
1855	49 (35)	4 (1)	45 (34)
1856	49 (89)	3 (5)	46 (84)

Source: *Abstracts of Oregon Donation Land Claims, 1852–1903* (Washington, D.C.: National Archives, National Archives and Records Service, General Services Administration), rolls 1–3.

Note: Claims filed as cash donations accounted for an increasing majority of land claims that were "exceptional" for being smaller than the allowable size. Another mitigating factor was arguably geographical: the latter claims were filed in southwestern Oregon, with its smaller valleys.

*Exceptions refer to claims of less than 600 acres for marrieds and less than 300 acres for singles.

**The cash donation law was passed on February 15, 1854, and went into effect on July 17, 1854, after the March and June recordings were completed; thus, no cash donations were recorded before October 1854, the year's last book.

collected approximately $25,000. The citizen land speculators demanded that Preston's replacement, Charles Gardiner, refrain from similar survey speculating, which eventually they accomplished.[129]

Because land speculations were stymied by the four-year clause that prohibited dividing claims prior to patent, colonials sent territorial representative Joseph Lane to Washington, D.C., to rectify the situation. Lane deflected accusations of rampant speculation by Oregonians, arguing that, since the Donation Land Act, land sales had ceased (except for town lots, the sale of which were still permitted under the federal law). Regardless, the sale of one's land, according to Lane, was a "right."[130] The solution that Lane affected in 1853 allowed for "cash donations," through which colonists could gain title if they occupied the land for only two years (soon modified to one year in 1854) and paid $1.25 per acre. The number of cash donations grew steadily, and they had the unsurprising effect of diminishing the size of claims. (See Tables 1 and 2.)

The usual Western gender-ratio imbalance among the colonists was reflected in the types of certified claims between 1853 and 1856, with the number of single claims continuing to increase annually. Yet, although the gender ratio does help explain the number of single-male claimants, the presence of single-female claimants is surprising. Between 1853 and 1856, five women filed as single claimants—not as heirs or widows, but as independent settlers. (See Table 1.) Their claims caused some apprehension at the general land office in Washington, D.C. The scrawls of confused clerks are still apparent in the ledger books: "female settler?—is she entitled?" The answer was yes; each of these women's claims was patented in 1862. The women (Janet Pugh, Sally Goodman, Mary Center, Mary Canada, and Delilah White) seem to have exploited some confusion created by the 1850 law's allowance for limited married women's property rights.[131] The provision granted up to 320 acres to wives in conjunction with their husband's claim, and widows could take claims as heirs.[132] The Oregon law does not suggest nascent proto-feminism, of course. Rather, the common view of women as keepers of hearth and home was responsible. In an 1854 congressional debate, Lane explained that men could not be trusted to refrain from speculating their lands, but women could, thus preserving homesteads and fledgling communities.[133] The law did not address nonwidowed single women, and colonials allowed these five to file claims. Congress rejected similar women's property provisions in the 1854 land law of New Mexico Territory. The five Oregon women who gained land patents were notable exceptions to the exclusivity of settler colonialism as the domain of white males.

As the missionaries of the Oregon Mission had found, colonial realities often confounded ideals, and squatter sovereignty as enacted by the donation land laws proved disappointing to Euro-American colonists. Similarly, whereas the ideal of imperialism might be considered the orderly acquisition and maintenance of power and influence, expansionist nations such as the United States rarely realized such order. In the case of Oregon, the citizenry pushed imperialism forward by initiating colonization before the nation had secured dominion vis-à-vis competing empires and indigenes. They attempted to create their ideal of squatter sovereignty, and, with the legitimacy of their territorial government, they pressed their goals but did not fully realize them. The mixture of economic speculation and racialized republicanism produced a form of colonialism that featured aggressive acquisition and trading of Native lands and that left no room for the Indian population. To realize their colonial goals of unfettered control over Native lands and resources, the citizen colonials would need to ignite a wider war comparable to the Cayuse War to achieve similar effects. Before, the goal was territorial recognition; now, it was dominion.

CHAPTER SEVEN

Polaklie Illahee (Land of Darkness)

Identity and Genocidal Culture in Oregon

Between 1846 and 1850, Euro-Americans benefited from the Oregon Treaty with Great Britain and succeeded in achieving territorial acquisition by the United States and some protections of their land claims. Clearly, however, the empire republic was not easily manipulated from the periphery. Divisions, constant deal making, and problematic compromises formed the heart of federal operations and inhibited distant manipulation, leaving colonials dissatisfied in many respects. Subsequent colonization would further highlight the limitations of territorial power. Importantly, the years between 1851 and 1858 saw intermittent armed conflict among Native peoples and colonials in western Oregon Territory. (In 1853, Congress formally separated Oregon and Washington territories at the Columbia River.) Conflicts produced tragic losses of life, land, and property for colonials and indigenes and exacerbated intraterritorial political feuding and federal-territorial tensions. During the tumultuous and often violent 1850s, colonists quickly claimed the lands of the Willamette and lower Columbia River valleys, then moved on to the southern valleys of the Umpqua, Rogue, and Coast Range Mountains.[1]

Newcomers found the valleys of southwestern Oregon attractive both because the climate was like "baby bear's porridge," drier than the Willamette Valley, wetter than California's Sacramento Valley. Also, the proximity to the goldfields in the Oregon-California borderlands provided a market for cattle and produce.[2] From the colonialist perspective, however, this border region had a serious drawback: the Native people had not been strongly integrated into the earlier fur-trade economy. Whereas, as we saw, relations between fur traders and Indians could be dicey, the mutual economic benefit contributed to a relatively peaceful coexistence. In the Oregon-California borderlands, however, relations would be shaped by the extremist acquisitiveness

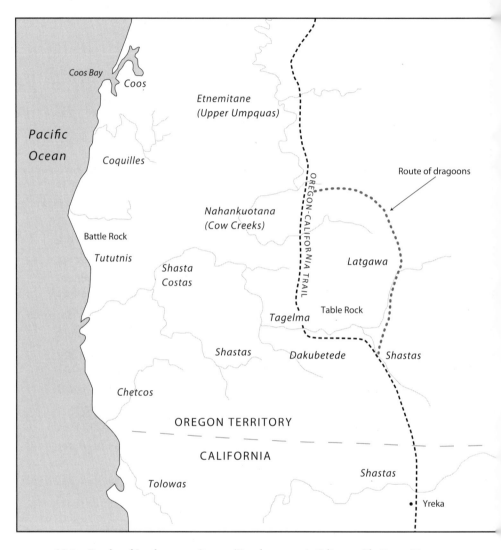

Native Peoples of Southwestern Oregon (Based on maps in Schwartz, *The Rogue River Indian War*)

of the gold rush. As well, the Native population was divided into numerous bands that in the 1850s were embroiled in a constant state of raiding, mostly for horses and women. The miners and other Indian people then traded for them. These Takelman- and Shastan-speaking bands of the interior valleys of northern California and southwestern Oregon remained a potent challenge despite their losses to disease since the 1830s and their fragmentation from raiding.

Attempted accommodations between Euro-Americans and Native peoples in the Oregon-California borderlands met with limited success. In 1851, a failed gold seeker named Thomas Smith, who had come west with an emigrant train called The Company of Equal Rights, arrived in the domain of the Bear Creek Shastas and their headman Tipsu Tyee ("bearded chief" in Chinook Jargon). Smith sought a place to grow crops for sale to miners and "chinamen." Tipsu Tyee may have been a mixed-blood man, but, if so, his "racial" heritage had no meaning to Shastas. He spoke only his Shasta dialect and the jargon, and he seems to have had no contact with his presumably fur-company father. His homeland surrounding modern Ashland, Oregon, sits below the Siskiyou Pass, which enters the high country between Oregon and California, and was well positioned for Smith's intent. Through Chinook Jargon (the sole English-speaking Shasta was apparently not present at the meeting), Tipsu Tyee made Smith pledge that he would not steal horses or women, activities in which some miners like some Indian men engaged. Mutually agreeing to stay out of each other's way and business, Tipsu Tyee consented to Smith's farm. They mostly avoided altercations. At one point in 1851, however, Smith blamed Tipsu Tyee for the theft of "some items" and threatened to summon a volunteer militia from Yreka, California to "kill all your men and burn your stick houses and destroy all your people." According to Smith's account, the tyee and other villagers exploded at the threat. Only the intervention of Tipsu Tyee's wife in the form of a thirty-minute monologue calmed the situation. Her "eloquence" held the people "spellbound" and led her husband to retrieve the few items that he could from a rival band of Shastas; much had already been traded down the Klamath River to non-Shastas, probably Karoks.[3]

In the region's tense atmosphere of the 1850s, such resolutions became increasingly difficult to achieve. In 1852, two crucial events enflamed tensions. First, Modoc Indians massacred an emigrant train on the Klamath Plateau, producing a retaliatory expedition from California and Oregon volunteer militias. Second, a packer named James Cluggage discovered gold on the Oregon side of the Siskiyous near modern Jacksonville. Over the next two years, the find attracted thousands of miners, settlers, and assorted entrepreneurs and speculators to the Rogue River Valley, the surrounding hills, and the coast. The colonists' seizure and destruction of Native land and resources made a precarious situation exceedingly dangerous.

To make matters worse for the Indians, newcomers had already decided that the Natives were irredeemable savages; theirs was the so-called Rogue country. The French Canadian fur trappers had only intermittent contact with the Takelma, Shasta, and Athapaskan bands in the 1820s and 1830s, and a few isolated problems produced the moniker "les coquins," the rascals, or the rogues. As discussed earlier, this derogatory nickname for Indians was common during initial encounters of the fur trade. Unfortunately for the Indians of the Oregon-California borderlands, they never received a new reputation. Largely because the fur trade was so limited in the region, resulting stable colonial relations never developed there. Beavers and other lucrative furbearers did not exist in large numbers, and the HBC's "fur desert" policy contributed to their near extinction. That beavers were a food source for the Indians did not help matters. At least by 1837, the nefarious reputation of the Native peoples produced an expectation among Euro-Americans for violent encounters, and at least one Shasta boy was killed by a nervous, trigger-happy traveler.[4] In 1847, Oregon's provisional Indian agent offered the following advice to a group of California-bound travelers: "After you get to the Siskiyou [M]ountains, use your pleasure in spilling blood . . . my only communication with these treacherous, cowardly, untamable rascals would be through my rifle." He explained that extermination was the only possible policy: "[t]he character of their country precludes the ideas of making peace with them, or ever maintaining treaties if made; so that philanthropy must be set aside in cases of necessity while self-preservation here dictates these savages being killed off as soon as possible."[5] The "Rogue" identity pressed on the region's Takelma, Shasta, and Athapaskan bands was fast becoming infused with the idea of irredeemable savagery and extermination. Settler colonialism did not allow for the incorporation or continued existence of Indians who challenged the birthrights of "white" citizens.

This logic gained force with time. Euro-Americans became more familiar with and desirous of the region, and the indigenous people came to be seen as obstacles to profitable pursuits or the "public welfare" in American settler-colonial discourse. In 1848, news of gold at Sutter's colony in the Sacramento Valley led many Willamette Valley colonists, such as famed "Indian fighter" John Ross and his "Oregon boys" (as he called his fellow settler-miners), to head south.[6] Supposedly, they had to fight their way from the north end of Umpqua canyon in southwestern Oregon to Scott's Valley on the California side of the Siskiyous.[7] To the waves of Euro-Americans in the 1840s and 1850s, the Native peoples of southwestern Oregon and neighboring northern-most California were simply "Rogues," and the river and the surrounding valleys bore the name. Through 1851, repeated references mention the "Rogue's river" or the "Rogue's valley."[8] As their spellings indicate, Euro-Americans understood the largely unknown region to be in the possession of rogues. Only with the increased presence of Euro-Americans and their land and mineral claims from 1852 onward did the Indians become literally divested of possession. Thereafter, they were more often defined in terms of the landscape, "Rogue Rivers" or "Rogue River Indians." As Euro-Americans took literal possession of the region, they maintained their perception of the "Rogue Indians" as naturally predisposed to thievery and violence.

As early as October 1849, with travel increasing between the Willamette settlements and the California goldfields, territorial governor Joseph Lane reported that the "Rogue river Indians . . . are a warlike and roguish people . . . it is to be feared that we will have trouble with these Indians."[9] Umpqua Valley colonist Jesse Applegate referred to the Oregon-California borderland as the "gauntlet of the Indians."[10] Indeed, each minor incident between colonists and the "Rogues" produced a new tale, which in turn grew with the telling, and justified whatever extreme retaliation the colonists' considered justified.[11] Smith's threat to destroy Tipsu Tyee's village and the Shasta's reaction were more indicative of this atmosphere than the peaceful settlement.

Early in the California Gold Rush, colonials put their extermination rhetoric into action. In 1849, while prospecting the area around Coloma, California, two "Oregonian" miners died, and their fellow colonists blamed the local Indians. John Ross and about twenty "Oregon boys" captured 130 Indians who were peaceably encamped near Coloma. An argument between "California miners and the Oregonians" over the fate of the Indians soon erupted. A man named Marshall tried to advocate for the Indians but was driven off at gunpoint, and the "Oregon boys" burst into a home to retrieve an Indian man "secreted" by a white woman in her home. They pronounced the secreted man and four others guilty and hung all but one who escaped. Probably in retaliation, another Oregon colonist was killed soon after. This time Ross and company did not bother pretending to determine the guilty parties and instead went Indian hunting, randomly slaughtering sixty people they came across.[12] The action of Ross and his "Oregon boys" was the first large-scale massacre of California Indians by Euro-Americans, a despicable trend that would continue for years throughout the gold rush and early colonization period and that would result in the extermination of entire bands.[13]

After a brief stint back in the Willamette Valley in which Ross discovered that another hardy pioneer had stolen his thresher, he rejoined some "Oregon boys," then prospecting along the Klamath River near the Oregon-California border. Over the next two years, Ross perpetrated or was involved in several more deadly expeditions against Shastas of the Klamath River and Scott's Valley and Modocs of the southern Klamath Basin. At Yreka, California, Ross led a popular revolt against so-called Indian resolutions that would have limited the rights of citizens to take violent retribution against Indians for thefts and other minor property offenses. Together with his colleague Benjamin Wright, a man who decorated his Yreka home's entrance with an Indian's scalp on a pole and who masterminded the massacre of 41 Modocs invited for peace talks in 1854, Ross carved out a niche for himself as the scourge of the Indians of the Oregon-California borderlands.[14] These deplorable actions explode the stereotypical paradigm of peaceable family-oriented Oregonians versus murderous individualist Anglo-Californians.

Such brutal violence helped Euro-Americans secure a more successful second treaty round with Indians of western Oregon to the north of the bloody borderlands. The treaties signed between 1853 and 1855 retroactively legalized ten years of intensive colonization and land speculations. Oregon Superintendent of Indian Affairs Joel Palmer effectively used his assertive personality and the threat of war; the latter proved the crucial ingredient that Dart had lacked in 1851 when treating with the Chinooks and the Clatsops. Understandably fearful, Indian people of the Willamette and Columbia valleys agreed to terrible conditions, including removal from their homelands. In the south, actual and rumored hostilities played crucial roles in 1853, when Palmer secured his first treaties with Takelmas of the Rogue River Valley and the Cow Creek Band of Umpqua. To end a brief conflict, the first treaties established terms of peace and reservations at Table Rock and Council Creek.

Still, the violent atmosphere persisted, and the colonists of southwestern Oregon clamored for federal troops to secure the area. Significantly, massacres of Euro-American emigrants on the Klamath Basin in 1852 and another near Fort Boise in 1854 led to brutal retaliations by volunteer militias. The brief clashes between Euro-Americans and bands of Shastas and Takelmas in the Rogue River Valley in 1851 and 1853 buttressed the colonials' case. In response, the U.S. Army built four forts—Fort Lane in the Rogue Valley, Fort Orford on Oregon's south coast, and Forts Reading and Jones across the pass in northern California—and maintained garrisons to monitor Indian-white relations and generally keep the peace. Despite pressures from local citizens, the aptly named Capt. Andrew Jackson Smith of Fort Lane saw little need for a fort on the Klamath Plateau or for policing the Indians too closely in the Siskiyous and adjacent valleys. Smith saw his fort near the new Table Rock Reservation as sufficient for the protection of Indian people and newcomers. Indeed, with independent, volunteer militias calling themselves "Squaw Hunters" and the "Exterminators" roaming the region at the first hint of violence, Smith and other federal officials tended to view Indians as the people needing protection.[15]

In 1854, the effectiveness of the army's Department of the Pacific was limited: Fewer than 1,000 men were spread out over a vast area including California, Utah territory, and the Pacific Northwest. Many were arranged to defend against an assault from an imperial rival such as Great Britain or Russia. The Crimean War was then raging, and Russian frigates in the Pacific made American officials and merchants nervous. Detachments sent to keep the peace between Indians and colonists were necessarily small, dispersed, and isolated. As had been the trend since the War of 1812, Congress allowed a large army only during war, slashing its size afterwards. With the notable exception of the conquest of Florida, so-called Indian wars usually did not compel Congress to increase the size of the regular armed forces.[16] In the midst of the rabid sectional politics caused partly by the recent, great land grab—the war with Mexico—the commander of the Pacific, Gen. John Wool, could not get Secretary of War Jefferson Davis even to approach Congress for more men and resources in 1854.[17] Wool had too few resources to guard the major harbors of California, Oregon, and Washington, the outlying settlements from the Pacific coast to Utah Territory, and the overland emigration routes from the new border with Mexico north to British Canada.[18] As well, he had to prevent private conquests, or "filibusters," against the Mexican state of Sonora and Hawai'i that were launched from California and involved a complicated diplomatic morass of French, Mexican, and American citizens.[19] Wool distrusted civilians and their colonial pursuits, and he saw independent militias such as those of Oregon as an affront to his authority.[20]

Oregon's speculative colonists probably did not know and certainly did not care about Wool's dilemmas, nor did they think much of his local representative, Captain Smith. Regular troops and volunteer militias often clashed over how to handle occasional thefts and violence, which according to the Euro-Americans were always the Indians' fault, and they were not too particular about which Native band they retaliated against. In one altercation in

September 1855, Captain Smith dispatched a lieutenant and forty dragoons to find the killers of a local Euro-American. The lieutenant refused the aid of volunteer militiamen and then gave up the cold trail as pointless in the steep rocky country. The colonials responded with emasculating taunts and threat to the regular troops: "[You are] just Squaws your Selves and we will clean you out too."[21] Some weeks later, Captain Smith made a similar violent threat against a volunteer militia in defense of Shasta and Takelma Indians on the Table Rock Reservation. The federals and the colonials had divergent goals and interests; again, empire did not always respond as those on its periphery wanted. The colonials wanted protection of their investments from Indians and the ability to take up claims securely and profitably in Indian Country (or the "unsurveyed public domain" in their conception of Oregon), duties for which the regular army was ill-equipped and unwilling to perform. In 1854, Oregon Territory revised its militia law to create an armed force, which could meet the goals of its citizenry.[22]

In early July of 1854, with the imminent approach of the "emigration season," Charles S. Drew petitioned Oregon Territorial Governor John Davis for permission to organize a volunteer militia to patrol the western stretch of the southern emigrant road. The southern, or Applegate, route ran between Fort Hall (in present-day southwest Idaho) and the settlements of the Rogue River Valley in southwestern Oregon. According to one disgruntled contemporary, a party of speculative "road hunters" led by Jesse Applegate established the route in 1846, because they wanted to divert emigrants to the upper Willamette and Umpqua valleys where they had land claims to sell.[23] A route through the Rogue Valley would bypass the older lower Willamette Valley settlements and the massive claims being divided and sold there. The southern route wound through the mostly arid homelands and frontiers of several bands of Shoshones, Northern Paiutes (known to Euro-Americans as "Snakes" and "Diggers"), Achumawi ("Pitt Rivers"), Modocs, Klamaths, and Shastas. The specter of an emigrant party massacred on the northeastern shore of Tule Lake in September 1852 continued to haunt Euro-American imaginations. To local Modocs the thin stretch of shoreline between the lake and a sheer wall of volcanic rock was *wagakanna* ("little canyon"). Henceforth, it became known to Euro-Americans as "Bloody Point."[24]

Drew stated that the evil deed was not repeated the following year only because "Captain" John Miller had led an independent militia of sixty volunteers to "Bloody Point" and prevented a similar massacre in 1853. Captain Smith of Fort Lane disagreed with this conclusion. Superintendent Palmer had visited the Klamath Basin and accepted pledges from the Indians that they would not attack emigrants again.[25] The commission led by Palmer probably met with Tule Lake and Lost River Modocs under the headman Schonchin, as well as several Klamath Lake bands that were then coalescing under the headmen Lileks and Chiloquin. Two Native historical accounts support Smith's and Palmer's claims that emigrants no longer had anything to fear on the Klamath Basin. Jeff Riddle, the son of Winema (the famous heroine of the 1873 Modoc War) and a local Euro-American, published a defense of his people in 1914. According to Riddle, the members of the Rock band of southern Modocs (Combutwaush) and certain individuals from the Lost River and Tule Lake bands who were responsible for the 1852 massacre had previously fled to the mountains and remained there.

Schonchin, having arisen as a principal headman around 1846, came to see his peoples' future as depending on peace with the increasing newcomers.[26] Indeed, Schonchin explained in an 1875 interview that he initially believed Euro-Americans to be far fewer in number. He lamented that "[w]e killed all we could; but they came more and more like new grass in the spring. I looked around and saw that many of our young men were dead and could not come back to fight." Schonchin ended his attacks on emigrants stating, "[m]y heart was sick. My people were few. I threw down my gun. I said, 'I will not fight again.' I made friends with the white man."[27] Schonchin's people remaining in the valleys around Tule Lake, however, would bear the wrath of the Euro-American citizen militias from Oregon and California from 1852 to 1854.

In the summer of 1854 militias from the Willamette and the Rogue valleys were dispatched to the Columbia Plateau and the Klamath Basin: the first to avenge a massacre and the latter supposedly to prevent one. Governor Davis, a temporary Democratic appointee, gave tenuous approval to the Klamath campaign "if it should be considered necessary." However, he advised Drew and Ross that the territorial government could not provide any monetary assistance or guarantee federal reimbursement, although "every proper effort will be made by this department to obtain compensation from the general Government for such outlay." He subsequently reminded Ross that "you will be compelled to rely upon the liberality and patriotism of our fellow citizens, who in turn will be compelled to rely upon the justness of the General Government for their compensation."[28] In a symbolic and strategic move, Ross ordered "Captain" Jesse Walker to establish his field headquarters at *wagakanna*/Bloody Point and to send detachments out to meet emigrants and arrange them into defensible groups. Of the Indian people, he said, "cultivate their friendship; but if necessary for the safety of the lives and property of the immigration, whip and drive them from the road."[29]

In both the Klamath Basin and the Snake River campaigns of 1854, the regular army at Forts Vancouver and Lane offered too little assistance to satisfy the colonists, acting under a different set of prerogatives than the territorial militias and constrained by limited manpower and resources. The army was not officially caught up in the profitability of Oregon, although the many desertions by soldiers to the goldfields might suggest otherwise. On the other side, volunteers from the Willamette and Rogue valleys acted similarly in their respective actions in the Snake River and Klamath Basin areas. Each campaign was partly protective, punitive, and vengeful. Despite the pleadings of Superintendent Palmer, the Snake River campaign was as brutally violent as the Walker expedition in which Modocs and Northern Paiutes were hunted and starved into submission.[30] Palmer instructed his subagent to determine the guilty and protect the innocent from revenge: "*It should not be forgotten that we are a civilized and [C]hristian people, and they savage and ignorant.* Women and children should, if possible, be saved, that they may, at the same time, be *impressed with a sense of our power, and our humanity*."[31] Palmer tried unsuccessfully to appeal to the rhetoric of benevolent, Christian civilization, about which most newcomers did not care. Even Palmer seemed ambivalent; in his call for a demonstration of American power, he echoed the same punitive ideas advocated by extremists. His advice to spare women and children "if possible," and a de facto instruction to kill the men, was not far removed from those of men such as Charles Drew who called for outright extermination.

These official, territorial campaigns were in addition to private militant actions by Euro-American citizens pursuing property, profit, and the extermination of Indian people who, in their opinion, inhibited their sacred birthrights to land and minerals. After the death of a miner, in August 1853, Benjamin Dowell, a Jacksonville lawyer and merchant, wrote that the "citizens mostly composed of miners . . . passed resolutions demanding the *Extermination of the Indian race*. The next day was death and destruction not only to the Shasta Indians but to any and all who were found by the Oregonians. Several Rogue River Indians were shot by whites without giving the Indians notice that the war had been commenced." Dowell also recounted the fate of an 8- to 10-year-old Indian boy, a laborer for Euro-Americans on Battle Creek, who came into town the evening two supposedly guilty Indians were hung for killing the miner. A mob seized the boy and went to hang him. Dowell claims to have intervened and proposed to hold him prisoner. "Just then," some volunteers rode into town who "had been out killing Indians" and "chanted, 'hang him! hang him!'" According to Dowell, the militia argued, " 'Our resolutions demand the Extermination of the whole indian race! Knits breeds lice!' " They hung the boy "not for any alledged crime, but for the purpose of exterminating the indian race."[32] Dowell's claim of nobility in attempting to protect the boy may be seen as self-serving and was perhaps fabricated to provide some distance between his murderous community and himself; the account comes from an 1878 interview with historian Hubert Bancroft. As a lawyer, however, Dowell made a career of pursuing remuneration claims for territorial militias and their suppliers, an effort that depended on support from Eastern members of Congress. His work would not be well served by embellishing "extermination rhetoric"; thus, his account would seem to have merit regarding the event and the public mood at the time.

Extermination of Indians for the sake of economic speculation was not limited to the immediate Jacksonville area. In the fall of 1853, an association of speculative colonials claimed land on the lower Chetco River for a town site that would serve the burgeoning mining population on the south coast. Athapaskan villagers on either side of the river mouth grudgingly acquiesced to the homesteads but refused to surrender their successful ferry business, by which they, too, profited from the gold rush. The Chetcos also refused to allow the speculators' leader, a man named Miller, to live in their village on the south bank. Indeed, Miller's proposed town-site claim encompassed that entire village. On February 15, 1854, Miller and some hirelings from nearby Crescent City, California (veterans of an 1853 massacre of Athapaskan Tolowas) slaughtered fifteen Chetcos and burned their two villages on either side of the river mouth. At a perfunctory hearing at Port Orford, Oregon, Miller offered no defense for his actions, and the surviving Chetco villagers could not legally testify because of their "race." Cleared for lack of evidence, Miller then took possession of his lower Chetco claim.[33] Desperate, some Chetcos raided settlements during the winter to survive. Although they did not kill any Euro-Americans, eleven more Chetco men "and several squaws were killed" by early May 1854.

Euro-Americans derided the Chetcos and other south coast victims as savage renegades, ignoring the manner in which the Athapaskan villagers had become homeless and desperate. Forty more "renegades" of the south-coast bands were killed in a militia raid during the Rogue River War in the spring of 1856.[34] Expeditions in 1856, 1857, and 1858 killed many more Native people of the Chetco and Pistol River bands near Port Orford during efforts to "bring in" the Indians.[35] For the 1857 "roundup," Indian Supt. James W. Nesmith contracted William Tichenor (the first land speculator on the south coast, founder of Port Orford) "for the purpose of securing and removing them to the reservation." However, the superintendent advised the commissioner of Indian affairs, "I have little hopes of his success, and see no way that the settlers in those infested neighborhoods can rid themselves of the nuisance, unless they can hit upon some mode for their extermination, a result which would occasion no regrets at this office."[36] An 1857 militia, the "Gold Beach Guard," failed to hit on such a mode, although, with the help of Tichenor, they did shoot seventeen more Chectos who reportedly tried to escape that year's roundup. That Tichenor previously placed hidden militiamen along the road at precisely the point where the Chetcos supposedly attempted their escape strongly suggests some forethought about the massacre. U.S. Army Lieutenant Shire from nearby Crescent City initially offered to help Tichenor, but, because he refused to consider extermination as an option, Tichenor sent him back to California. Tichenor later stated of his 1858 roundup, "[I] captured seventy-one . . . nine bucks with their families . . . if I had had my own way . . . I would have had to kill them." Indeed, he had told agent Nesmith that "[I] meant to quiet them, if I had to kill the last one of them."[37]

Most Native bands were small, and the massacre of one or two dozen people effectively exterminated some "tribes." On January 28, 1854, a few weeks before Miller's initial massacre of Chetcos and a short distance to the north, Euro-Americans staged a predawn surprise attack simultaneously on the three Nasomah (Miluk-Kusan speaking) villages on the lower Coquille River, shooting eighteen people indiscriminately as they fled their torched homes. The colonists claimed legitimate retribution for a damaged rope, a ricocheted shot meant for a duck but which passed near a ferry house, and a Nasomah man who reportedly uttered "God-damned Americans." When an Indian agent reached the area some months later, he indicated that two of the Nasomah villages were emptied, and only John's band (although probably a composite of survivors) of thirty-eight adults and twenty-one children occupied the third.[38] As a distinct people, the Nasomah never recovered from the massacre and dispossession soon to follow as they *had* recovered from successive disease epidemics since 1800.[39] Although some descendants now comprise part of the composite Coquille Indian Tribe, none can speak their Miluk language, and their traditions are fractured and lost in what one elder calls a "cultural black hole."[40]

Whereas colonials on the lower Coquille prepared a formal list of grievances before the massacre, many attacks on Indians occurred more randomly.[41] On the California side of the Siskiyous on May 24, 1854, colonists ambushed a band of Shastas from the Shasta Valley who had just come from a meeting with regular army captains of Forts Lane and Jones, in which they had been assured of their continued friendship and safety.[42] The excuse for the militia's attack on them was that a Shasta man, "Indian Joe," allegedly tried to rape a "white" woman. That the accused man was not present and was from a different band did not matter, nor did a history of attempts by the assailed band to maintain amicable relations with colonists around Yreka, California, and Ashland, Oregon. The headman, "Bill," had already killed his fellow Shasta headman Tipsu Tyee of the Rogue Valley, whose dwindling band was blamed for the alleged assault. "Bill" knew that colonial militias were not terribly discriminating in seeking revenge against Indians, and thus he killed Tipsu Tyee and his son to keep the peace with Euro-Americans. Still, "Bill" was among the victims on May 24. A confused and despondent Shasta elder who witnessed the massacre inquired why, if rape was such a horrific crime to Euro-Americans, did the colonists "constantly run down, sometimes by men on horse," and rape Native women. There is no record of how or if Captain J. C. Bonnycastle or any members of the Yreka militia—the self-ascribed "Squaw Hunters"—replied.[43]

Militias did not always find support for extermination among their fellow colonists. Captain Smith reported that, on February 3, 1854, nineteen miners attacked a village on southwestern Oregon's Illinois River, "in which there were but seven squaws, one boy, and two children, with the avowed intention of killing them all." After firing nine shots into a pregnant woman, killing her, the miners found themselves routed by three other women and the boy. When the miners attempted to recruit "an increased force . . . to wipe out the Indians . . . the better portion of the community interfered and delayed" them until the Indian agent arrived.[44] Still, by 1855, the ranks of the extermination-minded Euro-Americans swelled, counter-discourse waned, and no colonist did much to prevent the massacres of Native people.

In the summer of 1855, on the eve of the final Rogue River War, a group of Josephine County petitioners argued that they would lose "all invested here and if forced to leave by the hostility of the indians will be pecuniarly ruined and a mining locality capable of furnishing remunerative labor for thousands of men for years be again abandoned to be in unproductive idleness." They requested Gov. George Curry "*to expel from our midst these hostile indians and give us that security of our lives and property which is the birthright of all American citizens* [italics in original]."[45] Calls for the formation of militia companies came from all over southwestern Oregon beginning in the early summer and continuing through the autumn of 1855.[46] As John Ross put it to Governor Curry, the citizens of southern Oregon require "your aid in defending the inalienable rights of the people."[47]

The militia proponents used American settler-colonial discourse—the racialized republican language of citizenship—almost exclusively in their appeals for support and in defense of their actions. In their public appeals for funding, they consistently refer to themselves as "citizens" and the protection of their profitable pursuits as the "public welfare."[48] There were several reasons for such discourse: among them were attempts to legitimize extermination, to protect illicit land claims in Indian Country, and to receive federal remuneration for their militia activities. In the process, they voiced the underlying racialized notion of American citizenship as "white" and closed.

In Jacksonville, colonists held meetings about their "Indian problem," with voices for extermination being the strongest. As had happened a few years earlier in Coloma, extremists silenced one man who advocated for the Native people. Fearing for his life, John Beeson fled to San Francisco, then to New York, from where he published a highly critical tract against his fellow Oregonians and their advocacy of extermination.[49] The exiled Beeson claimed that "numbers of men made it a point" during the summer of 1855 "to shoot Indians wherever they could do it with safety to themselves."

In October, in a Jacksonville tavern, a local farmer and politician, James Lupton, hatched a scheme to avenge the deaths of two packers on the Siskiyou Pass and to instigate a final solution to the Indian problem. He formed a militia of local colonists, and in the predawn light of October 8, 1855, they assailed "Old Jake's" Quachis band of Shastas on Little Butte Creek in the shadows of Fort Lane and Table Rock. According to Beeson, the militia had "the avowed purpose of killing every Indian in the [Rogue River] valley, regardless of age or sex."[50] Trackers had previously determined the bands' guilt in waylaying and killing the two packers, at least to their satisfaction. The accompanying regular army officer disagreed with their assessment of the trail, particularly their conclusion that it led to Butte Creek and the Table Rock Reservation.[51] A justifiably doubtful Captain Smith refused to allow a vengeful Jacksonville militia access to the reservation to search for the suspects and ordered his federal troops to shoot the militiamen if they trespassed. Lupton's militia subsequently ended debate with a predawn massacre. They slaughtered approximately twenty-five Shasta men, women, and children. Lupton also died, despite the overwhelming odds of attacking sleeping families. A reconstituted Jacksonville militia soon killed more of this Shasta band as they tried to reach the protection of Fort Lane. Two "old squaws" were bashed to death with clubs, and "a child . . . was taken by the heels and its brains dashed out against a tree." According to General Wool, militias killed eighty "friendly Indians" to ignite the warfare of 1855–56 in southwestern Oregon;

others put the figure at 106. One volunteer stated that, although extermination made him feel bad, "the understanding was that [the Indians] were all to be killed. So we did the work."[52]

The final so-called Rogue River War had begun. "Colonel" William J. Martin of the territorial militia soon issued the following extermination order to the Oregon volunteer companies: "In chastising the enemy, you use your own discretion, provided you take no prisoners."[53] Another militia commander advised that "Treaties effected with powder and ball, and no other, *is the motto*."[54] In early November, Gen. John Wool reported to his superiors that "[i]n Rogue River valley the threats of the whites to commence a war of extermination against the friendly Indians on the reserve, and in the vicinity of Fort Lane, have been put into execution, despite the efforts of the officers of that post to prevent it."[55] On October 9, 1855, the day after the massacre on Little Butte Creek, many of the Indians remaining on the reservation fled to the protection of the rugged canyon country of the Coast Range Mountains. Agent Samuel Culver had earlier permitted some bands to leave the disease-ridden and poorly supplied reservation because the death rate had soared to 20 percent in the first year.[56] Native attempts to survive and remain sovereigns in their homelands and the militias' attempts to either kill or capture them continued for ten months into the early summer of 1856.

A self-fulfilling prophecy, the colonists had finally pushed the Native peoples into the extremely violent, widespread "race war" that they had forecast for years.[57] Subsequent massacres drove neutral bands into the conflict. At an Umpqua camp on the Arrington Ranch, ten Euro-Americans annihilated a camp of "old men, women, and children" while the men were hunting in the nearby Olalla Hills. The band had previously maintained amicable relations with the newcomers, some Umpquas labored on local farms, they regularly hung about the hotel, and some intermarriages occurred. The hunters, apprised of the Olalla Massacre by a boy who miraculously escaped, subsequently joined the warring bands along the lower Rogue River.[58] Such examples of Native peoples' traveling to assist in the fight against the colonials added fuel to the speculations regarding a pan-Indian threat.

Pan-Indian Militancy in *Illahee*

Indeed, a principal justification for the war by the colonists was defense against a perceived pan-Indian confederacy, which threatened extermination of the "whites." Thus, the colonialists' genocidal efforts supposedly mirrored Native intent and were thus morally defensible.[59] Not all "whites" were of a common mind regarding the pan-Indian threat. George Roberts, an English-man and administrator of the HBC's Puget Sound Agricultural Association, gruffly dismissed the popular beliefs of a pan-Indian threat as so much "public clamour." Roberts insisted that the notion of an inevitable race war was part of what he called an "earth hunger" that was born of an ignorant, nationalist belief in "Manifest Destiny" that was being carried out by "ruffians," "squat-ters," and the "vilest of the vile . . . hardy pioneers indeed." He was equally critical of the leadership among the Americans. He expressed his astonish-ment on hearing Joseph Lane, Oregon's preeminent early politician, "remark 'damn them [Indians], it would do my soul good to be after them.'"[60] The con-trast between Anglo and American interpretations of Indian behavior and intent had been obvious since the early 1840s. Henry Perkins of The Dalles mission had been convinced as early as 1843 that the Wascopam "Indians are endeavoring to form a general coalition for the purpose of destroying all the Boston people: that it is not good to kill a part of them, and leave the rest, but that every one of them must be destroyed."[61] Roberts, McLoughlin, and other HBC officials regularly discounted such beliefs, leading some American officials by the 1850s to portray the British as being part of the Indian con-spiracy.[62] "Earth hunger" certainly contributed to the Euro-American vision, but what were they witnessing among the Indians that was construed as a genocidal conspiracy?

Since the 1870s, historians of southwestern Oregon have focused mainly on American military maneuvers and political disputes over economic spec-ulation, but we are not much closer to understanding the Indians' actions after all this time: they have remained bit players in a nationalist, political drama. Historian E. A. Schwartz cast Native war efforts in 1855–56 as im-promptu defensive actions and dismissed the idea that any forethought was involved among Indian peoples. Similarly, he concluded that no ties existed among the bands of southern Oregon, Puget Sound, and the Columbia Pla-teau. Although the violent outbreaks all occurred nearly simultaneously in 1855 and concerned resource control, reservations, and increasing incidents of interracial violence, he considered them unrelated types of Indian war.[63] As well, he pointed to an intra-Indian conflict among the Shastas to demon-strate that Native wars were "formalized and almost benign" and not, in the least, extermination-minded.[64]

However, the action described seems to have been a settlement dance be-tween two Shasta bands, not a war—an elaborate ceremony common in the Oregon-California borderlands. The nature of Indian warfare was complex. Settlement dances did not always prevent further conflict; indeed, in their martial posturing and taunting they could instigate violence. As well, these ceremonies were distinct from horse and slave raids—in which all men were sometimes killed and villages exterminated— and should not be taken as the only representation of Indian warfare.[65] To do so is to give in to a well-intentioned but inaccurate interpretation of conflict among Native peoples and to inhibit a historical understanding of their actions in the colonial wars with Euro-Americans.

The Native peoples of the Columbia Plateau have received more scholarly attention, and the histories reflect greater imagination. In particular, Christopher Miller has portrayed the Native combatants as millenarians striving toward a revitalized world that was prophesized decades earlier, and which clashed with another millenarian movement, that of the Second Great Awakening and Manifest Destiny. Thus Miller, like Elizabeth Vibert, argues for a very early beginning to a concerted prophet movement on the Plateau.[66] Recently, however, anthropologist Theodore Stern debunked this cosmological thesis, arguing that the Plateau millenarian movement had yet to begin and would not reach maturity until the reservation era under Smohalla and the Dreamer Cult. The American millenarian movement was essentially over and in its post, or fulfillment, stage.[67] Instead, Stern explained the Plateau violence and the apparent Indian alliances through practical experiences, traditional spiritualities, and kinship ties that he compiled with the aid of Indians from the Umatilla Reservation in eastern Oregon. Furthermore, Stern did not find evidence of a larger Indian confederation in the Oregon Country.

Indeed, there was no grand confederacy of tribes from northern California to British Columbia, as claimed by nervous newcomers. In fact, there were no tribes, per the definition of a *tribe* as a coherent body politic, to form such a confederacy. Rather, the vast region was inhabited by groups of linguistically and culturally diverse peoples who were connected to other groups by kinship. Kinship ties largely shaped many forms of interaction such as trading, raiding, and distributing land and resources. This complex web of multilingual and multiethnic loyalties and identities inhibited a political confederacy, which relies on the organization of centralized authorities.[68] *Illahee* was simply too fragmented at the time.

As well, the unifying notion of race as understood by nineteenth-century Euro-Americans was not part of Native identities or politics. Certainly, Indians could and did distinguish between Natives and non-Natives, but the concept of race, as in the antebellum notion of "race war," was entirely foreign. American racial thinking in the 1850s was the product of two and a half centuries of a particular history of numerous, contingent power relations, which the various Native peoples of the Pacific Northwest obviously did not share.[69] White-male-supremacist notions of Manifest Destiny helped to define racial distinctions and to fuel Euro-American beliefs in the inevitability of race war, a clash between superior and inferior peoples. Granted, many Indian people who spoke the trade language Chinook Jargon used the term *siwash* quite freely to indicate a Native person. Few if any Indians, however, would have been aware that the word derived from *savage* (more properly, the French *sauvage*), or that Euro-Americans considered savages to be the lowest form of human being, or that Western thought had conceived of a Great Chain of Being, or Evolution. More commonly, Indians such as the multiethnic Wascopam used the jargon word *Tillicum,* or people, to distinguish themselves from slaves or other Native groups with whom they felt little affinity.[70]

The distinction Indians often made among whites throughout the Oregon Country—King Georges (British HBC men) and Bostons (Euro-Americans)—was presented to them by competing traders and was not in any sense racial. Other Native terms reflected the place Euro-Americans took in Native historical experience. The Modocs experienced devastating raids from the Columbia River peoples (*Yámakni* or north people) during the 1830s. The term *Yámakni* conferred a sense of ambivalence and trepidation as well as a cardinal direction. Later, the Modocs called Euro-American colonists *Yámakni Bóshtin*, probably for their similarly destructive presence, in addition to *Oregínkni* for the colonials' claimed identity, "Oregonians."[71] As noted in the previous chapter, Euro-Americans who raped or otherwise abandoned Native wives and mixed-blood children earned the name "moving people" on the south coast. Native terms for and considerations of the colonists were grounded in recent historical experiences and were often highly localized rather than sweepingly racial.

Simply put, racialization was a Western construction, not one that the Native peoples would easily have grasped, let alone employed in an attempt at unification.[72] Racial views helped justify extermination of Indians among Euro-Americans, but Indians had no such intellectual foundation. A union against "whites" would have to be based on a different set of intellectual beliefs such as defense of home or *Illahee.* In other words, Euro-Americans did not deserve death because of supposed natural, innate differences or a quasi-religious rationale, but because they threatened to drive all Native peoples from their homes. Along these lines, I do give some credence to Euro-American observations of pan-Indian efforts. They witnessed the complex relations among the Indians and interpreted them in ways that were advantageous and made sense for colonization; Euro-Americans reached rational, if inaccurate, conclusions such as the threat of a grand alliance.[73] The question becomes: What were Euro-Americans observing in *Illahee*?

Native kinship relations had been greatly expanded from their local networks of the early fur trade to encompass huge distances by the 1850s. Trade goods, slaves, and knowledge that would have passed slowly from one neighboring group to another now passed directly among groups that had formerly been separated by long distances and by Native intermediaries such as bands of Kalapuyas and Molalas. The deaths of so many Native peoples on the lower Columbia River and the lower Willamette Valley left a vacuum, which horse-riding Sahaptian peoples commonly called Klikitat Indians filled. As early as the 1830s, autonomous bands of Klikitats traveled from their homelands north of the lower and middle Columbia River to trade and raid among the Native peoples of the Willamette Valley and southern Oregon. By the 1840s, Klikitats outnumbered indigenous Kalapuyas and established relations with the Indians of southwestern Oregon, some settling in the Umpqua Valley. At the same time, Klamaths from south-central Oregon increasingly traveled to Oregon City and The Dalles on the Columbia River, both reflecting ties with peoples of these areas and facilitating further ties. By the 1850s, Shasta bands and possibly others from the Rogue River Valley and Siskiyou Mountains also had established relations with Native groups on the Columbia Plateau. The latter is especially notable because such people had formerly been only in the northern area as slaves of the Chinookan and Sahaptian peoples. Southern Oregon Natives had established more equitable relations through intermarriage and other forms of exchange.[74]

One observer noted that many of the Cayuse's 100 warriors in 1853 were, in fact, Shasta Indians.[75] Although he called them slaves, it is important to note that the Cayuse did not practice chattel slavery, but the Shasta men likely had lower status. Kinship ties among the Plateau peoples were long-standing and, at least by the 1840s, stretched across the Cascades from the Yakamas to the Nisquallys in the Puget Sound region. Together, I think it is quite clear that the Native peoples had extended their kinship networks throughout Oregon Territory by midcentury, although such relations hardly produced a pan-Indian alliance or confederacy. Instead, the Indians maintained lines of communication and had a roughly common cause of preserving their homelands.[76]

Euro-Americans often became unnerved when diverse bands of Indians gathered for trade fairs or ceremonies, or to settle disputes at locales such as The Dalles on the Columbia River, the Grande Ronde Valley on the Plateau,

Yainax Butte on the Klamath Basin, and Horse Creek on the upper Klamath River. These larger meetings were in addition to the much more frequent small-scale gatherings that had developed throughout the region. Although nearly all such gatherings had nothing directly to do with Euro-Americans, there is evidence that some meetings were held expressly to discuss the American colonization.

To illustrate, we can look at two famous examples from 1854 at Horse Creek and in the Grande Ronde Valley. In both cases, Native headmen subsequently informed Euro-Americans that the purpose was to determine a unified Native response to encroachments by emigrants, settlers, and miners as well as the looming possibility of removal and reservations.[77] In both cases, individual headmen reportedly argued for a regional pan-Indian effort to drive out the Euro-Americans and to seize their lands, and some called for their deaths or enslavement. Neither council produced such an alliance or an offensive—which is not surprising, given the extreme and unprecedented nature of such a union and the decentralized nature of Native politics and society.

Nevertheless, many of the hostilities that occurred in 1854 and 1855 as well as the final Rogue River War in late 1855 and 1856 featured a "combination of tribes," as Euro-American observers typically put it. Such combinations reflected kinship ties among supposedly distinct tribes as well as an outlet for militant individuals. The large councils of 1854 at Grande Ronde and Horse Creek allowed like-minded men to come together, even as the majority apparently rejected the larger plan of unification. Local bands had enough common experiences with troublesome emigrants, farmers, and miners for some individuals to become convinced of the necessity to fight.

Politics of Unity in *Illahee*

Euro-American colonization thrust a complex, political choice on Native peoples between fighting, best done united, and accommodation, best done separately on the local level. The numerous murders of Native headmen in the mid-1850s demonstrate the internal conflict tearing apart *Illahee*. The killing of Tipsu Tyee and his sons by "Bill's" band of Shastas is illustrative. As well, a Takelma headman, who worked diligently to maintain the peace between his people and the miners of the Jacksonville district, was gunned down, apparently for his resistance to fighting and, according to the Indian agent, to spark an Indian alliance.[78] On the coast, Lottie Evanoff, a Coos consultant for John Harrington, stated that this was a time when "[i]t seemed that every Ind[ian] chief [would] get murdered." Both her paternal and maternal grandfathers were killed, the first for his accommodative stance by a man who "wanted to kill off the White people awful bad. He foresaw the disappearance of the Ind[ian]s." Her second grandfather was killed for his militant stance by a group of men from his own village because "[h]e did not want to make friends with the white people."[79]

Evanoff's use of prophecy narrative indicates the continuity of communicating indigenous knowledge through an empowering framework. I will return to this issue of prophecy and its relation to Native unity later. First, however, I will briefly examine the underlying issue of violence among Indian peoples, a history that helps us understand Native divisions that hampered unity efforts in the 1850s.

As discussed earlier, slave raids by Columbia River peoples had spread south with the fur trade, reaching the Klamath Basin and the Rogue Valley, at least, by the 1820s. The Klamaths were able to transcend the position of raid victim within a decade. They succeeded in part because the Plateau Sahaptian peoples also desired cattle, and, rather than becoming dependent on the HBC, they sought the British company's source: John Sutter's colony in the Sacramento Valley in Alta California.[80] Centrally located, the Klamath Basin was a much-needed rest and supply point between the Plateau and the Sacramento. More importantly, the Klamaths learned to be the raiders instead of the raided, and Yainax Butte, within their domain, became an important Native trading site. Between 1842 and 1844, colonists noted slave-trade interactions between the Klamaths and Columbia River peoples, both in the Klamath Basin and around the settlements on the lower Willamette and The Dalles. Through this trade, the Klamaths obtained horses and guns, and thus they gained the advantage over their southern neighbors, such as the Native peoples of the Rogue and Pitt River valleys in the southwest Oregon–northern California borderland.[81]

As evidenced by Ogden's 1826–27 fur-expedition journal, this warfare was well under way by the late 1820s.[82] Because the Shoshone raids in the Oregon Country began in the late eighteenth century, the Klamaths had some prior experience—which may explain how they were able to turn the tables so quickly after the Sahaptian raids began. The aging warrior Chiloquin lumped all the conflicts together, saying: "[t]hose wars lasted a great many years. We found we could make money by war, for we sold the provisions and property captured for horses and other things we needed. . . . We made war because we made money by it and we rather got to like it anyhow."[83] Slave raids from the Klamath Basin and Klikitat raids from the Willamette Valley struck the

Takelma, Shasta, and Athapaskan peoples of southwestern Oregon particularly hard. Like the Klamaths, the Native people of the Rogue River region sought a better position and began raids of their own, forming temporary alliances across ethnic lines for security and to prosper through the slave trade.[84] By the mid-1840s, some headmen in southwestern Oregon sold their own people to the Klikitats. According to Native informants, the unfortunate individuals were "poor" who had lost their status through debts, and many were likely "bastard" children of "unpurchased" mothers.[85] Western colonization, as we have seen, had several indirect effects through the introduction of horses, cattle, guns, and the fur trade, as well as demographic pressures created by disease epidemics.

Colonization also directly caused the intra-Native raiding. David Hill (*Wawa'liks*), a "subchief" of the Klamath Lake band, evidenced this fact in his description of two of the three slave raids in which he was personally involved to linguist Albert Gatschet. He boasted of "the Lake tribe's" predominance over other southern Oregon Natives. However, the impetus for the raids in which he was involved was not Klamath but Euro-American. Regarding the first raid, he did not elaborate beyond mentioning that a Euro-American aided the raid on a band of Achumawi, or Pitt Rivers. In the second, however, he explicitly claimed that the raid began with an ox feast held by a Euro-American who "had become angry at the Pit Rivers." In a footnote, Gatschet explained that the instigator was a farmer on Lost River who, with other local colonists, wanted the Achomawis punished for an earlier attack on "whites."[86]

Euro-Americans were not the only people on the scene influencing political decisions. Metis and eastern Indians who had worked for the fur companies, government expeditions, and overland parties lived throughout Oregon Territory in the 1850s. The role of such individuals on the Plateau has been well documented, particularly that of Tom Hill and Joe Gray, Delaware and Iroquois, respectively, who explained American frontier history and Iroquois anticolonial tactics to Cayuse and Nez Perce audiences.[87] In southwestern Oregon, several Metis had established themselves near the mouth of the Rogue River. One, a man named Enos, had come to the region as a guide for the Wilkes Expedition in 1841. He apparently took an active role in joining coastal bands with interior Indians in the winter and spring of 1856. Taking advantage of his mixed-blood status to broker relations between colonists and indigenes, Enos had earlier convinced Euro-Americans that they had nothing to fear from the coastal bands. Euro-Americans subsequently hanged him for that service.[88]

The diverse Native peoples of southwestern Oregon never coalesced into a confederacy, contrary to incendiary and fearful reports.[89] Throughout the winter and early spring, most Indians remained in small bands of six to twenty individuals, surviving as best they could.[90] The long-established norm of Native life in the region was to occupy sedentary winter villages appropriately stored with harvests of roots, nuts, berries, smoked meats, salmon, and eels.[91] Roaming in the stormy winter of the Coast Range took its toll and contributed to the late spring–early summer surrender of almost all the Indians who managed to survive the elements and the militias. Many Native people in the region did their best to stay out of the fighting by refusing to leave the reservation or seeking refuge from federal agents and local settlers with whom they had highly localized friendly relations. Others, however, chose to fight, burning a swath of Euro-American structures throughout the Rogue River Valley, along the river's course, and torching Prattsville (now Gold Beach) at the mouth. They burned Euro-American ranches and killed entire families along the middle and lower Rogue River, temporarily clearing the area of most colonists. The violence was not random. Some ranches and colonists (mostly Metis) were spared because of previously peaceful relations, whereas others, such as Benjamin Wright, notorious for earlier massacres of Indians and abuse of women, was beheaded and his scalp ceremoniously danced over.[92]

According to combat reports and the eventual bureaucratic sorting of Indians for removal and confinement, the fighting had attracted Native people from well beyond the local villages. One local resident and witness to the burning of Prattsville noted the presence of "many strange Indians" taking part in the combat, and "Colonel" Drew of the volunteers claimed the participation of Klamaths.[93] The "Klamaths" probably referred to Shastas from northern California's Klamath River, as the Klamaths-proper never joined the conflict. Also, although many people fought as bands in small groups of about twenty, Tecumtum ("Elk Killer"), commonly known to Euro-Americans as "Old John," led a substantial interethnic force through the spring of 1856. Some reports claimed that he had hundreds of men.[94] Originally from Shasta Valley, California, and with kinship ties to the headwaters of the Applegate River (a tributary of the Rogue River) in Oregon, Tecumtum was well positioned to attract widespread allegiance. Tecumtum also had established relations with warring bands on the Columbia Plateau through his son-in-law, and he boasted of his intelligence regarding the activities of militias throughout Oregon and Washington territories.[95] The Metis Enos reportedly met with Tecumtum in the early winter of 1856 and coordinated efforts with coastal bands, also buttressed by relatives from across the California border, in the spring.[96]

Polaklie Illahee

Thus far, I have presented the Indian unity, as limited as it was, in political and kinship terms. The current literature on Indian alliances, such as the work of David Edmunds and Gregory Dowd, on Eastern, anticolonial movements suggests that a spiritual component was likely.[97] However, extensive interethnic connection through spirituality meant that Illahee would not have needed a new prophetic movement, but two features of the mid-1850s suggest that a new movement had emerged. In 1854, Leschi, a Nisqually man from the Puget Sound region, ventured hundreds of miles south to the Table Rock Reservation and surrounding environs in southern Oregon, telling of a vision. The vision was of a land of darkness, or *Polaklie Illahee* in Chinook Jargon, where Euro-Americans were going to take all the Indians, where the sun never shone, and where they would be damned to live out their days in a cold, dark, barren world. *Polaklie illahee* was the spiritual antipode of *nesika illahee*: a place of complete alienation where all Indians would be forced to reside, yet no Indian could live.[98] The prophecy spoke to the profound fear of forcible removal and relocation that spread through Indian Country west of the Cascade Mountains. It arose directly from the early dispossession and reservation experiences of western Washington, western Oregon, and perhaps northern California.

Indeed, early Seattle resident Dr. William Tolmie recalled that Leschi "shared at this time in the dread generally entertained by the Puget Sound Indians that the buying of their lands was a prelude to shipping them off in steamers to an imaginary dark and sunless country." Tolmie added that "the Indian agents of that day will remember how widespread and universal that apprehension was—how an Indian, seemingly convinced of its absurdity, would be back in a few days, as much alarmed as ever."[99] At the Table Rock reserve in southern Oregon, one fifth of the people had died in the first winter, and Native peoples throughout the Oregon Country were understandably distraught by the prospects of removal and confinement.[100] Likely, the Nisqually vision was well received by many among the Table Rock residents. That Leschi was from a distant country would not likely have rendered his message as foreign or alien. The Klamath seer and orator Cumutni ("living in a cave") reportedly consulted with many Native visitors who traveled as far as 200 miles to meet with him before his death in 1866.[101] A generation earlier, the peripatetic Kauxima-nupika offered another compelling example. Leschi's ethnicity would not have inhibited the spread of his message, but was Leschi a prophet of a militant nativist movement?

Although Indian historians have made important steps in the direction of recognizing the roles of indigenous worldviews, or "ethno-intellectual history," as Christopher Miller termed it, we should be careful not to look too hard for general Indian features such as prophet or revitalization movements.[102] The ethno-intellectual tradition should include room for Indians as being capable of making political decisions within preexisting, if badly tattered, relations even during periods of cataclysmic upheaval. As Michael Dorris, the Modoc novelist, chastised in Calvin Martin's *The American Indian and the Problem of History* (Oxford, 1987), Indians, as human beings, were quite capable of empiricism, and were not bound by "mysticism." Dorris attributes the insistence on mystical Indians to "the long standing tendency . . . to regard Indians as so 'Other,' so fundamentally and profoundly different, that [Europeans and Euro-Americans] fail to extend to native peoples certain traits commonly regarded as human."[103]

In line with Dorris's argument, and regarding the Columbia Plateau, I judge that Stern's version of the alliance achieved through family connections and practical, political decisions to be more viable than the workings of a millenarian movement. Similarly, the hostile "banditti" of the Puget Sound who attacked Seattle in 1856 can similarly be explained through kinship ties between the Nisquallys and the Yakamas as well as coercive threats from bands already at war with U.S. citizens.[104] The *Polaklie Illahee* vision was likely coded spiritually by the legitimacy accorded to prophetic dreams throughout much of the Native world and, perhaps, reflected the inherent problems of communicating through Chinook Jargon as well. The trade language seems to have lacked the nuances of a formal language and made literal translations of abstract concepts—such as removal and confinement—difficult. A contemporary governmental investigator offered a fairly accurate description, despite his racist phrasing, when he explained that "[i]t may readily be supposed that a rude and ignorant people, naturally prone to superstition, were not slow in giving credence to these fearful stories. Each tribe had its grievance from the north to the south. Common interest bound them in their compact against a common enemy."[105] Earlier, in 1853, Father Panderoy and Major Alvord at The Dalles had warned of the Wascopam and Plateau Indians' beginning to see a common cause and an effort "to unite the hearts of Indians . . . [because] the Americans are going to take [all] their lands."[106] Tecumtum in southwestern Oregon claimed a connection to these groups, and numerous south-coast Native peoples had joined him in an effort to re-claim their homes.[107] Regardless, their relations fall far short of a pantribal alliance, and *Polaklie Illahee* did not represent an underlying militant nativist movement.

Moreover, in 1855–56, the Native peoples certainly did not instigate the colonial "race wars." Yet, the manner in which so many bands came together and concerted their efforts so quickly following the attack on the Table Rock Reservation, as well as their possession of weaponry, supposedly banned to them previously, strongly suggests a good deal of contingency planning.[108] The unity that suggested an intertribal alliance to Euro-American observers and the numerous limitations that reduced the movement's effectiveness were shaped by the individual and collective Native historical experiences with co-lonialism in Oregon Territory. In 1855, confronted daily by Euro-Americans and the changes that they brought, the Native peoples were forced to make a decision—unite and fight or keep the peace and work toward other solutions. Some unity existed across cultural, linguistic, and geographic zones, but it was limited and appears to have been strictly defensive and mostly devoid of the extermination goal. The connections among the combative Indians in southern Oregon, the Columbia Plateau, and Puget Sound were tenuous and never approached the scope of a grand tribal alliance. Indeed, within each subregion, not all bands participated. Kinship relations could and most often did work in favor of settlement rather than war, but we do need to consider the more militant side as well in order to understand the complex resistance to colonialism in the Pacific Northwest. The limited Indian responses suc-ceeded only in stalling the volunteer militia campaigns, an effort aided by Oregon's winter storms that track from the Gulf of Alaska each season and allowed time for the U.S. Army to intervene. General Wool unequivocally viewed extermination as a colonial goal, not a Native one.

CHAPTER EIGHT

Extermination and Empire

Money, Politics, and the Oregon Wars, 1855–1856

In the early spring of 1856, the regular army ended the conflict, and, once again, the joint action by Oregon Territory and the United States produced considerable acrimony between federals and colonials. By early February 1856 it was obvious that the Oregon militias could not finish what they had begun, and even Charles Drew, a principal architect of the extermination efforts, was among eighty-one Jacksonville men to sign a petition begging General Wool to enter the fray. They, of course, blamed the "Barbarous Indians" who have "murdered whole families," "pillaged and burned," and kept the people from trading, mining, and tilling. The volunteers were "wholly inadequate . . . [poorly] organized, and though brave, are undisciplined."[1] Wool blamed the colonists for the widespread bloodshed in Oregon and Washington territories but promised troops to end it after the winter, and he made his stance against extermination clear. "Whilst I was in Oregon, it was reported to me, that many citizens, with a due proportion of volunteers, and two newspapers, advocated the extermination of the Indians." "This principle," he continued, "has been acted on in several instances without discriminating between enemies and friends, which has been the cause, in Southern Oregon, of sacrificing many innocent and worthy citizens, as in the case of Major Lupton and his party, (volunteers) who killed 25 Indians, eighteen of whom were women and children." Yet, he pledged federal forces to end the conflict.

Similarly, Wool advised Gov. Isaac Stevens of Washington Territory that he would close the war on the Columbia Plateau after the winter, "provided the extermination of the Indians, which I do not approve, is not determined on, and private war prevented, and the volunteers withdrawn from the Walla Walla country."[2] Stevens was of a different mind: "The beautiful Walla Walla can never be permitted to remain an uncultivated waste. It wants the flocks and herds of the Willamette. We have gold mines there. The treasure of these must be sought and obtained." Stevens concluded with a call for Wool's dismissal.[3] Similarly, the Oregon press lashed out, condemning the useless "brass buttons" of the regular army, and added many inflammatory, genocidal statements such as: "These Indians must be whipped, aye, they must be *exterminated* [italics in original], or there will be no peace or safety to any part or portion of the country."[4] The Oregon legislature censured Wool and dispatched a memorial to President Franklin Pierce requesting his removal from the office of commander of the Pacific Department.[5]

Wool had a different vision of the Rogue River War than the extermination-minded colonials: the mission was to "bring in" the Indians, protect them from the colonists, and remove them to the new Coast and Grand Ronde Reservations. His plan was to use three forces to converge on the lower Rogue River where most Indians had fled, "ferreting out . . . hostile bands" and establishing a peace council with the regions' headmen at Oak Flat.[6] This effort was mostly successful. In March 1856, Col. Robert Buchanon led a small regular army force to reinforce Smith's sole company of fifty dragoons and several dozen infantry. With the help of the militias and "friendly Indians" (those who fought colonialism with diplomacy and accommodation), he "rounded-up" most of the Native bands by early summer 1856. The militias' methods infuriated Buchanon, as reported by one of his captains in May; he reported to the colonel that the volunteers had sent "two squaws . . . to say if the Indians wanted peace they must send in the head of Enos. Col[onel was] in a rage at it."[7] The brutality of the request undermined the army's efforts.

However, although the regular army intended a forced removal strategy rather than one of extermination, green recruits became enraged by a "treacherous attack" against Captain Smith's unit, and retributive massacres resulted.[8] Capt. Edward Ord, who commanded a company of regulars, noted "that I am glad I didnt go down [to an Athapaskan village] for I should have attacked before day light and many women & children would have been killed. [F]or since the treacherous attack on Captain Smiths command [it is] difficult to show any quarter, the men are disposed to kill all."[9] As an imperial force charged with establishing and maintaining order in the Far West, the federal army did not initially have the same murderous intentions as the colonial militias. Oregon colonials advocated extermination of the Indians out of fear, vengeance, and greed, although they rendered it the public welfare. Wool's federals only slowly adopted the brutal tactics of mass slaughter and, then, only on their own terms of battlefield vengeance and never as outright policy. The U.S. Army certainly perpetuated several grotesque massacres of Native Americans. Yet, these massacres mostly occurred after the Civil War, when President Ulysses Grant backed a more powerful Army of the West to affect his ironically named "Peace Policy," and careerist army officers tried to wrest control of reservations from civilian administrators. Pre–Civil War massacres by federal troops tended to be singular instances of vengeance against noncombatants for embarrassing battlefield losses, such as the so-called Grattan Massacre in 1854.[10] In Oregon, during the Rogue River War, the army's "self-control" wavered under similar pressure.

Indeed, in practice, the combined force of regulars and volunteer militias approached the war similarly, attacking and torching Native villages regardless of evidence of any offense by the occupants: all Indians outside the temporary refugee camps on the lower Rogue River were fair game. Many of the coastal peoples probably did not know that their particular bands were at war with the Americans until they were attacked and rounded up. Through the late spring and early summer, hundreds of weak, sick, and hungry Indians, including those who had fled the Table Rock Reservation and those who had not yet experienced the horrific conditions of reservation life, turned themselves in to the federal authorities. The temporary camps grew daily with despondent Native refugees, and the regular army was careful to put its own troops in charge of guarding the "Rogues," not trusting the volunteer militias with this delicate task.[11] Career military man Captain Ord could barely contain his emotions witnessing the human misery surrounding him daily, as local Native villagers lost their homes, possessions, and family members despite having successfully removed the colonists from the lower Rogue River.[12] He complained to his diary that he could not sleep because of "the never ending melancholy wail of the Squaws in mourning from the officers tents" and the "old squaws . . . a howling the medicine song over sick babes." As well, the hills resounded nightly with the solemn rhythms of dancing and chanting men in the refugee camps who reached, perhaps, for some unattainable power at this excruciating time of loss.[13]

The Native peoples of southwestern Oregon were "removed" to a swath of land on the central coast (its rugged topography made it temporarily undesirable to most Euro-Americans and seemingly a natural barrier to escape) and the nearby Grand Ronde Reservation created for the Willamette Valley tribes.[14] The regular army had to detach a force to escort the Indians through the Umpqua and upper Willamette Valley settlements after citizens there had threatened to kill the surviving "Rogues" from the southwestern interior.[15] The army also established Fort Umpqua at the southern end of the Coast

Reservation to keep Indians from trying to return home and to protect them from vengeful militias. The colonists of nearby Empire City on Coos Bay announced their intention to kill any Native people who left the reserve, including those granted permission by Agent E. P. Drew to gather salmon for the winter.[16]

As mentioned earlier, subsequent militia endeavors such as the "Gold Beach Guard" and Tichenor's "round-ups" of Indians from the Chetco and Pistol rivers continued intermittently on the south coast through 1858 to rid the area of bands still "infesting" the south coast hills. Similarly, in the Rogue River Valley, in January 1857, colonists around Jacksonville attacked a small band of "Rogues" who had avoided the removals of the previous spring and summer. The militia killed all ten men and brought the sixty to sixty-five women and children to Jacksonville, where they remained in undisclosed conditions until their May 1857 removal to Grand Ronde.[17] The gross disparity in the band's sex ratio and the fate of the men suggest the powerful effect of the militias' hunting of Indian men during the 1850s in southwestern Oregon. A military post was erected in 1864 on the Klamath Basin, partly to keep the Rogue Valley environs clear of Indians from the east. The colonists of southwestern Oregon had not fought the Rogue River War, so Klamaths, Modocs, and Northern Paiutes could move into the region recently cleansed of the "Rogues," although exceptions for individual women continued.[18] An 1865 roundup at Kanaka Flats outside of Jacksonville included members, mostly women, of several Native ethnicities, including banished "Rogue" bands.[19] Similarly, on the coast, miners and loggers continued to harbor Native "wives," as the manual and sexual labors of Native women continued to be in demand in the remote camps.[20]

For Native women, marriage to or, more commonly, cohabitation with Euro-American men was a means of remaining in their homelands and avoiding the depredations of the reservations. Soldiers continued the rape and abuse of Native women that had been perpetrated by colonials before removal of the Indians.[21] In vain, headmen complained to a federal investigator about the violence against Native women as well as the deplorable conditions on the reservations, stating that it was not war but the peace that was killing their people.[22] Coquille Susan Ned explained the "choice" she faced: "sometimes when you are cold and hungry [on the reservation] you change your mind" and accept a Euro-American husband as a means of escape and survival.[23]

Some women who took that route were able to aid others who otherwise escaped from the reservations. Susan Adulsah Wasson, who married a

Scottish-Canadian, illegally housed her aged mother Gisgiu, who had miraculously evaded the soldiers and made her way down the rugged coastline from the Yachats Agency to her daughter's house on the South Slough of Coos Bay. She traveled at night, swimming the treacherous currents around the headlands and across river mouths. As a tribal storyteller, Gisgiu helped preserve the little that remains of Coquille oral history by relating many legends and tales to her children and grandchildren before her death in 1894. She also charged her fourth grandson with getting the tribal lands back. He was defeated by twentieth-century bureaucracy and racism, but successive generations of Wassons and their Coos-Coquille relatives have worked to keep his charge alive.[24] Susan Wasson was one of the nonreservation Coquilles who eventually claimed an allotment under section four of the Dawes Act. Her allotment, patented in 1895, was 160 acres of land adjacent to her "white" husband George's claim on the South Slough. Several Native relatives moved onto the allotment, as did the Wassons after George lost his land in a failed logging venture. Other Coquille Indians cited Susan Wasson as their relative in affidavits for allotments in the early 1900s and, ironically, for termination claims in 1954.[25] Following the Rogue River War and forced removal, Native peoples struggled to create new lives on the multiethnic reservations and some, mostly women, as minorities within colonial communities in their former homelands.

The Native peoples of southwestern Oregon joined the peoples of the Willamette Valley and lower Columbia River environs at the new Grand Ronde and Siletz reservations. Between March 1854 and January 1855, Indian Supt. Joel Palmer had affected treaties containing the removal clauses favored by Euro-Americans, which Dart had earlier failed to produce in 1851. Palmer took an effective tack of approaching the largest band (other than the Klikitats, who were ignored by the treaty commission), the Tualatin Kalapuyas, who reluctantly, but understandably, given the public mood among Euro-Americans, ceded their homeland.[26] The numerous smaller bands followed suit. The actual removal of the Willamette Indians did not occur until the outbreak of war to the north and south in October 1855, when the Euro-Americans' extermination cries reached a fevered pitch. The Willamette Indians did not resist, although some individuals obtained official permission to continue working as laborers on the farms and in the towns that had been their homelands twenty years earlier.[27] Even doing so could be dangerous, as evidenced by the citizens of Yamhill County, who resolved in the spring of 1856 that all off-reservation Indians "shall be declared enemies" and assumed to be in communication with the "hostiles."[28]

For citizens of Oregon Territory, the political struggle over the cause of the war was just beginning: Was it a speculative scheme of "private war" as charged by Wool and other critics? Money certainly was involved. The colonial warfare of 1855–56 in southwestern Oregon, the Puget Sound area, and the Yakama Country on the Columbia Plateau followed the arrival of monies from the national treasury, reimbursing militia expenses from the Cayuse War and the earlier, limited Rogue River War of 1853. As well, Drew and Ross—masterminds of the Walker Expedition to the Klamath Basin—were in the midst of trying to convince Governor Curry to make good on former Governor Davis's promise to obtain remuneration for their 1854 militia efforts. The best place to begin sorting out the supposed speculation schemes and conspiracies is with the political climate of the Oregon Territory, which produced the original accusations of speculation.

The control of Oregon territorial politics was at stake, with an old-line Democratic establishment known as the "Salem Clique" desperately trying to hold out against insurgents, particularly those from burgeoning Jacksonville in southwest Oregon. Although historian Rodman Paul dismissed the area as a "retarded subregion" of the California Gold Rush, the area was growing politically and economically powerful.[29] Indeed, Drew, Ross, and several of their compatriots—Whigs, disaffected Democrats, and Know-Nothings—were part of simultaneous movements to overcome the Salem Clique's stranglehold on territorial government and, more radically, to secede from Oregon. Their secession scheme called for stalling Oregon's statehood until southwestern Oregon and northern California were allowed to form a new territory as Washington had done the year before in 1853.[30] The new territory would remove substantial numbers of voters (necessary for statehood), the most mineral-laden portion of Oregon, and the remaining "unsettled" farmland of the southern valleys from the territory's resources. Not surprisingly, the clique cried foul. As the territorial representative to Congress was clique member Joseph Lane, the secession attempt was dead on arrival at Washington, D.C. Important for understanding the whole issue of economic speculation in the wars, the clique's newspaper that was owned by Democrat Ashael Bush, the *Oregon Statesman*, also attacked his rivals' remuneration attempt. The newspaper printed a lampoon of the 1854 Walker Expedition—"The Campaign to Fight the Emigrants"—and accused Ross, Drew, and company of speculating treasury funds to discredit them.[31]

Speculation, although engaged in by nearly all colonists, still carried the haunting image of moneyed interests infringing on the rights of citizens; thus, it was an effective political tool in the mid-nineteenth-century West.

William J. Martin, the author of the humorous spin on the expedition, asked rhetorically, "How can the Whigs be trusted in or out of office[?] They are all gobbling claims, ready to cheat Uncle Sam at all times whenever they can." Martin also called for an official investigation and recommended that Captain Smith of Fort Lane conduct it.[32] Through the pages of the *Oregonian*, a Whig newspaper, the southwestern Oregon colonists fired back and carefully explained why the Walker Expedition and future militia efforts were absolutely necessary to the "public welfare."[33] The outbreak of the 1855–56 Rogue River War added some new dimensions to the factional squabbling—control and supply of the militias, for example—but the speculation accusations soon waned in importance for territorial politicians. After Lupton's massacre of the Quachis Shastas on Little Butte Creek, the politicians collectively had a war to win and benefit from.[34] The rival newspapers and political factions largely agreed that extermination was the only practical solution to the Indian problem, although they disagreed on how long it would take.[35] Indeed, Martin, author of the incendiary lampoon, was the commander of the "southern army" who subsequently issued the "take no prisoners" order.[36]

Once conjured, however, the speculation genie could not be controlled, and federal officials subsequently grabbed hold and expanded the speculation charges to declaim the territorial factions as a single avaricious colonial entity. Martin's hyperbolic attack on the Walker Expedition had unwittingly added fuel to the fire by confirming Captain Smith's (and, in turn, Wool's) suspicions about the untrustworthy nature of territorial militias in 1854.[37] From early November 1855, General Wool was utterly convinced that the extermination efforts in southwestern Oregon—indeed, the entire volunteer effort in Oregon and Washington territories—were speculative endeavors to make money from war remunerations.[38] Again, if we look at the political context, the speculation charges can be understood.

Simply put, the colonial militias infringed on the regular army's turf—another case of colony and empire clashing. Much of Wool's criticism came from jurisdictional jealousies: the governors of Oregon and Washington territories had not requested his permission before putting militias into the field, and they operated independently of the regular officers representing Wool's command.[39] As Capt. T. J. Cram of the U.S. Topographical Engineers complained to Congress, "[t]o say nothing of the legality of those [volunteer military] measures, one familiar with military usage cannot fail to perceive in them either a marked contempt of the authority of the President's commander of the department [Wool], or else a total want of knowledge of that courtesy which of right and by usage is due to such officer." He also tied a condemnation of the territorial militias into a plea for more funding and men, explaining that "it is certainly much more economical to have sufficient force to prevent a war between the Indians and whites than to suffer it to be created, thereby affording a pretext for volunteers to be called out by the territorial governors, and afterward be obliged to bring the regular army into requisition to suppress it." Capitalizing on the speculation charges flying about, Cram concluded: "The truth of this will be fully sustained when the bills for the services of the Oregon and Washington volunteers are rendered to Congress."[40] The clashes between federal and territorial interests regarding the Indians, particularly regarding extermination, lasted for years. Wool and others effectively stymied federal remuneration efforts for the territorial militias for decades.[41] Other contemporary critics agreed with the regular army officers and saw the attempted extermination of Indians merely as despicable private wars to defraud the public treasury.[42]

Indeed, speculation probably played some role in the final Rogue River War, as charged by contemporary critics and as recently championed by historian E. A. Schwartz as the principal cause of the war.[43] After all, the entire colonial project of western Oregon was based on economic speculation. War profiteering and shenanigans with remuneration claims would be expected if countless other wars are indicative, including the "Cayuse War" of 1848 and the contemporaneous "Yakama War" of 1855–1856. Still, only one case of an illegal war claim from the Rogue River War was ever proven in court, and the scam actually occurred long after the war, during the protracted remuneration phase.[44] As well, the territorial government did not offer cash to suppliers or militiamen, offering instead pledges for future payment and scrip, which many merchants refused to accept.[45] Previous remuneration attempts had taken years, and the contemporaneous political morass regarding the Walker Expedition suggested that such payments were hardly automatic or immediately forthcoming. Thus, it seems doubtful that hundreds of individuals would launch into a bloody conflict because it might or might not bring payment at some indefinite point in the future. Indeed, as proclaimed in the *Oregonian* at the outset of the war, the federal government's inaction in "suppressing of Indian hostilities in years past, has destroyed the confidence of many, that the general government would render compensation for services rendered or supplies furnished, consequently the requisite supplies for this emergency are compelled to be raised by direct contributions of money, provisions &c from our citizens; a burden which they are illy able to bear."[46] Moreover, an 1857 investigation by the U.S. Treasury Department determined that remuneration speculations did not cause the war. Instead, the investigator J. Ross Browne faulted the discrepancies between imperial policies and colonial behavior and the role of violent racialism. In particular, he cited confusion over jurisdiction caused by the ill-considered Donation Land Laws, the failure to extinguish Indian title, and the "natural" results of a "superior race" coming into contact with an "inferior" one.[47]

Browne's conclusions are revealing: To comprehend the "Indian wars" of 1855–56, one must place them within the larger context of white supremacy and Euro-American settler colonialism in western Oregon. The Donation Land Laws (1850–54) had created a sovereignty swamp: as a territory, Oregon should have been legally Indian Country (until ceded by treaty), but the colonists were acquiring title preemption to aboriginal lands. Similarly, mining claims were completely unregulated, and Indians had no recourse from miners' intrusions and ecological devastation caused by their endeavors. Thus, it was "Indian Country and it is not," according to one befuddled Indian agent.[48] The result, in the words of a contemporary critic, was "the mischief-making policy of Squatter Sovereignty . . . and violence and outrage" against the Indians.[49] Investigator Browne concluded: "That [the confusion regarding sovereignty] has been a fruitful source of difficulty there can be no doubt. It was unwise and impolitic to encourage settlers to take away the lands of the Indians." He noted that Indians "could never be taught to comprehend that subtle species of argument by which another race could come among them, put them aside, ignore their claims, and assume possession, on the ground of being a superior people."[50] The supposed racial superiority represented popular folk beliefs linking whiteness, citizenship, and the rights of property, which undergirded this murderous example of Native dispossession.[51] Attributing the brutal slaughter of Native peoples, the open calls for their extermination, and the seizure of their lands solely to the speculative machinations of a handful of greedy men such as John Ross, James Lupton, and Charles Drew in 1855 misses the forest for the trees and takes at face value accusations leveled by self-interested political factions.[52]

Euro-American colonialists wanted to possess Oregon—more, to create Oregon according to a vision that left little or no room for the aboriginal inhabitants of *Illahee*. As postcolonial theorist Patrick Wolfe explained, "settler colonies . . . are premised on displacing indigenes from (*re*placing them on) the land." Indeed, they are "premised on the elimination of native societies."[53] From the mid-1840s, attempts at physical extermination by colonial militias occurred when Native bands contested colonization through "annoyances" and raids on mining camps, settlements, and emigration parties and when so-called Indian wars erupted intermittently from 1847 to 1856. Ending perceived and real threats to the "public welfare" involved eradicating feared bands of Indians—particularly the men, as women could still be useful for gaining larger land claims (320 acres for single men and 640 for married men) as well as domestic, agricultural, and sexual labors.[54] The extermination of the Native peoples of southwestern Oregon, defined as "rogues," comprised an important part of colonization as conceived and affected by Euro-Americans who were convinced that profitable exploitation of Oregon was their birthright as U.S. citizens. Nineteenth-century Euro-Americans understood extermination to be a component of conquest and colonization. Not all colonials favored extermination, nor did all militia members participate in massacres, but support for extermination was high and remained so for years after the war.[55]

Unlike many present-day historians, Victorian-era historian Frances Fuller Victor had no qualms about the link between Euro-American colonization and the extermination of Indians.[56] She wrote during an era of blatant U.S. imperialism overseas and local memory building at home, in which self-ascribed "Oregonians" constructed a past that legitimized, mythologized, and sanitized their oft-violent colonial actions.[57] Victor blamed the territory's "Indian wars" on the federal government's poor administration of Indian affairs and credited the "heroic pioneers" (to whom she dedicated her work) with guarding the frontier. "The preservation of their lives and property forced upon them the alternative of war, even to extermination, the end of which was . . . first conquest, and finally banishment for the inferior race . . . in consonance with that law of nature which decrees the survival of the fittest."[58] Such a grossly racist explanation suited the Gilded Age. Modern historians, however, should be able to analyze the relationship between colonization and extermination without the need to justify or deny it. Euro-Americans reserved settlement and economic speculation of Oregon's resources for themselves and ensured that "birthright" through extermination efforts. The discourse of American settler colonialism rationalized these endeavors as promoting the public welfare of the republican citizenry. Although they failed to either exterminate all the Indians or officially enlist the empire republic in their effort, the colonial actions did affect the forced removal of the Native population. That is, the fewer than 2,000 survivors of an estimated 1851 population of 11,500 were removed to the Coast Reservation in 1856.[59] The fact that Euro-Americans attempted genocide as a central component of settler colonialism makes it a crucial topic for historical analysis, one that should not be denied, buried in guilt and shame, or left to racist, archaic histories like Victor's to explain.

Conclusion

Illahee, "Indian Colonies," and the Paternalist State

When European and American mariners first encountered the Native peoples of the lower Columbia, they were not enacting some preordained plan of gradual imperial domination of the region and its inhabitants. Like the merchant explorers of the fifteenth and sixteenth centuries, their ultimate goal was to establish a profitable trade with Asia. The maritime traders recognized that their activities in the modern-day Pacific Northwest could facilitate a strong relationship with Chinese merchants. The Northwest Coast offered exploitable commodities, cheap indigenous labor, and (for the Russians, British, and Americans) a base of operations on the Pacific Ocean that was removed from the Spanish dominions. The imperial implications of this transoceanic trade were well established in the Atlantic World by the late eighteenth century. Captains Cook, Gray, and Broughton initiated a history much related to earlier colonization in eastern North America, Latin America, sub-Saharan Africa, and the Indian subcontinent. Great Britain, Spain, the United States, and Russia experimented with particular forms of imperialism to order their increasingly far-flung enterprises and to compete with one another more profitably. They cast their eyes on the Northwest Coast of North America with a vision sharpened by two centuries of overseas expansion, learning from both their countrymen and their competitors.

The United States, although young and relatively weak, was emerging as a nation-state at a time when the older European countries were similarly modernizing, coalescing into unified cultural, political, and economic states. Although internal divisions, contradictions, and contestation would play roles as large as unification in the ensuing national histories, coherent nation-states have remained the principal entities in the ongoing drama of domestic and global relations. As historian Peter Onuf argued, the "'nation,' a characteristically modern idea that Americans themselves helped invent, constituted an imaginative bridge across the great chasm between center and periphery, metropolis and provinces." Nation was inherently linked to empire in the eyes of America's visionary Thomas Jefferson and many of his contemporaries, friends and foes alike, in the United States and Europe. Moreover, American revolutionaries sought inclusion in the European world, not isolation from it. That inclusion meant economic competition for overseas markets and, by the early nineteenth century, spreading their democratic-republican ideals to distant lands.[1] Thus, the earliest colonial encounters in the lower Oregon Country were part of a larger national and international (imperial) equation. Inasmuch as local contingencies, circumstance, and individual agency shaped the historical events of the early- to mid-nineteenth century in the region, distant decisions and institutional memories of previous and contemporaneous colonial endeavors also shaped the early history of western Oregon.

An imperial context, however, certainly does not imply a simple historical picture. The land-based fur trade began as a competition between John Astor, a German-born American, and his erstwhile trading partners in Montreal, the nominally British Northwest Company, whose enterprise challenged the imperial monopoly of the Hudson's Bay Company. Although neither Astor nor the Northwesters sought to have nationalized companies, both sought to protect their investments by encouraging and fostering the imperial claims of their sponsor states. However, until the Oregon Treaty of 1846 finally established a boundary between the United States and British Canada in the Pacific Northwest, the competitors had to contend with the messy and confusing system of joint occupation. Importantly, the distant diplomatic mess of the metropoles affected life on the ground level. Such was evident in the relocation of Fort George, competition between the forts and American coasters, the "fur desert" strategy, and the consequent effects on relations between the colonial and indigenous traders.

The Christian American mission of the MEC offers one of the best examples of how murky and complex the relationship between colony and empire was in practice. From the outset, Jason Lee and his band attempted to operate within a paradoxical realm of mission and colony. The remote mission and its proposed Westernization project necessitated some degree of colonization. However, such actions encouraged the advent of settler colonialism, which was only slowly taking shape with the decline of the fur trade in the 1830s. Colonization undermined the plan of Christian conversion by attracting competition from individuals strictly interested in the economic possibilities of the land and invited criticism of the mission's supposedly secular activities. Moreover, what did it mean to spread Christian-American civilization? It meant conversion of the "savages," certainly, but folk tradition and governmental policies also suggested that occupation of the land and dispossession of the indigenous peoples were the more likely and preferred meanings. Elsewhere, Euro-American missionaries to the Indians had to contend with the dilemmas of disease epidemics, whether to attempt conversion or "civilization" first, and how to counter the corrupting influences of Westernism such as alcohol abuse and violence. In western Oregon, the competing imperial claims made the situation nearly untenable. In this situation, the Methodists became overwhelmed by the more powerful priorities of colonial land claims, and racial ideologies doomed their Christian mission.[2]

With the hordes of settler colonists from the mid-1840s onward, squatter sovereignty and white patriarchy regarding property ownership and citizenship emerged as the defining visions of western Oregon—a conglomeration of actions and discourse emblematic of settler colonialism. In the absence of a formal state, Euro-Americans drew on established precedents of national law, territorial government, and popular renderings of U.S. history to create a provisional government. Their provisional government granted them massive land claims throughout much of western Oregon and effectively dispossessed Native inhabitants, who were reeling from disease. The colonists espoused the ideals of classical republicanism and an unquestioned faith in white supremacy to provide rationales and legitimacy for their individual speculations, which were the economic base of settler colonialism in western Oregon.

From the earliest encounters of the 1790s through the fur trade and disease epidemics of the 1830s, the Native peoples evidenced a strong ability to adapt and change with historical circumstances. Thousands of individuals, mostly anonymous in the written record, went about their daily lives, balancing indigenous practices and beliefs with the new exigencies of manufactured goods, extremely high mortality, altered ecology, and the redistribution of land and resource sites. Such men and women also helped determine what the colonial traders ate, how well they profited, and how secure they felt and, indeed, were. Leaders such as Madame Coalpo, Concomly, and Casino variously challenged, inhibited, and aided the colonial traders, revealing constant Native efforts to benefit individually and communally for their villages and intervillage kin. Although malaria, smallpox, syphilis, and other diseases carried off catastrophically high numbers of Indians, a distinctive Native world continued to be evident through the dawn of settler colonialism and beyond.

I have often used the term *Illahee* instead of the larger and vaguer notion of "Indian Country" to specify experiences in western Oregon and to offer a parallel construction to "Oregon."[3] Just as Oregon has never had a single, fixed, uncontested meaning, *Illahee* was a composite Native realm with multiple meanings that changed over time in relation to Indian peoples' experiences with colonization. Intervillage communication, trade, and other forms of interaction on local and regional levels long predated encounters with Europeans and Euro-Americans, but there was no *Illahee* until there was an external imposition of imperialism. Scholars have long recognized the historical creations of the "other" by which indigenous peoples came to be defined against idealized self-identities of Westerners. Thus, there were no "Indians" or "savages" in the Americas before 1492. Similarly, the Americas as a place came into existence through Western cartography and attempts at imperial (or perhaps empirical) dominion. The idea of a Pacific Northwest or Oregon Country would have been meaningless to Native peoples initially. "Northwest of what?" Alexandra Harmon has examined the ways in which Europeans and Euro-Americans introduced the concepts of Indian identity to the Puget Sound region in the late eighteenth and nineteenth centuries and how Native peoples took up these identities and put them to use in the twentieth century. Katherine Morrissey has analyzed the cultural geography through which Euro-Americans created a place on the Columbia Plateau, the "inland empire," through their "mental mapping" and economic endeavors. Such creative phenomena had been ongoing on both macroscopic and microscopic levels, arguably, throughout human history. Constructions of identity and place are fundamentally historical creations, deriving from the ways in which people understand themselves, "others," and their environment.[4]

The planned and unplanned effects of the fur trade, missions, and settler colonialism created a dynamic and often dangerous world through which the Native peoples had to navigate. By the 1840s, many Indians of the Willamette Valley, lower Columbia environs, and Columbia Plateau took wage work on the farms and in the towns and industries that had displaced their traditional subsistence economies. In the 1851 treaty negotiations, local bands of Kalapuyas, Clatsops, and Chinooks requested only to maintain a core of their former homelands; these checkered holdings were *Illahee*. The Klikitats who took up land in the Willamette and Coquille valleys and the Umpquas who homesteaded along the river that bears their name established *Illahee*. *Illahee* existed in the two Chetco villages that combined a traditional economy with a ferry business servicing traveling colonists during the Gold Rush. More infamously, *Illahee* was evident in the limited defensive alliances from 1855 to 1856 and the political struggles for unified action that cost the lives of several headmen among the Coos, Takelmas, and others. Finally, there was the dystopian alternative vision of *Illahee*, the *Polaklie Illahee* prophecy of the land of darkness. Each of these manifestations of *Illahee* was simultaneously externally imposed (colonialist) and internally directed (indigenous), demonstrating continued Native adaptation and negotiation of historical change.

The causes of the so-called Rogue River Wars of the mid-1850s were complex, as evident from the previous chapters' analysis of economics, politics, and ideology. The California Gold Rush and the Oregon Land Rush collided in the canyons and river valleys of southwestern Oregon. The Native peoples there, who had been largely tangential to the fur trade and less devastated by disease than the Indians of the Willamette Valley, suddenly faced tremendous competition for resources. Colonials knew little of the Shastan-, Takelman-, Penutian-, and Athapaskan-speaking peoples other than that they were treacherous "rogues." Such Indians were not going to be allowed to stand in the way of a deserving citizenry. The earlier history of Willamette Valley colonization and the war with Mexico strengthened the Euro-Americans' beliefs in their racially exclusive birthright to possess Oregon. Congress obliged by granting territorial recognition and donation claims, and by remunerating the expenses of colonial militias from the late 1840s. The United States did little to prevent the resulting atrocities, and, indeed, the political ideology of the empire republic fostered white supremacist views of the land and its use. The genocidal wars of southwestern Oregon stemmed as much from the Euro-Americans' refusal to share resources with the Native peoples, which would have allowed Indians to adapt to the local colonial economy, as the fear of Indians' retribution for the destruction of their traditional subsistence economy. The discourse and actions of settler colonialism made the citizenry's extermination attempts seem warranted in the tense atmosphere of southwestern Oregon in the 1850s.

Throughout this history, colonials pressed the central government—which administered the American imperial apparatus of Indian treaties, land disposal, and foreign diplomacy—to secure the Oregon Country for U.S. citizens. Consistently, however, the political divisions of the empire republic stymied or stalled colonial pursuits even as they encouraged continued efforts. The American empire republic was not easily maneuvered from so far outside the halls of power in the East, but it nevertheless fostered an entrepreneurial settler colonialism, or "folk imperialism." Free to interpret their own versions of imperial institutions and with a weak imperial presence in the guise of a small federal force of officials, army officers, and regular troops, colonists seized land and resources and perpetrated massacres. Colonials drew on American tradition and law and simultaneously violated official American policy in the Far West to approximate their vision of Oregon.

Epilogue: "Postcolonial" Oregon

Removal, as well as confinement to reservations or, as Commissioner of Indian Affairs Charles Mix called them, "Indian colonies," in no way signaled the end of Native experiences with colonialism. In many ways, it was just the beginning, as their lives would be largely dominated by paternalist federal administration and shaped by their exclusion from dominant white society. When Treasury Department investigator Ross Browne interviewed the principal headmen of southwest Oregon at the Coast Reservation in 1857, they believed that their entreaties to the "Great Father," as Browne described the president, would have some effect. Cholcultah explained that he had never agreed to sell his homelands near Table Rock and Evan's Creek and had agreed to leave temporarily because "We are told that if we go back the white people will kill us all." He questioned Browne's paternalist depiction of the president, saying that if he "is our Great Father[,] Why, then should he compel us to suffer here?" He felt that the president should be able to control his people. "Let us go back to our homes," he implored, "and our hearts will be bright again like the sun."

Tecumtum had similar pleas based on his agreement to removal as having been temporary. As well, he noted the problem that the peoples of the southwestern interior did not know how to get food on the central coast; the country was foreign and "covered with great forests. It is hard to get through them." Agent Robert Metcalfe also noted the problem, saying that most of his charges "know nothing of the natural products," having never "seen this country" before confinement. As well, Tecumtum claimed that the president owed him, saying: "My son-in-law went to the Dalles to live with the Yakimas and Klikitats. I made peace, and sent word to him, and to all the hostile tribes, to quit fighting." Although certainly an overstatement of his authority, Tecumtum felt that credit was due. He said, "I told him to tell them I had made peace, and it was no use to fight any more. For this I think we deserve well of the President." His people could not stay on the reservation because "we are all dying." Indeed, the "Rogue Rivers" had the highest death rate among the reservation population, and this fact was hardly bemoaned by the Euro-Americans. Browne recorded the headmen's "many complaints" but advised them that they could not go home, ever. He expressed regret that Joel Palmer had misled them about their permanent removal, but "if they undertook to go back to their homes they would be shot down, and then the President's heart would be sad, because he could no longer protect them." The Native peoples would continue to press their case for returning home for several years, to no avail.[5]

The reservations were a stopgap measure to end the Rogue River War by removing Indian people from the path of Euro-American settlement and bullets. The majority of the Native peoples at the Siletz Agency did not even have a treaty agreement ratified by the Senate and were effectively "prisoners of war," according to their agent.[6] Without treaties, no annuity payments were forthcoming. Consequently, monies for food, clothing, and housing were completely unpredictable and fell far short of sustaining the reservation population. According to Superintendent Absalom Hedges in 1857, the Indians "must be fed . . . or must be fought," and he pressed for more funding.[7] Agent John Miller at Grand Ronde advised that, without government aid, the Willamette tribes would starve or leave; if they left, the Euro-Americans would renew "the war of extermination."[8] The secretary of the interior changed these reports somewhat, casting them as two policy alternatives. He advised in his annual report in 1858 that the federal government had to provide sustenance or "the only alternative . . . is to exterminate them."[9] He was probably striving for effect, however, rather than actually suggesting genocide. The business of administering Indian affairs proved quite lucrative for the agents involved, and the often corrupt men had a personal stake in increasing monies for the reservations.[10]

The Native desire to leave was strong initially. Siletz agent Robert Metcalfe worried that he could not keep the Indians on the reservation and suggested that some bands were conspiring to return home. Tecumtum reportedly tried to initiate such an effort to return to the Rogue Valley in 1858, and Agent Metcalf "banished" him and his son "Adam" (also known as "Cultus Jim," meaning "worthless" or "no good Jim" in Chinook Jargon). Military authorities agreed to take them to San Francisco's Alcatraz Island. Aboard the steamer *Columbia*, the two supposedly attempted escape while the ship was in Humbolt Bay near the California—Oregon border. In the fray, Tecumtum was shot through the nose, and his son suffered a broken leg, which was subsequently amputated. Five years later, after pleas from Tecumtum's daughters, Metcalfe's replacement, W. H. Rector, agreed to have the old warrior and his son returned to the reservation. The years on "the rock" understandably changed both men. According to their agent in 1863, "they exert a very salutary influence over other Indians in inducing them to remain at home [on the reservation] and live like white people."[11] Although agents would occasionally complain that members of south-coast bands threatened to burn reservation buildings in protest of their nonratified treaties, which meant no annuities and little provisions, the days of violent resistance to colonization were past.

In the first difficult years of reservation life, relations among the different Native ethnicities were often strained. Some violence occurred, because people blamed each other for the wars and removal. Sickness and disease were rampant, and resulting deaths were sometimes blamed on Native doctors who failed to produce a cure or who were believed to have conjured the illnesses. Grand Ronde agent John Miller cited "frequent serious quarrels," and in one instance the Takelmas had a bloody altercation or "open warfare" with the Umpquas. Tecumtum's son also had been implicated in a doctor killing, possibly related to this episode. Schoolmaster John Ostrander stated that one "doctress" sought blame for illnesses she could not cure, attempting to save her life. She blamed the school's trumpet for emitting sickness like "a mist" that settled "upon the camp." At a headman's request, Ostrander agreed not to sound his trumpet, sarcastically stating that he "was not such a monster . . . so the Indians 'still live.'" Siletz agent Metcalfe stated that the people "live in constant terror of their doctors and doctresses." He claimed that he knew "more than one hundred doctors and doctresses murdered, and many of them by the hands of their own brothers." His figure was certainly an exaggeration, and one soldier put the figure at six killed over the first thirty months. The death tolls from unknown diseases clearly had effects beyond individual deaths; they were assaulting Native belief systems and producing tremendous fear. Metcalfe aptly compared the situation to the Salem witch trials, which also occurred during a time of social upheaval. As late as 1871, Joel Palmer complained that "superstitious" ideas "that their 'medicine-men' can 'will' their death," was still maintained.[12] "Doctor killings," however, had apparently stopped.

Accommodation with the colonial administration also produced strained relations among Native peoples. The Kalipuyas, who had been working on Euro-American farms for years before removal, accepted agriculture much more readily than the recently removed bands from southwestern Oregon. There was not much good soil at Grand Ronde, but the Kalapuyas and the Umpquas were trying to make the best of it. Agent John Miller stated that, as a result, the name "Calapooias . . . has become a byword or term of reproach with the braver and more warlike Indians." At Siletz, Metcalfe similarly noted that "some in each tribe" castigate and discourage "those who will work, by calling them fools, slaves &c." Down the coast on California's lower Klamath River reservation, the agent also complained that many "look with contempt upon [agricultural] labor, and to taunt those who are willing to work with the epithet of 'white man's slave.'" For many Native people, to accept agriculture was to reject their identity.[13]

The few Native peoples who had tried "to live like white people" in the late 1850s found that some Euro-American citizens would not tolerate their land ownership. Louis Napesa and his Umpqua band had cultivated land and owned "improvements" in the Umpqua Valley, but they were compelled to depart for Grande Ronde in 1856 to avoid the wrath of Oregon militias. All their properties were seized by Euro-Americans. Napesa and his people spent years trying to recover equitable remuneration.[14] A Klikitat man known as Dick Johnson, his Umpqua wife, "Mummy," and some extended family occupied a homestead in the Umpqua Valley. Johnson had labored on Jesse Applegate's farm in the 1840s, and Rev. Josiah Parrish helped him get his own claim. Parrish wrote a letter of explanation for Johnson to show anyone who inquired, as he was ineligible to file an official claim at the land office, which barred nonwhites. Johnson and his family established their farm after the fashion of their Euro-American neighbors, complete with a house, fencing, and outbuildings. When the colonial wars broke out in 1855, Superintendent Palmer gave them special dispensation to remain on their claim and avoid removal. Well after the war, in November 1858, a small group of Euro-American men attacked the homestead, killing Dick and his brother-in-law. Mummy fled to relatives on the reservation, and, as an "Indian," she could not testify against the murderers. Indeed, the killers could not be tried without witnesses; and they subsequently filed a donation claim on the property, taking legal possession.[15] Indians were increasingly tolerated off the reservation as manual laborers, but property ownership—the prerogative of citizens—was exclusively for the "white" race.

By the 1860s, without money to provide sufficient food for the reservation population, agents issued "passes" so that Indians could leave to hunt, fish, and take work on the farms and towns of the Willamette and Umpqua valleys.[16] Many left without passes. Some returned to the reservation, others did not, and occasional roundups continued through the 1860s. Several young women fled to Portland, where they obtained domestic work and did their best to blend into the bottom rung of white society. Another group of 75 Molalas and Mohawk Valley Kalapuyas left Grande Ronde for six years before being forced to return in 1863.[17] The reservation population dropped when harvesting jobs were available and rose when those eligible for annuities could get them.[18] Illicit work, particularly prostitution, became a last resort for some women and their families, and alcohol abuse made the situation worse. Joel Palmer claimed to be putting an end to both alcohol abuse and Indian prostitution, which were annoying some citizens in the towns of the Willamette Valley in 1871. In 1878, however, Martha Minto claimed that "Today in Salem an Indian will take his squaw and meeting any white man or boy will offer her to them for money." She was likely exaggerating the frequency, but the problem had obviously not been solved by Parrish's renewed attempts at reservation confinement in 1871.[19] As mentioned, some women married Euro-American men to escape the reservations and the soldiers who raped them there, and to return to their former homelands. Others such as "Mummy Johnson" escaped to relative safety of family on the reservation. There were no easy answers, and Native people went back and forth from the reservations, as individual circumstances dictated, trying to forge lives in a hostile landscape.

Enumeration of Indians was as problematic as it had ever been and was still highly political. When the Oregon legislature petitioned Congress to open the reservation lands to Euro-Americans in 1870, the legislators claimed that there were only 800 Indians there. Contemporaneously, Indian officials whose living depended on the reservations claimed that there were 2,800: 2,300 at Siletz and 500 at the Alsea Agency.[20] Other enumeration problems stemmed from confusion about the rising mixed-blood population. In Coos County, for example, children of Euro-American fathers and Native mothers were "½ Ind" in 1860 and "white" in 1870.[21] Typically, however, mixed bloods were not considered white but were rather derided as "half-breeds" among Euro-Americans. The manner in which one lived seemed to determine identity among Indians. Without a biological conception of "race," Annie Miner Peterson considered herself and her children Indian, though she had a Euro-American father as did her children. Meanwhile, she spoke of another Native woman's children as "white person children," seemingly because they lived in town with their Euro-American father.[22]

Unlike the Indian-governmental relationship, the relationship between Oregon and the United States was no longer a colonial one after statehood in 1858. Territorial governments were politically akin to colonies in that the president of the United States appointed their governors, and territorial representatives to Congress could not vote. Statehood ended this dependency. Western states with small voting populations would not achieve the political power of Eastern states or California, but the notion that "empire and colony" continued to define the federal-state relationship in the West is not sustainable. Indisputably, Western communities would face famous "boom and bust" cycles and often be at the mercy of external capital and political decisions; but a true colonial relationship no longer existed.[23]

The ambivalent attitudes of the Oregon territorials regarding the federal government—desiring protection, free land, and full reimbursement for their wars without outside interference or limits imposed by "brass buttons" from Washington, D.C.—continues to be reflected today.[24] The current controversy over water rights in the Klamath Basin offers one such example, pitting local farmers and ranchers against federal biologists, Native peoples, and commercial fishers. The agriculturalists who castigated federal officials, illegally released irrigation water, and proudly trumpeted militant antifederal rhetoric to the media are, nevertheless, dependent on federal subsidies. The Klamath agriculturalists argue that the federal government owes them the right to farm and raise cattle on the land, based on promises from the turn of the last century, before public priorities included Native sovereignty and environmental protection. Similarly, voters of Grant County on the Columbia Plateau passed legislation in May 2002 granting themselves permission to harvest timber on public lands without approval from or restrictions of the U.S. Forest Service. Like their provision on the same ballot that declared the county a "U.N. Free Zone" to prevent a takeover by an international conspiracy aided by the federal government, the vote is legally meaningless. Recent events in Klamath and Grant counties, however, point to an ongoing tradition in rural Oregon of construing their demands for public monies and resources as rights and setting themselves off from the rest of the country (and the world) in a self-serving "us versus them" myth.[25] That they are citizens of a large republic that ideally tries to balance numerous, often conflicting, concerns instead of supporting only the desires of male Euro-Americans seems to elude their logic. By the late 1850s, Oregon was no longer a place disputed by imperial powers and populated by a subject "white" citizenry despite continued rhetoric and the legacies of frustration with the harsh economic realities of the Jeffersonian promised land.

Conversely, the Native peoples continue to experience the realities of colonialism, as they were legally and popularly defined as the "other," separated from dominant society, denied access to most of their resources, and refused both the legal recourse of citizens and a meaningful right of self-determination. Between 1856 and 1859, the U.S. Army forced the Sahaptian peoples of the Columbia Plateau onto reservations. In 1864, the Klamath

Tribes accepted a reservation within the range of their former homelands. In 1873, several Modocs went to war to avoid removal and lost. Later in the 1870s, it was the turn of the Northern Paiutes, the Shoshones, and then the Nez Perce. Chief Joseph's famous surrender near the Canadian border in 1877 ended the military subjugation of the Native peoples of the former "Oregon Country." In western Oregon, state officials, squatters, and speculators pressed for reductions of Indian reservation lands. In 1865, Yaquina Bay was removed from the Coast Reservation, splitting it into the Siletz Agency in the north and the Alsea and Yachats agencies to the south. In 1875, the two southern agencies were closed, and those lands as well as the vast majority of those of the Siletz Agency were seized for the public domain. In less than two decades, the Indians of western Oregon lost approximately 80% of their reservation lands.[26] The remainder was slowly reduced to zero by the mid-1950s, when Congress "terminated" the tribes of western Oregon. Tribes elsewhere in the region, notably the Klamath Tribes, had similar experiences. Only in recent years have some western tribes regained "federal recognition" and reclaimed a tiny fraction of land, which is nevertheless managed through the Bureau of Indian Affairs.

Neither the Native peoples nor the federal officials seemed to have had any idea in 1856 that the colonial relationship would continue indefinitely. The administration of "Indian affairs" and the nascent reservation system of the mid-1850s constituted the beginning of a paternalist structure that still dominates much of Native life, similar to the British bureaucratic regime in India until 1947 and the United States in the Philippines until 1934 and, arguably, in Puerto Rico to the present.

However, the colonial administration of the reservations had an ironic, unintended effect as well; it fostered Native unity and an Indian identity. At the Grand Ronde Agency, for example, the children spoke several different dialects and languages, which the teachers did not understand. The administration's initial solution was to teach in Chinook Jargon until the children could master English.[27] The children learned an identity; they were *tillicum*, the people. Where did they live? They lived in *Illahee*. Adults intermarried with peoples of different ethnic and linguistic backgrounds, sometimes causing problems, including unions between people who disagreed about cultural practices such as flattening the heads of infants.[28] Yet, Chinook Jargon, for a time, was likely the lingua franca of the reservation homes and facilitated a transition to an identity as "Indians."[29] Bureaucratic administration also created tribal identities by confederating different bands. Some, such as the confederation of "Rogue Rivers" and "Shastas," merged peoples who had previously fought with one another before removal. Certainly, the bands initially remained aloof, but shared experiences broke these barriers over time. Modern descendents know their lineage, but their legal and social identities stem from the confederations and the reservation experiences. Today, cultural heritage efforts at Grand Ronde include teaching children Chinook Jargon, which played such an important role in the formative years of the reservation community. Also, the Confederated Tribes of Siletz hold an annual powwow that they call *Nesika Illahee*, "Our Land." The Native peoples and their descendents continue to create ways to be and remain Indian in the face of changing realities and continued colonial administration.

Takelma Invocation for a New Moon[30]

I shall be blessed,
I shall go ahead.

Even if people say of me,
   "Would he were dead,"
I shall do just as you,
   I shall still rise.

Even if all kinds of things devour you,
   Frogs eat you,
Everything,
   Lizards,

Even if they eat you,
   Yet you shall still rise,
I shall do just as you from this on—
   "Bo——!"

Notes

Preface

1 Amy Kaplan, "'Left Alone with America,'" 15–19; Maria E. Montoya, "Claims and Prospects Of Western History: A Roundtable," 40–43; Patricia Nelson Limerick, "Going West and Ending Up Global," 5–23; and Jeffrey Ostler, *The Plains Sioux and U.S. Colonialism*.

2 Jurgen Osterhammel, *Colonialism: A Theoretical Overview*, 4, 10–12, 21–22, 25; Ian Copland, *The Burden of Empire: Perspectives on Imperialism and Colonialism*, 2; and Richard White, *The Middle Ground*, xi.

3 Richard White, "Indian Peoples and the Natural World: Asking the Right Questions," 94; see also the editors' introduction in Richard White and John M. Findley, eds., *Power and Place in the North American West*, x; and James Carson Taylor, "Ethnogeography and the Native American Past," 769–88.

4 Philip J. Deloria, "Historiography," 21.

Chapter One

1 Consultant, Charles Cultee, in Franz Boas, *Chinook Texts*, 275–78.

2 For detailed analyses of the relationships between indigenous knowledge, stories, and places, see Keith H. Basso, *Wisdom Sits in Places*; and Julie Cruikshank, *The Social Life of Stories*.

3 Frederick Jackson Turner, "The Significance of the Frontier in American History," 199–227; for an important detractor, see Patricia Nelson Limerick, *The Legacy of Conquest*; and, for a critical synthesis, see Kerwin Lee Klein, *Frontiers of Historical Imagination*.

4 Verne Frederick Ray, "Lower Chinook Ethnographic Notes," 93.

5 Hubert Howe Bancroft, *The Works of Hubert Howe Bancroft*, vol. 27, *History of the Northwest Coast*, vol. 1, 260.

6 Scott Byram and David G. Lewis, "Ourigan."

7 Bruce Trigger, "Early Native North American Responses to European Contact."

8 Allan Richardson, "The Control of Productive Resources on the Northwest Coast of North America."

9 A. L. Kroeber and E. W. Gifford, "World Renewal"; Cora DuBois, Tututuni (Rogue River) Fieldnotes, microfilm 2216, reel 6, Bancroft Library, University of

California, Berkeley (hereafter cited as BL), MS CU-23.1, frames 307–44; personal communication, Robert Kentta, cultural resources director, Confederated Tribes of Siletz, August 19, 2004; and personal communication, Dr. George B. Wasson Jr., Coquille Indian Tribe, July 12, 2004.

10 Ray, "Lower Chinook Ethnographic Notes," 79, 84.

11 Yvonne P. Hajda describes such linkages as social and religious belief networks in "Regional Social Organization," 2.

12 House, *Report of J. Ross Browne*, 44–47.

13 Stephen Dow Beckham, *The Indians of Western Oregon*, 95–96.

14 Abe Logan regarding Megwin and Joshua Tututni peoples, in Philip Drucker, Field Notes, 1934, vol. 3, 30, 31.

15 Albert Samuel Gatschet, *The Klamath Indians of Southwestern Oregon*; Leslie Spier, "Klamath Ethnography"; and Theodore Stern, "The Klamath Indians and the Treaty of 1864."

16 Isaac J. Stevens, Indian Treaty File: Klickatat Indians, 4.

17 Alexandra Harmon, *Indians in the Making*. See also John Lutz, "Making 'Indians' in British Columbia: Power, Race, and the Importance of Place," in White and Findley, eds., *Power and Place*, 61–84.

18 James Clifford and George E. Marcus, *Writing Culture*.

19 For an example of attempting to make Richard White's "middle ground" paradigm of mutual accommodation fit western Oregon, see Nathan Douthit, *Uncertain Encounters*.

20 Peter S. Onuf, *Jefferson's Empire*, 5–6; Bradford Perkins, *Cambridge History of Foreign Relations*; Gary Lawson and Guy Seidman, *The Constitution of Empire*; and Reginald Horsman, "The Dimensions of an 'Empire for Liberty.'"

21 Whaley, "'Complete Liberty'?"

22 Whaley, "'Trophies' for God."

23 Whaley, "Oregon, *Illahee*, and the Empire Republic."

24 Dart to CIA, November 7, 1851, in Coan, "The First Stage of the Federal Indian Policy," 66–75.

25 Palmer to CIA, June 23, 1853, in William G. Robbins, "Extinguishing Indian Land Title," 14.

26 For a related discussion, see James Ronda, "Coboway's Tale," in White and Findley, eds., *Power and Place*.

27 For related discussions regarding Oregon, see Beckham, *The Indians of Western Oregon*; Nathan Douthit, *Uncertain Encounters*; E. A. Schwartz, *The Rogue River Indian War*; and in the West generally, see David Svaldi, *Sand Creek and the Rhetoric of Extermination*; Reginald Horsman, *Race and Manifest Destiny*; James J. Rawls, *Indians of California*; and Albert L. Hurtado, *Indian Survival*.

28 Disputes between volunteer territorial and federal forces occurred in much of the West, sometimes including the issue of extermination. See Hurtado, *Indian Survival*, 125–48; David Rich Lewis, *Neither Wolf nor Dog*, 84–88; Francis Paul Prucha, *The Great Father*, 452–59; Rawls, *Indians of California*, 179–83; Sherry L. Smith, *View from Officer's Row*, 119–25; and Robert A. Trennert Jr., *An Alternative to Extinction*, 94–130.

Chapter Two

1 Robert F. Jones, ed., *Annals of Astoria*, 44.

2 Robert H. Ruby and John A. Brown, *The Chinook Indians*, 15, 17. McDougall recorded the item as "clemels," in Jones, *Annals of Astoria*, 46, 77, 93, 95, 108, 130, 182, 197, 200, 208, 212, 214, 217. Alexander Henry called them "clemens," describing some of Tillamook manufacture as "war garments made of thick red deerskins [elk] dress in the grain with urine," Elliott Coues, *New Light*, 858.

3 Leland Donald, *Aboriginal Slavery*, 225, 231; and Hajda, "Regional Social Organization," 193.

4 James R. Gibson, *Otter Skins*, 16–17.

5 Theodore Stern, *Chiefs and Chief Traders*, 18–33.

6 The importance of the blue beads was noted by Lewis and Clark, vol. 6, 123, 134, 164–66, 215–16. They continued in importance through the early land-based fur trade, Jones, *Annals of Astoria*, 215; into the Willamette Valley; and the "fashion" developed that only one of the three sizes was acceptable by 1814, Coues, *New Light*, 815, 817, 888.

7 See Cole Harris, *The Resettlement of British Columbia*; D. W. Meinig, *The Great Columbia Plain*; and Ronda, *Lewis and Clark*.

8 For the descriptive term for the region, see Hajda, "Regional Social Organization."

9 Thomas Vaughan and Bill Holm, eds., *Soft Gold*, ix.

10 Gary E. Moulton, ed., *Journals of Lewis and Clark*, vol. 6, editor's note 1, 432.

11 House, *Military Posts—Council Bluffs to the Pacific Ocean. Report of the Committee on Military Affairs*, 27th Cong., 2nd Sess., 1842, Doc. 830, Serial 410, 12–13.

12 Ibid.; and Dorothy O. Johansen, *Empire of the Columbia*, 40–43.

13 Moulton, *Journals of Lewis and Clark*, vol. 6, 433, 437–38, n. 5.

14 This useful regional designation covers from the Quinalt to the Alsea rivers, both sides of the Columbia up to The Dalles, up the Cowlitz and Willamette rivers (to Willamette Falls), and some peripheral interior areas, Hajda, "Regional Social Organization."

15 The word *Clatsop* derived for pounded salmon, but, as Lewis noted, that commodity came mostly from "the river above, to the grand falls inclusive. . . . The bay in which this trade is carryed on" was in the Clatsops' territory, Moulton, *Journals of Lewis and Clark*, vol. 6, 76 (n. 1), 201.

16 Ibid., 155 and fn 159.

17 Ibid., Lewis 164, Clark 165.

18 Richard Glover, *David Thompson's Narrative*, 361, 373–74.

19 Moulton, *Journals of Lewis and Clark*, vol. 6, 429, 431.

20 Ronda, *Lewis and Clark*, 4–9.

21 Ibid., 1–4.

22 Moulton, *Journals of Lewis and Clark*, vol. 6, 336–37.

23 James Kendall Hosmer, ed., *Gass's Journal*, 170; and Glover, *David Thompson's Narrative*, 370.

24 Moulton, *Journals of Lewis and Clark*, vol. 6, 286.

25 Ibid., 234.

26 "2 cases Chinook Hats" are listed on the "Bill of Ladings" from Fort George for the interior trade, April 4, 1814, in B. C. Payette, ed., *The Oregon Country under the Union Jack*, 172. As late as 1825, the Hudson's Bay Company priced "1st quality" Chinook hats at four large, prime beaver skins, Dorothy Nafus Morrison, *Outpost*, 151.

27 Ross Cox, *The Columbia River*, 41–42.

28 For a discussion of such depictions in the neighboring "upper Oregon Country," see Elizabeth Vibert, *Traders' Tales*.

29 Meriwether Lewis, *The Lewis and Clark Expedition*, 482, 530.

30 November 21, 1805, and March 15, 1806, incidents, Ibid., 482, 542; Moulton, *Journals of Lewis and Clark*, vol. 6, 73–75, 416–18; and March 24, 1806, incident, Milo M. Quaife, ed., *Journals*, 331.

31 Moulton, *Journals of Lewis and Clark*, vol. 6, 75.

32 Donald Jackson, ed., *Letters of the Lewis and Clark Expedition*, 503.

33 Moulton, *Journals of Lewis and Clark*, vol. 6, 75.

34 Hosmer, *Gass's Journal*, 204.

35 Moulton, *Journals of Lewis and Clark*, vol. 6, 239, 241.

36 Quaife, *Journals*, 331, 26.

37 Moulton, *Journals of Lewis and Clark*, vol. 6, 120, 123, 136, 360. Stern, *Chiefs and Chief Traders*, 26–27.

38 Ibid., 365–66.

39 Hajda, "Regional Social Organization," 178, 182; Ray, "Lower Chinook Ethnographic Notes," 51–54, 69–70; and Donald, *Aboriginal Slavery*, 233.

40 Ray, "Lower Chinook Ethnographic Notes," 53.

41 Donald, *Aboriginal Slavery*, 233–35.

42 Ronda, *Lewis and Clark*, 208.

43 Francis Paul Prucha, ed., *Documents of United States Indian Policy*, 16–17.

44 Following the English "financial revolution" of the 1690s, which established a national bank, a national debt, and a wealthy and politically powerful class of London investors, England became increasingly oriented toward controlling overseas markets. The grants of monopolies for products such as tea and the bureaucratization and militarization of its colonies were innovative efforts to meet the challenges of expanding and maintaining its empire in the face of indigenous resistance and imperial competition. The ideology of "free trade," first apparent in the domestic economy, took hold more slowly in colonial administration, P. J. Cain and A. G. Hopkins, *British Imperialism*, 53–104.

45 James P. Ronda, *Astoria and Empire*, 42–64.

46 Jones, *Annals of Astoria*, 204.

47 Osterhammel, *Colonialism*, 25–26.

48 Ronda writes of the fort's hierarchy in terms of labor performed and excludes the Kanakas from his calculations, *Astoria and Empire*, 209–14.

49 Ibid., 218–19.

50 Jones, *Annals of Astoria*, 20.

51 Robert F. Jones, ed., *Astorian Adventure*, 100, 124.

52 Jones, *Annals of Astoria*, 132–33; and Ronda, *Astoria and Empire*, 218–19.

53 Coues, *New Light*, 891, 908.

54 Jones, *Annals of Astoria*, 125.

55 Jones, *Astorian Adventure*, 133.

56 Jeremie also was reprimanded for playing sick to avoid work, Jones, *Annals of Astoria*, 29. He pledged no more escapes in writing but broke the written promise, 36; Alexander Ross, *Adventures of the First Settlers*, 93; see also Ronda's discussion of runaways, particularly Paul Jeremie, in *Astoria and Empire*, 216.

57 Gabriel Franchere, *Adventure at Astoria*, 115.

58 Glover, *David Thompson's Narrative*, 361–62, 370.

59 Robert Boyd, *People of The Dalles*, 145.

60 Jones, *Annals of Astoria*, 16–17.

61 Ibid., 27.

62 Ibid., 148.

63 Ibid., 138, 150.

64 Ross, *Adventures of the First Settlers*, 102–3.

65 Jones, *Annals of Astoria*, 152–53.

66 Ray, *Lower Chinook Ethnographic Notes*, 110–11.

67 For a contrary assessment of the economic-ecological pressures of fur traders, see Jay Zucker, Kay Hummel, and Bob Hogfoss, *Oregon Indians*, 61.

68 Coues, *New Light*, 817.

69 Franchere, *Adventure at Astoria*, 100.

70 Jones, *Astorian Adventure*, 116; *Annals of Astoria*, 186, 206–7; and Franchere, *Adventure at Astoria*, 76. See also Coues, *New Light*, 831, 837.

71 Jones, *Annals of Astoria*, 216.

72 Ibid., 186.

73 Coues, *New Light*, 817.

74 Jones, *Astorian Adventure*, 144–45.

75 Coues, *New Light*, 862.

76 Phrase borrowed from Sylvia Van Kirk, *Many Tender Ties*.

77 Ray, "Lower Chinook Ethnographic Notes," 72–73.

78 Jones, *Annals of Astoria*, 203–4 and fn. 98.

79 Coues, *New Light*, 901.

80 Jones, *Astorian Adventure*, 116.

81 Hajda, "Regional Social Organization," 179–82.

82 Ross, *Adventures of the First Settlers*, 107.

83 Cox, *The Columbia River*, 159–62.

84 Coues, *New Light*, 790, 800, 805; Frederick Merk, ed., *Fur Trade and Empire*, 104; and McLoughlin to Donald Manson, August 18, 1829, in Burt Brown Barker, ed., *Letters of Dr. John McLoughlin*, 46.

85 Coues, *New Light*, 891.

86 From the various sources of Forts Astoria (George) and Vancouver, the Iroquois and Algonkian women all appear to have been wives of trappers hired at Montreal and Michilimackinac.

87 Matthew Dennis, *Cultivating a Landscape of Peace*, 28, 108–9; and Daniel K. Richter, *The Ordeal of the Longhouse*, 18–24, 43–44.

88 Coues, *New Light*, 891.

89 Jones, *Annals of Astoria*, 237.

90 Ross, *First Settlers*, 130–31.

91 Coues, *New Light*, 908; Cox, *The Columbia River*, 268; and Jones, *Astorian Adventure*, 134.

92 Corney in Grace P. Morris, "Development of Astoria, 1811–1850," 417.

93 Simpson in Morrison, *Outpost*, 154.

94 Recollections of George B. Roberts, MS P-A 83, 15. See also Van Kirk's discussion of "daughters of the country," *Many Tender Ties*, 95–122.

95 Coues, *New Light*, 910.

96 Cox, *The Columbia River*, 158, 166, 172.

97 Van Kirk, *Many Tender Ties*, 53–74.

98 Anne M. Butler, *Daughters of Joy*; Frances Finnegan, *Poverty and Prostitution*; Timothy J. Gilfoyle, *City of Eros*; and Linda Mahood, *The Madgalenes*.

99 Cox, *The Columbia River*, 166.

100 Coues, *New Light*, 754, 849.

101 Gass likely started the observational trend with his 1811 publication, Hosmer, *Gass's Journal*, 176; see also Ross, *First Settlers*, 106.

102 Glover, *David Thompson's Narrative*, 362.

103 Cox, *The Columbia River*, 87.

104 Glover, *David Thompson's Narrative*, 357, 376.

105 Cox, *The Columbia River*, 156.

106 Coues, *New Light*, 908–9.

107 ox, *The Columbia River*, 156, 158.

108 Controlling Barnes would have been imperative for the creation and maintenance of a moral order; as Michel Foucault argues, morality is a complex interplay of regulations, restrictions, and the interplay of individual behavior with these codes, *The Use of Pleasure*, 22–32.

109 Coues, *New Light*, 825–26.

110 Jones, *Annals of Astoria*, 140, 141.

111 Coues, *New Light*, 835–36.

112 Jones, *Annals of Astoria*, 2, 10, 31, 39, 66, 108, 133, 153, 158, 159, 191, 201.

113 Coues, *New Light*, 836, 911, 859.

114 Jeremie's medical experiment, Jones, *Annals of Astoria*, 136–37.

115 Ibid., 141–42.

116 Coues, *New Light*, 890, 891, 806, 859.

117 Franchere, *Adventure at Astoria*, 117.

118 Hajda, "Regional Social Organization," 182.

119 Cruikshank, *The Social Life of Stories*, particularly 118, 122, 136. See also James Clifford and George E. Marcus, *Writing Culture*; Eugene S. Hunn, *Nchi-i-Wana*; Claude Schaeffer, "The Kutenai Female Berdache"; Leslie Spier, *The Prophet Dance*; and Elizabeth Vibert, "'The Natives Were Strong to Live.'"

120 For discussions of transgender among Indian people, see Richard C. Trexler, *Sex and Conquest*; Evelyn Blackwood, "Sexuality and Gender"; and Will Roscoe, "The Zuni Man-Woman," 136, 143. See also Sue-Ellen Jacobs, Wesley Thomas, and

Sabine Lane, *Two-Spirit People*; and Walter L. Williams, *The Spirit and the Flesh*. For examples specifically from western Oregon, see H. G. Barnett, Indian Tribes of the Oregon Coast: Field Notes, vol. 1, 1934, 4, 85; Field Notes, vol. 2, 1934, 24, 26; and Philip Drucker, Field Notes, vol. 4, 1934, 47.

121 Schaeffer, "The Kutenai Female Berdache," 216.

122 For discussions of the Prophet Movement and the possible role of Kauxuma-nupika, see Schaeffer, "The Kutenai Female Berdache"; Spier, "The Prophet Dance"; Vibert, " 'The Natives Were Strong to Live' "; and Christopher L. Miller, *Prophetic Worlds*.

123 Barbara Belyea, ed., *Columbia Journals*, 160; and Glover, *David Thompson's Narrative*, 367.

124 Ross, *The First Settlers*, 144–45; and Schaeffer, "The Kutenai Female Berdache," 206–7.

125 Franklin narratives quoted in Schaeffer, "The Kutenai Female Berdache," 207–8.

126 Ibid., 211–12.

127 Franchere, *Adventure at Astoria*, 130–31, and editor's note 5, 133.

128 Jones, *Annals of Astoria*, 33, 37; and Franchere, *Adventure at Astoria*, 56.

129 Jones, *Annals of Astoria*, 42, 44.

130 Ibid., 191–95; and Ronda, *Astoria and Empire*, 235–37.

131 Belyea, *Columbia Journals*, 162.

132 Moulton, *Journals of Lewis and Clark*, vol. 7, 104–10; and Ronda, *Lewis and Clark*, 216–17.

133 Philip Ashton Rollins, ed., *The Discovery of the Oregon Trail*, 55–59.

134 Jones, *Annals of Astoria*, 81, 113.

135 Hosmer, *Gass's Journal*, 177–78.

136 Jones, *Astorian Adventure*, 109, 113–14.

137 Lewis O. Saum, *The Fur Trader*, 40, 47.

138 Rollins, *Discovery of the Oregon Trail*, 61, 54; also see Ross, *Adventures of the First Settlers*, 129.

139 Ross, *Adventures of the First Settlers*, 129.

140 White, *The Middle Ground*.

141 Jones, *Annals of Astoria*, 105–14.

142 Raccoon, at one point, convinced McDougall that the Chinooks planned "to take away" the *Dolly*, and, although they could not sail a sloop, McDougall considered it a "probable" plot, Jones, *Annals of Astoria*, 115.

143 Ibid., 103–14.

144 Henry noted their presence as common, Coues, *New Light*, 879.

145 Jones, *Annals of Astoria*, 104–5, 107, 110.

146 Rollins, *Discovery of the Oregon Trail*, 34–37.

147 Belyea, *Columbia Journals*, 162.

148 Rollins, *Discovery of the Oregon Trail*, 53.

149 Jones, *Astorian Adventure*, 105.

150 Glover, *David Thompson's Narrative*, 363.

151 Jones, *Annals of Astoria*, 197.

152 Cox, *The Columbia River*, 122, 124–25.

153 Coues, *New Light*, 785.

154 Payette, *The Oregon Country under the Union Jack*, 24–25.

155 Coues, *New Light*, 785; Cox, *The Columbia River*, 148–49; and Franchere, *Adventure at Astoria*, 93–95.

156 Coues, *New Light*, 785, 788–89; for Seton's description of "Fort Calipuyaw," see Jones, *Astorian Adventure*, 133–34.

157 Jones, *Annals of Astoria*, 83, 149, 156, 178.

158 Coues, *New Light*, 793, 797.

159 Ibid., 798–809; and Franchere, *Adventure at Astoria*, 98–99. Cox or his editor gave a literal meaning to "covering the dead," writing that the goods were burial wealth; however, Henry and Franchere do not support this rendering, *The Columbia River*, 148.

160 Coues, *New Light*, 821.

161 Ibid., 820, 824.

162 Ibid., 853, 856, 879.

163 Stern, *Chiefs and Chief Traders*, 32–33; and Merk, *Fur Trade and Empire*, 106.

164 Perkins, *Cambridge History of Foreign Relations*; and Donald R. Hickey, *The War of 1812*.

165 Their little ship *Dolly* flew the Northwest Company flag, the crew hoping that it would appear neutral, Coues, *New Light*, 848.

166 Ronda gives a full discussion of Astor's machinations and "Astoria at War," *Astoria and Empire*, 243–76; see also Franchere, *Adventure at Astoria*, 86–87.

167 Franchere, *Adventure at Astoria*, 74.

168 Jones, *Annals of Astoria*, 150.

169 Ibid., 172–73.

170 Jones, *Astorian Adventure*, 128–29.

171 Franchere, *Adventure at Astoria*, 79.

172 Jones, *Annals of Astoria*, 219–20.

173 Franchere, *Adventure at Astoria*, 89.

174 Coues, *New Light*, 852.

175 Cox, *The Columbia River*, 119.

176 Coues, *New Light*, 850.

177 Jones, *Annals of Astoria*, 174, 188.

178 Cox, *The Columbia River*, 147–48.

179 Franchere, *Adventure at Astoria*, 90–91.

180 Coues, *New Light*, 866–67, 878.

181 Ibid., 902, 905, 907, 912–15.

182 Franchere states "most," *Adventure at Astoria*, 87.

183 Coues, *New Light*, 889–90, 902, 906–7.

184 For an analysis of all the machinations of Astor and his Northwestern competitors, see Ronda, *Astoria and Empire*; and the classic diplomatic history of the imperial fight for Oregon remains Frederick Merk, *The Oregon Question*.

185 Payette, *The Oregon Country under the Union Jack*, 177–78. See also Ronda, *Astoria and Empire*, 308–15.

186 Payette, *The Oregon Country under the Union Jack*, 36–61.

187 Ibid., 180, 660, 662, 666, 668.

188 Ibid., 183.

189 Franchere, *Adventure at Astoria*, 115.

Chapter Three

1 Nikolai N. Bolkhovitinov, "Russia and the Declaration," 104–6, 110; Bradford Perkins, *The Creation of a Republican Empire*, 159–61; and William Appleman Williams, *The Contours of American History*, 215–18.

2 The Red River colony and the fur-trade wars have been covered numerous times by historians. For two monographs that make explicit connections with the Oregon Country, see Morrison, *Outpost*; and John S. Galbraith, *The Hudson's Bay Company*.

3 Simpson in Merk, *Fur Trade and Empire*, 65.

4 The rationale for Britain's imperial monopolies was to provide clear order far from the metropole, a rarely achieved ideal but one for which Simpson and his contemporaries strove. For treatments of the ideals and changing practices of the British Empire, see James Muldoon, *Empire and Order*; Cain and Hopkins, *British Imperialism*; and Robert G. Wesson, *The Imperial Order*.

5 Gov. J. H. Pelly to Hon. George Canning, London, December 9, 1825, in Merk, *Fur Trade and Empire*, 258.

6 John K. Townsend quoted in Morris, "Development of Astoria," 422.

7 Hajda, "Regional Social Organization," 46.

8 Galbraith, *The Hudson's Bay Company*, 91.

9 Ibid., 89.

10 Ibid., 88.

11 Jeff LaLande, ed., *First over the Siskiyous*, 13.

12 Ibid., 15, 34–35.

13 Theodore Stern, *The Klamath Tribe*, 3–21.

14 LaLande, *First over the Siskiyous*, 39 and note on 134.

15 Gatschet, *The Klamath Indians*, 192.

16 Stern, *The Klamath Tribe*, 22–24.

17 Chiloquin quoted in ibid., 23.

18 Gatschet, *The Klamath Indians*, vol. 1, 16.

19 The relevance of the spelling with and without possessive "s" is discussed more completely in chapter 4.

20 LaLande, *First over the Siskiyous*, 59–60. LaLande notes that Ogden's reference may have been to Finan McDonald's trapping expedition to the Klamath River the previous year, 135.

21 Ibid., 59–60, 64, 122–23.

22 Dennis J. Gray, *The Takelma*, 40, 73.

23 Ibid., 88–92; and Robert F. Heizer and Thomas Roy Hester, "Shasta Villages," 119–30.

24 LaLande, *First over the Siskiyous*, 65, 69–71.

25 Ibid., 79–91.

26 See also Lewis A. McArthur, *Oregon Geographic Names*, 719–20.

27 Father Blanchet wrote of the Rogue Valley, "its name from the Indians whose territory it waters, and whose predatory habits have acquired them the rather unpleasant *sobriquet* of the "Rogues." Blanchet lumped the coastal Athapaskan "Port Orford Indians" with the Rogues; "[t]he similarity of their language, the friendly intercourse that exists between them, their disposition and decided taste for plunder, are strong proofs that they form but one tribe," *A Comprehensive, Explanatory, Correct, Pronouncing Dictionary*, 60, reprinted in appendix of Thomas Vaughn, ed., *Paul Kane*. See also Overton Johnson and Wm. H. Winter, *Route across the Rocky Mountains*, 50; and for an early "scientific" classification of "the Rogue or Rascal Indians," see Horatio Hale, "Ethnography and Philology," 221.

28 Letter from McLoughlin to Smith, September 12, 1828, in Maurice S. Sullivan, ed., *The Travels of Jedediah Smith*, 109.

29 Coues, *New Light*, 867.

30 Ibid., 109.

31 For the rape charge, see Nathan Douthit, "The Hudson's Bay Company," 44; and for a discussion refuting the charge, see John Phillip Reid, "Restraints of Vengeance," 72–73.

32 LaLande, *First over the Siskiyous*, 91.

33 Letter from McLoughlin to McLeod, September 12, 1828, in Sullivan, *The Travels of Jedediah Smith*, 109.

34 Morrison, *Outpost*, 176–78.

35 Letter from McLoughlin to McLeod, September 12, 1828, in Sullivan, *The Travels of Jedediah Smith*, 109.

36 Gustavus Hines, *Life on the Plains of the Pacific*, 104–5.

37 Jones, *Astorian Adventure*, 134.

38 Barker, *Letters of Dr. John McLoughlin*, 83.

39 Douthit, "The Hudson's Bay Company," makes the case that the colonial traders instigated the violence in the southern Oregon trade. Reid developed a sophisticated legal history for the clashes in John Phillip Reid, *Patterns of Vengeance*.

40 Barker, *Letters of Dr. John McLoughlin*, 18–26, 41, 118–19.

41 Ibid., 41.

42 The Astorians were keen observers of the various conflicts of the lower Columbia Native peoples, always watchful of alliances that might turn against them, Jones, *Annals of Astoria*, 37, 109–10, 206–9; Coues, *New Light*, 855, 867, 879–81; Franchere, *Adventure at Astoria*, 115–17; and Ross, *Adventures of the First Settlers*, 102–3.

43 Barker, *Letters of Dr. John McLoughlin*, 21.

44 McLoughlin quoted in Morrison, *Outpost*, 175.

45 For European constructions of the "Indian," see Robert F. Berkhofer Jr., *The White Man's Indian*. For the developing Native notions of Indian identity, see Alexandra Harmon, "Lines in the Sand"; and Harmon, *Indians in the Making*. For racial constructions of "white" colonialists, see Audrey Smedley, *Race in North America*.

46 Barker, *Letters of Dr. John McLoughlin*, 46, 163, 170, 181.

47 Morris, "Development of Astoria," 421.

48 Boyd, *People of The Dalles*, 156–57; Donald, *Aboriginal Slavery*, 140–42, 224–28, 232–33; and Hajda, "Regional Social Organization," 191–95.

49 Thomas E. Fessett, ed., *Reports and Letters of Herbert Beaver*, 132.

50 Hajda, "Regional Social Organization," 179–80, 195.

51 Donald, *Aboriginal Slavery*, 229–31.

52 McLoughlin letters to McGillivray, February 27, 1832, and to Simpson, March 15, 1832, in Barker, *Letters of Dr. John McLoughlin*, 254–55, 258.

53 McLoughlin to McGillivray, March 15, 1832, in ibid., 258.

54 Theodore Stern, *Chiefs and Change*, 150–51; and Boyd, *People of The Dalles*, 78.

55 McLoughlin to William Connolly, July 2, 1830, in Barker, *Letters of Dr. John McLoughlin*, 109.

56 McLoughlin to LaFramboise, April 1832, May 9, 1832; to James Birnie, May 15, 1832, in ibid., 268, 272–73.

57 T. C. Elliott, "Journal of Peter Skene Ogden," 370.

58 Saum, *The Fur Trader and the Indian*, 42.

59 Cox, *The Columbia River*, 119, 167–68.

60 Recollections of George B. Roberts, BL, MS P-A 83, 14.

61 Morrison, *Outpost*, 209–10, 211.

62 Robert Boyd, *The Coming of the Spirit*, 109.

63 Hajda, "Regional Social Organization," 35–46.

64 P. L. Edwards, *Sketch of the Oregon Territory*, 15–16.

65 Boyd, *The Coming of the Spirit*, 97–99.

66 Ibid., 84, and see tables, 323–29.

67 Ibid., 329. Rev. John Frost was responsible for the lower estimate, and, as discussed in the next chapter, his reasons for undercounting the Native population related to his desire to leave his mission post.

68 Ibid., 131–34.

69 Ibid., 109; Nellie B. Pipes, "Journal of John H. Frost," 140–41; and, more generally, Alfred W. Crosby Jr., "Virgin Soil Epidemics."

70 Ray, "Lower Chinook Ethnographic Notes," 86.

71 Roberts, "Recollections," 14.

72 Boyd, *The Coming of the Spirit*, 46–47.

73 Cox, *The Columbia River*, 170. Irving's narrative was originally published five years after Cox's in 1836, Washington Irving, *Astoria*.

74 Recollections of George B. Roberts, BL, MS P-A 83, 14; Boyd, *People of The Dalles*, 173; and Boyd, *Coming of the Spirit*, 46, 109, 112–15.

75 Hines, *Life on the Plains of the Pacific*, 105–12.

76 These events have been much covered by historians. For a recent discussion, see Morrison, *Outpost*, 231–41.

77 Jones, *Annals of Astoria*, 89–90, n 17; and Cox, *The Columbia River*, 45.

78 Fessett, *Reports and Letters of Herbert Beaver*, 42, 54, 85, 131.

79 English settler colonialism dated back to the 1780s, but migration increased in the 1840s, as did the colonization of New Zealand. Like the Far West of the United States, emigration was spurred by a gold rush. See Cain and Hopkins, *British Imperialism*, 229–31, 243–58.

80 Simpson in Merk, *Fur Trade and Empire*, 65, 101.

81 Fessett, *Reports and Letters of Herbert Beaver*, 35, 40, 50, 54, 57, 86, 117–21.

82 Ibid., 140, 145, 147–48.

Chapter Four

1 "Diary of Rev. Jason Lee," *Oregon Historical Quarterly*, 408, 254.

2 Robert J. Loewenberg, *Equality on the Oregon Frontier*, 4–6; William G. McLoughlin, "Cherokees and Methodists 1824–1834"; and Christine Leigh Heyrman, *Southern Cross*.

3 Antonio R. Gualtieri, *Christianity and Native Traditions*, 3–9.

4 Robert F. Berkhofer Jr., *Salvation and the Savage*, 69.

5 H. W. Perkins to Waller, January 1, 1841, Oregon Historical Society, Portland, Ore. (hereafter cited as OHS), MS 1210, folder 9.

6 H. K. Perkins to Cyrus Shepard, December 6, 1839, OHS, MS 1219, folder 2b.

7 Diary of Alvan F. Waller, OHS, MS 1210, folder 11, 4.

8 Loewenberg, *Equality on the Oregon Frontier*, 112. See also Nathan Hatch, *Democratization of American Christianity*; John Wigger, *Taking Heaven by Storm*; and Cynthia Lynn Lyerly, *Methodism and the Southern Mind*.

9 See Gregory Evans Dowd, *A Spirited Resistance*; and White, *Middle Ground*.

10 Robert J. Loewenberg, "Saving Oregon Again: A Western Perennial?"

11 For a discussion of Lee's supporters and critics, see Gene Herbert Hovee, "Jason Lee," 43–55.

12 Jason Lee, OHS, MS 1212, folder 4, *Christian Advocate and Journal*, June 13, 1834, 3–4.

13 Frederick Merk, *Manifest Destiny*.

14 David Leslie, OHS, MS 1216, folder 3, 10–11; McLoughlin, "Cherokees and Methodists 1824–1834"; Hugh T. Hodges, "Charles Maclay"; Haunani-Kay Trask, *From a Native Daughter*; and Kenton J. Clymer, "Religion and American Imperialism."

15 Leslie, OHS, MS 1216, folder 3, 10; folder 5, Henry Perkins to Leslie, February 8, 1844.

16 Horsman, *Race and Manifest Destiny*. For comparable studies of empires and mission, see Norman Etherington, ed., *Mission and Empire*, and Bernard Bailyn, *Atlantic History*.

17 Perkins, *Cambridge History of Foreign Relations*.

18 Alvan F. Waller, OHS, MS 1210, folder 8, J. P. Durbin to Waller, October 9, 1857.

19 The ABCFM was a union of the Congregationalist, Presbyterian, and Dutch Reformed churches.

20 Jonathan S. Green, *Journal of a Tour*, 10–11.

21 Ibid., 17.

22 Address printed in the *Missionary Herald*, December 1827, 396–97, in ibid., 17–19; Archer Butler Hulbert and Dorothy Printup Hulbert, eds., *The Oregon Crusade*, 29; and O. A. Bushnell, *The Gifts of Civilization*, 221–22.

23 Green, *Journal of a Tour*, 37–38.

24 Ibid., 103. Green's report was reprinted in the *Missionary Herald*, April 1831, in Hulbert and Hulbert, *The Oregon Crusade*, 76–78, 83.

25 Mission Board in Robert Moulton Gatke, "A Document of Mission History," 73.

26 Bangs in ibid., 74.

27 Charles Henry Carey, "Methodist Annual Reports," 305.

28 Ibid., 306.

29 Because of my focus on western Oregon, I mostly discuss the Methodists. Others, however, notably the Catholics and the ABCFM, also heeded the Macedonian Call. Still, Jason Lee and his band were first.

30 "Diary of Rev. Jason Lee," 242.

31 The Plateau peoples' belief in the missionaries' powers to control disease—inflict it and heal it—would later figure in the Whitman Massacre after a number of Cayuse, Wallawalla, and Shoshones faulted the ABCFM missionaries for an outbreak of measles and dysentery in 1847, Stern, *Chiefs and Change*, 170–71.

32 "Diary of Rev. Jason Lee," 241–42, 255; and Stern, *Chiefs and Change*, 43–45.

33 "Methodist Mission Record Book, 1834–1838," MS 1224, folder 1, 11; and "Diary of Rev. Jason Lee," 255.

34 Lee's sermon in Hovee, *Jason Lee*, 107–8.

35 Daniel Lee and J. H. Frost, *Ten Years in Oregon*, 127.

36 Cyrus Shepard, OHS, MS 1219, folder 5, *Christian Advocate and Journal*, January 10, 1835, 1.

37 Carey, "Methodist Reports," 307–8.

38 Gatke, "Document of Mission," 74–76.

39 Carey, "Methodist Reports," 310.

40 For the Jason Lee quotation, see Robert J. Loewenberg, "New Evidence, Old Categories," 356; and Hubert Howe Bancroft, *History of Oregon*, 174.

41 Cushing Eells Letters, 1843–1859, OHS, MS 1218, folder 2, Eells to Greene, vol. 248, letter 101, September 21, 1846, 74.

42 For Choctaw mission-agricultural schools, see Clara Sue Kidwell, "Choctaws and Missionaries," letter October 2, 1839, printed in *Missionary Herald*, June 1840, reprinted in Stern, *Chiefs and Change*, 51.

43 For the criticism of Indian students' education, see Lee and Frost, *Ten Years in Oregon*, 148.

44 Fessett, *Reports and Letters of Herbert Beaver*, 78, 130.

45 Cyrus Shepard, OHS, MS 1219, folder 2b, Cyrus Shepard to "Addison" William A. Horve, April 9, 1838, 1–2; Lee, OHS, MS 1212, folder 4, *Christian Advocate and Journal*, September 2, 1836; Shepard, OHS, MS 1219, Susan Shepard to sister Ann, September 15, 1839, 2.

46 For Slacum's views, see his letter to Jason Lee and others, January 18, 1837, in Hines, *Life on the Plains of the Pacific*, 22–23.

47 For Slacum, see Cornelius J. Brosnan, *Jason Lee, Prophet*, 84–85. For the role of Jason Lee and the figures, see Lee and Frost, *Ten Years in Oregon*, 146. Lee and Frost put Slacum's donation at only $50.

48 Lee's sermon recounted in *Zion's Herald*, February 6, 1839, and his speech to the Mission Board, Jason Lee MS Collection, OHS, are quoted in Hovee, *Jason Lee*, 53–54, 106–12.

49 Lee in Hovee, *Jason Lee*, 54.

50 "Diary of Rev. Jason Lee," 241, 264–65, 401–2.

51 Lee, OHS, MS 1212, folder 4, *Christian Advocate and Journal*, February 6, 1835, Jason Lee to Mission Board, 13–14; Cyrus Shepard, OHS, MS 1219, folder 1, diary, 1834–1835, May 2, 1834, and Susan Shepard to sister Mrs. Joseph A. Lloyd, November 1, 1837, 2; Eells, OHS, MS 1218, folder 2, Eells to Rev. David Greene, vol. 248, letter 96, November 9, 1843, 51.

52 Minutes of the Annual Meetings of the Oregon Mission, OHS, MS 1224, folder 3, 32.

53 Ibid., 1842 meeting, May 20, 1842, Resolution to accept invitation for open communication with the Sandwich Island Mission regarding "all subjects of common interest to our missionary work," 27; Cyrus Shepard, OHS, MS 1219, folder 2b, Susan Shepard to Sister Ann, August 5, 1836, 3, and January 31, 1837.

54 Lee testimony to the board, July 2, 1844, in Brosnan, *Jason Lee, Prophet*, 257; Pipes, "Journal of John H. Frost," 360.

55 Fessett, *Reports and Letters of Herbert Beaver*, 4.

56 Letter, Margaret Smith, dated "Fort Vancouver, April 10th, 1838," in *Oregonian and Indians' Advocate*, November 1838, I, 58–61, reprinted in Brosnan, *Jason Lee, Prophet*, 82.

57 Thomas Edward Harper, *Chinook*, 75.

58 Leslie, OHS, MS 1216, folder 5, Henry Perkins to Leslie, February 8, 1844.

59 Cushing Eells Letters, 1843–1859, OHS, MS 1218, folder 2, 50–51; Henry Perkins to David Leslie, February 8, 1844, in David Leslie, OHS, MS 1216, folder 5.

60 Gustavus Hines Diary, September 6, 1845, OHS, MS 1215, see entries 10/2/45, 12/10/45, 1/11/46, 2/21/46.

61 Hines, *Life on the Plains of the Pacific*, 105.

62 Pipes, "Journal of John H. Frost," 360.

63 Ibid., vol. 3, 72–73.

64 Kone in Robert Moulton Gatke, "A Document of Mission History," 87; for Lee, see Frances Fuller Victor, *The Early Indian Wars*, 14.

65 For a discussion of regional networks, see Hajda, "Regional Social Organization," 2, 22, 24.

66 Stern, *Chiefs and Change*, 19; for a recent collection of essays that attempts to comprehend Native agency, see Nicholas Griffiths and Fernando Cervantes, eds., *Spiritual Encounters*. See, particularly, Griffiths's historiographic discussion of Indian conversion, "Introduction," 3–7.

67 Tracy Neal Leavelle, "'We Will Make It Our Own Place,'"; Pamela T. Amoss, "The Indian Shaker Church." Regarding syncretism, see Leslie Spier, *The Prophet Dance*; James Mooney, *The Ghost-Dance Religion*; and Cora Alice DuBois, *The Feather Cult*.

68 "Mission Record Book, 1834–1838," OHS, MS 1224, folder 1, 9.

69 Ibid., 128–29. Deaths include "William Brooks," who died on Jason Lee's first fundraising trip back east.

70 "Diary of Rev. Jason Lee," 255–56; "Mission Record Book," folder 1, 128–29; folder 5, 175.

71 Sheppard in Hulbert and Hulbert, *The Oregon Crusade*, 197.

72 "Mission Record Book," folder 1, 29–30.

73 Stern, *Chiefs and Change*, 44–46, 170–72; Robert Boyd, "The Pacific Northwest Measles"; and Hurtado, *Indian Survival*, 80.

74 Pipes, "Journal of John H. Frost," 363; Jason Lee in *Christian Advocate and Journal*, September 2, 1836, 3; and Waller, OHS, MS 1210, folder 11, 5–6.

75 "Mission Record Book," folder 5, 141, 147, 175.

76 Lee and Frost, *Ten Years in Oregon*, 263–64; Waller, OHS, MS 1210, folder 11, 6–7; Hamilton Campbell to 'Bro. & Sister Whitcomb,' October 25, 1843, OHS, MS 1225, folder 2, 4; Chloe A. Clark to Mary A. Norton, May 22, 1840, OHS, MS 1225, folder 12, 4; and *North American*, June 5, 1839, reprinted in Brosnan, *Jason Lee, Prophet*, n. 70, 39–40.

77 David Leslie, OHS, MS 1216, folder 3, 2; "Westward to Oregon: Diary and Letters of Almira David Raymond and W. W. Raymond, Oregon pioneers with Rev. Jason Lee/introduction, commentary and family notes by Leon Thomas David," OHS, MS 2997, 16, 31, 34; and David Leslie to T. C. Peirce, April 21, 1842, OHS, MS 1216, folder 5.

78 "William Brooks' Boston Speech," *Zion's Herald*, February 13, 1839, 27, in Brosnan, *Jason Lee, Prophet*, 112.

79 Ibid., 121.

80 Ibid., 124.

81 Ibid., 137.

82 Bernd C. Peyer, *The Tutor'd Mind*, 20. See also Dale T. Knobel, "Know Nothings."

83 *Christian Advocate and Journal*, October 4, 1839, 25, and *Columbian Weekly Register*, January 12, 1839, in Brosnan, *Jason Lee, Prophet*, 113.

84 Ibid., note, 140.

85 Jason Lee, OHS, MS 1212, folder 4, *Zion's Herald* and *Christian Advocate and Journal*, April 30, 1834.

86 Ibid., *Christian Advocate and Journal*, June 13, 1834, 5.

Chapter Five

1 Alvan F. Waller, OHS, MS 1210, folder 5, 2–5.

2 Ibid.

3 Ibid., folder 10, Narcissa Whitman to Waller, May 31, 1844, and folder 13, Waller's petition to Genessee Conference.

4 Cyrus Shepard, OHS, MS 1219, folder 2b, Shepard to Brother and Sister Jenkins, October 8, 1839. Regarding the first petition for territorial acquisition in 1838, Shepard to William A. Horve, April 9, 1838, 3.

5 Cyrus Shepard, OHS, MS 1219, folders 105 and 13; Alvan F. Waller, OHS, MS 1210, folder 11, August 11, 1845, 15.

6 For the Genesee Conference, see *Christian Advocate and Journal*, April 4, 1834, in Hulbert and Hulbert, *The Oregon Crusade*, 122–24; for the subsequent attempt, see Clifford M. Drury, "The Oregonian and Indian's Advocate," *Pacific Northwest Quarterly*, and Clifford Merritt Drury, ed., *The Mountains We Have Crossed*, 314–16.

7 Stern, *Chiefs and Change*, 50–51.

8 J. Orin Oliphant, "Lee-Greene Correspondence."

9 For a defense of Whitman's actions, see Myron Eells, OHS, MS 1218, folder 3, Frances Fuller Victor to Myron Eells, April 3, 1883; Myron Eells to J. G. Prentiss, May 18, 1882, 3; and folder 4, Eells, "Indian Missions on the Pacific Coast," 15–17.

10 Pipes, "Journal of John H. Frost," 56.

11 Ibid., 150.

12 Ibid., 362.

13 Ibid.

14 Celiast also is known as Helen Smith from her marriage to Euro-American colonist Solomon Smith. She was the middle daughter of Coboway, the principal headman of the Clatsops during the early fur trade. Celiast had earlier married a French Canadian and resided at Fort Vancouver. Thus her conversion may well have occurred before the Oregon Mission and/or been aided by earlier acculturation. See David Peterson-del Mar, "Intermarriage and Agency"; and Eugene O. Smith, "Solomon Smith."

15 Pipes, "Journal of John H. Frost," 73.

16 Ray, "Lower Chinook Ethnographic Notes," 75–76.

17 Pipes, "Journal of John H. Frost," 359–60.

18 Ibid., 364.

19 Ibid., 160.

20 Ibid., 161.

21 For recent studies of this phenomenon, see Shari M. Huhndorf, *Going Native*; and Philip J. Deloria, *Playing Indian*.

22 Pipes, "Journal of John H. Frost," 372.

23 Hines, *Life on the Plains of the Pacific*, 104–5.

24 Lee to Fisk, March 15, 1836, in Brosnan, *Jason Lee, Prophet*, 80; Jason Lee sermon, in ibid., 111–12.

25 Jason Lee sermon, in Brosnan, *Jason Lee, Prophet*, 111–12.

26 Carey, "Methodist Reports," 318–19, 322, 324.

27 For complaints from Elijah White, J. P. Richmond, George Abernethy, and William Kone, see Gatke, "Document of Mission," 81–89, and Joseph Whitcomb's pro-Lee testimony, 164–68; and Hines's damning letter of the mission, 171–81, Loans to Emigrants, in Carey, "Methodist Reports," 361.

28 OHS, MS 1225, folder 3, George Gary to Isaac Stone, December 8, 1846.

29 Ibid., 360.

30 Gatke, "Document of Mission," 173.

31 Charles Henry Carey, "Diary of Rev. George Gary," 81.

32 Carey, "Methodist Reports," 348–49.

33 Frederick V. Holman, "A Brief History," 123.

34 Gatke, "Document of Mission," 164–65, 167.

35 Waller, OHS, MS 1210, folder 8, Gary to Waller, July 24, 1844.

36 Gatke, "Document of Mission," 78–79.

37 Carey, "Methodist Reports," 318.

38 Gatke, "Document of Mission History," 91.

39 Ibid., 88–89.

40 Ibid., 90–91.

41 Ibid., 170.

42 Gary finished the job of disposing of mission properties in 1846, OHS, MS 1225, folder 3, George Gary to Isaac Stone, December 8, 1846.

43 Carey, "Methodist Reports," 361.

44 Daniel Lee to David Leslie, January 20, 180, OHS, MS 1216, folder 5; Jason Lee in Loewenberg, "New Evidence, Old Categories," 363.

45 Samuel Parker, *Journal of an Exploring Tour*, 269, 271.

46 Lee and Frost, *Ten Years in Oregon*, 105.

47 For the best overview of the relationship between "Anglo-Saxon" Americans and their perceived destiny to possess most of North America, see Horsman, *Race and Manifest Destiny*. In the mid-nineteenth century, the identity of white slowly encompassed non-Anglo immigrants such as Germans and Irish and later Eastern and Southern Europeans, Matthew Frye Jacobson, *Whiteness of a Different Color*; David R. Roediger, *The Wages of Whiteness*; and James R. Barrett and David Roediger, "Inbetween Peoples."

48 Slaiha Belmessous, "Assimilation and Racialism"; for an insightful discussion of "Indian hating," see White, *The Middle Ground*, 383–96; for race, see Richard White, *It's Your Misfortune and None of My Own*, 320–22; Smedley, *Race in North America*; and Edmund S. Morgan, *American Slavery*.

49 Heyrman, *Southern Cross*.

50 Jason Lee, OHS, MS 1212, folder 4, *Christian Advocate and Journal*, June 13, 1834, 5.

51 Lee in Hovee, *Jason Lee, A Rhetorical Criticism*, 54.

52 Mission Record Book, 1834–1838, OHS, MS 1224, folder 1, 34.

53 Lee's testimony July 2, 1844, in Brosnan, *Jason Lee, Prophet*, 258.

54 "Diary of Rev. Jason Lee," 249–50.

55 Ibid., 412, and Hovee, *Jason Lee*, 54.

56 Carey, "Methodist Reports," 317.

57 Ibid., 258.

58 "Petition of Felix Hathaway" in Loewenberg, *Equality on the Oregon Frontier*, 134.

59 Fessett, *Reports and Letters of Herbert Beaver*, 48–54, 57, 86, 116.

60 Loewenberg, *Equality on the Oregon Frontier*, 135.

61 John Minto, Early Days of Oregon, BL, MS P-A 50, 9.

62 Letter from Jason Lee, February 5, 1834, reprinted in *Christian Advocate and Journal*, February 21, 1834, and Hulbert and Hulbert, *The Oregon Crusade*, 136.

63 Loewenberg, *Equality on the Oregon Frontier*, 123, 124.

64 Harald E. L. Prins, "To the Land of the Mistigoches"; *Zion's Herald*, October 17, 1838, 9, 167; and *Christian Advocate and Journal*, December 14, 1838, 13, 66, in Brosnan, *Jason Lee, Prophet*, 98.

65 Carey, "Diary of Rev. George Gary," 85.

66 Ibid., 84–86; and "Minutes of the Annual Meetings of the Oregon Mission, For the Years 1841, 1842, 1843," OHS, MS 1224, folder 3, 37.

67 Carey, "Diary of Rev. George Gary," 84–86.

68 For a full exploration of the notion of Indians' school, reflecting the agency of the students, versus a school for Indians, see K. Tsianina Lomawaima, *They Called It Prairie Light*.

69 Hamilton Campbell to Ezekial Pilcher, September 12, 1840, OHS, MS 1225, folder 4; "Minutes of the Annual Meetings," 37; and Hamilton Campbell to 'Bro. & Sister Whitcomb,' October 25, 1843, OHS, MS 1225, folder 2.

70 Carey, "Diary of Rev. George Gary," 84.

71 Lee testimony to the Board, July 2, 1844, in Brosnan, *Jason Lee, Prophet*, 257.

72 A. F. Waller to Amos Cooke, August 2, 1843, OHS, MS 1210, folder 7.

73 Carey, "Diary of Rev. George Gary," 91.

74 Ibid., 84.

75 Susan Shepard to Mrs. Joseph A. Lloyd, November 1, 1837, OHS, MS 1219, folder 2b; and Jason Lee in *Christian Advocate and Journal*, September 2, 1836.

76 For the assumptions of mutability within the monogenetic view, see Robert E. Bieder, *Science Encounters the Indian*, 11–12, 91. Race scientists did, however, combine Darwinian evolution with monogenesis to rank civilizations, chart the presumed decline of "primitives," and predict the inevitable extinction of Indians and freed blacks, Smedley, *Race in North America*, 163, 166, 229–40. Such beliefs would not have been very prevalent among nineteenth-century missionaries, who were dedicated to uplifting "lesser" peoples of the world, and who continued to advocate the civilizing effects of education. See House, "Memorial of The Board of Managers of the American Indian Mission Association," 29th Cong., 1st Sess., January 13, 1846, Doc. 73, Serial 483, 1.

77 Green, *Journal of a Tour*, 10.

78 Horsman, *Race and Manifest Destiny*, 190; see also 189–207.

79 Smedley, *Race in North America*, 163, 166, 174–76, 229–40; and Bieder, *Science Encounters the Indian*, 11–12, 91; and for the dominance of racial thinking in Indian-white relations, see Horsman, *Race and Manifest Destiny*, 189–207.

80 Pipes, "Journal of John H. Frost," 239. For a discussion of craniometry and its chief creator, Dr. Samuel Morton, see Smedley, *Race in North America*, 230–33.

81 *Congressional Globe*, 29th Cong., 1st Sess., May 28, 1846.

82 For border claims, see Carey, "Methodist Reports," 325.

83 Gatke, "Mission Document," 82.

84 Ibid.

85 Pipes, "Journal of John H. Frost," 360.

86 Lee testimony, July 2, 1844, in Brosnan, *Jason Lee, Prophet*, 257.

87 For example, see Gatke, "Methodist Document," 88.

88 Josiah L. Parrish, Anecdotes of Intercourse with the Indians, BL, MS P-A 59, 16.

89 Carey, "Methodist Reports," 357.

90 Ibid., 359.

91 Minutes of the Annual Meetings, OHS, MS 1224, folder 3, May 8, 1841, 10.

92 Parrish, *Anecdotes of Intercourse*, 37.

93 "Minutes of the Annual Meetings," 41.

94 Parrish, *Anecdotes of Intercourse*, 19, 34–47.

95 Hamilton Campbell to 'Bro. & Sister Whitcomb,' October 25, 1843, OHS, MS 1225, folder 2, 2–3.

96 Minto, *Early Days*, 2, 20–21.

97 Joseph Holman, The Peoria Party, BL, MS, 1, 2, in Brosnan, *Jason Lee, Prophet*, 101–2.

98 Edwards, *Sketch of the Oregon*, 6–7.

99 Ibid., 19–20.

100 Minto, *Early Days*, 6.

101 Lee and Frost, *Ten Years in Oregon*, 96, 100, 104–5, 261, 262.

102 Carey, "Methodist Reports," 326.

103 Lee and Frost, *Ten Years in Oregon*, 140–41; Irving, *Astoria*; Blanchet in Vaughn, *Paul Kane*, 64–65; and Joel Palmer, *Journal of Travels*, 136–41.

104 Lee and Frost, *Ten Years in Oregon*, 130–31.

105 Hines, *Life on the Plains of the Pacific*, 101–2; and Elizabeth Vibert, *Traders' Tales*.

106 Hines, *Life on the Plains of the Pacific*, 104–5. See chapter 1 for a discussion of the massacre.

107 Ibid., 105–12.

108 Ibid., 112–18.

109 Ibid., 117–18.

110 Ibid., 101–3; speech, 104–5; and warning about missionaries, 106.

111 Fessett, *Reports and Letters of Herbert Beaver*, 78, 31, 22, 85, 131, 129.

112 For editor's discussion of Harrison, see ibid., 16.

113 Carey, "Methodist Reports," 364.

114 House, "Memorial of The Board of Managers," 29th Cong., 1st Sess., January 13, 1846, Doc. 73, Serial 483, 1.

115 House, *Annual Report of the Commissioner of Indian Affairs (ARCIA) 1857* (1858), 35th Cong., 1st Sess., Ex. Doc. 2, Serial 919, 369, Mary C. Ostrander to John F. Miller, July 1857.

116 Frederick E. Hoxie, *A Final Promise*.

Chapter Six

1 For land claims, see Lottie LeGett Gurley, ed., *Genealogical Material in Oregon*. For demography and birthplaces of the initial colonists, see William Bowen, "The Oregon Frontiersman"; and Holman, "A Brief History."

2 Under the provisional government, claims larger than 640 acres usually were business partnerships; see Gurley, *Genealogical Material*, Book 1, for example. Seeking an amendment to sales of land claims in 1854, Oregon representative Joseph Lane admitted that the original claims taken under the provisional government and sanctioned by the 1850 federal law were overly large in size. He also had to defend his speculative constituents from some amusingly sarcastic criticisms from fellow representatives regarding the Oregonians' propensity for economic speculation. *Congressional Globe*, 33rd Cong., 1st Sess., May 4, 1854, 1076.

3 For related discussions, see Paul W. Gates, "The Role of the Land Speculator"; Jerry A. O'Callaghan, *The Disposition of the Public Domain*; Paul W. Gates and Robert W. Swenson, *History of Public Land Law*; Roy M. Robbins, *Our Landed Heritage*; and Malcolm J. Rohrbough, *The Land Office Business*.

4 Merk, *The Oregon Question*.

5 The land office reflected the growing unease among the Euro-American colonists that new emigrants would jump their claims, Holman, "A Brief History," 135–36.

6 Ronald Spores, "Too Small a Place," 173.

7 Benjamin Dowell argued, for example, that since 1841 "[i]n Oregon and California every settler upon the public lands, whether 'surveyed or unsurveyed' had, and still has the guarantee of an act of Congress for a perfect title before the Indians title is extinguished." BL, MS P-A 133, folder 4, 7.

8 Gurley, *Genealogical Material*, 215.

9 Ibid., 68.

10 As early as 1825, the British had indicated that they were willing to abandon all the lands south of the Columbia River, modern-day Oregon, and the location of most Euro-American colonial settlements. HBC chief factor John McLaughlin continued to act under that belief until the 1846 treaty, Holman, "A Brief History," 121; and Merk, *The Oregon Question*, 72.

11 Spores, "Too Small a Place," 172; and Boyd, *The Coming of the Spirit*, 323–29.

12 The California Gold Rush caused the actual numbers of Euro-Americans to fluctuate, making their numbers hard to determine. For the approximate figure of 9,000, see Holman, "A Brief History," 132, 136. President Polk's address to Congress in 1848 put the figure at 12,000, Senate, *Message of the President of the United States*, 30th Cong., 1st Sess., 1848, Doc. 47, Serial 508. The 1850 figure is from the Corrected United States Census, Oregon, 1850, Bowen, "The Oregon Frontiersman," 184.

13 Robbins, "Extinguishing Indian Land Title," 11; and Spores, "Too Small a Place," 173.

14 For detailed studies of environmental change in the Pacific Northwest, see William G. Robbins, *Landscapes of Promise*; Robert Bunting, *The Pacific Raincoast*; Richard White, *Land Use, Environment, and Social Change*; and Peter Boag, *Environment and Experience*.

15 Spores, "Too Small a Place," 173, 176.

16 Joseph Lane, Autobiography, BL, MS P-A 43, 99; Thomas Smith, Account of the Rogue River Indian Wars, BL, MS P-A 94, 44; Parrish, Anecdotes of Intercourse, BL, MS P-A 59, 71; Reminiscences of Southern Oregon Pioneers, MS CB H629, Knight Library, Finnis Dillard, 3, Jennie Bealman Dewald, 5, Clara Stevens White, 5; and Ruby and Brown, *Indian Slavery*, 66, 98, 114.

17 Perkins in Boyd, *People of The Dalles*, 69.

18 Senate, *Report of the Secretary of the Interior*, 33rd Cong., 2nd Sess., 1854, Ex. Docs., Serial 746, 456.

19 House, *Report of J. Ross Browne*, 35th Cong., 1st Sess., 1858, Ex. Doc. 38, Serial 955, 7.

20 Spores, "Too Small a Place," 172–74; Robbins, "Extinguishing Indian Title," 11; and C. F. Coan, "The First Stage of the Federal Indian Policy," 52–53.

21 House, *Report of J. Ross Browne*, 8.

22 Washington territorial governor Isaac Stevens would eventually effect their removal in his 1855 negotiations with the support of the Yakama Nation, Isaac J. Stevens, Indian Treaty File: Klickatat Indians: Council Notes, Hazard Stevens, AX 42/8/22, Knight Library.

23 There were approximately 3,950 filings noted in Gurley, *Genealogical Material*, a figure that includes repeated filings by individuals for the same claim, as the provisional claims lasted only six months.

24 Ibid., 89, 107, 109, 110, 111; value consideration, 110; and indentures and crop liens, 89, 90, 163, 196.

25 Ibid., 117, 128.

26 Ibid., low 209, high 264; and Clatsop Plains, Supt. Anson Dart to Commissioner of Indian Affairs, November 7, 1851.

27 For a strong, recent treatment of the topic, see Woody Holton, *The Forced Founders*.

28 Gurley, *Genealogical Material*, 159, 160, 163.

29 Ibid., 164.

30 Richard H. Chused, "The Oregon Donation Act of 1850," 77.

31 Gurley, *Genealogical Material*, high price 209, low price 214.

32 Ibid., 91.

33 James M. Bergquist, "The Oregon Donation Act," 32; Charles H. Carey, *A General History*, 344.

34 White, *Land Use, Environment, and Social Change*, 78.

35 James G. Swan, *The Northwest Coast*, 19.

36 Gurley, *Genealogical Material*, 246; and Carey, *A General History*, 390.

37 For a general description, see *Oregon Sentinel*, February 5, 1879; for the 1861 legal suit, see B. F. Dowell, BL, MS P-A 139, 206.

38 In 1830, chief factor John McLaughlin of the HBC's Fort Vancouver sent salted salmon with a Captain Simpson to Monterrey and south to Valpraiso, Lima, and Buenos Aires to see whether there was a market for them, Barker, *Letters of Dr. John McLoughlin*, 163, 170, 181. Joseph Holman cited the potential profits of salmon packing for his 1839 emigration, *The Peoria Party for Oregon*, BL, MS, 1, 2, in Brosnan, *Jason Lee, Prophet*. Regarding shellfish, see Swan, *The Northwest Coast*, 33, 63.

39 Swan, *The Northwest Coast*, 33, 59.

40 Ibid., 36.

41 Ibid., 42.

42 Ray, "Lower Chinook Ethnographic Notes."

43 Swan, *The Northwest Coast*, 33.

44 Ibid., 58–59.

45 Superintendent Dart's assessment of the colonists' reliance on Indian labor was that it was temporary, "at this time," Dart to CIA, November 7, 1851.

46 Mike Davis, *Prisoners of the American Dream*, 28–29.

47 David Alan Johnson, *Founding the Far West*, and Charles Sellers, *The Market Revolution*.

48 Johnson, *Founding the Far West*, 181–87, 270, 180; Sean Wilentz, *Chants Democratic*; Paul E. Johnson, *A Shopkeeper's Millennium*; Mary P. Ryan, *Cradle of the Middle Class*; and Daniel Feller, *The Jacksonian Promise*.

49 Holman, "A Brief History," 110–11.

50 For example, see David D. Smits, "'Squaw Men'"; George Martinez, "Mexican Americans and Whiteness"; David G. Gutierrez, *Walls and Mirrors*; and Tomas Almaguer, *Racial Fault Lines*.

51 Organic Laws of Oregon (Article 2, part 10), quoted in Reuben Gold Thwaites, *Early Western Travels*, vol. 30, 306.

52 Lansford W. Hastings, *The Emigrant's Guide*, 105, 113; Palmer, *Journal of Travels*, 100. See also Overton Johnson and Wm. H. Winter, eds., *Route across the Rocky Mountains*, 107. For an official report containing similar racial language, see "Account of Oregon, by Lieut. Wilkes, Commander of the late Exploring Expedition," in Thwaites, *Early Western Travels*, vol. 29, 99.

53 Puget Sound Agent M. T. Simmons to Superintendent Nesmith, June 30, 1858, in Senate, *ARCIA, 1858*, 35th Cong., 2nd Sess., 1858, Ex. Docs. 1, Serial 974, 224. For the Fort Vancouver population as "mongrel," see Palmer, *Journal of Travels*, 100.

54 Holman, "A Brief History," 104–5.

55 *Eighth United States Census Manuscripts, 1860*; Matthew Aeldun Charles Smith, "Wedding Bands," 49–51, 66–73. Smith makes much of the small increases in the numbers of intermarriages from 1850 through 1870 but does not account for the drastically increased population size or the ratio of intra- and interracial unions.

56 Initially, under Article 4 of the 1843 Provisional Land Laws, each man was entitled to 640 acres, but, by the passage of the 1850 Donation Land Law, the full section was for married couples only, *United States Statutes at Large*, 31st Cong., 1st Sess., Chap. 76, 1850, Section 4.

57 "Vandolf V. Otis," *Cases in the Supreme Court, Territory of Oregon, December 1854*.

58 Much of the following discussion of bride purchase derives from my unpublished paper, "The 'Value' of Women."

59 Jay Miller and William R. Seaburg, "Athapaskans of Southwestern Oregon," 585; Daythal L. Kendall, "Takelma," 591; Henry B. Zenk, "Siuslawans and Coosans," 575–76; Roberta L. Hall, *The Coquille Indians*, 53; and Beckham, *The Indians of Western Oregon*, 95–96. For some Native informant statements about exogamy, see Philip Drucker, Field Notes, vol. 1, 1934, 23; Melville Jacobs, "Coos Narrative and Ethnologic Texts," 84–88; and John P. Harrington, *Harrington Papers*, roll 25, frame 1023.

60 H. G. Barnett, Indian Tribes of the Oregon Coast: Field Notes, vol. 1, 1934, 71; and Philip Drucker, vol. 3, 41.

61 Barnett, vol. 1, 64; and Philip Drucker, vol. 2, 88.

62 Ethnographies: Lottie Evanoff in *Harrington Papers*, roll 24, frame 889; Nellie Lane in Drucker, vol. 3, 39; Jim Buchanan, Harry Hull St. Clair, Coos Linguistic Material, vol. 1, Field Notes, 1903, 1. For linguistic evidence from the Hanis Coos language, Drucker noted the word *getummol*, which he defined two ways: first, his interpretation, "old maid," and second, the literal translation from informant Frank Drew, "wouldn't marry," Drucker, vol. 1, 79. Annie Peterson used a very similar Hanis Coos word, *ketammul*, to describe a woman who "refused an offer of marriage," Barnett, vol. 1, 19.

63 Kendall, "Takelma," 591.

64 Barnett, vol. 1, 75.

65 Drucker, vol. 1, 23.

66 *Harrington Papers*, 25, 905.

67 Ibid., 943.

68 Barnett, vol. 2, 21–22.

69 Drucker, vol. 1, 23, 77, 25.

70 Peterson in Jacobs, "Coos Narratives," 81–88.

71 Drucker, vol. 4, 36.

72 For Euro-American recognition of this problem, see *ARCIA 1871*, 316, 319.

73 Reminiscences of Southern Oregon Pioneers, MS CB H629, Knight Library, Richard Cannon, 4.

74 Emil R. Peterson and Alfred Powers, *A Century of Coos and Curry*, 261.

75 Doyce B. Nunis Jr., ed., *The Golden Frontier*, 56.

76 Reminiscences, Lucretia Ollivant, 3.

77 House, *ARCIA, 1871*, 319.

78 Jacobs, "Coos Narratives," 118.

79 Supt. Anson Dart to Commissioner of Indian Affairs L. Lea, November 7, 1851.

80 Nunis, *The Golden Frontier*, 45.

81 Ibid., 46.

82 David D. Smits, "The 'Squaw Drudge.'" Some Native scholars assert that "squaw" derives from an Iroquoian word for *vagina* and is, therefore, racist; see Joy Harjo and Gloria Bird, *Reinventing the Enemy's Language*, 44. Marge Bruchac (University of Massachusetts, Amherst) counters that "it does not come from the Kanienke-hake (Mohawk) word "otsikwa" or "otsioskwa" (which actually translates to "corn-meal mush"). It *does* come from a phoneme—variously spelled "squa," "skwa," "esqua," "kwe," "queh," etc.—a sound common to all Algonkian languages that indicated "female," not "female reproductive parts," <H-Amindian@H-Net.msu .edu>, February 2, 2001. For a recent etymology and an overview of the current debate as it has applied to place names, see William Bright, "The Sociolinguistics of the 'S-Word.' "

83 *Harrington Papers*, 25, 943.

84 Ibid., 24, 921.

85 Ibid., 698.

86 Ibid., 694.

87 Ibid., 921, 1004.

88 Stern, *Chiefs and Change*, 229.

89 Boyd, *The Coming of the Spirit*, 328.

90 *Congressional Globe*, 31st Cong., 1st Sess., May 28, 1079. For a contemporary criticism of Oregon's "Whites Only" policy, see "Who May Be Citizens of the United States."

91 Janice K. Duncan, *Minority without a Champion*, 15–16.

92 Kanaka Flats Inventory, April 12, 1865, Takelma Indians File, Southern Oregon Historical Society, Medford, Ore.

93 Jesse Applegate in Bowen, "The Oregon Frontiersman," 183.

94 *Oregon Sentinel*, December 21, 1857.

95 *Congressional Globe*, May 28, 1850, 1079.

96 Ibid., 1080.

97 Allan R. Millett and Peter Maslowski, *For the Common Defense*, 136.

98 Paul W. Gates and Robert W. Swenson, *History of Public Land Law Development*, 390.

99 Drew to Oregon Territorial Gov. George Curry, December 30, 1854, in Dowell, BL, MS P-A 133, folder 4.

100 Dorothy Sutton and Jack Sutton, eds., *Indian Wars of the Rogue River*, 166, and Old John of Rogue Or Red River.

101 *Congressional Globe*, April 23, 1850.

102 President James K. Polk to Congress, May 29, 1848, Senate, *Message of the President of the United States, In Relation to the Indian Difficulties in Oregon*, 30th Cong., 1st Sess., 1848, Doc. 47, Serial 508, 2.

103 Based on a comparison between land-office records and remuneration claims, at least 76 percent of the militia had land claims in the Willamette Valley. Adjusting for matching surnames (in the case of young men who volunteered for Indian fighting but who were not old enough to take land claims) and garbled French surnames, the figure may have been closer to 90 percent. Such would explain the failure to accept bounty claims in Cayuse country. Data are from Gurley, *Genealogical Material*; and Senate, *Memorial of the Legislature of Oregon*, 31st Cong., 2nd Sess., 1851, Misc. Doc. 29, Serial 592.

104 Territorial Gov. George Abernethy to President Polk, in Victor, *The Early Indian Wars*, 236–37.

105 For an excellent recent narrative of the Cayuse War, particularly regarding Indian actions, see Stern, *Chiefs and Change*, Section 5.

106 John Minto, Early Days of Oregon, BL, MS P-A 50, 37.

107 Ibid., 39.

108 Gurley, *Genealogical Materials*, 52, 53, 71, 102, 116, 118, 126, 139, 191, 194, 204, 224, 232, 241, 259.

109 Minto, Early Days, 41–45.

110 Ibid.

111 Senate, *Message of the President of the United States, In Relation to the Indian Difficulties in Oregon*, 30th Cong., 1st Sess., 1848, Doc. 47, Serial 508, 2–7.

112 *Senate Executive Journal*, 5, 2.

113 Statement of Comptroller Elisha Whittlesey to Secretary of the Treasury James Guthrie, House, *Expenses of the Cayuse War*, 33rd Cong., 1st Sess., 1854, Doc. 45, Serial 721, 6–8.

114 George H. Hines, ed., "Diary of Samuel Royal Thurston," 171–73, 175–76, 179–88, 191–98, 200.

115 Robbins, "Extinguishing Indian Land Title," 12.

116 *United States Statutes at Large*, 27th Cong., 1st Sess., Chap. 16, 1841.

117 *Journal of the House of Representatives of the United States, 1789–1873*, May 29, 1850, 978–79; *Senate Executive Journal*, May 6, 1850, 324; August 6, 1852, 434; and March 9, 1854, 262.

118 *Journal of the House of Representatives of the United States*, May 29, 1850, 978–79; *Senate Executive Journal*, May 6, 1850, 324; August 6, 1852, 434; and March 9, 1854, 262.

119 *Congressional Globe*, 31st Cong., 2nd Sess., January 13, 1851, 103.

120 Ibid., 1st Sess., September 25, 1850, 1703–4.

121 Dart to CIA, in Coan, "The First Stage of the Federal Indian Policy," 67; and Elmer G. Million, "Frontier Legal Process."

122 Dart to CIA, in Coan, "The First Stage of the Federal Indian Policy," 66–69.

123 Dart to CIA; "Treaty with Lower Band of Chinook," August 9, 1851, in Coan, "The First Stage of the Federal Indian Policy," 69–70.

124 Spores, "Too Small a Place."

125 Bergquist, "The Oregon Donation Act," 30.

126 Harlow Zinser Head, *The Oregon Donation Acts*, 65–70.

127 Bergquist, "The Oregon Donation Act," 29; and *Abstracts of Oregon Donation Land Claims*, rolls 1–3.

128 Preston in Head, "The Oregon Donation Acts," 70.

129 Head, *The Oregon Donation Acts*, 69.

130 *Congressional Globe*, 33rd Cong., 1st Sess., May 4, 1854, 1075.

131 *Abstracts of Oregon Donation Land Claims*, rolls 1–3, certificates 44, 57, 79, 376, 380.

132 Sections 5 and 8, *United States Statutes at Large*, 31st Cong., 1st Sess., Chap. 76, 1850.

133 *Congressional Globe*, 33rd Cong., 1st Sess., May 4, 1854, 1076.

Chapter Seven

1 Head, "The Oregon Donation Claims," 56–58.

2 Smith, Account of the Rogue River Indian Wars of 1853 and 1855, BL, MS P-A 94, 6–7.

3 Ibid., 3–15.

4 Victor, *Early Indian Wars*, 12–13; and Stephen Dow Beckham, *Requiem for a People*, 34.

5 Quoted in Victor, *Early Indian Wars*, 238.

6 The dichotomy typical of the region's historiography—settler versus miner—is misleading. The settlers, or "hardy pioneers," were the initial miners of the California Gold Rush and continued to feed the ranks for years, particularly in southwestern Oregon, which was a northern extension of the rush. Such notables of southern Oregon history as William Packwood, Pleasant Armstrong, Charles Brown, John Groslius, Peter Hunter, John Kirkpatrick, John B. Long, James Lowe, Dr. James McBride, and Benjamin Wright had filed provisional land claims before moving south to the goldfields of California and southwestern Oregon. See Gurley, *Genealogical Material*, respectively, 103, 33, 19, 95, 111, 213, 230, 219, 102, and 231.

7 Ross, *Narrative*, 11.

8 For example, see Hastings, *The Emigrant's Guide*, 65; Palmer, *Journal of Travels*, 90; Johnson and Winter, *Route across the Rocky Mountains*, 50; and passage from Gen. George B. McClellan's Mexican War diary quoted in Sutton and Sutton *Indian Wars*, 20.

9 Senate, *Message of the President of the United States of America to Congress*, 31st Cong., 2nd Sess., 1851, S. Ex. Doc. 1, Serial 587, 164. See also Anson Dart to William Spaulding, October 14, 1850, *Oregon Superintendent: Letters Received, 1824–1881*, roll 607, frame 730.

10 Applegate in Victor, *Early Indian Wars*, 149.

11 For a narrative of early Indian-white conflicts, see Beckham, *Requiem for a People*, 23–46. The depredations against Euro-American travelers served the purpose of justifying colonial bellicosity and militia remuneration, although the accounts did not explain provocations by colonists or the number of Indians wounded or killed. See, for example, the "history" provided by territorial secretary B. F. Harding in his attempt to secure remuneration for the 1854 militia campaigns to the Snake River and Klamath Basin, House, *Papers Transmitted by the Secretary of Oregon Territory*, 35th Cong., 2nd sess., 1859, Misc. Doc. 47, Serial 1016, 57–60.

12 Ross, *Narrative*, 13–17.

13 See, for example, Hurtado, *Indian Survival*; Rawls, *Indians of California*; Sherburne F. Cook, *The Conflict*; and Clifford E. Trafzer and Joel R. Hyer, eds., *Exterminate Them!*

14 For a description of Wright's décor, see Ross, *Narrative*, 24. The massacre of the Modocs generated some controversy; see A. B. Meacham, *Wigwam and War-Path*, 677–78; and for a Native account see Gatschet, *The Klamath Indians*, 13.

15 Senate, *Message of the President of the United States*, 33rd Cong., 2nd Sess., 1855, Ex. Doc. 16, Serial 751, 15, 18–19; Dowell, BL, MS P-A 133, 5–6.

16 Millett and Maslowski, *For the Common Defense*, 122, 136.

17 Davis to Wool, December 13, 1854, in Ex. Doc. 16, 125–27.

18 Wool to Major General Winfield Scott, February 28, 1854, in ibid., 11.

19 Ibid., 50–58.

20 Frustrated with the volunteer militias authorized by territorial governors, Wool claimed the sole right to call for militias and that he "should have all the staff departments within his command under his immediate and direct control," Wool to Jefferson Davis, January 7, 1854, in ibid., 5–6. Wool blamed the Oregon volunteers, "mustered into service, by the authority of the governor," for speculating supply funds; Wool to L. Thomas, Headquarters of the Army, New York, September 14, 1854, in ibid., 103–4.

21 Smith, Account of the Rogue River Indian Wars, 68.

22 Section 15 of the 1854 territorial militia law; see Drew to Davis, July 7, 1854, in 35th Cong., 2nd Sess., 1859, Misc. Doc. 47, 3–5. The national Militia Act of 1792 had stipulated that all states and territories maintain trained, equipped, and regulated militias, but few localities abided by its tenets, which required regular musters, self-support (taxation), and a subservience to federal command during war. Numerous debacles from the War of 1812 and the 1847 conquest of Mexico spoke to the deficiencies of the law in practice. Indeed, military historians generally agree that militias of this design had withered into nonexistence by 1830, Jerry Cooper, *The Militia and the National Guard*; Jerry Cooper, *The Rise of the National Guard*; Tom D. Dillard, "An Arduous Task to Perform"; and James B. Whisker, *The Rise and Decline*. The frontier versions—like those of Oregon, Washington, and California in the 1850s—were distinct from federal law in their independent, temporary, and racially charged anti-Indian actions. Nonetheless, the mid-nineteenth-century far-western militias certainly drew on a preexisting cultural tradition of volunteer Indian fighting, which they carried with them from the earlier eastern frontiers, Mary Ellen Rowe, "The Sure Bulwark of the Republic."

23 Broadside circulars in 1847 "informed" the public of these supposed speculations regarding the "road of starvation," George N. Belknap, *Early Oregon Imprints*, 30–31; see also Buena Cobb Stone, "Southern Route into Oregon."

24 Jeff C. Riddle, *The Indian History of the Modoc War*, 22.

25 Senate, *Report of the Secretary of the Interior, 1854*, 33rd Cong., 2nd Sess., 1854, Ex. Docs., Serial 746, 470.

26 Riddle, *The Indian History*, 27.

27 Schonchin quoted in Stern, *The Klamath Tribe*, 38–39.

28 Drew to Davis, July 7, 1854; Davis to Ross, July 17, 1854; Ross to Davis, August 5, 1854; and Ross to Curry, November 10, 1854; all in Dowell, BL, MS P-A 133, folder 4.

29 Ross to Walker, August 8, 1854, in ibid.

30 Walker to Ross, November 11, 1854, in ibid.

31 Palmer letter appointing a subagent for eastern Oregon, September 28, 1854, in folder 47, box 1/4 "1851–1855" in Cayuse, Yakima, and Rogue River Wars Papers (1847–1858), MS 72–322, box 47, Knight Library.

32 Dowell, BL, MS P-A 133, 5.

33 *Report of the Secretary of the Interior*, 1854, 465–67.

34 Sutton and Sutton, *Indian Wars*, 258.

35 William Tichenor, Among the Oregon Indians, BL, MS P-A 84, 25–31, 82–85, 105–6; Senate, *ARCIA, 1857*, 35th Cong., 1st Sess., Ex. Doc. 2, 1858, Serial 919, 324; and A. Z. Hedges to Commissioner George Manypenny, November 19, 1856, *Oregon Superintendent*, roll 609, frame 244.

36 Senate, *ARCIA, 1857*, 324.

37 Tichenor, *Among the Oregon Indians*, 25, 27.

38 *Report of the Secretary of the Interior*, 1854, 476–95.

39 Roberta L. Hall and Don Alan Hall, "The Village at the Mouth," 107.

40 George Bundy Wasson Jr., "The Coquille Indians and the Cultural 'Black Hole.'"

41 *Report of the Secretary of the Interior*, 1854, 480–81.

42 Bonnycastle to Wool, May 28, 1854, S. Ex. Doc. 16, 80–83.

43 Ibid., 78.

44 Ibid., 14–15.

45 *Cayuse Papers*, folder 1, box 6, "Undated; fragments"—a petition from Josephine County residents to Curry, probably summer of 1855, given reference to an early July event and Curry's position.

46 Dowell, BL, MS P-A 137, 31, 102, 136, 152, 160, 164, 180, and 230.

47 Ibid., 230.

48 For numerous examples of such discourse, see Dowell, BL, MS P-A 133 and 137. Dowell was an attorney for numerous federal remuneration claims on behalf of Oregon citizens, seeking to recover costs and damages from fighting Indians. His scrapbooks are replete with relevant testimony, editorials, and personal correspondence, much of which predates the remuneration attempts but served subsequently as evidence.

49 John Beeson, *A Plea for the Indians*.

50 Beeson in *Oregon Superintendent*, roll 609, frame 19.

51 Smith, Account of the Rogue River Indian Wars, BL, MS P-A 94, 73.

52 House, *The Topographical Memoir*, 35th Cong., 2nd Sess., 1859, Ex. Doc. 114, Serial 1014, 44–46. For a recent discussion of the Lupton Massacre, see Schwartz, *The Rogue River Indian War*, 85–86. For the volunteer's quote, see Beeson, *A Plea*, 54–55.

53 Sutton and Sutton, *Indian Wars*, 172.

54 Dowell, BL, MS P-A 137, 172.

55 Wool to Thomas, November 3, 1855, in Dowell, BL, MS P-A 138, 131.

56 *Report of the Secretary of the Interior*, 1854, 463.

57 An anonymous letter (probably from Charles Drew) to the editor proclaimed that "the predictions . . . have been more than realized," *Oregonian,* October 12, 1855.

58 For the Olalla massacre, see Reminiscences, Virginia McKay, 5–6.

59 Victor, *Indian Wars*, 423.

60 Recollections of George B. Roberts, BL, MS P-A 83, 20, 32, 34, 39, 41, 77, 90, and 94.

61 Hines, *Life on the Plains of the Pacific*, 143–44.

62 Isaac Stevens address to "Fellow Citizens of Portland and Oregon Territory," *Standard*, October 16, 1856, in Dowell, BL, MS P-A 134, 100.

63 Victor, *The Early Indian Wars*; Beckham, *Requiem for a People*; and Schwartz, *The Rogue River Indian War*.

64 Schwartz blithely concluded regarding interethnic Native relations, "They do not seem to have gotten on well with their Shasta neighbors," *The Rogue River Indian War*, 3–4, 11. Beckham noted issues such as slave raiding and "fighting" but did not analyze them, *Requiem for a People*, 10, 22. The original description is found in James A. Cardwell, Emigrant Company, BL, MS P-A 15, 17–18.

65 Regarding intra-Indian extermination, see Coquille Thompson in *Harrington Papers*, 25, 907–8; and Tichenor, Among the Oregon Indians, 105–6. For a discussion of settlement ceremonies in the region, see Gray, *Takelma*, 40, 60, 73, 88–92; Lucy Thompson, *To the American Indian*, 185–88; Kroeber and Gifford, "World Renewal," 110, 128; Philip Drucker, "The Tolowa," 251; A. L. Kroeber, "A Yurok War Reminiscence"; and William W. Elmendorf, *The Structure of Twana Culture*, 466–68, 475.

66 Miller, *Prophetic Worlds*, and Vibert, "The Natives Were Strong to Live."

67 Stern, *Chiefs and Change*, 93.

68 See intermarriage discussion, chapter 4. As well, the above statements are in keeping with contemporary anthropological scholarship. For a good introduction, see the several applicable articles in Wayne Suttles, *Handbook of North American Indians*, vol. 7, Northwest Coast. For excellent analyses of Native identity over time in the neighboring Puget Sound region, see Harmon, *Indians in the Making*; and Harmon, "Lines in the Sand."

69 Smedley, *Race in North America*; and Theodore W. Allen, *The Invention of the White Race*.

70 Boyd, *People of The Dalles*, 112.

71 Gatschet, *The Klamath Indians*, vol. 2, 617.

72 For the history of race in early U.S. history, particularly regarding Indians and westward expansion, see Almaguer, *Racial Fault Lines*; James Campbell and James Oakes, "The Invention of Race"; Richard Drinnon, *Facing West*; Barbara Fields, "Ideology and Race in American History"; Ramon A. Gutierrez, *When Jesus Came*; Horsman, *Race and Manifest Destiny*; Hurtado, *Indian Survival*; Patricia Nelson Limerick, *The Legacy of Conquest*; and Tessie Liu, "Race."

73 Social action may be immoral and based in ignorant fear, but, when directed by common purpose such as "Manifest Destiny," it is not irrational, Pierre Bourdieu, *Practical Reason*.

74 Boyd, *People of The Dalles*, 157, and House, *Report of J. Ross Browne*.

75 House, *Report of Brevet Major Benjamin*, 34th Cong., 3rd Sess., 1856–1857, Doc. 76, Serial 906, 11.

76 See Tecumtum's speech in House, *Report of J. Ross Browne*, 44–47.

77 For Horse Creek, see House, 35th Cong., 2nd Sess., 1854, Misc. Doc. 47; Senate Misc. Doc. 59; and Senate, *ARCIA*, *1854*, 262, 277, 278. Also see correspondence, C. S. Drew to Oregon Governor Davis, July 7, 1854, in Dowell, BL, MS P-A 133. For Grande Ronde, see Stern, *Chiefs and Change*, 275–76.

78 Senate, *Report of the Secretary of the Interior, 1854*, 33rd Cong., 2nd Sess., 1854, Ex. Docs., Serial 746, 464.

79 *Harrington Papers*, reel 24, frames 937, 939.

80 Stern, *Chiefs and Change*, 170–72; regarding Sutter, see Hurtado, *Indian Survival*, 80–81.

81 Boyd, *People of The Dalles*, 157; Donald, *Aboriginal Slavery*, 141; and Gatschet, *The Klamath Indians*, vol. 1, 20.

82 LaLande, *First over the Siskiyous*, 34–35, 39.

83 Chiloquin quoted in Stern, *The Klamath Tribe*, 23.

84 Gray, *The Takelma*, 17, 18, 52, 62; Robert F. Heizer and Thomas Roy Hester, "Shasta Villages and Territory," 144.

85 Ruby and Brown, *Indian Slavery*, 211; Coquel Thompson in *Harrington Papers*, 25, 944; and Peterson in Jacobs, "Coos Narratives," 84–88.

86 Gatschet, *The Klamath Indians*, vols. 1, 16, 20, 26. This may be the same incident covered in "The Late Indian Outrages in Pitt River Valley," *Yreka Union*, February 12, 1857.

87 Stern, *Chiefs and Change*, 71, 111.

88 Tichenor, Among the Oregon Indians, BL, MS P-A 84, 39; and Beckham, *Requiem for a People*, 173–76. For "culture brokers," see Alan Taylor, "Captain Hendrick Aupamut"; and Clara Sue Kidwell, "Indian Women as Cultural Mediators."

89 The belief was especially acute regarding the events of 1855; see correspondence from J. W. Nesmith, Superintendent of Indian Affairs for Oregon and Washington territories, to J. Denver, Commissioner of Indian Affairs, September 1, 1857, Senate, *ARCIA*, *1857*, 35th Cong., 1st Sess., 1858, Ex. Doc. 2, Serial 919, 315.

90 Dowell, BL, MS P-A 137, 172, 208.

91 Kay Atwood and Dennis J. Grey, *People and the River*; and Gray, *The Takelma*.

92 Nunis, *The Golden Frontier*, 95. South-coast Indians removed to the Siletz agency after the war ceremoniously re-created Wright's death nightly, dancing around his

scalp. The agent, Robert Metcalf, sent soldiers to capture and threaten the lives of two Native men unless the Indians surrendered their trophy, which they reluctantly did, in House, *Report of J. Ross Browne*, 48.

93 Palmer's annual report included a letter from W. H. Dunbar, November 22, 1855: "He states that he [a survivor hiding in a thicket] saw the Too-too-to-teis [and] . . . Many strange Indians have made their appearance well armed and have actually committed many depredations," in Dowell, BL, MS P-A 133. C. S. Drew to Col. Williams, January 4, 1856, reports that the Indians involved in recent shooting were not " 'Johns' Indians' they are Klamaths," in Dowell, BL, MS P-A 138, 21.

94 For recent narratives of the spring 1856 campaigns, see Beckham, *Requiem for a People*, 147–90; and Schwartz, *The Rogue River Indian War*, 136–47.

95 House, *Report of J. Ross Browne*, 44–47; and Senate, *ARCIA, 1856*, 34th Cong., 1st Sess., 1856, Ex. Docs., Serial 810.

96 Ord, April 13, 1856, entry, in Tichenor, Among the Oregon Indians, 39; and Sutton and Sutton, *Indian Wars*, 201.

97 Dowd, *A Spirited Resistance*; Joel W. Martin, *Sacred Revolt*; Joel W. Martin, "Before and Beyond the Sioux Ghost Dance"; and R. David Edmunds, "Tecumseh."

98 House, *Report of J. Ross Browne*, 11–12; Senate, *ARCIA, 1858*, 226–27; Dr. William F. Tolmie to Governor Fayette McMullen, in Ezra Meeker, *Pioneer Reminiscences*, 448; and Ruby and Brown, *Indian Slavery*, 191.

99 Dr. William F. Tolmie to Gov. Fayette McMullen, in Meeker, *Pioneer Reminiscences*, 449.

100 *Report of the Secretary of the Interior, 1854*, 463.

101 Gatschet, *The Klamath Indians*, vol. 1, ix and *Overland Monthly*, June 1873, 540.

102 Miller, *Prophetic Worlds*.

103 Michael Dorris, "Indians on the Shelf," 101.

104 Henry L. Oak, "Notes on Indian Wars in Washington Territory, 1855–1856," BL, MS P-B 69, 8–9; and Dr. William F. Tolmie to Gov. Fayette McMullen, in Meeker, *Pioneer Reminiscences*, 448–49. Gov. Isaac Stevens coined "banditti" for the Seattle assailants to distinguish them from the Yakamas, *ARCIA, 1857*, 34th Cong., 3rd Sess., 1857, Ex. Doc. 37, Serial 899.

105 House, *Report of J. Ross Browne*, 12.

106 Ibid., 10; Stern, *Chiefs and Change*, 273.

107 House, *Report of J. Ross Browne*, 44–47; and Sutton and Sutton, *Indian Wars*, 133–34.

108 Euro-Americans asserted that much of the weaponry was obtained through prostitution, Sutton and Sutton, *Indian Wars*, 74–75.

Chapter Eight

1 Petition of citizens of Jacksonville to Wool, February 2, 1856, in Dowell, BL, MS P-A 138, 40–45.

2 Wool quotations appear in an unnamed newspaper clipping from February 12, 1856, in Dowell, BL, MS P-A 134.

3 *Standard*, October 16, 1856.

4 *Oregonian—Extra*, March 28, 1856.

5 House, *Topographical Report of Captain T. J. Cram*, 104–5.

6 For Wool's strategy, see ibid., 48–49.

7 Edward Ortho Cresap Ord, BL, MS C-B 479, box 7, May 6, 1856.

8 House, *Topographical Report*, 51–53. It remains unclear whether the "Battle of Big Meadows" was a failed truce attempt resulting from poor communication or a sneak attack by Tecumtum and his people, as charged by Euro-Americans.

9 Ord diary entry, June 6, 1856.

10 For the Grattan Massacre and the politics of the Peace Policy on the Plains, see Ostler, *The Plains Sioux*, 40–105.

11 Ord diary entry, June 17, 1856.

12 Ibid., June 8, 1856.

13 Ibid., June 7 and 12, 1856.

14 For a geographical description, see House, *Topographical Report*, 53–54.

15 Ibid., 46; and Sutton and Sutton, *Indian Wars*, 216.

16 E. P. Drew Umpqua agency to Nesmith, June 30, 1858. Drew had allowed "a party of Indians to return to Kowes river and Ten-mile creek for the purpose of subsisting themselves for a time, and also to procure salmon for their winter's use." However, "The residents of Empire City . . . urgently petitioned this office to recall them, stating, in their petition, that the prevailing opinion in that vicinity was to the effect 'that any Indian found off the reserve could at once be shot, and no law or justice reach the offender,'" Senate, *ARCIA, 1858*, Doc. 1, 254–57.

17 S. Ex. Doc. 2, 361–62.

18 House, *Report of the Secretary of the Interior*, 38th Cong., 1st Sess., 1864, Ex. Doc. 1, Serial 1182, 171.

19 Kanaka Flats Inventory, April 12, 1865, Takelma Indians File, Southern Oregon Historical Society, Medford, Ore.

20 Royal Augustus Bensell in Shannon Applegate and Terence O'Donnell, eds., *Talking on Paper*, 56.

21 Beverly Ward, *White Moccasins*, 57–58.

22 House, *Report of J. Ross Browne*, 44–47, and J. W. Nesmith to Commissioner J. W. Denver, September 1, 1857, in Senate, *ARCIA, 1857*, 316.

23 Ned quoted in Ward, *White Moccasins*, 58. See also Johnny Waters statement regarding his grandmother, in *Harrington Papers*, roll 24, frame 797.

24 George Bundy Wasson Jr., *Growing Up Indian*, 187, 217–20.

25 The land also served the purpose of a burial ground until 1934 and remained in the Wasson family until 1956. In 1956 an anonymous descendant sold the property to Coos Head Timber Company, and, in January 1979, the land became an ecological sanctuary of the state of Oregon, Hall, *The Coquille Indians*, 114–15, 68, 70–73. Several of Susan Wasson's descendants still live in the immediate area.

26 Spores, "Too Small a Place," 181.

27 Ibid., 185.

28 Incomplete newspaper clipping following the March 1856 attack on the Cascades settlement, in Dowell, MS 34.

29 Rodman Wilson Paul considered southwest Oregon to be part of the northern California mines and thus, also, a retarded subregion, *Mining Frontiers*, 11, 37.

30 Sutton and Sutton, *Indian Wars*, 121–23.

31 See *Oregon Statesman*, June 2, 1855, for the initial charge and use of the phrase, which appeared as a broadside against a faction of supposed Know-Nothings.

32 *Oregon Statesman*, May 20, 1855; July 14, 1855; and Benjamin Franklin Dowell, MS 209, OHS, 89–191.

33 *Oregonian*, June 13 and October 12, 1855. The newspaper rivalry was fierce. The *Oregon Statesman* (December 8, 1855) charged that "Last Spring [Charles Drew] formed a partnership with the *Oregonian* to incite Indian hostilities south, for the patriotic purpose of furthering the payment of the yet unpaid bills of the famed expedition to 'fight the emigrants' and opening an opportunity for another grab."

34 Schwartz, *The Rogue River Indian War*, 93–112.

35 For examples of this factional sniping regarding the Walker Expedition, see Dowell, MS 209, 154–56, 189–91; and ibid., MS 34, 23. For disagreements about the required time for extermination, see ibid., 72–73. For the proposed territorial secession, see Sutton and Sutton, *Indian Wars*, 121–23. For an early accusation of speculation, see Ashael Bush editorial, *Oregon Statesman*, October 8, 1855; and for an attempted retraction of this position, *Oregon Statesman*, May 4, 1858.

36 Sutton and Sutton, *Indian Wars*, 172.

37 Wool to L. Thomas, September 14, 1854, in S. Ex. Doc. 16, Serial 751, 103–5.

38 Wool in House, *Topographical Memoir*, 125.

39 Ibid., 7.

40 Ibid., 72.

41 Wool to Secretary of War John B. Floyd, January 28, 1858, in House, *Topographical Memoir*, 124–26.

42 Of particular frustration to the Oregon politicians and their newspapers were editorials from San Francisco that called the Rogue River War a hoax and an invention to market surplus produce to troops, Dowell, BL, MS 209, 75.

43 Schwartz, *The Rogue River Indian War*, "pork-barrel" thesis, xii, 45–46, 69–90.

44 Longtime Salem Clique member turned U.S. District Court judge Matthew Deady gave loaded jury instructions regarding his rival Charles Drew on December 14, 1878, reprinted in the *Albany Register*, January 17, 1879, evidencing that Deady still held to his former political enmity. *United States v. William Griswold* concerned a falsified muster roll, a copy of the original made for submission to the Treasury. The case alleged that Drew and Griswold added false claims to the original and had John Ross sign it in attorney Benjamin Dowell's presence. Drew testified that he never signed the false document and disavowed knowledge of the addition of false claims; handwriting experts confirmed that the signature did not match. Dowell, however, swore that he witnessed Drew sign but that he must have "signed in a disguised hand, so that he might deny it at some future time." Although Drew was not on trial, Deady instructed the jury that he all but admitted to having forged the papers. The substitution of papers was done some time after 1860. The originals were said to have been lost, but Deady advised the jury that it was unlikely that the papers were really lost. The jury ruled in favor of the United States in the amount of $35,228, Dowell, BL, MS P-A 139, 390–407.

45 Dowell, BL, MS P-A 137, 106; and Sutton and Sutton, *Indian Wars*, 295.

46 "Forest Dale" (probably Charles Drew) to editor, *Oregonian*, October 12, 1855.

47 House, *Report of J. Ross Browne*, 4.

48 Agent M. T. Simmons to Nesmith, June 30, 1858, Senate, *ARCIA, 1858*, 225. Although Simmons was describing his district of the Puget Sound, the same conditions had existed in western Oregon.

49 Editorial from southwestern Oregon settler John Beeson to the *True Californian*, in *Oregon Superintendent: Letters Received, 1824–1881*, roll 609, frame 20.

50 House, *Report of J. Ross Browne*, 4.

51 For racism as a folk belief, see Smedley, *Race in North America*. For whiteness as property, see Cheryl Harris, "Whiteness as Property."

52 The political explanation can be found most recently in Schwartz, *The Rogue River Indian War*, which, while containing commendable research, nevertheless reinforces the "naturalness" of extermination by not critically examining it.

53 Patrick Wolfe, *Settler Colonialism*, 1, 2.

54 White men vastly outnumbered white women, 5,268 to 1,428, or approximately 3.7 to 1, in the six counties of southwestern Oregon (Coos, Curry, Douglas, Jackson, Josephine, and Umpqua). Still, in 1860, after Indian removal, there were only 32 intermarriages on record in the six counties, *Eighth United States Census Manuscripts, 1860*. Reminiscence accounts consistently cite land claims for the few intermarriages; see, for example, Reminiscences of Southern Oregon Pioneers: Virginia Estes Applegate, 5; "Stonewall" Jackson Chenoweth, 2–3; and Virginia McKay, 3. Unofficial relations certainly occurred as well, although it would be misleading to regard them as necessarily long-lasting. In the words of Lottie Evanoff, a Coos woman: "The early whites here were just like Coyote—they would make a baby & just keep on going," *Harrington Papers*, roll 24, frame 694.

55 Locked in a tough election and seeking Jacksonville votes, the Salem Clique ran an *Oregon Statesmen* article on May 4, 1858, that included a series of earlier quotes demonstrating that the Democrats had supported the Rogue River War and the extermination of the Indians all along. Thus, extermination advocacy appears to have continued to be a bellwether political issue for Rogue Valley residents even after the war and Indian removal.

56 Victor, *The Early Indian Wars*. For an argument that suggests that historians do not address extermination, see Richard White, in Eric Foner, ed., *The New American History*; and for a recent example of taking an approach with no villainy (except human ignorance of the environment), see Elliott West, *The Way to the West*. For historical treatment of extermination, see Svaldi, *Sand Creek*; and for select chapters, Horsman, *Race and Manifest Destiny*; Rawls, *Indians of California*; and Hurtado, *Indian Survival*.

57 Gray H. Whaley, "Indians Twice Removed," 84–85. For the preeminent works on the subject, see Richard Slotkin, *The Fatal Environment*, and Slotkin, *Regeneration through Violence*.

58 Victor, *The Early Indian Wars*, 424.

59 Beckham, *Requiem for a People*, 9; and Schwartz, *The Rogue River Indian War*, 149. As Schwartz notes, the 1857 census figure of 1,943 did not include the few individuals, mostly women, who had avoided removal.

Chapter Nine

1 For a detailed discussion of the modern nation-states and their relation to imperialism, see Bill Ashcroft, Gareth Griffiths, and Helen Tiffin, *Key Concepts*, 149–55; and Peter S. Onuf, *Jefferson's Empire*, 5–6.

2 In other regions, conversely, Methodism would emerge as nearly synonymous with local dominant society. For an excellent review essay of recent works on American Methodism and Euro-American culture in the eighteenth and nineteenth centuries, see Richard D. Shiels, "More New Light," published as "Review of Dee E. Andrews," H-SHEAR, H-Net Reviews, January, 2002, <http://www.h-net .msu.edu/reviews>.

3 I use quotation marks here to stress the continuing evolution and presence of cultural geography, the definition of places, and the assignment of names and meanings. Terms such as *western Oregon*, *Oregon-California borderland*, and *Columbia Plateau* are modern creations, a "necessary evil" for conveying this narrative.

4 The literature on identity of self and others is voluminous; see, for example, Berkhofer, *The White Man's Indian*; Karen Kupperman, *Settling with the Indians*; and Harmon, *Indians in the Making*. For the "inland empire" example of cultural geography, see Katherine G. Morrissey, *Mental Territories*.

5 House, *Report of J. Ross Browne*, 47–48; and Senate, *ARCIA 1858*, 252–53.

6 Senate, *ARCIA 1857*, 358; Senate, *ARCIA 1861*, 772; House, *ARCIA 1871*, 316.

7 House, Hedges to CIA Manypenny, 34th Cong., 3rd Sess., H. Ex. Doc. 37, serial 899.

8 Senate, *ARCIA 1857*, 368.

9 Ibid., *ARCIA 1858*, 137.

10 Schwartz devotes much of his discussion of the early reservations to exploring possible corruption, *The Rogue River Indian War*, 161–213.

11 Senate, *ARCIA 1858*, 252; House, *ARCIA 1862*, 399; Sutton and Sutton, *Indian Wars*, 261–62.

12 Senate, *ARCIA 1857*, 361, 369; Senate, *ARCIA 1859*, 793; House, *ARCIA 1871*, 323; and Sutton and Sutton, *Indian Wars*, 261.

13 Senate, *ARCIA 1857*, 364; *ARCIA 1859*, 795; and *ARCIA 1858*, 286–87.

14 Senate, *ARCIA 1857*, 363–64.

15 Senate, *ARCIA 1859*, 796–97; Meacham, *Wigwam and War-Path*, 667–69; Josiah L. Parrish, MS 2320, OHS; and Beckham, *Land of the Umpqua*, 106–7.

16 For some examples of passes, see Senate, *ARCIA 1860*, 441; Senate, *ARCIA 1861*, 773; and House, *ARCIA 1871*, 323.

17 House, *ARCIA 1863*, 201. See also Schwartz, *The Rogue River Indian War*, 171, 175.

18 House, *ARCIA 1862*, 420.

19 House, *ARCIA 1871*, 323; and Martha Ann Minto, Female Pioneering, BL, MS P-A 51, 26.

20 Schwartz, *The Rogue River Indian War*, 183.

21 *Eighth United States Census Manuscripts, 1860*, Coos County, Ore., 1860, 1870.

22 Melville Jacobs, "Coos Narrative and Ethnologic Texts," 102.

23 Although I disagree with William Robbins's larger attempt to describe the West, he offered the best case study of a coastal Oregon community, Coos Bay, and

its repeated booms and busts. William G. Robbins, *Hard Times in Paradise*; and Robbins, *Colony and Empire*.

24 For a discussion of antipathy toward the federal government among residents of the West, see Limerick, *Legacy of Conquest*.

25 For the Klamath controversy, see the *Register Guard*'s coverage from July through September 2001; and for Grant County's vote, see the same newspaper, June 3, 2002, 1.

26 Cynthia Viles and Tom Grigsby, "The Confederated Tribes of Siletz," 106.

27 House, *ARCIA 1863*, Doc. 23, 204.

28 *Harrington Papers*, roll 24, 868.

29 Dell Hymes and Virginia Hymes, "Chinook Jargon," 257.

30 The invocation, originally entitled "A Takelma Invocation," is meant to be shouted at a new moon, per contributor Frances Johnson in Dell Hymes, "Languages and Their Uses," in Buan and Lewis, eds., *The First Oregonians*, 34.

Bibliography

Primary Sources

Abernathy [Abernethy], George. MS 929. Oregon Historical Society, Portland, Ore.

Abstracts of Oregon Donation Land Claims, 1852–1903. Washington, D.C.: National Archives, National Archives and Records Service, General Services Administration. Rolls 1–3.

Applegate, Shannon, and Terence O'Donnell, eds. *Talking on Paper: An Anthology of Oregon Letters and Diaries*. Corvallis: Oregon State University Press, 1994.

Bancroft, Hubert Howe. *History of Oregon*. Vol. 1. San Francisco: History Company Publishers, 1886.

———. *History of the Northwest Coast, Part 1: 1543–1800*. Vol. 27 of *The Works of Hubert Howe Bancroft*. San Francisco: A. L. Bancroft & Co. Publishers, 1884.

Barker, Burt Brown, ed. *Letters of Dr. John McLoughlin Written at Fort Vancouver, 1829–1832*. Portland: Binfords and Mort for the Oregon Historical Society, 1948.

Barnett, H. G. Indian Tribes of the Oregon Coast: Field Notes. Vol. 1. Southwestern Oregon Research Project, Box 2, Knight Library Special Collections, University of Oregon, 1934.

———. Indian Tribes of the Oregon Coast: Field Notes. Vol. 2. Southwestern Oregon Research Project, Box 2, Knight Library Special Collections, University of Oregon, 1934.

Beeson, John. *A Plea for the Indians; With Facts and Features of the Late War in Oregon*. New York: John Beeson (self), 1857.

Belknap, George N. *Early Oregon Imprints in the Oregon State Archives*. Worcester, Mass.: American Antiquarian Society, 1981.

Belyea, Barbara, ed. *Columbia Journals, David Thompson*. Montreal and Kingston: McGill-Queen's University Press, 1994.

Boas, Franz. *Chinook Texts*. Vol. 20. Washington, D.C.: Smithsonian Institution, Bureau of Ethnology, 1894.

Brosnan, Cornelius J. *Jason Lee, Prophet of the New Oregon*. New York: Macmillan, 1932.

Cardwell, James A. *Emigrant Company*. MS P-A 15. Bancroft Library, University of California, Berkeley.

Carey, Charles H. "Diary of Rev. George Gary." *Oregon Historical Quarterly* 24, no. 1 (1923): 68–105.

———. *A General History of Oregon, Prior to 1861.* Portland, Ore.: Metropolitan Press, 1935.

———. "Methodist Annual Reports Relating to the Willamette Mission (1834–1848)." *Oregon Historical Quarterly* 23, no. 4 (1922): 303–64.

Cayuse, Yakima, and Rogue River Wars Papers (1847–1858). MS 72–322, Box 47, Knight Library, University of Oregon.

Christian Advocate and Journal.

Coues, Elliott, ed. *New Light on the Early History of the Greater Northwest: The Manuscript Journals of Alexander Henry and of David Thompson, 1799–1814.* Minneapolis, Minn.: Ross & Hanes, Inc, 1965.

Cox, Ross. *The Columbia River.* Edited by Edgar I. Stewart and Jane R. Stewart. Norman: University of Oklahoma Press, 1957.

"Diary of Rev. Jason Lee." *Oregon Historical Quarterly* 17, no. 2–4 (1916): 116–46, 240–66, 397–430.

Dowell, B. F. MS P-A 133. Bancroft Library, University of California, Berkeley.

———. MS P-A 134. Bancroft Library, University of California, Berkeley.

———. MS P-A 137. Bancroft Library, University of California, Berkeley.

———. MS P-A 138. Bancroft Library, University of California, Berkeley.

———. MS P-A 139. Bancroft Library, University of California, Berkeley.

Dowell, Benjamin Franklin. MS 209. Oregon Historical Society, Portland, Ore.

Drucker, Philip. Field Notes. Vol. 1. Southwest Oregon Research Project, Box 3, 4516, File 78, Knight Library Special Collections, University of Oregon, 1934.

———. Field Notes. Vol. 2. Southwest Oregon Research Project, Box 3, 4516, File 78, Knight Library Special Collections, University of Oregon, 1934.

———. Field Notes. Vol. 3. Southwest Oregon Research Project, Box 3, 4516, File 78, Knight Library Special Collections, University of Oregon, 1934.

———. Field Notes. Vol. 4. Southwest Oregon Research Project, Box 3, 4516, File 78, Knight Library Special Collections, University of Oregon, 1934.

DuBois, Cora. Tututuni (Rogue River) Fieldnotes. Microfilm 2216, Reel 6, MS CU-23.1. Bancroft Library, University of California, Berkeley.

Edwards, P. L. *Sketch of the Oregon Territory, or Emigrants' Guide.* Liberty, Mo.: Herald Office, 1842.

Eells, Cushing. Letters, 1843–1859. MS 1218, Folder 2. Oregon Historical Society, Portland, Ore.

Eells, Myron. MS 1218. Oregon Historical Society, Portland, Ore.

Elliott, T. C. "Journal of Peter Skene Ogden; Snake Expedition, 1827–1828." *Oregon Historical Quarterly* 11, no. 4 (1910): 355–96.

Fessett, Thomas E., ed. *Reports and Letters of Herbert Beaver, 1836–1838: Chaplain to the Hudson's Bay Company and Missionary to the Indians at Fort Vancouver.* Portland, Ore.: Champoeg Press, 1959.

Franchere, Gabriel. *Adventure at Astoria, 1810–1814.* Translated and edited by Hoyt C. Franchere. Norman: University of Oklahoma Press, 1967.

Gatke, Robert Moulton. "A Document of Mission History, 1833–43." *Oregon Historical Quarterly* 36, nos. 1–2 (1935): 71–94, 163–81.

Gatschet, Albert Samuel. *The Klamath Indians of Southwestern Oregon.* Washington, D.C.: U.S. Government Printing Office, 1890.

Glover, Richard. *David Thompson's Narrative 1784–1812*. Toronto: Champlain Society, 1962.

Green, Jonathan S. *Journal of a Tour on the North West Coast of America in the Year 1829*. New York: Chas. Fred. Heartman, 1915.

Gurley, Lottie LeGett, ed. *Genealogical Material in Oregon: Provisional Land Claims, Abstracted*. Vols. 1–8, 1845–1849. Portland, Ore.: Genealogical Forum of Portland, 1982.

Hale, Horatio. "Ethnography and Philology." *United States Exploring Expedition. During the Years 1838, 1839, 1840, 1841, 1842. Under the Command of Charles Wilkes, U.S.N*. Ridgewood, N.J.: Gregg Press, 1968.

Harper, Thomas Edward. *Chinook: A History and Dictionary of the Northwest Coast Trade Jargon*. Portland, Ore.: Metropolitan Press Publishers, 1935.

Harrington, John P. *The Papers of John Peabody Harrington in the Smithsonian Collection, 1907–1957*. Millwood, N.Y.: Kraus International Publications, 1981.

Hastings, Lansford W. *The Emigrant's Guide to Oregon and California*. Reprint of 1st 1846 ed. New York: Da Capo Press, 1969.

Hines, George H., ed. "Diary of Samuel Royal Thurston." *Oregon Historical Quarterly* 15 (1914)" 153–205.

Hines, Gustavus. Diary Sept. 6, 1845, to. MS 1215. Oregon Historical Society, Portland, Ore.

———. Letters. MS 1215. Oregon Historical Society, Portland, Ore.

———. *Life on the Plains of the Pacific*. Buffalo, N.Y.: George H. Derby and Co., 1851.

Hosmer, James Kendall, ed. *Gass's Journal of the Lewis and Clark Expedition*. Chicago: A. C. McClurg & Co., 1904.

Hulbert, Archer Butler, and Dorothy Printup Hulbert, eds. *The Oregon Crusade: Across Land and Sea to Oregon*. Denver, Colo.: Stewart Commission of Colorado College and the Denver Public Library, 1935.

Irving, Washington. *Astoria, or Anecdotes of an Enterprise beyond the Rocky Mountains*. Philadelphia: Carey, Lea, & Blanchard, 1836.

Jackson, Donald, ed. *Letters of the Lewis and Clark Expedition with Related Documents, 1783–1854*. Chicago: University of Illinois Press, 1978.

Jacobs, Melville. "Coos Narrative and Ethnologic Texts." *University of Washington Publications* 8, no. 1 (1939): 1–126.

Johnson, Overton, and Wm. H. Winter. *Route across the Rocky Mountains*. Reprint of 1846 ed. Princeton, N.J.: Princeton University Press, 1932.

Jones, Robert F., ed. *Annals of Astoria: The Headquarters Log of the Pacific Fur Company on the Columbia River, 1811–1813*. New York: Fordham University Press, 1999.

———, ed. *Astorian Adventure: The Journal of Alfred Seton, 1811–1815*. New York: Fordham University Press, 1993.

Kanaka Flats Inventory, April 12, 1865. Takelma Indians File. Southern Oregon Historical Society. Medford, Ore.

LaLande, Jeff, ed. *First over the Siskiyous: Peter Skene Ogden's 1826–1827 Journey through the Oregon-California Borderlands*. Portland: Oregon Historical Society Press, 1987.

Lane, Joseph. Autobiography. MS P-A 43. Bancroft Library, University of California, Berkeley.

Lee, Daniel, and J. H. Frost. *Ten Years in Oregon.* New York: J. Collord, 1844.

Lee, Jason. MS 1212. Oregon Historical Society, Portland, Ore.

Leslie, David. MS 1216. Oregon Historical Society, Portland, Ore.

Lewis, Merriwether. *The Lewis and Clark Expedition.* 1814 Ed. Unabridged. Vol. 2. New York: J. B. Lippincott Co., 1961.

Meacham, A. B. *Wigwam and War-Path; or the Royal Chief in Chains.* Boston: John P. Dale and Co., 1875.

Meeker, Ezra. *Pioneer Reminiscences of Puget Sound: The Tragedy of Leschi.* Seattle, Wash.: Lowman & Hanford Stationary and Printing Co., 1905.

Merk, Frederick, ed. *Fur Trade and Empire: George Simpson's Journal; Remarks Connected With the Fur Trade in the Course of a Voyage From York Factory to Fort George and Back to York Factory, 1824–1825.* Cambridge, Mass.: Harvard University Press, 1931.

Methodist Mission. MS 1225. Oregon Historical Society, Portland, Ore.

Methodist Mission Record Book, 1834–1838. MS 1224. Oregon Historical Society, Portland, Ore.

Minto, John. Early Days of Oregon. MS P-A 50. Bancroft Library, University of California, Berkeley.

Minto, Martha Ann. Female Pioneering in Oregon. MS P-A 51. Bancroft Library, University of California, Berkeley.

Minutes of the Annual Meetings of the Oregon Mission, For the Years 1841, 1842, 1843. MS 1224. Oregon Historical Society, Portland, Ore.

Moulton, Gary E., ed. *The Journals of the Lewis and Clark Expedition: November 2, 1805–March 22, 1806.* Vol. 6. Lincoln: University of Nebraska Press, 1990.

———. *The Journals of the Lewis and Clark Expedition: March 23–June 9, 1806.* Vol. 7. Lincoln: University of Nebraska Press, 1990.

Nunis, Doyce B., Jr., ed. *The Golden Frontier: The Recollections of Herman Francis Reinhart, 1851–1869.* Austin: University of Texas Press, 1962.

Oak, Henry L. Notes on Indian Wars in Washington Territory, 1855–1856. MS P-B 69, Bancroft Library, University of California, Berkeley.

Old John of Rogue or Red River, Oregon (From Army and Navy Journal—1855). MS 286. Oregon Historical Society.

Oliphant, J. Orin. "Lee-Greene Correspondence, 1839." *Oregon Historical Quarterly* 35, no. 3 (1934): 263–68.

Ord, Edward Ortho Cresap. Edward Ortho Cresap Ord Papers. MSS C-B 479, Box 7, Bancroft Library, University of California, Berkeley.

Oregonian.

Oregon Sentinel.

Oregon Statesman.

Oregon Superintendent: Letters Received, 1824–1881. M 234, no. 607–30.

Overland Monthly.

Palmer, Joel. *Journal of Travels over the Rocky Mountains.* Reprint of 1847 ed. Fairfield, Wash.: Ye Galleon Press, 1983.

Parker, Samuel. *Journal of an Exploring Tour beyond the Rocky Mountains, Under the Direction of the A.B.C.F.M.* 4th ed. Ithaca, N.Y.: Andrus, Woodruff, and Gauntlett, 1844.

Parrish, Josiah L. Anecdotes of Intercourse with the Indians. MS P-A 59. Bancroft
    Library, University of California, Berkeley.
———. MS 2320. Oregon Historical Society, Portland, Ore.
Payette, B. C., ed. *The Oregon Country under the Union Jack: A Reference Book of
    Historical Documents for Scholars and Historians*. Montreal: Payette Radio Ltd, 1962.
Pipes, Nellie B. "Journal of John H. Frost, 1840–43." *Oregon Historical Quarterly* 35,
    nos. 1–4 (1934): 50–73, 139–67, 235–62, 348–75.
Prucha, Francis Paul, ed. *Documents of United States Indian Policy*. 2nd expanded ed.
    Lincoln: University of Nebraska Press, 1990.
Quaife, Milo M., ed. *The Journals of Captain Meriwether Lewis and Sergeant John
    Ordway*. 2nd ed. Madison: State Historical Society of Wisconsin, 1965.
Register Guard, The.
Reminiscences of Southern Oregon Pioneers. MS CB H629. Knight Library,
    University of Oregon, 1938.
Riddle, Jeff C. *The Indian History of the Modoc War and the Causes That Led to It*.
    Medford, Oregon: Pine Cone Publishers, 1973.
Roberts, George B. Recollections of George B. Roberts. MS P-A 83. Bancroft Library,
    University of California, Berkeley.
Rollins, Philip Ashton, ed. *The Discovery of the Oregon Trail: Robert Stuart's
    Narratives*. New York: Charles Scribner's Sons, 1935.
Ross, Alexander. *Adventures of the First Settlers on the Oregon or Columbia River,
    1810–1813*. Lincoln: University of Nebraska Press, 1986.
Ross, John E. *Narrative of an Indian Fighter*. MS P-A 63. Bancroft Library, University
    of California, Berkeley.
St. Clair, Harry Hull. Coos Linguistic Material. Vol. 1, Field Notes. Southwest Oregon
    Research Project, Box 2, 1822, Special Collections, Knight Library, University of
    Oregon, 1903.
Schoolcraft, Henry R. *Information Respecting The History, Condition And Prospects Of
    The Indian Tribes Of The United States: Collected And Prepared Under The Direction
    Of The Bureau Of Indian Affairs*. Vol. 3. Philadelphia: Lippincott, Grambo & Co.,
    1853.
Shepard, Cyrus. MS 1219. Oregon Historical Society, Portland, Ore.
Smith, Thomas. Account of the Rogue River Indian Wars of 1853 and 1855. MS P-A 94.
    Bancroft Library, University of California, Berkeley.
Standard, The.
Stevens, Isaac J. Indian Treaty File: Klickatat Indians: Council Notes. Hazard Stevens,
    AX 42/8/22. Knight Library, University of Oregon, 1956.
Sullivan, Maurice S, ed. *The Travels of Jedediah Smith: A Documentary Outline,
    Including the Journal of the Great American Pathfinder*. Santa Ana, Calif.: Fine Arts
    Press, 1934.
Swan, James G. *The Northwest Coast; or, Three Years' Residence in Washington
    Territory*. New York: Harper & Brothers, Publishers, Franklin Square, 1857.
Thompson, Lucy. *To the American Indian: Reminiscences of a Yurok Woman*. Berkeley,
    Calif.: Heyday Books, 1991.
Thwaites, Reuben Gold. *Early Western Travels, 1748–1846*. Cleveland, Ohio: Arthur H.
    Clark Co., 1906.

Tichenor, William. Among the Oregon Indians. MS P-A 84. Bancroft Library, University of California, Berkeley.

Trafzer, Clifford E., and Joel R. Hyer, eds. *Exterminate Them! Written Accounts of the Murder, Rape, and Enslavement of Native Americans during the California Gold Rush*. East Lansing: Eastern Michigan State University Press, 1999.

United States Exploring Expeditions. Voyage of the U.S. Exploring Squadron, Commanded by Captain Charles Wilkes, of the United States Navy, in 1838, 1839, 1840, 1841, and 1842. Philadelphia: C. Sherman, 1861.

U.S. Congress. *The Congressional Globe.*

U.S. House of Representatives. *Annual Report of the Commissioner of Indian Affairs, 1862*. 37th Cong., 3rd Sess., 1862, Ex. Docs., Serial 1157.

———. *Annual Report of the Commissioner of Indian Affairs, 1863*. 38th Cong., 1st Sess., 1863, Ex. Docs., Serial 1182.

———. *Annual Report of the Commissioner of Indian Affairs, 1871*. 42nd Cong., 2nd Sess., 1871, Ex. Docs., Serial 1505.

———. *Expenses of the Cayuse War*. 33rd Cong., 1st Sess., 1854, Doc. 45, Serial 721.

———. *Journal of the House of Representatives of the United States, 1789–1873*. Washington, D.C.: U.S. Government Printing Office.

———. *Memorial of the Board of Managers of the American Indian Mission Association*. 29th Cong., 1st Sess., January 13, 1846, Doc. 73, Serial 483, 1.

———. *Military Posts—Council Bluffs to the Pacific Ocean. Report of the Committee on Military Affairs*. 27th Cong., 2nd Sess., 1842, Doc. 830, Serial 410.

———. *Papers Transmitted by the Secretary of Oregon Territory, Relative to the Protection Afforded by the Volunteers of Oregon and Washington Territories to Overland Immigrants in 1854*. 35th Cong., 2nd Sess., 1859, Misc. Doc. 47, Serial 1016.

———. *Report of Brevet Major Benjamin*. 34th Cong., 3rd Sess., 1856–1857, Doc. 76, Serial 906.

———. *Report of J. Ross Browne on Indian Affairs in the Territories of Oregon and Washington, 1857*. Special Agent of the Treasury Department J. Ross Browne, 35th Cong., 1st Sess., 1858, Ex. Doc. 38, Serial 955.

———. *Report of the Secretary of the Interior*. 38th Cong., 1st Sess., 1864, Ex. Doc. 1, Serial 1182.

———. *The Topographical Memoir and Report of Captain T. J. Cram, Relative to the Territories of Oregon and Washington, in the Military Department of the Pacific*. 35th Cong., 2nd Sess., 1859, Ex. Doc. 114, Serial 1014.

———. *U.S. Pacific Railroad Explorations and Survey. 47th and 49th Parallels*. 33rd Cong., 1st Sess., 1855, Ex. Doc. 129.

U.S. Senate. *Annual Report of the Commissioner of Indian Affairs, 1856*. 34th Cong., 1st Sess., 1856, Ex. Docs., Serial 810.

———. *Annual Report of the Commissioner of Indian Affairs*. 34th Cong., 3rd Sess., 1857, Ex. Doc. 37, Serial 899.

———. *Annual Report of the Commissioner of Indian Affairs, 1857*. 35th Cong., 1st Sess., 1858, Ex. Doc. 2, Serial 919.

———. *Annual Report of the Commissioner of Indian Affairs, 1858*. 35th Cong., 2nd Sess., Ex. Docs., 1858, Serial 974.

———. *Annual Report of the Commissioner of Indian Affairs, 1859.* 36th Cong., 1st Sess., Ex. Docs., 1859, Serial 1023.

———. *Annual Report of the Commissioner of Indian Affairs, 1860.* 36th Cong., 2nd Sess., Ex. Docs., 1860, Serial 1078.

———. *Annual Report of the Commissioner of Indian Affairs, 1861.* 37th Cong., 2nd Sess., 1861, Ex. Docs., Serial 1117.

———. *Journal of the Executive Proceedings of the Senate of the United States, 1789–1875.* Washington, D.C.: U.S. Government Printing Office.

———. *Memorial of the Legislature of Oregon, Praying an Appropriation for the Payment of Expenses Incurred by the Provisional Government of Oregon in the Cayuse War.* 31st Cong., 2nd Sess., 1851, Misc. Doc. 29, Serial 592.

———. *Memorial of the Legislature of Oregon, Praying for the Extinguishment of the Indian Title and the Removal of the Indians from Certain Portions of That Territory; Payment of the Debt Growing out of Recent Indian War, etc.* 31st Cong., 2nd Sess., 1851, S. Misc. Doc. 5, Serial 592.

———. *Message of the President of the United States, In Relation to the Indian Difficulties in Oregon.* 30th Cong., 1st Sess., 1848, Doc. 47, Serial 508.

———. *Message of the President of the United States of America to Congress.* 31st Cong., 2nd Sess., 1851, Ex. Doc. 1, Serial 587.

———. *Message of the President of the United States, Communicating . . . the Instructions and Correspondence Between the Government and Major General Wool.* 33rd Cong., 2nd Sess., 1855, Ex. Doc. 16, Serial 751.

———. *Report of the Secretary of the Interior, 1854.* 33rd Cong., 2nd Sess., 1854, Ex. Docs., Serial 746.

United States Census. *Manuscripts.* 1860, 1870.

United States Statutes at Large. 27th Cong., 1st Sess., Chap. 16, 1841.

———. 31st Cong., 1st Sess., Chap. 76, 1850.

"Vandolf v. Otis." *Cases in the Supreme Court, Territory of Oregon, December 1854.* 1 Oregon 153 (1853).

Vaughn, Thomas, ed. *Paul Kane, The Columbia Wanderer: Sketches, Paintings, and Comment, 1846–1847.* Portland: Oregon Historical Society, 1971.

Victor, Frances Fuller. *The Early Indian Wars of Oregon, Compiled from the Oregon Archives and Other Original Sources with Muster Rolls.* Salem, Ore.: Frank C. Baker, State Printer, 1894.

Waller, Alvan F. MS 1210. Oregon Historical Society, Portland, Ore.

Ward, Beverly. *White Moccasins.* Cottage Grove, Ore.: B. H. Ward, 1986.

"Who May Be Citizens of the United States." *Harper's Weekly* (1858), 306.

Wilkes, Charles. *Narrative of the United States Exlporing Expedition. During the Years 1838, 1839, 1840, 1841, 1842.* 5 volumes, atlas. Philadelphia: C. Sherman, 1844.

Yreka Union.

Zion's Herald.

Secondary Sources

Allen, Theodore W. *The Invention of the White Race.* Vols. 1–2. New York: Verso, 1994.

Almaguer, Tomas. *Racial Fault Lines: The Historical Origins of White Supremacy in California*. Berkeley: University of California Press, 1994.

Ambrose, Stephen E. *Undaunted Courage: Meriwether Lewis, Thomas Jefferson, and the Opening of the American West*. New York: Simon & Schuster, 1996.

Amoss, Pamela T. "The Indian Shaker Church." In *Handbook of North American Indians*, vol. 7. Washington, D.C.: Smithsonian Institution, 1990, 633–39.

Ashcroft, Bill, Gareth Griffiths, and Helen Tiffin. *Key Concepts in Post-Colonial Studies*. New York: Routledge, 1998.

Atwood, Kay, and Dennis J. Grey. *People and the River: A History of the Human Occupation of the Middle Course of the Rogue River of Southwestern Oregon*. Vol. 1. Medford, Ore.: USDI—Bureau of Land Management, 1996.

Bailyn, Bernard. *Atlantic History*. Cambridge, Mass.: Harvard University Press, 2005.

Barrett, James R., and David Roediger. "Inbetween Peoples: Race, Nationality and the 'New Immigrant' Working Class." *Journal of American Ethnic History* 16, no. 3 (Spring 1997): 3–44.

Basso, Keith H. *Wisdom Sits in Places: Landscape and Language among the Western Apache*. Albuquerque: University of New Mexico Press, 1996.

Beckham, Stephen Dow. *The Indians of Western Oregon: This Land Was Theirs*. Coos Bay, Ore.: Arago Books, 1977.

———. *Land of the Umpqua: A History of Douglas County, Oregon*. Roseburg, Ore.: Douglas County Commissioners, 1986.

———. *Requiem for a People: The Rogue Indians and the Frontiersmen*. Corvallis: Oregon State University Press, 1971.

Belmessous, Slaiha. "Assimilation and Racialism in Seventeenth and Eighteenth Century French Colonial Policy." *American Historical Review* 110, no. 3 (2005): 322–49.

Bergquist, James M. "The Oregon Donation Act and the National Land Policy." *Oregon Historical Quarterly* 58 (1957): 17–47.

Berkhofer, Robert F., Jr. *Salvation and the Savage: An Analysis of Protestant Missions and American Indian Response, 1787–1862*. New York: Atheneum, 1972.

———. *The White Man's Indian: Images of the American Indian rom Columbus to the Present*. New York: Alfred A. Knopf, 1978.

Bieder, Robert E. *Science Encounters the Indian, 1820–1880: The Early Years of American Ethnology*. Norman: University of Oklahoma Press, 1986.

Blackwood, Evelyn. "Sexuality and Gender in Certain Native American Tribes: The Case of Cross-Gender Females." *Signs* 10 (1984): 27–42.

Boag, Peter. *Environment and Experience: Settlement Culture in Nineteenth Century Oregon*. Berkeley: University of California Press, 1992.

Bolkhovitinov, Nikolai N. "Russia and the Declaration of the Non-Colonization Principle: New Archival Evidence." *Oregon Historical Quarterly* 72, no. 2 (1971): 101–26.

Bourdieu, Pierre. *Practical Reason: On the Theory of Action*. Stanford, Calif.: Stanford University Press, 1998.

Bowen, William. "The Oregon Frontiersman: A Demographic View." In *The Western Shore: Oregon Country Essays Honoring the American Revolution*. Edited by Thomas

Vaughn, 181–98. Portland, Oregon Historical Society and the American Revolution Bicentennial Commission of Oregon, 1976.

———. *The Coming of the Spirit of Pestilence: Introduced Infectious Diseases and Population Decline Among Northwest Coast Indians, 1774–1874*. Seattle: University of Washington Press, 1999.

Boyd, Robert. "The Pacific Northwest Measles Epidemic of 1847–1848." *Oregon Historical Quarterly* 95, no. 1 (1994): 6–47.

Boyd, Robert. *People of The Dalles, The Indians of Wascopam Mission: A Historical Ethnography Based on the Papers of the Methodist Missionaries*. Lincoln: University of Nebraska Press, 1996.

Boyd, Robert T., and Yvonne Hajda. "Seasonal Population Movement along the Lower Columbia River: The Social and Ecological Context." *American Ethnologist* 14, no. 2 (1987): 309–26.

Buan, Carolyn M., and Richard Lewis, eds. *The First Oregonians: An Illustrated Collection of Essays on Traditional Lifeways, Federal–Indian Relations, and the State's Native People Today*. Portland: Oregon Council for the Humanities, 1991.

Bunting, Robert. *The Pacific Raincoast: Environment and Culture in an American Eden, 1778–1900*. Lawrence: University Press of Kansas, 1997.

Bushnell, O. A. *The Gifts of Civilization: Germs and Genocide in Hawai'i*. Honolulu: University of Hawai'i Press, 1993.

Butler, Anne M. *Daughters of Joy, Sisters of Misery: Prostitutes in the American West, 1865–90*. Chicago: University of Illinois Press, 1985.

Byram, Scott, and David G. Lewis. "Ourigan: Wealth of the Northwest Coast." *Oregon Historical Quarterly* 102, no. 2 (2001): 126–57.

Cain, P. J., and A. G. Hopkins. *British Imperialism: Innovation and Expansion, 1688–1914*. New York: Longman, 1993.

Campbell, James, and James Oakes. "The Invention of Race: Rereading White over Black." *Reviews in American History* 21, no. 1 (1993): 172–83.

Cannon, William B. "John Wesley's Years in Georgia." *Methodist History* 1, no. 4 (1963): 1–7.

Carson Taylor, James. "Ethnogeography and the Native American Past." *Ethnohistory* 49, no. 4 (2002): 769–88.

Chused, Richard H. "The Oregon Donation Act of 1850 and Nineteenth Century Federal Married Women's Property Law." *Law and History Review* (1984): 44–78.

Clifford, James, and George E. Marcus, *Writing Culture: The Poetics and Politics of Ethnography*. Berkeley: University of California Press, 1986.

Clymer, Kenton J. "Religion and American Imperialism: Methodist Missionaries in the Philippine Islands, 1899–1913." *Pacific Historical Review* 49, no. 1 (1980): 29–50.

Coan, C. F. "The First Stage of the Federal Indian Policy in the Pacific Northwest, 1849–1852." *Oregon Historical Quarterly* 22 (1921): 46–89.

Cook, Sherburne F. *The Conflict between the California Indian and White Civilization*. Berkeley: University of California Press, 1976.

Cooper, Jerry. *The Militia and the National Guard in America since Colonial Times: A Research Guide*. Westport, Conn: Greenwood Press, 1993.

———. *The Rise of the National Guard: The Evolution of the American Militia, 1865–1920*. Lincoln: University of Nebraska Press, 1997.

Copland, Ian. *The Burden of Empire: Perspectives on Imperialism and Colonialism*. Melbourne: Oxford University Press, 1990.

Crosby, Alfred W., Jr. *The Columbian Exchange: Biological and Cultural Consequences of 1492*. Westport, Conn: Greenwood Press, 1972.

———. "Virgin Soil Epidemics as a Factor in the Aboriginal Depopulation in America." *William and Mary Quarterly* 33 (1976): 289–99.

Cruikshank, Julie. *The Social Life of Stories: Narrative and Knowledge in the Yukon Territory*. Lincoln: University of Nebraska Press, 1998.

Davis, Mike. *Prisoners of the American Dream: Politics and Economy in the History of the US Working Class*. London: Verso, 1986.

Deloria, Philip J. "Historiography." In *A Companion to American Indian History*, edited by Philip J. Deloria and Neal Salisbury. Malden, Mass.: Blackwell Publishing, 2004.

———. *Playing Indian*. New Haven, Conn.: Yale University Press, 1998.

Dennis, Matthew. *Cultivating a Landscape of Peace: Iroquois-European Encounters in Seventeenth-Century America*. Ithaca, N.Y.: Cornell University Press, 1993.

Dillard, Tom D. "An Arduous Task to Perform: Organizing the Territorial Arkansas Militia." *Arkansas Historical Quarterly* 41 (1982): 174–90.

Donald, Leland. *Aboriginal Slavery on the Northwest Coast of North America*. Berkeley: University of California Press, 1997.

Dorris, Michael. "Indians on the Shelf." In *The American Indian and the Problem of History*, edited by Calvin Martin, 98–105. New York: Oxford University Press, 1987.

Dorsey, Peter A. "Going to School with Savages: Authorship and Authority among the Jesuits of New France." *William and Mary Quarterly* 55, no. 3 (1998): 399–420.

Douthit, Nathan. "The Hudson's Bay Company and the Indians of Southern Oregon." *Oregon Historical Quarterly* 93, no. 2 (1992): 25–64.

———. *Uncertain Encounters: Indians and Whites at Peace and War in Southern Oregon, 1820s to 1860s*. Corvallis: Oregon State University Press, 2002.

Dowd, Gregory Evans. *A Spirited Resistance: The North American Indian Struggle for Unity, 1745–1815*. Baltimore: Johns Hopkins University Press, 1992.

Drinnon, Richard. *Facing West: The Metaphysics of Indian Hating and Empire Building*. Minneapolis: University of Minnesota Press, 1980.

Drucker, Philip. "The Tolowa and Their Southwest Oregon Kin." *University of California Publications in American Archaeology and Ethnology* 36, no. 4 (1937): 221–300.

Drury, Clifford M. "The Oregonian and Indian's Advocate." *Pacific Northwest Quarterly* 56, no. 4 (1965): 159–67.

Drury, Clifford Merrill, ed. *The Mountains We Have Crossed: Diaries and Letters of the Oregon Mission, 1838*. Lincoln: University of Nebraska Press, 1999.

DuBois, Cora Alice. *The Feather Cult of the Middle Columbia*. Menasha, Wis.: George Banta Publishing Co., 1938.

Duncan, Janice K. *Minority without a Champion: Kanakas on the Pacific Coast, 1788–1850*. Portland: Oregon Historical Society Press, 1972.

Edmunds, R. David. "Tecumseh, the Shawnee Prophet, and American History: A Reassessment." *Western Historical Quarterly* 14 (1983): 261–76.

Elmendorf, William W. *The Structure of Twana Culture: With Comparative Notes on the Structure of Yurok Culture by A. L. Kroeber.* Pullman: Washington State University Press, 1992.

Etherington, Norman, ed. *Mission and Empire* (Oxford History of the British Empire Companion Series). New York: Oxford University Press, 2005.

Feller, Daniel. *The Jacksonian Promise: America, 1815–1840.* Baltimore: Johns Hopkins University Press, 1995.

Fields, Barbara. "Ideology and Race in American History." In *Region, Race, and Reconstruction,* edited by J. Morgan Kousser and James M. McPherson. New York: Oxford University Press, 1982.

Finnegan, Frances. *Poverty and Prostitution: A Study of Victorian Prostitutes in York.* New York: Cambridge University Press, 1979.

Foner, Eric, ed. *The New American History.* 2nd ed. Philadelphia: Temple University Press, 1997.

Foucault, Michel. *The Use of Pleasure.* Vol. 2 of *The History of Sexuality.* Translated by Robert Hurley. New York: Pantheon Books, 1985.

Fraser, Steven, and Gary Gerstle. *Ruling America: A History of Wealth and Power in a Democracy.* Cambridge, Mass.: Harvard University Press, 2005.

Galbraith, John S. *The Hudson's Bay Company as an Imperial Factor, 1821–1869.* Berkeley: University of California Press, 1957.

Gates, Paul W. "The Role of the Land Speculator in Western Development." In *The Jeffersonian Dream: Studies in the History of American Land Policy and Development,* edited by Allan G. and Margaret Beattie Bogue, 6–22. Albuquerque: University of New Mexico Press, 1996.

Gates, Paul W., and Robert W. Swenson. *History of Public Land Law Development.* Washington, D.C.: U.S. Government Printing Office, 1968.

Gibson, James R. *Otter Skins, Boston Ships, and China Goods: The Maritime Fur Trade of the Northwest Coast, 1785–1841.* Seattle: University of Washington Press, 1992.

Gilfoyle, Timothy J. *City of Eros: New York City, Prostitution, and the Commercialization of Sex, 1790–1920.* New York: W. W. Norton and Co., 1992.

Goddard, Peter A. "Converting the *Sauvage*: Jesuit and Montagnais in Seventeenth-Century New France." *Catholic Historical Review* 84, no. 2 (1998): 219–39.

Gray, Dennis J. *The Takelma and Their Athapascan Neighbors: A New Ethnographic Synthesis for the Upper Rogue River Area of Southwestern Oregon.* University of Oregon Anthropological Papers 37. Eugene: University of Oregon, 1987.

Griffiths, Nicholas, and Fernando Cervantes, eds. *Spiritual Encounters: Interactions between Christianity and Native Religions in Colonial America.* Lincoln: University of Nebraska, 1999.

Gualtieri, Antonio R. *Christianity and Native Traditions: Indigenization and Syncretism among the Inuit and Dene of the Western Arctic.* Notre Dame, Ind.: Cross Cultural Publications, Cross Roads Books, 1984.

Gutierrez, David G. *Walls and Mirrors: Mexican Americans, Mexican Immigrants, and the Politics of Ethnicity.* Berkeley: University of California Press, 1995.

Gutierrez, Ramon A. *When Jesus Came, the Corn Mothers Went Away: Marriage, Sexuality, and Power in New Mexico, 1500–1846*. Stanford, Calif.: Stanford University Press, 1991.

Hajda, Yvonne P. "Regional Social Organization in the Greater Lower Columbia, 1792–1830." Ph.D. diss., University of Washington, 1984.

Hall, Roberta L. *The Coquille Indians: Yesterday, Today, and Tomorrow*. Lake Oswego, Ore.: Smith, Smith and Smith Publishing Co., 1984.

Hall, Roberta L., and Don Alan Hall. "The Village at the Mouth of the Coquille River: Historical Questions of Who, When, and Where." *Pacific Northwest Quarterly* (1991): 101–8.

<H-Amindian@H-Net.msu.edu>.

Harjo, Joy, and Gloria Bird. *Reinventing the Enemy's Language: Contemporary Native Women's Writings of North America*. New York: W. W. Norton. 1997.

Harmon, Alexandra. *Indians in the Making: Ethnic Relations and Indian Identities around Puget Sound*. Berkeley: University of California Press, 1998.

———. "Lines in the Sand: Shifting Boundaries between Indians and Non-Indians in the Puget Sound Region." *Western Historical Quarterly* 26, no. 4 (1995): 429–53.

Harris, Cheryl. "Whiteness as Property." In *Black on White*, edited by David R. Roediger, 103–18. New York: Schocken Books, 1998.

Harris, Cole. *The Resettlement of British Columbia: Essays on Colonialism and Geographical Change*. Vancouver: University of British Columbia Press, 1997.

Hatch, Nathan. *Democratization of American Christianity*. New Haven, Conn.: Yale University Press, 1989.

Head, Harlow Zinser. "The Oregon Donation Acts: Background, Development and Application." Master's thesis, University of Oregon, 1969.

———. "The Oregon Donation Claims and Their Patterns." Ph.D. diss., University of Oregon, 1971.

Heizer, Robert F., and Thomas Roy Hester. "Shasta Villages and Territory." *Contributions of the University of California Archaeological Research Facility: Papers on California Ethnography* 9 (1970): 119–58.

Heyrman, Christine Leigh. *Southern Cross: The Beginnings of the Bible Belt*. New York: A. A. Knopf; Distributed by Random House, 1997.

Hickey, Donald R. *The War of 1812: A Forgotten Conflict*. Urbana: University of Illinois Press, 1989.

Hinderaker, Eric, and Peter C. Mancall. *At the Edge of Empire: The Backcountry in British North America*. Baltimore: John Hopkins University Press, 2003.

H-Net Reviews. <http://www.h-net.msu.edu/reviews>.

Hodges, Hugh T. "Charles Maclay: California Missionary and San Fernando Valley Pioneer—Part I." *Southern California Quarterly* 68, no. 2 (1986): 119–66.

———. "Charles Maclay: California Missionary and San Fernando Valley Pioneer—Parts II, III." *Southern California Quarterly* 68, no. 3 (1986): 207–56.

Holman, Frederick V. "A Brief History of the Oregon Provisional Government and What Caused Its Formation." *Oregon Historical Quarterly* 13, no. 2 (1912): 89–139.

Holton, Woody. *The Forced Founders: Indians, Debtors, Slaves, and the Making of the American Revolution in Virginia*. Chapel Hill: University of North Carolina Press, 1999.

Horsman, Reginald. "The Dimensions of an 'Empire for Liberty': Expansion and Republicanism, 1775–1825." *Journal of the Early Republic* 9. no. 1 (1989): 1–20.

———. *Race and Manifest Destiny: The Origins of American Racial Anglo-Saxonism*. Cambridge, Mass.: Harvard University Press, 1981.

Hovee, Gene Herbert. "Jason Lee: A Rhetorical Criticism of His Sermon on the Oregon Mission." Master's thesis, University of Oregon, 1963.

Hoxie, Frederick E. *A Final Promise: The Campaign to Assimilate the Indian, 1880–1920*. New York: Cambridge University Press, 1992.

Huhndorf, Shari M. *Going Native: Indians in the American Cultural Imagination*. Ithaca, N.Y.: Cornell University Press, 2001.

Hulme, Peter. *Colonial Encounters: Europe and the Native Caribbean, 1492–1797*. New York: Routledge. 1986.

Hunn, Eugene S. *Nchi-i-Wana, "The Big River": Mid-Columbia Indians and Their Land*. Seattle: University of Washington Press, 1990.

Hurtado, Albert L. *Indian Survival on the California Frontier*. New Haven, Conn.: Yale University Press, 1988.

Hymes, Dell, and Virginia Hymes. "Chinook Jargon as 'Mother Tongue.'" *International Journal of American Linguistics* 38, no. 3 (1972): 207.

Jacobs, Sue-Ellen, Wesley Thomas, and Sabine Lang. *Two-Spirit People: Native American Gender Identity, Sexuality, and Spirituality*. Urbana: University of Illinois Press, 1997.

Jacobson, Matthew Frye. *Whiteness of a Different Color: European Immigrants and the Alchemy of Race*. Cambridge, Mass.: Harvard University Press. 1998.

Johansen, Dorothy O. *Empire of the Columbia: A History of the Pacific Northwest*. 2nd ed. New York: Harper and Row, Publishers, 1967.

Johnson, David Alan. *Founding the Far West: California, Oregon, and Nevada, 1840–1890*. Berkeley: University of California Press, 1992.

Johnson, Paul E. *A Shopkeeper's Millennium: Society and Revivals in Rochester, New York, 1815–1837*. New York: Hill and Wang, 1978.

Kaplan, Amy. "'Left Alone with America': The Absence of Empire in the Study of American Culture." In *Cultures of United States Imperialism*, edited by Amy Kaplan and Donald E. Pease. Durham, N.C.: Duke University Press, 1993.

Kelley, Robin D. G. *Yo' Mama's DisFunktional! Fighting the Culture Wars in Urban America*. Boston: Beacon Press, 1997.

Kendall, Daythal L. "Takelma." In *Handbook of North American Indians*, vol. 7, edited by Wayne Suttles, 589–92. Washington D.C.: Smithsonian, 1990.

Kidwell, Clara Sue. "Choctaws and Missionaries in Mississippi before 1830." *American Indian Culture and Research Journal* 11, no. 2 (1987): 51–72.

———. "Indian Women as Cultural Mediators." *Ethnohistory* 39, no. 2 (1992): 97–107.

Klein, Kerwin Lee. *Frontiers of Historical Imagination*. Berkeley: University of California Press, 1998.

Knobel, Dale T. "Know Nothings and Indians: Strange Bedfellows?" *Western Historical Quarterly* 15, no. 2 (1984): 175–98.

Krech, Shepard, III, ed. *Indians, Animals, and the Fur Trade: A Critique of Keepers of the Game*. Athens: University of Georgia Press, 1981.

Kroeber, A. L. "A Yurok War Reminiscence: The Use of Autobiographical Evidence." *Southwestern Journal of Anthropology* 1 (1945): 318–32.

Kroeber, A. L., and E. W. Gifford. "World Renewal, A Cult System of Native Northwest California." *University of California Publications in Anthropological Records* 13, no. 1 (1952): 1–155.

Kupperman, Karen. *Settling with the Indians: The Meeting of Indian and English Cultures in America, 1580–1640.* Totowa, N.J.: Rowman and Littlefield, 1980.

Lawson, Gary, and Guy Seidman. *The Constitution of Empire: Territorial Expansion and American Legal History.* New Haven, Conn.: Yale University Press, 2004.

Leavelle, Tracy Neal. "'We Will Make It Our Own Place': Agriculture and Adaptation at the Grande Ronde Reservation, 1856–1887." *American Indian Quarterly* 22, no. 4 (1998): 433–56.

Lewis, David Rich. *Neither Wolf nor Dog: American Indians, Environment, and Agrarian Change.* New York: Oxford University Press, 1994.

Limerick, Patricia Nelson. "Going West and Ending Up Global." *Western Historical Quarterly* 32, no. 1 (2001): 5–23.

———. *The Legacy of Conquest: The Unbroken Past of the American West.* New York: W. W. Norton and Co., 1987.

Liu, Tessie. "Race." In *A Companion to American Thought*, edited by Richard Fox and James Kloppenberg, 564–67. New York: Blackwell, 1995.

Loewenberg, Robert J. *Equality on the Oregon Frontier: Jason Lee and the Methodist Mission, 1834–43.* Seattle: University of Washington Press, 1976.

———. "New Evidence, Old Categories: Jason Lee as Zealot." *Pacific Historical Review* 47, no. 3 (1978): 343–68.

———. "Saving Oregon Again: A Western Perennial?" *Oregon Historical Quarterly* 78, no. 4 (1977): 332–50.

Lomawaima, K. Tsianina. *They Called It Prairie Light: The Story of Chilocco Indian School.* Lincoln: University of Nebraska Press, 1994.

Lloyd, T. O. *The British Empire: 1558–1995.* Short Oxford History of the Modern World. 2nd ed. New York: Oxford University Press, 2000.

Lyerly, Cynthia Lynn. *Methodism and the Southern Mind, 1770–1810.* New York: Oxford University Press, 1998.

Mahood, Linda *The Madgalenes: Prostitution in the Nineteenth Century.* New York: Routledge, 1990.

Martin, Calvin. *In the Spirit of the Earth.* Baltimore: Johns Hopkins University Press, 1992.

———. *Keepers of the Game: Indian-Animal Relationships and the Fur Trade.* Berkeley: University of California Press, 1978.

———, ed. *The American Indian and the Problem of History.* New York: Oxford University Press, 1987.

Martin, Calvin Luther. *The Way of the Human Being.* New Haven, Conn.: Yale University Press, 1999.

Martin, Joel W. "Before and Beyond the Sioux Ghost Dance: Native American Prophetic Movements and the Study of Religion." *Journal of the American Academy of Religion* 59 (1991): 677–701.

———. *Sacred Revolt: The Muskogees' Struggle for a New World*. Boston: Beacon Press, 1991.

Martinez, George. "Mexican Americans and Whiteness." In *Critical White Studies: Looking behind the Mirror*, edited by Richard Delgado and Jean Sefancic, 210–13. Philadelphia: Temple University Press, 1997.

McArthur, Lewis A. *Oregon Geographic Names*. Portland: Oregon Historical Society, 1992.

McKevitt, Gerald. "Jesuit Missionary Linguistics in the Pacific Northwest: A Comparative Study." *Western Historical Quarterly* 21, no. 3 (1990): 281–304.

McLagan, Elizabeth. *A Peculiar Paradise: A History of Blacks in Oregon, 1788–1940*. Portland, Ore.: Georgian Press, 1980.

McLoughlin, William G. "Cherokees and Methodists, 1824–1834." *Church History* 50, no. 1 (1981): 44–63.

Meinig, D. W. *The Great Columbia Plain: A Historical Geography, 1805–1910*. Seattle: University of Washington Press, 1968.

Merk, Frederick. *Manifest Destiny and Mission in American History: A Reinterpretation*. Cambridge, Mass.: Harvard University Press, 1963.

———. *The Oregon Question: Essays in Anglo-American Diplomacy and Politics*. Cambridge, Mass.: Belknap Press of Harvard University Press, 1967.

Merritt, Jane T. "Metaphor, Meaning, and Misunderstanding: Language and Power on the Pennsylvania Frontier." In *Contact Points: American Frontiers from the Mohawk Valley to the Mississippi, 1750–1830*, edited by Andrew R. L. Cayton and Fredrika Teute. Chapel Hill: University of North Carolina Press, 1998.

Miller, Christopher L. *Prophetic Worlds: Indians and Whites on the Columbia Plateau*. New Brunswick, N.J.: Rutgers University Press, 1985.

Miller, Jay, and William R. Seaburg. "Athapaskans of Southwestern Oregon." In *Handbook of North American Indians*, vol. 7, edited by Wayne Suttles, 580–88. Washington, D.C.: Smithsonian, 1990.

Millett, Allan R., and Peter Maslowski. *For the Common Defense: A Military History of the United States of America*. New York: Free Press, 1984.

Million, Elmer G. "Frontier Legal Process: Parrish Vs. Gray, 1846." *Oregon Historical Quarterly* 73, no. 3 (1972): 245–56.

Montoya, Maria E., in Virginia Scharff, et al., "Claims and Prospects of Western History: A Roundtable." *Western Historical Quarterly* 31, no. 1 (2000): 40–43.

Mooney, James. *The Ghost-Dance Religion and the Sioux Outbreak of 1890*. Washington, D.C.: U.S. Government Printing Office, 1896.

Morgan, Edmund S. *American Slavery, American Freedom: The Ordeal of Colonial Virginia*. New York: Norton, 1975.

Morris, Grace P. "Development of Astoria, 1811–1850." *Oregon Historical Quarterly* 38, no. 4 (1937): 413–24.

Morrison, Dorothy Nafus. *Outpost: John McLoughlin and the Far Northwest*. Portland: Oregon Historical Society Press, 1999.

Morrissey, Katherine G. *Mental Territories: Mapping the Inland Empire*. Ithaca, N.Y.: Cornell University Press, 1997.

Muldoon, James. *Empire and Order: The Concept of Empire, 800–1800*. New York: St. Martin's Press, Inc., 1999.

Nash, Gerald D. *Creating the West: Historical Interpretations, 1890–1990*. Albuquerque: University of New Mexico Press, 1991.

O'Callaghan, Jerry A. *The Disposition of the Public Domain in Oregon: Memorandum of the Chairman to the Committee on Interior and Insular Affairs, United States Senate*. Washington, D.C.: U.S. Government Printing Office, 1960.

Okihiro, Gary Y. *Margins and Mainstreams: Asians in American History and Culture*. Seattle: University of Washington Press, 1994.

Onuf, Peter S. *Jefferson's Empire: The Language of American Nationhood*. Charlottesville: University Press of Virginia, 2000.

Osterhammel, Jurgen. *Colonialism: A Theoretical Overview*. Princeton, N.J.: Markus Wiener Publishers, 1997.

Ostler, Jeffrey. *The Plains Sioux and U.S. Colonialism from Lewis and Clark to Wounded Knee*. New York: Cambridge University Press, 2004.

Paul, Rodman Wilson. *Mining Frontiers of the Far West, 1848–1880* revised, expanded. Edited by Elliott West. Albuquerque: University of New Mexico Press, 2001.

Perkins, Bradford. *Cambridge History of Foreign Relations: Vol. 1, The Creation of a Republican Empire, 1776–1865*. New York: Cambridge University Press, 1993.

Peterson, Emil R., and Alfred Powers. *A Century of Coos and Curry: History of Southwest Oregon*. Portland, Ore.: Binfords and Mort, Publishers, 1952.

Peterson del Mar, David. "Intermarriage and Agency: A Chinookan Case Study." *Ethnohistory* 42, no. 1 (Winter 1995): 1–30.

Peyer, Bernd C. *The Tutor'd Mind: Indian Missionary-Writers in Antebellum America*. Amherst: University of Massachusetts Press, 1997.

Prashad, Vijay. *The Karma of Brown Folk*. Minneapolis: University of Minnesota Press, 2000.

Prins, Harald E. L. "To the Land of the Mistigoches: American Indians Traveling to Europe in the Age of Exploration." *American Indian Culture and Research Journal* 17, no. 1 (1993): 175–95.

Prucha, Francis Paul. *The Great Father: The United States Government and the American Indians*, vol. 2. Lincoln: University of Nebraska Press, 1984.

Rawls, James J. *Indians of California: The Changing Image*. Norman: University of Oklahoma Press, 1984.

Ray, Verne Frederick. "Lower Chinook Ethnographic Notes." *University of Washington Publications in Anthropology* 7, no. 2 (1938).

Reid, John Phillip. *Patterns of Vengeance: Crosscultural Homicide in the North American Fur Trade*. Sacramento, Calif.: Ninth Circuit Historical Society, 1999.

———. "Restraints of Vengeance: Retaliation-in-Kind and the Use of Indian Law in the Old Oregon Country." *Oregon Historical Quarterly* 95, no. 1 (1994): 48–92.

Richardson, Allan. "The Control of Productive Resources on the Northwest Coast of North America." In *Resource Managers: North American and Australian Hunter-Gatherers*, edited by Nancy M. Williams and Eugene S. Hunn. Boulder, Colo.: Westview Press, Inc., 1982, 93–112.

Richter, Daniel K. *The Ordeal of the Longhouse: The Peoples of the Iroquois League in the Era of European Colonization*. Chapel Hill: University of North Carolina Press, 1992.

Robbins, Roy M. *Our Landed Heritage: The Public Domain, 1776–1936*. Princeton, N.J.: Princeton University Press, 1942.

Robbins, William G. *Colony and Empire: The Capitalist Transformation of the American West*. Lawrence: University of Kansas Press, 1994.

———. "Extinguishing Indian Land Title in Western Oregon." *Indian Historian* 7, no. 2 (1974): 10–14, 52.

———. *Hard Times in Paradise: Coos Bay, Oregon, 1850–1986*. Seattle: University of Washington Press, 1988.

———. *Landscapes of Promise: The Oregon Story, 1800–1940*. Seattle: University of Washington Press, 1997.

Roediger, David R. *The Wages of Whiteness: Race and the Making of the American Working Class*. New York: Verso, 1991.

Rohrbough, Malcolm J. *The Land Office Business: The Settlement and Administration of American Public Lands, 1789–1837*. New York: Oxford University Press, 1968.

Ronda, James P. *Astoria and Empire*. Lincoln: University of Nebraska Press, 1990.

———. *Lewis and Clark among the Indians*. Lincoln: University of Nebraska Press, 1988.

Roscoe, Will. "The Zuni Man-Woman." In *Ethnographic Studies of Homosexuality*, edited by Wayne R. Dynes and Stephen Donaldson, 358–70. New York: Garland, 1992.

Rowe, Mary Ellen. "The Sure Bulwark of the Republic: The Militia Tradition and the Yakima War Volunteers." Ph.D. diss., University of Washington, 1988.

Ruby, Robert H., and John A. Brown. *The Chinook Indians: Traders of the Lower Columbia River*. Norman: University of Oklahoma Press, 1976.

———. *Indian Slavery in the Pacific Northwest*. Spokane, Wash.: Arthur H. Clark Co., 1993.

Ryan, Mary P. *Cradle of the Middle Class: The Family in Oneida County, New York, 1790–1865*. New York: Cambridge University Press, 1981.

Said, Edward W. *Culture and Imperialism*. New York: Knopf; Distributed by Random House, 1993.

Saum, Lewis O. *The Fur Trader and the Indian*. Seattle: University of Washington Press, 1965.

Schaeffer, Claude. "The Kutenai Female Berdache: Courier, Guide, Prophetess, and Warrior." *Ethnohistory* 12, no. 3 (1965): 193–236.

Schwartz, E. A. *The Rogue River Indian War and Its Aftermath, 1850–1980*. Norman: University of Oklahoma Press, 1997.

Schwarz, Henry, and Ray Sangeeta, eds. *A Companion to Postcolonial Studies*. Malden, Mass.: Blackwell Publishers, 2000.

Sellers, Charles. *The Market Revolution: Jacksonian America, 1815–1846*. New York: Oxford University Press, 1991.

Slotkin, Richard. *The Fatal Environment: The Myth of the Frontier in the Age of Industrialization, 1800–1890*. New York: Atheneum, 1985.

———. *Regeneration through Violence: The Mythology of the American Frontier, 1600–1800*. Middletown, Conn.: Wesleyan University Press, 1973.

Smedley, Audrey. *Race in North America: Origin and Evolution of a Worldview*. 2nd ed. San Francisco: Westview Press, 1999.

Smith, Eugene O. "Solomon Smith, Pioneer: Indian-White Relations in Early Oregon." *Journal of the West* 13, no. 2 (1974): 44–58.

Smith, Matthew, and Aeldun Charles. "Wedding Bands and Marriage Bans: A History of Oregon's Racial Intermarriage Statutes and the Impact on Indian Interracial Nuptials." Master's thesis, Portland State University, 1997.

Smith, Sherry L. *View from Officer's Row: Army Perceptions of Western Indians.* Tucson: University of Arizona Press, 1990.

Smits, David D. "The 'Squaw Drudge': A Prime Index of Savagism." *Ethnohistory* 29, no. 4 (1982): 281–306.

———. " 'Squaw Men,' 'Half-Breeds,' and Amalgamators: Late Nineteenth-Century Anglo-American Attitudes toward Indian-White Race-Mixing." *American Indian Culture and Research Journal* 15, no. 3 (1991): 29–61.

Spence, Mark David. *Dispossessing the Wilderness: Indian Removal and the Making of the National Parks.* New York: Oxford University Press, 1999.

Spier, Leslie. "Klamath Ethnography." *University of California Publications in American Archaeology and Ethnology* 30 (1930).

———. *The Prophet Dance of the Northwest and Its Derivatives: The Source of the Ghost Dance.* New York: AMS Press, 1979.

Spores, Ronald. "Too Small a Place: The Removal of the Willamette Valley Indians, 1850–1856." *American Indian Quarterly* 17, no. 2 (1993): 171–93.

Stern, Theodore. *Chiefs and Change in the Oregon Country: Indian Relations at Fort Nez Percés, 1818–1855.* Vol. 2. Corvallis: Oregon State University Press, 1996.

———. *Chiefs and Chief Traders: Indian Relations at Fort Nez Percés, 1818–1855.* Corvallis: Oregon State University Press, 1993.

———. "The Klamath Indians and the Treaty of 1864." *Oregon Historical Quarterly* 57, no. 3 (1959): 229–73.

———. *The Klamath Tribe: A People and Their Reservation.* Seattle: University of Washington Press, 1966.

Stone, Buena Cobb. "Southern Route into Oregon: Notes and a New Map." *Oregon Historical Quarterly* 47, no. 2 (1946): 135–54.

Suttles, Wayne, vol. ed. *Handbook of North American Indians*, vol. 7: Northwest Coast. William C. Sturtevant, series ed. Washington, D.C.: Smithsonian, 1990.

Sutton, Dorothy, and Jack Sutton, eds. *Indian Wars of the Rogue River.* Grants Pass, Ore.: Josephine County Historical Society, 1969.

Svaldi, David. *Sand Creek and the Rhetoric of Extermination: A Case Study in Indian-White Relations.* New York: University Press of America, 1989.

Taylor, Alan. "Captain Hendrick Aupamut: The Dilemmas of an Intercultural Broker." *Ethnohistory* 43, no. 3 (1996): 431–57.

Trask, Haunani-Kay. *From a Native Daughter: Colonialism and Sovereignty in Hawai'i.* Honolulu: University of Hawai'i Press, 1999.

Trennert, Robert A., Jr. *An Alternative to Extinction: Federal Indian Policy and the Beginnings of the Reservation System, 1846–1851.* Philadelphia: Temple University Press, 1975.

Trexler, Richard C. *Sex and Conquest: Gendered Violence, Political Order, and the European Conquest of the Americas.* Ithaca, N.Y.: Cornell University Press, 1997.

Trigger, Bruce. "Early Native North American Responses to European Contact: Romantic versus Rationalist Interpretations." *Journal of American History* 77 (March 1991): 1195–1215.

———. "The Jesuits and the Fur Trade." *Ethnohistory* 12, no. 1 (1965): 30–53.

Turner, Frederick Jackson. "The Significance of the Frontier in American History." *Annual Report of the American Historical Association for the Year 1893.*

Van Kirk, Sylvia. *Many Tender Ties: Women in Fur-Trade Society, 1670–1870.* Norman: University of Oklahoma Press, 1980.

Vaughan, Thomas, and Bill Holm, eds. *Soft Gold: The Fur Trade and Cultural Exchange on the Northwest Coast of America.* Portland: Oregon Historical Society, 1982.

Vibert, Elizabeth. "'The Natives Were Strong to Live:' Early-Nineteenth-Century Prophetic Movements in the Columbia Plateau." *Ethnohistory* 42, no. 2 (1995): 197–229.

———. *Traders' Tales: Narratives of Cultural Encounters in the Columbia Plateau, 1807–1846.* Norman: University of Oklahoma Press, 1997.

Viles, Cynthia, and Tom Grigsby. "The Confederated Tribes of Siletz." In *The First Oregonians: An Illustrated Collection of Essays on Traditional Lifeways, Federal-Indian Relations, and the State's Native People Today,* edited by Carolyn M. Buan and Richard Lewis, 105–8. Portland, Oregon, Council for the Humanities, 1991.

Wasson, George Bundy, Jr. "The Coquille Indians and the Cultural 'Black Hole' of the Southwest Oregon Coast." Master's thesis, University of Oregon, 1994.

———. "Growing Up Indian: An Emic Perspective." Ph.D. diss., University of Oregon, 2001.

Wesson, Robert G. *The Imperial Order.* Berkeley: University of California Press, 1967.

West, Elliott. *The Way to the West: Essays on the Central Plains.* Albuquerque: University of New Mexico Press, 1995.

———. *The Contested Plains: Indians, Goldseekers, and the Rush to Colorado.* Lawrence: University Press of Kansas, 1998.

Whaley, Gray H. "'Complete Liberty'? Gender, Sexuality, Race, and Social Change on the Lower Columbia River, 1805–1838," *Ethnohistory* 54, no. 4 (2007): 669–95.

———. "Creating Oregon from *Illahee*: Race, Settler-Colonialism, and Native Sovereignty in Western Oregon, 1792–1856." Ph.D. diss., University of Oregon, 2002.

———. "Indians Twice Removed: Historical Representations of the Native People of Southwestern Oregon." In *Changing Landscapes: "Telling Our Stories," Proceedings of the Fourth Annual Coquille Cultural Preservation Conference, 2000,* edited by Jason Younger, Mark A. Tveskov, and David G. Lewis, 79–92. North Bend, Ore.: Coquille Indian Tribe, 2001.

———. "Oregon, *Illahee*, and the Empire Republic: A Case Study of American Colonialism, 1843–1858." *Western Historical Quarterly* 36, no. 2 (2005): 157–78.

———. "'Trophies' for God: Native Mortality, Racial Ideology, and the Methodist Mission of Lower Oregon, 1834–1844." *Oregon Historical Quarterly* 107, no. 1 (2006): 6–35.

Whisker, James B. *The Rise and Decline of the American Militia System.* Selinsgrove, Pa.: Susquehanna University Press, 1999.

White, Richard. "Indian Peoples and the Natural World: Asking the Right Questions." In *Rethinking American Indian History*, edited by Donald L. Fixico. Albuquerque: University of New Mexico Press, 1997.

———. *It's Your Misfortune and None of My Own: A New History of the American West*. Norman: University of Oklahoma Press. 1991.

———. *Land Use, Environment, and Social Change: The Shaping of Island County, Washington*. Seattle: University of Washington Press, 1980.

———. *The Middle Ground: Indians, Empires, and Republics in the Great Lakes Region, 1650–1815*. New York: Cambridge University Press, 1991.

White, Richard, and John M. Findley, eds. *Power and Place in the North American West*. Seattle: Center for the Study of the Pacific Northwest and the University of Washington Press, 1999.

Wigger, John. *Taking Heaven by Storm: Methodism and the Rise of Popular Christianity in America*. New York: Oxford University Press, 1997.

Wilentz, Sean. *Chants Democratic: New York City and the Rise of the American Working Class, 1788–1850*. New York: Oxford University Press, 1984.

Williams, Walter L. *The Spirit and the Flesh: Sexual Diversity in American Indian Culture*. Boston: Beacon Press, 1992.

Williams, William Appleman. *The Contours of American History*. Chicago: World Publishing Co., 1961.

Wolfe, Patrick. *Settler Colonialism and the Transformation of Anthropology: The Politics and Poetics of an Ethnographic Event*. New York: Cassell, 1999.

Zenk, Henry B. "Siuslawans and Coosans." In *Handbook of North American Indians*, vol. 7, edited by Wayne Suttles, 572–79. Washington D.C.: Smithsonian, 1990.

Zucker, Jay, Kay Hummel, and Bob Hogfoss. *Oregon Indians: Culture, History, and Current Affairs: An Atlas and Introduction*. Portland, Ore.: Western Imprints, 1983.

Index